P9-CKQ-929

LOST IN THE FUNHOUSE

THE LIFE AND MIND OF ANDY KAUFMAN

"Comprehensive . . . if you want the facts, this is the only [book] you need."
—*The New York Times Book Review*

"If I had lost the Andy Kaufman I first met in 1975, I found him again in *Lost in the Funhouse*."
—Lorne Michaels, *Saturday Night Live*

"Fascinating and frequently hilarious."
—*Kansas City Star*

"Insightful."—*The Plain Dealer* (Cleveland)

"Nobody, not his family or his 'best friend,' got as close to the truth about Andy as did Bill Zehme in *Lost in the Funhouse*. His six years of research unmasks the distortions and allows the reader to meet the real Andy."
—Stanley L. Kaufman (Andy's father)

"Entertaining . . . comprehensive . . . [Zehme] interviewed more than 200 people who had known or worked with Kaufman; had full access to Kaufman's family as well as the comic performer's personal papers; utilizes his manager's diaries; and did some diligent reporting. . . . Zehme's a pro."
—*Chicago Tribune*

Please turn the page for more extraordinary acclaim. . . .

"What a gift . . . to have a book that helps you enjoy once again Andy Kaufman's wild and wondrous mind. It's brilliant!"
—Carl Reiner

"Excellent."
—*Esquire* (England)

"Bill Zehme's bio of Andy Kaufman gets a firm grasp on the slippery master. . . . Zehme's book hasn't a dull page."
—*Artforum*

"Bill Zehme was dedicated to revealing the true Andy Kaufman story and I'm so grateful for that. This book is the interesting, funny, sad, unique and—finally and completely—true story of a very special life!"
—George Shapiro, Andy Kaufman's manager and co–executive producer of *Man on the Moon*

"Ingenious . . . the best possible guess of what this singular comedian was all about."
—*St. Petersburg Times*

"Zehme writes with a verve that is rare among biographers, sometimes letting the prose go into a voice reminiscent of Kaufman's own speech patterns."
—*Ft. Worth Star-Telegram*

BILL ZEHME

LOST IN THE
FUNHOUSE

THE LIFE AND MIND

OF ANDY KAUFMAN

DELTA TRADE PAPERBACKS

A Delta Book
Random House, Inc.
1540 Broadway
New York, New York 10036

Copyright © 1999 by Bill Zehme

All rights reserved. No part of this book may be reproduced or transmitted
in any form or by any means, electronic or mechanical, including photo-
copying, recording, or by any information storage and retrieval system,
without the written permission of the Publisher, except where permitted
by law. For information address: Delacorte Press, New York, N.Y.

Delta ® is a registered trademark of Random House, Inc., and the
colophon is a trademark of Random House, Inc.

ISBN: 0-385-33372-2

Reprinted by arrangement with Delacorte Press

Book design by Brian Mulligan
Photo insert design by Julie Schroeder
Cover and title page photograph by Wayne Williams

Cover design by John D. Sparks

Photograph on page 363 courtesy of Shapiro/West and Associates, Inc.

Manufactured in the United States of America
Published simultaneously in Canada

January 2001

10 9 8 7 6 5 4 3 2 1

BVG

For Lucy Ellen,
with love very extremely

LOST IN THE
FUNHOUSE

THE LIFE AND MIND

OF ANDY KAUFMAN

1

Everyone lives in his own fantasy world, but most people don't understand that. No one perceives the *real* world. Each person simply calls his private, personal fantasies the Truth.

—Federico Fellini

Um. *Ummm . . .*

He came late. Mommy and Daddy tried to make him three times and each time they got a new baby started something bad happened to Mommy and she cried. He was made the fourth time, finally, and so was his invisible twin brother, Dhrupick, but nobody cared about Dhrupick, although Dhrupick would later help him do special things. No, *really.* He had to name Dhrupick himself, because nobody else ever saw Dhrupick, or they didn't know that they saw him even when they saw him. And also, since Dhrupick was his exact replicate, *he* could be Dhrupick when he wasn't himself, which was often, eventually more and more so. Anyway, Dhrupick made being somebody else easy, he learned. Of what was mathematically considered to be his childhood (just yearwise), he would later tell some person, "Every once in a while, every week or two, I would wake up in the morning and I would say, 'I think I'll be Dhrupick.' D-h-r-u, I think, p-i-c-k. I chose that name for a logical reason, but I forget what it was."

And so his eyes opened thirty-five years and four months before they stopped seeing anything anymore ever again. Once opened, they were stroboscopic! They were two very big bright blue dancers! They spun and spun inside white orbs even bigger! They said come-here-and-help-me-play-and-please-just-help-me-and-here-I-am-and-I'm-not-here-at-all-and-oh-yes-I-am-no-really. He was seven pounds eleven ounces (a craps-table baby!) and Daddy later joked that his eyes had weighed four pounds alone. Daddy proudly designed his birth announcement with a picture of a baby rolling dice, come seven and eleven; pounds, ounces, natch. He (and Dhrupick) came out of Mommy just after two o'clock on the afternoon of January 17, 1949, in a bed in Kew Gardens Hospital in Queens, New York. Mommy started calling him Pussycat almost right away. He purred for her most always, but he learned to yell sometimes, too. That came a bit later.

He got his own name from maternal favor: Mommy had a grandmother named Ann and an uncle named George, and so he became Andrew Geoffrey Kaufman—firstborn child of a frustrated-dreamer second-generation costume jewelry salesman who would manage to do well for himself in a very tough racket and his pretty wife who was a former teen fashion model with piercing green eyes. He was adored most thoroughly, for he was also the first grandchild of both grandmas and both grandpas, each of whom bestowed assorted legacies of color and character and individuality upon the small pink boy. To them, he was *delicious*, this fine grandson whose cheeks they pinched, whose head they nestled, a sweet bubelah who could have anything he wanted, whom they indulged in ways he never knew he wanted but came to require when grown. It was the grandmas and the grandpas, more than anyone, who made him special, and for this he would love them and credit them always. Being special would be his singular excuse; not that he ever really tried to be that way or decided that specialness was his intention; he just was; and he was mostly glad about it—no matter that Daddy often hollered at him, no matter that other kids called him crazy, no matter that everyone thought he was crazy. Everyone did think he was crazy—either a little or a lot. He was crazy. He was crazy like everyone never knew. But he knew just precisely how to be crazy. He knew everything he wanted to know.

———————

Hello, this is George Shapiro. These are my personal notes to myself regarding Andy Kaufman. Today is Friday, September 1, 1978, and I'm about to go over to see Andy as he's taping a new television series called *Taxi* for ABC-TV.

I've been Andy's personal manager for approximately two years. He came to my attention through my darling uncle and client, Carl Reiner, who saw Andy in a nightclub in New York called Catch a Rising Star, and Carl told me how unusual and different he was. Well, that may be one of the greatest understatements in the history of mankind. He is very close to being from another planet.

I am, for the most part, greatly enjoying working with Andy, because he has great creativity and spontaneity and it's very interesting being around him. There are some very positive aspects of his nature and some very negative ones. One of the biggest shortcomings to his professionalism is his need to come late to every situation that he is in. Including being late to performances in major arenas such as Town Hall in New York. He was scheduled for an eight-thirty curtain, normal for Broadway, and he probably went on at five minutes to nine. Kept a very restless audience waiting. It was a sellout crowd and he opened his show as Tony Clifton, which is in Andy's mind a secret, but many, many people in the industry and in the audience were aware that he was portraying another person, in makeup, in full makeup. He had a chin piece, a nose piece, his eyes were made up to be puffy, and he had a huge black wig covering his hair. His main line of patter, as you may know, is insulting the audience. He says, "I don't have to be here—you're lucky to have me!" That nature of thing.

Anyway, he did quite well in his opening of the show as Tony Clifton, then went backstage to take off his makeup. There was a scheduled twenty-minute intermission and it took close to forty minutes, and he came back and he actually killed the crowd, ending with a standing ovation. It was a very exciting evening. In fact, I would say it was the most exciting evening that I spent with Andy thus far. Of course, it was New York City, a sellout crowd, there was snow on the ground, people were coming in the snow and being turned away. So it was extremely exciting.

Andy's major television work thus far has been on *Saturday Night Live,* where he's done about six or seven appearances, and I think this show has made a tremendous impact on the college-age students. The youth of America watch this show and he became their favorite, above many of them. He still is not known in many areas of the country and his star is rising right now. He also appeared about five or six times on *The Tonight Show;* his first appearance was with Steve Allen, who filled in for Johnny Carson; Steve Allen has a great appreciation of Andy's talent. He was one of the first people to discover him. Other people who have discovered him besides the aforementioned Carl Reiner, who was very quiet about his discovery, are Alan King and Dick Ebersol, who is truly way up front in discovering him. Dick Ebersol is an NBC executive at this time; by the time anyone listens to this tape, I don't know where he will be—you know how it is with network executives. They go from one network to another network to independent productions to a third network, then starting all over at the first network again. Dick Ebersol brought him to the attention of Lorne Michaels, who is the producer of *Saturday Night Live.* And that started that part of his career. He also appeared about four times on *The Midnight Special.* Soon after I met Andy, I brought him to the Dick Van Dyke series, which I think was a quality series that was short-lived. The producers were Allan Blye and Bob Einstein and they truly appreciated Andy's talent and used him to great advantage on the show. He did only the Foreign Man characterization on the Dick Van Dyke show, from which he sprung into his imitations. He did Elvis Presley to great success on that show.

Following the Van Dyke series, he did a pilot for ABC, a half-hour situation comedy entitled *Stick Around,* in which he played a humanoid, a domestic robot, who did the chores and maid services around the house. Andy scored quite well on it, but the pilot did not sell. And as a tie-in to the deal, on his behalf, I received a payment of $25,000 for him to write a pilot script, which he later did with his friend Bob Zmuda. This was called *Fingers and Knuckles* and was presented to ABC, whose executives felt that the character Andy portrayed, Knuckles (short for Knucklehead), was a little bit too slow, too retarded, for a television series. They said that a man who couldn't find his way to an elevator is a little slow for our network and turned down the pilot script, which was written quite well by Andy and Bob. I have to admit this character was quite slow, but he had a certain appeal. Well, we'll see. I predict that somewhere in the future we will hear from Knuckles.

In addition to the guarantee of the pilot script, I had also negotiated for Andy six guest appearances on ABC within one year at $5,000 each, for a total of $30,000. He ended up doing only one appearance, on the Redd Foxx variety show, and he ended up earning $30,000. That was very nice for Andy. I also negotiated on Andy's behalf a ninety-minute late night special for ABC. He received $110,000 for the production and we formed a production company called KSW Productions, for Kaufman, Shapiro, and my partner Howard West. We did the special, although it looked like we were going to go way over budget, but we were able to bring it in so that we didn't go into a loss position. ABC didn't react real hot for this special. As a matter of fact, they refuse to telecast it. It *was* a little bit unusual. Andy did part of his act, which was very powerful, at the opening of the show, and he also had Cindy Williams on the show. Her spot was rather controversial because he had her come on pretending that she didn't know a song she was going to sing and Andy sort of pushed her on the stage to do the song anyway. Not what you would call one of your "commercial" spots . . . My opinion of the special was that it was very different and there were some things redeeming about it and some things that were a little slow. Hopefully this special will be telecast someday. . . .

Anyway, the last time Andy appeared in the Main Room of the Comedy Store, Ed. Weinberger came in with his associates who were about to write a script for a new series entitled *Taxi*. Ed. Weinberger's associates were Jim Brooks and Dave Davis and Stan Daniels. They asked Andy if he would go into the series. My feeling was it would be a nice boost for his career because it was a guaranteed "on-the-air" series and he would be playing a character that he knew very well, the Foreign Man—this particular character speaks no English in *Taxi* and his name is Latka Gravas. At this point, we do not know the reaction to the show, because it will not be telecast until September 12 and today is September 1. I think he will get great recognition and I feel this would bolster his career and personal appearances and will put him more in demand. He will receive more money, which will enable him to spend more money on his act and do the things that he wants to do. And when he has money, he wants to do outrageous things. I think this should prove very, very interesting.

He would never care much about money because Daddy seemed to care about it so intensely. He would see Daddy become angry about it, and about many other things, too, but down deep it was money matters that roiled most all aggravations that spewed forth onto the family. Daddy yelled a lot. Upon reflection, in fact, Daddy would sometimes lament that he really didn't feel alive unless he was angry.

Daddy came with a story, about which his son also cared little, but with which the son would become familiar enough, although never so much as to expend much empathy or acknowledgment. That, of course, is the province of fathers and sons before sons become their fathers. Nevertheless, here was Stanley Lawrence Kaufman, born of Flatbush, thus of Brooklyn, on August 31, 1922. Later, he would blame his birth sign, Virgo, for his passionate need to order the life in which he lived: "Gotta have control, gotta have control," he would tell intimates. He would also say, "I start my day writing a list and the best part of my day is when I check that list off at night." He was produced by people less meticulous and very boisterous, origin German-Jewish, though American-born: His father, Paul, especially, was nothing if not a (barely) repressed showman whose youthful antics on the Lower East Side caught the fancy of a vaudeville producer who had sent Eddie Cantor and Al Jolson into the world. It was Paul's formidable young wife, the former Lillie Goldberg, who told him to *oy* knock it off with even thinking about such fun and games and to get a decent job thank you, which turned out to be hawking cheap baubles and beads, which grew into a costume jewelry business that served better department stores throughout North America. They had two sons, six years apart, Stanley first, Jackie second, both of whom were to be good boys who followed in their father's jaunty, bejeweled footsteps.

So, young Stanley was thus: a street-savvy hail-fellow-well-met; a dashing and *wiry* little guy from a girth-endowed gene pool—these life-loving Kaufmans packed poundage!—and also he was *fast*; they called him Speedy Stanley on the track teams at school; he was quick with numbers, too, and took a business degree at Penn before the Army got him in '44 and sent him over to Normandy five days after D-Day. In one year of fight, of blood and chaos, he went down thrice, three Purple Hearts attendant. He received some minor German shrapnel first, was mended; then a prisoner he was escorting back from the lines of the Black Forest stepped on a land mine, killing the prisoner and searing Stanley's face and nose and neck (marks forever carried, though obscured), but he was mended again; then, out along the French-German border, a Nazi shell loaded with nails and tacks exploded in his chest, which sent him home, elated, with at least one tack lodged so deeply that it showed up in X rays for all time thereafter. He went home to the little girl he left behind, in whom he had found his first and only soul mate, whom he had vowed and yearned to marry immediately upon his return, so long as the Nazis hadn't killed him.

This love—which would come to bear a boy with big eyes—had struck him four springs earlier, in 1941. He had a fraternity brother at Penn who had a beautiful cousin on Long Island, in Belle Harbor, with whom he wanted to set Stanley up. Her name was Janice Terry Bernstein, a mere fifteen and a half years old, but so very poised, the only child of a menswear manufacturer named Cyril and his plucky wife, Pearl. Stanley was eighteen, shy with girls, dated hardly at all. But he agreed to meet this lovely thing who modeled in New York under the name Janice Terry for the tony John Robert Powers and Conover agencies. (Her specs, per professional data sheet: size 9 to 12; height five foot five, but really five-three; weight 104; eyes green; hair light brown; contours 32–23–32^1/$_2$.) She had already appeared, most prominently, in a *Parade* magazine photo spread as a glamorous urchin called The Runaway Girl. On a weekend home from school, Stanley and the frat brother whisked Janice and another girl off on a blind double-date in the city, a night of dancing and laughter during which hours flew and suddenly he was driving her home at four in the morning as her father paced the sidewalk in a bathrobe waiting and fuming. The blame fell upon Stanley's friend, Janice's cousin, for which he thanked God, and he himself didn't get back to Brooklyn until five, whereupon his mother lit into him and he stopped her with the proclamation, "*Mom, I want you to know that this is the girl I'm gonna marry!*" To which she responded most wearily, "Yeah yeah yeah." But he knew what he knew, which was that no one had ever made him so happy, so comfortable in his own skin. They went out again the very next night and his attentions from then on simply overwhelmed her. He doted tenaciously, as was his wont—a gift-giver like she had never known—thereby cementing his future and theirs.

They wed June 5, 1945. This was just ten days after he had returned stateside, where—as one of the walking wounded—he was kept as an outpatient at the Camp Edwards army base hospital on Cape Cod. Janice was ordered by Stanley to cease her wavering liberal studies at Moravian College in Bethlehem, Pennsylvania, so as to take his hand and make a life with him already. She complied, because what else could she do? He would have it no other way. Her mother—the gregarious Pearl—plotted the ceremony with great haste, pulling together three hundred celebrants, an officiating rabbi, and a matrimonial canopy for the event, which was held at a swank Long Island hotel. The groom was twenty-three, the bride was twenty; they took a brief honeymoon at Grossinger's Resort in the Borscht Belt before he had to return to Camp Edwards to complete his recuperation. A second honeymoon came immediately thereafter, for Stanley wanted to see the United States, so for three unforgettable months they drove thirteen thousand miles across the nation, plus up into Canada, plus down into Mexico, in an old Plymouth convertible with both of their mothers along for the ride— a screwball touch that gave him cocktail party patter forevermore.

And then came that which he could not escape, that which were he to have done it all over again he would have run like hell the other way from. But he did what he did, which he came to hate: He went to work for his father. The war was over and jobs were precious and fate was done. The company, located smack in the middle of Manhattan's jewelry district, was called KARU, for the partnership Kaufman and Ruderman, which was a mostly fractious partnership forged in the twenties but sufficiently profitable enough, no matter the ever squabbling egos therein, to keep from dissolving. Stanley had worked there, if briefly, before going to war, odd-jobbing in the shipping department, making cartons, sweeping floors. But now, in January of 1946, resigned and not too thrilled about it either, he officially began the only career he would ever know. He started in sales, with the understanding that one day he would rise up through the ranks, such as they were. He drove around New York, no real assigned territory, lugging samples in the car trunk, calling on any store he found that carried costume jewelry. "I would take an order here, an order there." He turned out to be a colorful performer—not quite the mammoth ham that his father was, but a warm and engaging and funny pitch artist. He got 10 percent commission on whatever sold. That first year he made about $8,500; within three years, he was making $12,500 per, which could maybe support a family. He and Janice were living in a sweet but small one-bedroom apartment in a nice building called The Fresh Meadows, in Queens. There they awaited the stork, coming close a few times with unhappy results, before the egg properly took and grew and grew inside Janice's belly. She would have to stay in bed most of this time to prevent another loss and was thrilled to feel the strengthening thump-thump-thumps within, like a little conga drum. Sometimes she played her records, listening to the music, feeling the bouncy little thumps beating along, sometimes (she thought) kind of in a rhythm all its own.

"I am from Caspiar. Eet ees an island. Eet's in the Mediterranean Sea and eet's a small island maybe many miles north of Tripoli, you know, in Africa. I know Tripoli because I know you have to go to Tripoli to get to Caspiar. We always get food from Tripoli so we always send to Tripoli. So you know eet's a small island not on the map. And we live, you know, not very many people. Mostly we fish. Just to eat. And food. And trees. I don't mean eat trees—but what grow on trees! People think I am eating trees! No, fruit and de vegetables! And we have bread, yah. But I wanted to be in show business, but I was going to stay on my island, but one day I go fishing and I go come back and my island ees not there. My island sink. Because eet's not there, I row de boat to Tripoli to go to United States to New York. Citizen I want to be. I want to be in show business."

Mommy and Daddy bought a little portable Victrola (well, they called it that) and put it on the dresser next to the crib to make music to soothe the baby. Grandpa Paul had gotten him plastic records, brightly colored ones, that played happy songs about Henry's wagon and about chick-chicks here and oink-oinks there and the monkey chasing the weasel and, through the bars of the crib, he would watch the colors spin and see how the needle went from one edge to the other edge to make the sounds come out. "Whenever it was on, he was totally content," Mommy recalled. She would later tell him that when he was nine months old, he could pull himself up in the crib and reach through the bars and push the needle down on the records and start the music all by himself. She would come into the room and find him laughing and jumping and the music playing. Sometimes—or so he eventually convinced himself—he would move his mouth along with the words on those records, "lip-synching" (he said) before he knew what such a thing was. "And all the relatives would come around into the room," he would boast, based on what he was told, "and watch and clap and laugh and everything." Anyway, he loved that story always and made Mommy tell it to new friends throughout his whole life. He saw this, quite proudly, as his first significant act on earth.

Daddy remained both impressed and incredulous whenever conjuring the memory of this small feat of dexterity and purpose: "He could play his own records. He was independent."

Channel 5 was purchased by Stanley early in the first year of his son's life. This would be where much invaluable laboratory work was completed, where the beginnings of the material would take shape. All performances were to be televised via unseen imaginary cameras installed beneath painted plaster drywall in the small bedroom where the infant would grow into his seventh year. Rehearsals began with the delightful phonograph exhibition, but the station would not be fully operational until the boy became familiar with actual television programming, still in its own technical nascency, as broadcast locally and nationally and viewed in the flickering snow-fuzzed black-white-blue glow of the family console, a wood-paneled Dumont.

It was no coincidence that Channel 5 was located at 5 Robin Way in the relatively modest Saddle Rock Estates section of Great Neck, Long Island. The closing price was $24,000, give or take, for which

Stanley assumed the mortgage on this handsome two-story red-brick home, tall and narrow, fashioned in the colonial style with white columns flanking the front door. There were three bedrooms and deep lawns fore and aft dotted with trees—an altogether suitable step toward upward mobility, a suburban family dwelling whose monthly nut worked out to be roughly ten dollars more than what renting a bigger apartment would have cost in The Fresh Meadows building. Not that Stanley wasn't nervous about the move: By this time, the company had handed him a major sales region in the South, encompassing Mississippi, Alabama, Georgia, and Florida, which forced him out onto the road more than he liked (six miserable weeks at a time!) and now there was much more at stake.

Great Neck itself had long represented the flush life. A century earlier, New York barons had begun building shrines to their great fortunes on these peninsular shores of the Long Island Sound. Formidable mansions owned by Vanderbilts and Chryslers and Annenbergs and the like hulked on manicured greens in privileged pockets of town. Swells had made much merry, especially during the Jazz Age, thusly inspiring F. Scott Fitzgerald, who in the summer of 1923 began to write *The Great Gatsby* while briefly ensconced with his wife Zelda in their Great Neck Estates home at 6 Gateway Drive—less than a mile from Stanley Kaufman's new source of debt. Show people had once swarmed Great Neck as well—from George M. Cohan to Florenz Ziegfeld to Fanny Brice to Groucho Marx. Mostly, however, it came to be understood that here was where upper-middle-class Jews went to live and raise families, a very safe thirty minutes removed from urban grit. Paul and Lillie Kaufman had settled into a house of their own on Wensley Drive five years before Stanley and Janice and the baby took up residence. That their little grandson would now be so close caused much kvelling, to be sure. And Janice's parents in Belle Harbor—Papu Cy and Grandma Pearl Bernstein—were no more than forty minutes away, for which what could be better?

Baby Andrew loved company and play. Daddy was away often— when he was home there was always commotion, sometimes happy, sometimes not so happy, mostly because of work stories. (He wanted to quit, to move his family to California, to do *anything* else though he knew not what—but his parents would hear none of it.) Anyway, the grandmas came around constantly to help Mommy with her musical Pussycat boy. And Grandpa Paul popped in regularly and made a wonderful ruckus, like a human carnival of noises and horseplay. But Papu Cy simply entranced him. Stanley would eventually call his father-in-law the love of his son's life. Papu dandled the boy and spoke sweetly and quietly sang to him. The child was mesmerized and would imprint and store these moments in his secret psyche and speak of them later: "I was just a real infant, you know, but I remember it. He was a real gentle man—he was always gentle, never yelled. He wasn't just that way with me, but with everybody. He loved me very, very much and I loved him. And he used to sit with me in the living room at night and sing this one song that he taught me, which was our song that the two of us had together. It was 'The Grandfather's Clock' . . . 'The grandfather's clock stood ninety years on the wall, but it stopped short never to go again when the old man died. . . .' You know that song?"

And so he would sing and he would laugh, unless he wept, as babies will (although hardly ever if Papu Cy was around); and when he wept, he held his breath, nobody knew why, he just held it until he turned the color of a grape, until his eyes protruded from their sockets, scaring the bejesus out of everyone. "You stop your crying!" Stanley would order him, sitting in a chair by the crib. "I would try to stare him down," he later recalled. "And I would take him and put him down. He'd get right up. And then he'd cry and hold his breath, a real good tantrum, and he'd turn blue and black from not breathing. Finally, I'd give him a couple of smacks so he'd open his mouth. Within the year, we noticed that when he howled and cried like that, there was a bulge in his groin. That was the first indication that Andy had a hernia."

Lots of whiteness, fingers poking down there, he was brave, a little soldier, barely one year old. "We were probably more frightened than he was. He was fine. There was no evidence of his being frightened," Daddy says. *They went inside and fixed him up and he came home from the hospital after a few nights during which he never squawked and right away Mommy took him down to Florida where both grand-mas and both grandpas were staying together in a big hotel—what great friends the grandmas and grandpas had become! Daddy put him and Mommy on the train.* "I remember saying goodbye to them at the station, and he was absolutely the most beautiful little boy, very hand-some, very very handsome, in his beautiful little outfit with a little cap to match." *The tonsils came out next, just months later.* "He had a lot of colds. We promised him ice cream." *Ice cream! He liked to mush it so it went down smoothly in his throat, which felt scratchy. Mush and smush it with his spoon. He would always want it just like that.* "I wonder if it all started with the tonsils. . . . His ice cream was a ritual all his life. He never ate the ice cream while it was hard. He took a spoon—it was like making butter. He'd get a tremendous bowl and he'd mix the chocolate with the vanilla. You would hear him stir-ring and stirring." *Then Mommy went away because there was another baby inside of her and this baby would be his brother, his little brother, and it was the day after New Year's Day—just before he would turn two—that Michael, Michael Alan Kaufman, came out. Mommy and Daddy and the bundle returned home from the hospital and everybody was happy but he wasn't very happy, or so it seemed to the grown-ups, and now there was another crib in the room and somebody else in it.* "When I was born, he would look out the window," Michael says. "This is what I was told. He was like normal before I was born, but then he started looking out the window." *Through the living room window, he would stare out at the grass and the trees and into the—where?* "When my brother was born," he would say, because Mommy told him this, "I started standing in the living room and I would stare out the window—just stare—and I would be very sad. Just sad." *He looked and looked for something, out that window. Maybe for Dhrupick to come play with him. Or Papu Cy. Papu made him feel better after Michael came to the family but then Papu stopped coming very much and Mommy said Papu wasn't feeling well and had to be in the hospital for a while.* "I remember he was in the hospital and I would see him less and less. And I would think, Oh! I was getting sad because I wasn't seeing him." *Papu had stomach cancer which was not good and he didn't come over anymore at all and then that November Mommy and Grandma Pearl and everybody looked very very sad, which made him even sadder.* "When he died, they didn't tell me— because I didn't know anything about death. So they told me that he went away. And I said, 'Well, when's he coming back?' And I kept waiting for him to come back and he never did." *He stood and stood in the window watching.* "I would just keep asking every once in a while, 'When's he coming back, when's he coming back?' And they said, 'Well, he's never coming back. He went on a long trip and he's never coming back.' " *Very lost very empty, big tears big eyes, almost three years old, so confusing—how?* "When I got older, my mother said that they realized that it was a mistake for them to tell me that. Because I kept saying, 'Well, why didn't he take me with him—if he was my friend, you know?' And then they said that God—who I just thought was this other guy—that God took him away with Him. God wanted him. So I pictured him driving along, that he had gone on a vacation and all of a sudden God lifted him up out of the car and He wasn't letting him come back. At first, I think I resented the fact that he didn't take me with him. But when they explained to me about God lifting him up and stuff, then it was all right." . . . *And the clock stopped short never to go again when the old man died.* . . . *He watched the window less and stayed in front of the television set and began watching the people and the cartoons inside the glass very very closely.*

2

Out of the blue, in the middle of the action, an extremely clever comic began counting, very slowly, and with great concentration: one, two, three, four . . . enunciating each of the numbers with the utmost deliberation, as if they had gotten away from him and he was gathering them up again: five, six, seven, eight. . . . When he reached fifteen, the audience began to laugh, and by the time he had slowly, and with greater and greater concentration, made his way up to a hundred, people were falling off their seats. . . .

Yes, cross the border and you hear that fateful laughter. And if you go farther, beyond laughter?

—Milan Kundera,
The Book of Laughter and Forgetting

Kiddie City, recording booth, Little Neck, New York, father, son, 1954:

"It's the Andy Kaufman Jamboree! And here's the great old troubadour himself with his guitar, Andy Kaufman! Good evening, Andy, how are you tonight?"

"Fine."

"How 'bout a little song for us. You got anything in mind that you'd like to sing? Maybe some original piece that you've written?"

"Yep!"

"What's the name of it, Andy?"

" 'Playin' on Me Ol' Guitar!' "

"Okay, Andy, let's see how it sounds! Introducing Andy Kaufman

with an original piece just written and being heard for the first time on radio and television—Andy Troubadour Kaufman!"

"O-lay-ee-oh, o-lay-ee-oh, o-lay-ee-oh, brrr-um-bum, brrr-um-bum, brrr-um-bum, brrr-um-bum, brrr-um-bum; playin' on the ol' guitar, playin' on the ol' guitar, gotta keep it old but I don't know how, playin' on the ol' guitar, bumbadumbum, bee-hee bee-hee bee-hee, brrr-um-bum; look at that man over there, he's wearin' no underwear, gotta keep it old but I don't know how, playin' on me ol' guitar, bee-hee bee-hee bee-hee. . . ."

"That was a terrific number, Andy. I'm sure that before very long, you're gonna be hearing that number from coast to coast and it'll be on top of the hit parade! Andy, is there one more number you have in mind?"

"I have—'What Time Is It.' "

"Is that another original composition?"

"Yep!"

"Okay, Andy, I guess all the folks would like to hear that number. Take it away!"

"What time is it? What is the time? It's only one o'clock. What time is it? What time is it? It's only one-thirty, it's only one-thirty. What time is it? What time is it? It's only two o'clock, it's only two o'clock. What time is it? What time is it? It's only two-thirty, it's only two-thirty. What time is it? What time is—"

"It's time to stop this song right now! Thank you, Andy, that was terrific! By the way, Andy, what time would you have ended that song?"

"Twelve-thirty."

"You mean you would have gone all the way up to twelve-thirty? My goodness, Andy! You know this program goes off the air in exactly one minute, and I don't think we would have made it. What do you think?"

"Wellll, that's not quite a long song!"

"I thought it was going to be a verrry long song. . . ."

Time was amorphous, meant very little. Hours passed, usually in solitude, though he was never alone, though he was mostly alone.

(He and/or Dhrupick became many characters and now the characters were working regularly. They made noises that burst out of him; he was a crowd; he was a spectacle; nobody saw or was supposed to.) Channel 5, of 5 Robin Way, upstairs bedroom, beamed daily telecasts beginning in 1953: "I really thought there was a camera in the wall and that there were millions of people watching me somewhere out in TVland. I don't know where—but *somewhere*—and I really believed this." No one was in the room with him. "No one was in the room with me." Little Michael would be gone, maybe downstairs or somewhere with the housekeeper, Margaret E. English, of Denmark, South Carolina—a shy and kindly young black domestic who had come to work for and live with the family the year before. Upstairs, Andy made his rumpus. Margaret saw him as a peripheral blur: "He would jump around, always on the go." Concentration was focused on the afternoon block of programming: "I had about four hours of programming every day," he would soberly recount to a television psychologist thirty years in the future. "Ohhh, I had all kinds of different shows—adventure shows, horror shows, old-time movies, cartoons. I would just run around the room playing all the parts." Eventually, he would break the afternoon down into eight half-hour shows. He would sing and dance, play heroes and apes, judges and defendants, villains and monsters, damsels and dogs, cowboys and . . . "I don't remember much of them. I remember one that was like an old-time silent movie show—'cause in those days on television they showed a lot of silent movies instead of cartoons. I didn't understand what was going on in these movies—all I knew was that these people were walking around faster than usual, with music playing. So when I was re-creating them for myself, there wasn't any plot. It was just me for a half hour walking around fast and doing all kinds of faces and falling down and stuff like that. . . .

"My parents would say, 'Why don't you go out and play?' And I would say, 'I can't! I'm putting on my shows!' "

Having gone inward when his grandfather died, he stayed inward, coming out only when alone. But he had also found a friend who lived across the backyard—she was real; her name was Cathy

Bernard—and he showed her the magic of inwardness, how to find secret places, the thrill of shared sanctuary, of hiding from. "He had a great imagination. We'd make tunnels in the backyard. This kid across the street had a tree house and we'd hang out there and make up stories and play house. There was another kid who lived next door to me who we hated. Andy would come up with all kinds of ways to torment him. We would make different bird sounds from the tree to confuse him. We'd say he could come over to play and then we'd hide. The kid would just go nuts. Andy liked finding ways to keep people from knowing where we were. He was into getting people wound up. My family had a basement with catacombs and we were always going in there. Sometimes he'd sneak down there unbeknownst to me and he'd make weird noises to scare us. One time, a house down the block caught fire and Andy said, 'Let's go jump on the fire engine!' So we hid on the engine while the firemen were putting out the fire. They didn't find us until they had pulled away and gone a few blocks.

"Mostly, I remember a lot of hiding in the family cars, then scaring the hell out of his parents when they looked inside. We'd crouch down in the back and his parents would be yelling, '*Andy, where are you!*' They had someplace to go or something to do. And he'd say, 'Let 'em go crazy, let 'em find us!' And his mother—she was a funny lady, too—she used to get so mad, and then she'd laugh because we were right there all along. The truly funny part was she never figured out that that's where we *always* were!"

Michael: "*One Saturday night, we were outside playing with Margaret. My parents were going to a formal dance in Manhattan and it's getting dusky and Margaret told us it's time to come in. Suddenly, 'Where is Andy?' She couldn't find Andy.*" Margaret: "*His mother and pop left for their dinner and it's dark and no Andy. I'm going around to different houses saying, 'Andy! Andy!' Nobody'd seen Andy. I got frightened.*" Stanley: "*As we're just about to go over the Fifty-ninth Street Bridge into Manhattan, I look in my rearview mirror—and I see this dirty little face popping up with a big, big grin, like, 'Surprise!' I was in shock. I didn't know what to do. I said, 'Janice, guess who's in the car with us?' She turns around and screams! What are we gonna do? We're late to this dinner dance, this kid is in the car, we're thirty-five minutes from home, Margaret's got to be frantic. So we immediately go to a telephone, call Margaret and tell her we have Andy with us. And then we call my mother-in-law, who now had an apartment in the city, and thank God she's home. Of course, she's thrilled because we bring her little grandson over to her. But Andy was so pleased that he had put this one over on us. So it all started very early, didn't it?"*

"Cut the kiddin', Kid McCoy!"

Was what Grandma Pearl always told him.

He never listened.

He loved to play for her.

(And for Grandpa Paul and sometimes Grandma Lillie.)

But most of all for Grandma Pearl, who lost Papu.

Like him.

Stanley and Janice noticed that he still had that sad face.

Somber almost. Sullen.

Unless he was making those noises behind that door.

(Or when he hid on them. Him with the surprises always.)

Or when he was with Pearl.

"Cut the comedy, Kid McCoy!"

"Cut the clownin', Kid McCoy!"

Pearl loved it, really.

Such energy, enthusiasm! A delight!

Then later the withdrawal, the shell, the lonesome eyes.

Janice: very concerned, then—

Preschool teacher said he's not right maybe.

Worriedly mentioned "imagination" to Janice.

Imagination = Delusional?

Teacher had glimpsed him alone, happily flailing-jabbering.

Like he was somewhere/someone else.

Then back again, so quiet again.

Perhaps and only if she would like . . .

The name of a reputable child's psychologist in the area?

Little tests could tell things . . .

It was probably nothing at all.

Was what Janice told herself.

He was four the first time. "When we saw that sad little face, we couldn't stand it, and we took him for psychological testing," his mother remembered. "Apparently, he was playacting all the time, really a showman." Which was to say, he was playacting even for the doctor lady, so how could anyone know the truth? "I would play with the toys the psychiatrist had. There were toy guns. I especially liked this air gun with red Ping-Pong balls. You pump it up and then you shoot it. I used to aim it at the psychiatrist. And she'd say, 'Now, you don't want to shoot me with that.' So I said, 'Okay.' " He always left the sessions smiling brightly—as though he had spun good ones in there. His father thought little of such examinations—*since when is imagination a bad thing?* The only conclusion that emerged was that, well, *here* was quite the lively lively mind! But where oh where oh where did he get such fanciful ideas?

Hi, Howdy.

Ho-ho! Well, hi, Andy!

How are you?

Ho, boy! I'm fine. And how about you?

I'm fine, thank you. Wow—thanks for coming on my show.

Oh, well, thank you for having me on your show, Andy. Boy, it sure feels great to be here!

Well, it's great having you. You know, Howdy, I was watching you ever since I was a real little boy. I used to every day go into the living room and I'd sit down before the television and turn on your show, at five-thirty. Every day. And I just thought it was great.

Ho, gosh! Well, thank you, Andy.

You know, you're even older than me. Your show came on in 1947, and I was born a couple years after that. So that means I was watching you since the time I could just first perceive images or sounds. Before I ever even knew what a television set was, I was watching you! So, like, you're the first friend from television I ever had—and probably the closest, I think. And, uh, I always wanted to meet you, and now I finally am.

Well, Andy, I . . . I'm glad to meet you, too.

(Laughter. Why are they laughing?)

You know, I was once in your Peanut Gallery, when I was five years old. You know? And I was just sitting there, and . . . I was kind of depressed, because I could see the man who was working your strings. And, I must say, even though I could see your strings and everything— to me you're just as real as anyone else who's on this show. And I feel like I'm really talking to a real person. But, anyway, one thing I wanted to do that day—and they wouldn't let us 'cause there was too many kids—and I always wanted to do this. And I'm wondering if maybe I could. And that was to touch you. Do you think I could maybe touch you?

Sure, Andy, go ahead—you can touch me.

Okay . . . (Laughter. What's so funny?) *Wow. You know, another thing that I always wanted to do was shake your hand. Do you think maybe I could shake your hand?*

Ho-ho! Sure, Andy!

Okay . . . (Laughing again—why?) *You know, this is just like a fantasy fulfilled for me. 'Cause I always used to want to be on your show.* (And again.) *And I thought that your show—you know, in Doodyville? That's where your show was . . .* (And again—please don't, okay?) *And I thought Doodyville was inside of the television. You know, like if television was this box—and if I went inside the box that was a television, I'd be in Doodyville. And I always wanted to be on your show. Now, here it is about, I guess, twenty-five years later, and I have my own show, and you're on my show!*

That's right, Andy. . . .

* * *

Kindergarten. Trauma.

[As depicted in epic semiautobiographical novel always and ever in progress—these portions written October 25, 1979, one week after the author had wrestled women on *Saturday Night Live* for the first time.]

Um.

First day of class. Mommy had fed him breakfast, got him dressed neatly. **"Hold it, honey," she said, and fixed his collar and buttoned his top button. "There you go . . . fit as a fiddle."** Always hated top button buttoned. Mommy made him always. She waved as bus pulled away. **He wanted to cry, but was too shy in front of all these strangers.** At school, teacher goes around room asking each child to introduce him/herself. **As it got closer to the little boy's turn, he became very very extremely nervous, repeating his name in his head over and over again so he would get it right. Finally, when it was his turn, he couldn't do it. A little voice in his head said, "Come on, just say your name," and he wanted to very much, but no voice would come out of his mouth.**

"And what's your name?" The teacher was looking directly at him. "No? Not today? Oh, all right." And she smiled understandingly at him and directed her attention to the next child. "And what's *your* name?"

If he had ever felt like crying, now was really the time. He had never felt such embarrassment in his whole five-year-old life. He sat there, forcing his jaw to stay open, knowing that if he let it close, he would definitely cry and then be even more embarrassed than he already was. . . . As he sat there and saw all the other kids saying their names, he felt that they were all looking at him and saying to theirselves, "Look at that baby. What a baby! Well, I'll never play with him! He should be totally ashamed of himself. So very very extremely ashamed that he should hang his head down so he's looking at the ground and when he walks he should keep his head between his legs." When he looked up, he noticed that no one was watching him. . . .

Well . . . some would watch when he wasn't looking, when he was off alone/oblivious behind the school playground, obscured by the little cluster of trees, where he repaired to continue his riotous broadcasts. School had seriously interfered with his ritual of afternoon bedroom performances. Now at Saddle Rock Elementary, he relegated programming to lunch recess period; other children played amongst themselves; he played amongst himselves (for the entertainment pleasure of unseen millions as usual). Once he had reached first grade onward, he could compress his sprawling cavalcade to a solid solitary outdoor half hour of extravaganza, and he thrilled at his own ability to make it such a tremendous success. Out in TVland, his loyal viewership had come to adore his every song dance fall leap spin face voice character movement gyration yodel instrument solo symphony fight victory defeat commercial trick and tale. He was a smash! Huge and very very extremely famous. He knew this certainly and one day so would everyone else.

Later, much later, after people, many people, certainly not *everyone*, had begun to sort of know who he was and journalists came to ask him about how he got to be the way that he was—*this was all according to master plan, of course*—he would recall his excellent work in the woods behind the school. He would conjure and reenact these performances for whoever poked deeply enough. He would coalesce *years* of stored recess broadcasts (all the way up through fifth grade, in fact), slipping into each splendid reverie with fresh conviction. . . .

"I could only do one program a day. . . . For a while, I did my version of *American Bandstand* where I played the Dick Clark part. I was the emcee Andy. Then I would be each of the performers—the rock-and-roll stars. Then I would be the kids dancing. Finally, I would be all these things at the same time. . . . For a few months, I put on a monster show called *Horror House*. I'd be strangling myself, yelling, going, 'Get away from me! Get away from me!' Then I'd turn around and do the other part: '*Errggh, I'm going to keel you!*' 'No! No!' '*Errggh!*' So if someone had been watching me, they'd think I was crazy. . . . Oh! And I'd do wrestling, too! I put on a wrestling show where I'd play both parts—I'd be both the bad guy and the good guy and wrestle myself.

"One day a kid was chasing a ball and he came into the woods where I was doing a horror show: *'Getcha hands off me!'* 'No! No!' And I'd be serious. I wasn't trying to be funny, but it would look like a crazy man. He stayed there and watched. The next day another came. A few more every day. The word got around. And do you know that after a while I had an actual audience! I really did!

"They'd be clapping. . . .

"I was just a nut doing this stuff. . . .

"I was serious about it, but I suppose to them it was funny. . . .

"They were laughing. . . .

"I wasn't trying to be funny. . . .

"They thought I was nuts and that's what they were laughing at. . . .

"I wouldn't care, you know. I'd still continue doing my shows the same way. *But they would be watching me.* . . .

"Then, one day in the second or third grade, something funny happened. My show ran overtime and I was announcing the closing credits on the way back to the building after recess. Real serious. I was saying, *'That's all from* The Andy Kaufman Show! *This program was brought to you live by—'* All of a sudden, by my side, I heard a voice go, *'No, this program was brought to you dead!'* I said, *'No, it was live!'* *'Maybe yours was live,'* this voice said, *'but mine was dead.'* A kid who was watching me had begun doing the same thing on the other side of the playground. We finished our two shows together. We looked at each other and started laughing. We were exactly on the same wavelength! It was beautiful. We became best friends.

"Every day we started putting on shows together. It was a partnership. Before that, I never had any friends—I was 'nuts.' I still remember his name: Alfred Samuels. After a while my parents thought he was crazy because he talked to himself and they forbid me to be friends with him. They also thought there was something wrong [with me], but not nuts like this guy. I was their son, so they loved me. . . . The funniest thing, though, is that his parents thought the same thing about me! His parents ended up moving out of town. I never saw him again. I wonder what ever happened to him. . . ."

Um.

Stanley and Janice never knew of any Alfred Samuels.

Nor did anyone else who knew their son.

Nor, quite apparently, was there ever such a boy.

Except for one.

Not counting Dhrupick.

Howdy had Buffalo Bob and what great pals they were! One really couldn't exist without the other (they even sort of sounded alike), it seemed to him. And they had other good friends like Flub-a-Dub and Mr. Bluster and Dilly Dally and, of course, the antic mute Clarabell the Clown (see—quiet could be fun!). Then on *Terrytoon Circus* (on which host Claude Kirchner told him every evening to go to bed afterward like "all good boys and good girls"—for which he and Michael were inspired to throw things at the Dumont screen), Heckle had Jeckle and vice versa (and they looked an awful lot alike; magpies, whatever). Mighty Mouse, meanwhile, had other identities, disguises, kept pretty much to himself (unless Mr. Trouble a.k.a. the idiot cat came to hang around). Superman was two guys who were one guy. Popeye ate spinach and became a different/same Popeye. And then there was *Winky-Dink and You,* which was really Winky-Dink and him: Equipped with his very own Official Winky-Dink Kit, he could draw directly on the TV screen—with magic crayon over green cellophane—so as to interact with (and often make fun hiding places for) his cartoon pal with the star-shaped head. As such, essential lessons in friendship and in persona had washed over him and stuck deep. "It seems to me that he took so many of those programs very seriously," Stanley would say. "They gave him ideas that he never forgot."

Lessons at school were less intriguing. He was disinterested in his studies, always would be, would always be thinking of other things instead. "He didn't work hard at all," his father recalled. "He didn't work any harder than he had to. He got average marks without studying. He was a very, very smart kid, but he never wanted anyone to know it. For whatever reason. It was always my impression that whatever his ability was, he didn't want it to be known. It was his secret." Thus there were teacherparentconferences unending. He hated Mrs. Sanders of the second grade. "He would make faces at her, drive her crazy," Cathy Bernard recalled. "He mimicked her. She was the type who said, '*You do this, you do that!*' There was no room for anything other than what she told you to do. For someone like Andy, that was the perfect foil."

Eventually, the debut was at hand. *The time had come.* "At school," he said, "every week or two, I was bored with being myself." *As such.* "I'd go off into fantasyland." *Always nicer there.* "Sometimes I'd be my twin brother Dhrupick." *Of course.* His father had traveled to Japan on jewelry business and returned with kimonos for the family. And so it was that Dhrupick, finally, flamboyantly, officially, came out of his closet. "One day, in second or third grade, I was looking in my closet and saw the kimono and I decided to wear it to school. I forgot I had it on. When the teacher asked, 'Why are you wearing that, Andy?' I said, 'I'm not Andy. I'm Andy's twin brother Dhrupick.'" He remembered being immediately sent to the school psychologist . . . or was it just that the teacher shrugged, rolled her eyes, as usual, and let him be? Or was it both? Or did it ever happen at all? Well, that was how he remembered it anyway. He always liked the kimono story. Everyone seemed to like the kimono story. It was a good story.

Meanwhile . . .

Janice would become pregnant with Carol. The house on Robin Way would begin to shrink. Always there was ruckus. Michael broke Andy's neck. Well, they liked to say that—it was a bad strain, really. They wrestled a lot. They imitated the Spanish wrestlers on TV. Margaret watched her gospel shows and the boys made fun of her and switched the channel over to the wrestlers whenever she turned her back. Andy was in traction for maybe three weeks with the neck. It never hurt all that badly. He was very very proud. He liked the traction thing, the ropes. He liked the broken neck thing very much. Once he and Michael stole all the newspapers from everyone's front stoop, then threw them down the sewer. Stanley went crazy (yell-yellyell), went out and bought the neighborhood new papers, delivered them with beet-faced apology. Andy liked blaming Michael for everything. Like the time he snipped all the buds off the rosebush in front, then said Michael did it. Stanley went crazy (yellllll); Michael got spanked. Perfect crime. The brothers decided to repaint the living room furniture one Christmas to surprise their parents. Wood, upholstery, everything. Some great-aunt gave them the paint kit. Redyellowgreenblue, everywhere. Stanley went crazy (yelllllllllll-llllll), rolled each son into a ball and threw them across the room onto a (painted) couch; they bounced and bounced. Thank God for the homeowner's insurance. Big fat Grandpa Paul kept bringing stuff. He got them a movie projector and reels and reels of movies, shorts and features: funny cowgirls singing on stick ponies. The Little Rascals trapped in a spookhouse. Boris Karloff as the Mummy. The Creature from the Black Lagoon. He also kept bringing them new records, then took them to make their own records, took the whole family to the small-fry amusement park Kiddie City, ten minutes from home, again and again, to sing songs in the recording booth. They were little blue records. Paul and Stanley loved taking turns in the booth with the boys, making like corny Hit Parade announcers. Michael Troubadour Kaufman sang children's favorites. Andy Troubadour Kaufman sang both original compositions and hits of the day. He sang "Your Cheatin' Heart"; nobody knew where he learned it. He sang "Love and Marriage" and "My Baby Don't Love Me No More" and "Let Me Go, Lover" and, very frequently, "It's Howdy Doody Time." He was never shy when he sang, only shy when he didn't. Or so his family noticed, with continued amazement. At such moments, he was without all inhibition and rather dazzling. He rarely forgot a single lyric. Such focus, precision. Odd. Carol was named after Papu Cyril. She was very beautiful like her mother. She was born the day before Andy's seventh birthday. Stanley and Janice said she was his birthday present. He was not thrilled especially. Within months, the cameras in his bedroom walls had to be removed. They were reinstalled in a much larger house where he would eventually perfect the (friendly) world which only he would, or could, inhabit.

3

"Your place looks like the world's fair," I said.

"Does it?" He turned his eyes toward it absently. "I have been glancing into some of the rooms. Let's go to Coney Island, old sport."

—Nick Carraway to Jay Gatsby,
F. Scott Fitzgerald
The Great Gatsby

Paths are taken but also given. Fate, stars, moons—he would later listen carefully to what they told him about who he was and why and how and where he would go. He shared his birthday with Cassius Clay/Muhammad Ali, which he would take as a sign—identities/invincibility. (Others born January 17, about which he cared less: Benjamin Franklin, Al Capone, acting theorist Konstantin Stanislavsky, silent-comedy director Mack Sennett—all of whom, like him, followed their divergent instincts unyieldingly.) His day of birth, he would discover, came with an astrological mandate—that he would do exactly what he was supposed to do and do it no matter what anyone else thought and no one would ever tell him otherwise. (*Was anyone else really there?*) He would never ask permission nor would he ever understand the meaning of permission. Thus, the hollerings of his father would increasingly become mere racket to him, an unpleasant din he would drown by whatever means most amused him. He lived for amusement, so much so that he became amusement—and that was his path and he went forth determined and oblivious. Now whenever a new passion enraptured him, he absorbed it entirely, became proficient at it, commanded it, finally showed it off to others (this last was most imperative to the plan). A new and finer hyperkinesia flamed throughout his awkward body, made it adroit, precise, confidant. When amused, when amusing, he beamed, he was beautiful. When his father forced him to attend athletic summer camp or play Little League baseball—well, there would be photographs in family albums of a boy sodden in unspeakable misery, quite limp/lost, quite out of context. Stanley later regretted doing that to him, humiliating his son by assuming that he was like any/every other template of American boyhood, that his son was anything at all like the boy that even he himself had been. No, here was a different boy with a mission. (*Very serious about it . . . maybe funny to others . . . wasn't trying to be funny . . .*) And there would be, in all actuality, without metaphor, a different drummer—a very very extremely different drummer—and the different boy found the different drummer's drumming in short order and then great changes took hold. Hence, the march of a lifetime ensued.

Everything enlarged. Beginning with the house. They moved to the best part of town, to King's Point, long considered the most prestigious corner of Great Neck—albeit to a relatively new and modest subsection therein. This was summer 1956; the property at 21 Grassfield Road cost $52,000; houses here were built on lush berms and set far back from the street. Now there were five bedrooms, including Margaret's on the lower level near a laundry facility and a smallish den which would become a sanctum most hallowed (and often forbidden)—the place a certain mind's eye pictured whenever feats were performed in the outside world that had been born and practiced endlessly down there. Anyway, this would be the last family home they would all know together.

Stanley Kaufman's career in costume jewelry had obviously also enlarged, though not without struggle and frayed nerves and ongoing dreams of escape and hopeless irritability attendant. He would eventually call this house—sturdily spread, tri-leveled, prefab-sided, with attached two-car garage, on enormous lot—"the best investment of my life." His job responsibilities were by now more than commensurate with his talents—besides fully engaging his bright business acumen, he was even designing KARU product lines of earrings and pendants and such. Still, however, working with his father and his father's partner gave him much *tsouris*, much doubt. "The truth is, I had just bought the house and things were terrible downtown. You've got to understand—at no time in all the years I was with my father did I ever have any feeling of security. I had to be a very, very conservative person because I could be out of a job at any moment. These two men were at it almost every day of the week—'We're gonna break up this goddamned business!' I'd not only hear it at the office, I used to drive home with my father maybe three days out of five and it was always a rehash. I thought, *Forget it!* It was awful. Nothing pleasant about it at all. So the commitment of the new house came with the headache of *Can I sustain this?"*

Chaos at work required perfect o-r-d-e-r at home—order unimaginable, thus unachievable, in a household where three young children grew and cavorted. And so, too, the rages enlarged. Janice took/accepted the brunt. Stanley, the otherwise good and loving husband and father, would have to vent and rant for years to come. (Was there no aspect of his world that he could control?! How he tried—picking out furniture and decor for the house, selecting clothes for Janice and the kids, shopping for groceries, designating basic tasks for all—but damned if the results ever turned out exactly as he wished.) His frustrations and furies were to be a Grassfield Road continuum. His wife heaved her sweet deep sighs and patiently understood—she once wrote a poem and handed it to him and left the room—

"I'm wishy washy, dull as can be;
No one asked you to marry me.

But you liked those traits and gave me a boost;
For that I let you Rule the Roost. . . .
If I choose something that I like to wear,
You say, "No. Wear this." As if you care.
But other times, I don't know why,
You're so indifferent, you make me cry.
Now try to be nice—let's not fight,
Tell me, which dress should I wear tonight?"

The children, however, could not abide the storms. They witnessed their father carping at their mother, wishing she could stop him, knowing that she wouldn't. "For the most part," Michael remembered, "she just took it. Here was this fragile little woman—I was amazed that she didn't cry when he yelled at her. She hardly ever did. Sometimes she would even start it by asking him a stupid question. She drew it out. Carol, Andy, and I would look at each other and go, 'Why is she doing it?' We'd see it coming and think, 'Watch out! Let's head for our rooms!' But they somehow were able to have a sense of humor about it. I think he once had a T-shirt made up for her that said, DON'T YELL AT ME! And she had one made for him that said, I'M NOT YELLING!"

Carol turned from infant to teen with the cacophony ever resounding, wincing at it always. "I saw her as a doormat, a victim," she recalled. "He'd bark, 'You left the lights on!' 'Burnt steak again!' 'Where'd you get this meat from?!' I'd be sitting there with knots in my stomach. It was almost like having an alcoholic father, in terms of not wanting your friends to see what was happening—and sometimes they did. I remember seething inside and thinking, 'Just tell him to shut up!' Later, I'd sometimes tell her, 'Leave. Just pack your bags, take us and leave.' Mostly, I just went and turned up the stereo."

Andy kept silent about it. Then and for always. Excused himself from the table, from the room, from the family, from the reality. He rarely spoke of his father's noise to anyone for the rest of his life; it never really came up in normal conversations; of course, he would make an inadvertent point of never actually having normal conversations; they never really came up. (Certainly, he would personally withstand gusts of that same anger as he grew and tested paternal patience.) But he paid enough attention to the tone of the torrents—shrill, nasal, sibilant, snappish, relentless. Strangely, he would one day know a particularly bilious lounge singer who seemed to replicate, bleat for bleat, the singular staccato of Stanley Kaufman's fulminations. Enlarged on them, even. And though he would have a very special affection for the unpleasant lounge singer, he never really approved of all that terrible yelling. It just wasn't very nice.

Storms came and went, trailing wakes of regret. Regret brought reprieves, big fun happy ones. Coney Island was best. It became a family ritual, beginning when Carol was tiny, continuing on through always. Janice loaded the kids into the car and Stanley took the D train from town after work and they'd meet in the parking lot and nights of wonder unfolded. Rainbow lights swirled and spun; saltwater breeze swept calliope music into the muddle of screams, laughter, shills, nonsense. Such was Coney—that, plus neat sideshow freaks. (Upon arrival, every time, two big wide eyes got bigger and wider and danced better dances. What was seen here, heard here, was what lived behind those eyes since forever. Home. This. Best place anywhere. Absolutely. He always said so.) Food came first, per ritual. Stanley filled the bellies of his brood with fabulous Nathan's Famous hot dogs and french fries, then chow mein on rolls, then corn on the cob, then custard, then jelly apples and cotton candy. (Cotton candy: *Oh!*) Then they rode everything, repeatedly—the Steeplechase, the Parachutes, the Rotowhirl, the Wonder Wheel and the mountainous, monsterous Cyclone. But of course—the Cyclone!—towering behemoth, legendary roller coaster of the gods, famous for its seemingly ninety-degree plunge toward certain death. It was, to be sure, Andy's favorite, would always be. He made a prop of it. For every turn on the ride, he created elaborate performances around the bliss/terror. He liked to announce in shrieks at the apex: *"We're all going to die!!"* He liked to feign desperate protests before boarding—*Oh please, no, please-please-please, I-don't-wanna, noooooo!!!* Best of all, he liked to disembark weeping hysterically, until his father or mother or some- one told him to knock it off, at which point his face resumed repose and he smiled and said, "Okay." (Could turn on a dime. Like that. Liked doing that like that. Interesting. Was only fooling. No, really.)

Coney Island stayed inside of him.

Performances picked up. Got more daring. He had transferred to Baker Hill Elementary after the move to King's Point, then quickly found a new wooded nook behind the school playground for his stage- craft. Boy in bushes continued apace with aforementioned flights. He would recall spending weeks in class expressing himself only in the voice of Jerry Lewis. ("And I had never seen Jerry Lewis." *Nasal, hy- perspastic, self-infantilizing.* "I just could not talk unless I talked like a little boy." *More and more teacherparentconferences redux.*) In cold weather, he furthered his inadvertent study of response testing: At his mother's insistence, he wore layer upon layer upon layer upon layer of clothing to prevent chill. Then, upon entering school, he method- ically—never hurriedly—removed each layer after layer after layer after layer, which incited laughter and discomfort and derision among his classmates and teachers alike. He grew to enjoy each beat of the process, each pursuant guffaw and groan and glare.

He began to add even more layers.

He never did it to be funny, of course, possibly.

Anyway, they all got bored with it.

He was, after all, nuts.

Meanwhile, in his new bedroom on Grassfield Road, the wall- camera business began wearing upon his mother. In his ninth sum- mer, she demanded that he just stop. He would choose to remember it this way: "She said, 'You cannot do these shows anymore unless you have an audience. Even if it's only one person watching you.' She thought, *Now he can't do them anymore—ha ha ha!* This was very bad, in that he was onto something big by now. Panicked, he sought solution; his brother could not have been less interested, was always outside playing, anyway; friends were not an option, really; finally, he noticed another person in his family, female, two years of age, very malleable. "My sister loved bubble gum. So what I would do was bribe her. I'd give her a piece of bubble gum every day if she would just sit in the room. Also, I wasn't shy in front of her, because she didn't know how to talk. So she would be my audience — and that was my loophole. I got my mother on that one."

Big break came the year before. Out of the blue. Changed everything. Started everything. Thus the panic and the desperate need for practice. Finally, for once, he had acquired a proper audience — not a gaggle of bemused/hectoring onlookers (as with schoolyard), or a loophole (as would his sister become), but an actual rapt assemblage that sat in little folding chairs to watch him. "I had a movie projector, and a friend of the family asked me if I would show some movies at his daughter's birthday party. I said sure and I did some stuff between films." Whatever the stuff, no memory would be retained. Musical chairs? Fun with phonograph? Magic tricks? All very likely. Certainly all would figure later, very much later, and also sooner. But this was his fleeting debut at something really real. It was a taste. It filled him with ideas. He got to do in public that which was previously private or semi-such. Gently, tentatively, he had performed for children who *wanted* and *expected* him to perform for them. And they seemed to kind of enjoy him. Little birthday party children, they liked him. This was very very good. He would do more. He could see it very clearly.

February 13, 1975 (3:04 A.M.):
He had left the club, loaded his stuff back into his father's car, driven the quiet Long Island Expressway from town back to Great Neck, back to Grassfield Road. Things had gone well enough — his work with the pitiful F. Man was only getting better and better and more fragile so as to almost crumble like brittle ash but never really. "Laughing at me? Or . . . laughing weeth me?" Grandma Pearl always told him with with with. Also E. was probably perfect by now, at least for these crowds — voice very strong, legs and hips electric, needed only better costume. Phonograph, drums, songs, fooling, teasing, lying in/for fun — fine so far. Good nights, okay nights, bad nights, just moving for-

ward. Anyway, Budd and Rick really liked him and always gave him time, and the NBC people were supposed to come to see him work soon, something about some new show that might happen, and he already did that Dean Martin summer thing last year, so it was building and building. Mommy and Daddy were sleeping, of course, and he smushed his ice cream and took it down to his room and opened his sand-colored Pen-Tab Wire Bound Theme Book (90 Sheets; 69 cents) on which he had chicken-scrawled across the cover, as he did with everything he wrote in, "This book belongs to Andy Kaufman." (He had started this one last May, slowly filling it with short stories and ideas, almost always in the dead of night, because it was quiet and he needed to sleep all day, anyway.) Now he would make notes for the novel, whatever the novel would be whenever he got around to writing it. It would be huge, he knew that, and it would be about a boy who grew up to become the world's greatest entertainer (himself, he hoped; you have to write what you know plus make-believe things) and it would deal with a mountain and getting over the mountain that no one had ever gotten over before and it would have lots of cataclysmic adventures and amusement park rides. He dated the page, checked the clock, recorded the time, and wrote the word **earthquake** *and then filled line after line with other brief notions, scene ideas, diagrammatic plot points like* **seeing of beautiful "angel" at foot of mountain** *and* **occasional meetings w/future self; as star, businessman, bum, intellectual writer, millionaire, etc.** *Mainly, the plan here was to flash forward and backward a lot by way of fantasies and he was remembering now about how he first started out, way back at the birthday parties, which would be how this character—who was going to have the name Huey Williams—also started and he wrote:*

> **entertaining the kids—great performance,**
> **his ego is up—after he leaves then,**
> **he meets future self (star) & is inspired . . .**

*   *   *

He was very inspired, of course. But he had to wait wait wait after that first party and better prepare himself for the next one. He knew this was going to be his racket: the birthday parties. He would be a kid entertainer, making amusement amid cake and candles and ice cream and cookies. (Oh!) Grandpa Paul always created big hambone spectacles at his grandchildren's parties—he would bring new cartoons for the projector and do old magic tricks and tease the kids and make everyone laugh. What Grandpa Paul did, he could do, too. He just needed a little more practice. Carol watched him practice until he was ready.

April 4–9, 1980 (past midnight), Maharishi International University, Fairfield, Iowa:

Seven months into the novel now, actually writing, finally writing, whenever he could; Huey Williams was him, most certainly; he had been departing from his outline notes, taking more and more unplanned flights directly into barely veiled autobiography. To wit: Little Huey was very very shy, played alone behind schoolyard in woods with imaginary friends (some had names—there was Harry, **the nicest guy in the world. Whenever you have a problem, you can just tell him and he'll listen and try to help you no matter how busy he is;** *Eddie, who was* **very mean, so if you're in a bad mood, you can always pick a fight with him, and if you want, you can always win;** *and Marcia,* **the most beautiful girl in the world and she loves you more than anyone has ever loved anyone and ever will love anyone.)** *There was also a sweet Mommy who called Huey her Pussycat; the Daddy had an irrational temper, screamed often; there was a little brother (Waldo) and baby sister (Kate); and there was a Grandpa who was both Cyril Bernstein (profound love connection with grandson) and Paul Kaufman (wonderful fat irrepressible performer). Now—here in this quiet quiet timeless place where he liked to come and stay and learn and settle himself—he would write about Grandpa's performances at children's parties and how he taught Huey to follow suit. Grandpa showed cartoons, of course, and did a strange song and dance involv-*

ing noodles and wore fangs as he did so. He also had a wind-up phono-graph, a Victrola, on which he played funny old-fashioned records, next to which he **stood in place, bobbing his roly-poly body up and down, pointing his finger in the air and wriggling it to and fro in rhythm with the music. In the middle of the song, the record had a scratch . . . and a phrase kept repeating several times as he just kept bobbing and wriggling his finger, until he smiled to attract the attention to his face . . .** *He followed with magic tricks which he intentionally messed up which made the children laugh because his face was creased with* **utter dismay which he put on for their benefit.** *Also he produced a large peculiar musical instrument called the Wamagadoon and he* **started banging it in such a silly, untalented way, but with such technique that it fascinated the kids and had them totally entertained.** *Later, very movingly, in a private moment, he revealed to Huey* **all his tricks and secrets . . . how to keep up the people's attention and fascinate them. He showed him the "art" of playing the Victrola so that people would watch, and last but not least, he showed him how to play the Wamagadoon.**

All of it was pretty much the way it really happened, except the part about the Wamagadoon. But this stuff wasn't supposed to be completely true, anyway.

Ponpongaba, ponpongaba. Now came the thumping, and with the thumping came the rest of everything. Babatunde Olatunji, enormously tall, draped in dashiki, flamed of fingertips, mystical Nigerian—he appeared like a miracle, unprecedented, without warning, performing for school assembly in the auditorium of Baker Hill Elementary (*most unusual booking*) in the spring of 1959. It was, maybe, a divine intervention. Virtuoso of West African percussion, first and most famous exporter of such, Olatunji had just made his best-selling debut album, *Drums of Passion,* for Columbia Records—an awakening sound, all new, deeply ancient—whose liner notes explained inexplicable primitive beliefs: "The drum, like many exotic articles, is charged with evocative power . . . [it is] not only a musical instrument, [but] also a sacred object . . . endowed with a mysterious power, a sort of life-force which has been incomprehensible to many missionaries and early travelers, who ordered its suppression by forbidding its use." And so Olatunji brought his forbidden drums to school that day—drums of hollowed trees and stretched ramskins, congas large and small, over which he leapt and pounced, danced and chanted, beating his rhythms of *gangan* and *dundun* and *bembe* and whatever else they were called. Grades one through six beheld the exhibition, some of whom endured squirmingly, others most certainly rendered agog.

One member of the fourth grade, in particular, could not believe his eyes or ears. "That was definitely an epiphany moment," said Gregg Sutton, a very new friend who would become much more. "I was sitting right next to Andy and we were both completely entranced, mesmerized. If we had been bored for a second, we would have started doing stupid shit. We never even looked at each other—except to say 'This is pretty great!' We had never seen a black guy like that. The only black people in Great Neck we had contact with were domestics that worked for our parents and grandparents or else the occasional cab driver. So here all of a sudden was this giant black man with a different vibe—and his music was wild! That's when Andy probably went, *Hey, I could do that!*"

Olatunji's thrall engulfed him entirely. Those sounds—he couldn't get them out of his head, maybe they had always been there. He knew this much—that he would chase down Olatunji, hound him relentlessly, beg private lessons from him, become his special friend, one day do him proud. Gregg Sutton would bear witness to this, to almost everything pertinent, as years unspooled. In Sutton, meanwhile, he had recognized with happy alarm (oh!) a new sort of kindred spirit—an eccentric kid, temperamental, musical, rebellious, dangerously smart. Sutton came from garment industry money imperceptible; he was, in fact, a well-bred but scraggly fellow with a most erratic demeanor. He earned Andy's unending admiration during a classroom party by smashing a pineapple upside-down cake on the head of a boy nobody much liked. "It

started a riot. The teacher had a nervous breakdown right there—
she had to lay down on her desk—and we never saw her again. I was
psychotic that day. Andy loved it. He never let me forget about it."

Their bond was forged in other ways, too: Sutton had been friends
with another Andy Kaufman at school (there were, astonishingly, two
of them at Baker Hill, although a Kaufman in Great Neck would be
as rare as a Smith or Johnson anywhere else). The other Andy
Kaufman (regular kid) either moved away like Alfred Samuels before
him or sought the need for individuating anonymity. In any case,
Sutton found dark amusement in switching over to this new Andy,
the one with the eyes. Much more important, however, was the fact
that they would share an increasingly unpopular fondness for Elvis
Presley. They could endlessly debate merits of each Presley single
and its flipside, their first nexus being thus: "We both thought 'Fame
and Fortune' was bullshit and that 'Stuck on You' was okay, but not
nearly as good as the other stuff. It just came up one day out of
nowhere. Then we realized that we were the only two kids who even
cared. Nobody we knew ever talked about Presley. We looked at each
other and went, *Wow!*"

*"When I was five years old my parents took us to Tennessee. When
we were there, my dad took us to a theater. A man was doing an act
which involved singing and shaking his hips a lot. When I got home
from my trip, I jumped around as if I were that guy. I practiced my
singing and after a while I started to sound like him. Then, in 1960, I
saw Elvis for the first time and I couldn't believe it. Elvis was doing the
same thing I was doing and the same thing that guy in Tennessee was
doing. I never knew that guy's name, but he was my inspiration, not
Elvis."*

As with so much treasure, Grandpa Paul brought Elvis to him.

This, of course, was the presumptive wont of Paul Kaufman. He
was the uncommon senior—sixty-five the year of Presley's emer-

gence—who embraced all newness with unnerving zeal. He could not help but help himself—and his loved ones—to whatever suddenly struck his epic fancy. *Was it so wrong to enjoy? To enjoy spreading enjoyment?* He believed in living in, and of, the moment and saw no reward in acting his age, whatever that meant. Among friends and acquaintances, for instance, he would be the first owner of a color television set, gleefully paying upwards of $3,500 for the distinction. He proudly drove a 1957 Chrysler Imperial outfitted with its own dashboard phonograph which spun specially designed records that he blared through rolled-down windows so as to remind neighbors of his youthful abandon. "You know what record he played most?" Stanley would say. " 'Davy Crockett' from the Walt Disney program! My father was a big kid."

And so now the youngsters were making the new music, especially the southern boy with the guitar who did the wiggling with the waist. He thought that his eldest grandson should have this buoyant noise in his ears. And so he brought "Hound Dog" and "Don't Be Cruel" and "Blue Suede Shoes" and "Tutti Frutti" and, well, Andy was indifferent and disinterested—did not get it at all—and Michael danced and jumped and made the records his own. Michael took to Elvis first, along with a generation (slightly older) and much of the free-thinking world, while Andy patiently waited for . . . Fabian. He waited for Fabian Forte of Philadelphia, teen prettyboy with street-punk voice and glandular energy, whose frenetic sounds would spill from radios nearly three years thereafter. Anyway, when the time came, without even being asked, Grandpa Paul brought Fabian to him as well.

Fabian's would be the first rock-and-roll music that mattered to him—perhaps because it was executed by an adolescent only six years his senior, eight years Elvis Presley's junior. He could, would, see himself doing likewise, if a little differently, as soon as possible. So he remained loyal whenever pressed: "Fabian was my favorite singer, and then Elvis," he averred. "I chose Fabian over Elvis because he was the first guy I ever heard." Which was to say, he may have listened to Elvis but did not *hear* him until he was ready. Truth was ever negotiable, though, and he would conjure other legends to serve him when necessary, such as the one about an early life-altering trip to Memphis with his family where he saw a mystery man shake hips. ("Did not happen," said Stanley.) "See, when Elvis went into the Army, Fabian came on the scene, and that was when I really got into liking rock and roll. Fabian became my idol." He would most clearly remember the summer of 1959 when his grandfather presented him with three pivotal singles: "Got the Feeling" by Fabian, "Mary Lou" by Ronnie Hawkins and the Hawks, and "I Need Your Love Tonight" by Elvis. This was the first morsel of Presley that truly resonated—bouncy, plaintive, leghappy—*"Oh! Oh! I love you so! Uh-oh! I can't let you go!"* He would know it intimately. But Fabian took greater hold and, in short order, the entire Fabian singles discography would be entered (sides A and B together) in the coveted top thirteen positions of Andy's first real record collection—a stout plastic box of fifty 45s, meticulously inventoried in quavering penmanship on two separate insert sheets. There were, in an order of his own devising, "I'm a Man" (#1), "Lilly Lou" (#2), "Turn Me Loose" (#3), "Tiger" (#4), "Got the Feeling" (#5), "Hound Dog Man" (#6), the flip side of which was "This Friendly World"—

Ohh!

Right away, he liked this song very very much. It would, in fact, never ever leave his life. It rarely even left his head for very long.

In this friendly friendly world . . .

He heard it as a gentle anthem of kindness . . .

With each day so full of joyyyyyy . . .

And understanding . . .

Why should any heart be lonelyyyy . . .

And not making fun of people who were different . . .

The world is such a won-der-ful place to wander throuuugh . . .

Like reallyreally different . . .

When you've got someone you love to wander along with youuu . . .

Slow haunting corny rhythm put him in the mind of people—all kinds of people—locking arms and swaying back and forth and being very very, well, *friendly* with one another. It was probably the quietest, most earnest song Fabian would ever sing (so strange), a saccharine message song he had sung in the movie *Hound Dog Man* (not about Elvis), and it went all the way to number twelve on the radio charts just a few weeks before Christmas 1959. Andy learned the words instantly, played it over and over again, sang along and beat along, very gently, on the twin bongo drums he had asked his father to buy him. (Actually, he wanted a big set of congas, but was encouraged to start small, to which he grudgingly agreed.) He would beat along to most every song he played on his phonograph, which his mother made him move all the way downstairs to the small den, so as to not disturb the house or little Carol's afternoon naps, especially now with all the drumming. He could not stop the drumming. It didn't matter which of his records was on the turntable: "I'm Sorry" by Brenda Lee (#15), "That's Why (I Love You So)" by Jackie Wilson (#20), "Muskrat Ramble" by Freddy Cannon (#26), "The Twist" by Chubby Checker (#31), "Alley Oop" by Dante and the Evergreens (#33), "Theme from *A Summer Place*" by Percy Faith & Orchestra (#39), "Sink the Bismarck" by Homer and Jethro (#41), "The Chipmunk Song" by David Seville and the Chipmunks (#50). He kept drumming and drumming and then he found Olatunji's *Drums of Passion* long-playing album and the drumming got wilder and more fun and he had to get his own conga drum now and his father finally relented (they got it in Greenwich Village) and he would stand in front of the large narrow drum on its three-legged pedestal and pretend he was Olatunji, very tall, very black, a West African possessed of mad new/old rhythms, and he beat along until he knew exactly when to thump hard (palm of hand) and when to thump softly (fingertips) and he would close his eyes while he beat and there was nothing else in the world and he imagined how his thumps could transform people and make them deliriously uninhibited and forgetful of all worries and problems and he just got very very extremely lost.

He banged on the Wamagadoon and as he did it made him feel happier and happier. The instrument contained some magical qual-

ity which made tones, tunes, and sounds that moved through one's soul with such a joyous carefree quality that one just felt more and more waves of bliss going through his or her body and soul, no matter how young or old, no matter how smart or ignorant. These waves were felt especially by the person perpetrating them; that is, playing the instrument, which in this case was Huey. . . . He was too shy to sing at first, so he just played, and the children, feeling these unavoidable waves of happiness, got up and danced. After a while, the intensity of the feeling in the room became so high and Huey felt so good that he actually did start singing. "Come on, we're playing the Wamagadoon," he said with a carefree air. "Yes, yes, everyone play with me, the Wamagadoon." . . . It all worked like a charm and everyone clapped along and loved him, as the adults watched from the doorway and commented, "He's so good with the children."

". . . With a C,
And an O,
And an N,
And an F,
And an I,
And a D,
And an ENCE!
Put 'em all together and what have you got?"

How the act came together: He learned to play the guitar from a friend named Charlie—the simplest chords, really, so as to be able to strum with minor proficiency—and this helped greatly. Also, Mommy had forced piano lessons on both him and Michael and they drove their teacher crazy, actually once made the poor guy cry, which was fun, but he did pick up the basics of the keyboard. So he would sit at the piano in the living room where Mommy always played and sang her music and he plink-plunked until he came up with a little melody of his own and made it a song about animals and the noises they made, which he could maybe have the young children sing along with him. *("Say! I've got an idea! Let's all sing the song together!")* He could play it on the guitar, too, in case there wasn't a piano in somebody's house. *Ohhhhhhhh*—it began—*hhhhhhhhh, the cow goes moo and the dog goes woof and the cat goes meow and the bird goes tweet and the pig goes oink and the lion goes roarrrrr and that's the way it goes!* The idea was to get the kids to make the noises *("This time I'll sing the name of the animal and you sing what the animal says, okay? Okay? Every time I say okay, everybody say okay, okay?")*, since everybody liked doing that with "Old MacDonald Had a Farm," which he had practiced on the phonograph in the den, using the big orange record with the Humpty Dumpty label that Grandpa Paul had given him long ago. It was a funny old version of the song sung by the ensemble of Billy Williams and his Cowboy Rangers, in which a bunch of western galoots took turns doing the animal sounds as directed by Mr. Billy, who did the chickchick part himself and then Little Tex did the quackquacks and Joe did the gobblegobbles and Eddy did the oinkoinks and Gabe finished off with the moomoos. He practiced all the different parts, which he knew well anyway, then decided that he would be Mr. Billy (moving his lips in perfect synchronization with the record) and have children at parties come up and play the other cowboys while he comically pulled them back and forth as they pantomimed their parts. He nervously tried it out at one party in the neighborhood and it all worked like a charm and everyone clapped along and loved him—and laughed at how silly the whole exercise looked. (The production became even funnier once he began wearing a straw farmer's hat.) He showed the Little Rascals film (*Hide and Shriek*) and old cartoons (*Thomas Jefferski*, about racial tolerance, was a favorite) and scary bits of *The Creature from the Black Lagoon* for good measure and then got the musical chairs going and pin-the-tail-on-the-donkey, too, and did some magic with intentional ineptitude (the Ball Cup and the Mummy Case were always good for bad close-up) so the children could gigglingly try to foil him and deduce his (fumbling) sleight of hand, which was the best part of any trick anyway. Sometimes, for added novelty, he brought along a big reel-to-reel tape recorder (Grandpa Paul got it) on which he would record every kid's voice, then play it back and make them all happily cringe. He always left his drum at home, however, because the drumming was kind of a private thing that sort of helped him to feel brave and not so shy, which was essential if he was going to be performing in front of people, even such small people.

The business began—once he had really decided that it was, in fact, a business—by word of mouth. It was a very occasional enterprise at first, starting really in his tenth year. But he was adamant about his own professionalism and showed uncommon poise when he took control of a party, summoning depths of adrenaline to combat all shyness. (Still, he preferred that the adults leave when he began the act.) "At eleven years old, he was a businessman," his father remembered. "Nobody had ever been doing this. Parents who had birthdays for their five-year-olds just dreaded throwing these parties. When Andy started taking over, they were absolutely thrilled. They actually left their homes with him in charge. And the children idolized him. We got accolades." The commitment to show business, as such, was fortified so much so that, by age fourteen (Andy's memory; others claim earlier), he drew up an advertisement for his services and, unbeknownst to his family, paid ten dollars to place it in the *Great Neck Penny Saver* newspaper—and, suddenly, the calls started coming with impressive regularity. "He began by charging five dollars for two hours of entertainment and worked his way up to twenty-five dollars for one hour," said Stanley. "Eventually, he was working parties as far as twenty miles from our home. Since I delivered him by car to his jobs, I had to lug the movie projector, which felt like it weighed a hundred pounds. Several years later, I had a hernia repair—and all I could think of was that goddamned projector."

These performances would now become the most important part of his life and he worked and worked to think of new things to do. "I was very successful and I kept doing this through junior high and high school and for a year after, when everyone else went to college," he recalled, ever proud of his initiative. His parents were also proud, if amazed and baffled by what was happening here. They had been raising an unusual boy, they knew, and now they realized that they might have to try harder to respect his eccentricities, which grew exponentially. It was, oftentimes, a most difficult challenge. The clamor from the den below—the thumpings and the rock and roll and the voices and the strange yelpings—took on a certain fevered intensity, bigger, broader, louder. Thank God he could close the door to the room, which he did, always with a solemn sense of purpose. No one dared to enter without invitation. His father would state, "When he closed the door in the den, he closed the door. That was that. It was his inner sanctum."

4

. . . The madman drove me home to New York.

Suddenly, I found myself on Times Square . . . and right in the middle of a rush hour, too, seeing with my innocent road-eyes the absolute madness and fantastic hoorair of New York with its millions and millions hustling forever for a buck among themselves, the mad dream. . . .

—Jack Kerouac,
On The Road

He made himself a freak, which was fine, because everything was always fine; whenever asked how he was, he was fine—*um, fine*—was how he always was, no more, no less. He was visibly unflappable in his freakishness, unruffled by accompanying torment: ostracism, fine; humiliation, fine; you're-such-a-freakin'-freak, fine, *um*, thank you. But he was not meant for peer approval, not until he had peers who were also freakish. That would happen soon enough—the American sixties, psychedelia, peacelove, whatever-turns-you-on, friendly friendlier world—but first, he was made to thoroughly understand his lowly place in the local adolescent firmament. One recollection, for instance: "I have never been an athlete in my life. I was always the worst. As a matter of fact, in gym, when we were kids, like if all the classes got together and played coed sportings events—all the girls and all the boys together—they wouldn't choose me till last, after all the boys and all the girls were chosen. It was very embarrassing." It was also very fine; he didn't dislike it that way; he just accepted it; plus, he always embellished these tales for greater obfuscation of truth; no, really. Nonetheless, he didn't mind that he threw like a girl. He wasn't suited for ball sports or team sports, anyway. It never occurred to him to adapt or to change or to be better or to dedicate himself to any popular endeavor that disinterested him. His nonconformity was not meant as a statement, although it would be taken as such. If it was rebellion, it was causeless rebellion, which was, um . . . fine.

Nevertheless: Another shrink, when he was in sixth grade, he said. "I saw another psychologist when I was in the sixth grade." If so, it would be forgotten by all else and examinations would have been brief and cursory and not illuminating. (Attention deficiency/imagination, of course.) Janice saw same shrink this time, he said. "My mother did, too." If so, she wanted to know what was really happening down in that den and how it related to the very poor schoolwork. Gradewise, he flatlined always, a D-minus dunce with a million better notions of what he wanted to learn. Pattern came to be that teachers uniformly gave him 65s on everything, so as not to flunk him, which he often deserved, so as not to get him back the following year, which they felt they did not deserve. Stanley signed his report cards with heavy heart, also with disgust, and would give the boy unholy hell. That he demonstrated an industrious bent in the birthday business did not make up for lack of academic luster. Goddamned door of den sealed off too goddamned much reality (only little Carol or the family dog, a small Yorkshire terrier named Snoopy, were occasionally privy to fantastic obstreperousness within; Michael somewhat, too). Stanley was never home, except for dinner/weekends, gave up on son, refused to give up on son, looked the other way, could not ignore it, bore down upon him when energy permitted, goddamned jewelry business sucked him dry, and this kid with his lousy grades and off-center ideas—well, he tried and tried to impart paternal wisdom, new approaches, to jar the kid into living in the same world all else inhabited. HOUR MAGAZINE: What type of work was your dad involved in? Was it a normal childhood? One of you must know. CAROL: Oh, yeah, it was real normal. MICHAEL: Oh, yeah, it was wonderful. ANDY: Every night he would come home for dinner, and he'd sit down—we'd all sit down at the table and eat. CAROL: And he'd ask us, "What'd you learn today? Let's review current events." ANDY: And if we didn't know, then we couldn't watch television. You know, he wouldn't let me watch Soupy Sales if I didn't know the answers.

Stanley proudly read *The New York Times* each day he rode the Long Island Rail Road to work. "When I came home at night and we all sat at the table for dinner, I would try to find out what my children knew about the world and the current events of the day. So I would ask questions—about world politics, national politics, crime, sports, it depended. And the kids did very, very well with their answers. If they didn't, it was nothing. I would just tell them what was going on. I was the big shot who read *The New York Times*.

"But one time—I don't exactly remember what it was—I had apparently asked a question which required an answer that was correct. No other answer would be satisfactory. And Andy answered this particular question and I said, 'No, Andy, that's wrong,' and he said, 'No, Dad, it's right,' and we started getting into a very heated debate. Maybe I'm known for being stubborn, dogmatic, whatever—but if I know something is right, *it's right!* Goddamn it! You don't disagree with me! We got into a real tussle. Then I made the analogy, 'Goddamn it, isn't two and two four?' And he looks me in the eye and he says, 'Not necessarily.' So I just threw my hands up and said, 'I can't go any further! That's it!' He's a kid, for crying out loud—eleven, twelve! Later on in life I learned that two and two maybe in Eskimo language doesn't make four. Two and two can be something else entirely. This was what he was getting at. He had a perception of life that was always questioning everything."

Still, punishments were levied for bad grades and slack attitudes. The requisite rumpwhacks or, far far worse, television deprivation—which cut to the bone and severed the lifeline—were enforced by Janice when Stanley worked, which felt like conspiracy, which he ostensibly took just fine, although he simmered and stewed and plotted revenge within. His anger, he learned, was best dealt with on paper,

with pen or pencil, which was nicer than his father's methods of release. He made sure, however, to let them read or to recite for them
exactly what scorn he was feeling.

Upon the eve of his thirteenth birthday, scratched in longhand,
composed in seventeen minutes, presented immediately to assemblage on Grassfield Road—this:

Jan. 16, 1962 (11:05 P.M.)

My Last Will and Testament: Andy Geoffrey Kaufman

I would like all my belongings (including money and possessions)
to be divided in this way. (As I am writing this, I do not think much
of my mother and father, but I must give them what I am going to
give them because what they have given to me has amounted to
something. I owe it to them.)

I would like Grandma Pearl M. Bernstein to be the guardian of my
beloved dog, Snoopy. I would like Snoopy to live [the] best life.

I would like my belongings (possessions) to [be] divided evenly
between (if any of the following should die before the will is read,
the money is still to be divided between the remaining folks):

(Mother) Janice T. Kaufman	Grandma Lillie
(Father) Stanley L. Kaufman	Grandpa Paul
(Michael) My Brother	[Great] Grandma Rachel
(Carol) My Sister	Grandma Pearl
Aunt Fran	(Maid) Margaret E. English
Uncle Jackie	

[signed] Andy G. Kaufman (11:22 P.M.)
[witnessed and signed by:]
Pearl M. Bernstein
(Father) Stanley L. Kaufman Jan. 16, 1962 (11:27 P.M.)

*   *   *

Boy had no fear of death, saw it as kind of romantic, really. Nothing much scared him back then. And the things that actually did scare him he liked because being scared was fun and fun never scared him. Things grotesque generally pleased him—also, physical, mental, behavioral ugliness; the reviled, the aberrant. Certainly, as with most boys, he loved monsters. But he loved real ones as well as unreal ones. Per the latter, he never missed the classic black-and-white horror films shown late every Saturday night on local New York television—specifically *Shock Theater* as hosted by the comical pasty-faced ghoul Zacherle (pronounced, with ominous emphasis, Zack-er-LEEE!), who emerged from a coffin each week to introduce the movies. Stanley and Janice would often socialize on these nights with another Great Neck couple whose son was roughly Andy's age, and so Jimmy Krieger, a rather straight-arrow kid, quick and self-assured, became Andy's regular partner in various macabre and offbeat predilections.

"We did this almost every Saturday night between the ages of ten and fourteen," Krieger would recall. "Our parents would put us together, either at their house or at ours, and we'd stay up way past midnight watching these movies. We were both fascinated by them. We used to act out *Frankenstein Meets the Wolf Man*—that was the biggie. Andy was absolutely frightened stiff of Lon Chaney, Jr., as the Wolf Man, the only monster that really bothered him. So I would be the Wolf Man and wear the fangs and stand behind a door to scare him. His parents hated that. He wasn't thrilled, either. It's ironic to think that Andy would later be thought of as the Boy Who Cried Wolf—and he was petrified over the Wolf Man. We also saw *The Mummy* maybe a thousand times on his sixteen-millimeter projector. Andy used to wrap himself in toilet paper and did that shuffling Mummy walk with the dangling hand. Sometimes it would be the Wolf Man versus the Mummy and we'd argue technically over who would win."

By sheer force, it was usually Jimmy Krieger who won—a dynamic that had marked their relationship since early childhood. Stanley used to seethe whenever he caught Jimmy happily pouncing on and clobbering his impassive son: "Andy wouldn't fight back. I got so mad once, I said, 'Goddamn it, Andy, why don't you hit him back?' " Krieger would remember the horseplay more lightheartedly: "Even though I was a year older than Andy, he was bigger than me. And he was a wimp, so what did that make me? Although I did beat up on him, it was all theatrical—nothing to really hurt him—just playing out what we saw on TV. A parent wouldn't necessarily see it that way, though, I suppose."

Still, the boys collaborated in hatching many superb schemes: "Our greatest accomplishment happened when Zacherle very creepily started asking viewers what ever became of Alan Freed, the disc jockey who coined the term *rock and roll*. [Freed was famously fired for accepting record company payola in 1959, after which he seemed to just disappear.] Andy and I wrote in to Zacherle in the guise of a pseudo–Alan Freed Fan Club and sent along what we claimed were Alan Freed's gruesome remains—just a bunch of iodine-dyed twine which we said was his nervous system. Zacherle read the letter and showed the guts on the air. It was a major triumph."

Before this and throughout their youthful companionship, there was always TV wrestling—of course, the wrestling! the fights! the matches! oh!—Saturday night grappling cards broadcast from Sunnyside Gardens and beyond, thunderfleshed hulks snarling and bellowing, slamming sweat-slicked torsos against ropes and onto canvas, hair-pulling face-biting blood-spurting throat-stomping eye-gouging jeer-spewing thespianic guys with remarkable coifs and dumb names. And it was—had to be, couldn't be anything else—a big lie, a phony deal, fabulous fakery probably kind of all-made-up. They were only fooling—in fun—probably. Anyway, this was stuff very very extremely thrilling to behold—loud, bellicose, prancing, giant assholes in heaving combat! It was the only sport that remotely held any appeal for him, so he clung to it proudly and defiantly: "Wrestling is the finest and oldest sport known to man," he declared many years later. "It's been around since the caveman, before the ball and the wheel were invented!" Stanley, on son: "He went bananas for wrestling as a kid." As kid grew, he remained bananas for such. Jimmy Krieger: "We loved to watch Killer Kowalski and Haystack Calhoun—they were the two biggies for a while. Kowalski was just vicious; he once ripped a guy's ear off, according to legend. [Truth! He stepped on it and off it tore. Kowalski demurred, 'It was so cauliflowered, it would have fallen off by itself if it had a chance to.'] Haystack Calhoun was the only guy who could beat him, because he was so big and fat that he would just fall on The Killer." (Haystack, weighing in at six hundred pounds, would happily exult from every ring he trod, "There are going to be a lot of *human pancakes* around here before I get finished!") "The meaner they were, the more Andy liked 'em," said Krieger.

He needed to see them up close, so Stanley or Grandma Pearl would take Andy and Michael (another fan) out to Commack Arena or Suffolk Forum on Long Island, when pro matches came through the territory. "We saw Wild Red Berry and The Kangaroos, 'Brute' Barney Bernard [with his sixty-three-inch chest], Cowboy Bob Ellis, Skull Murphy, and Johnny Valentine," Michael recalled. "Andy's favorite was Buddy 'Nature Boy' Rogers—the blond pretty boy bad guy. He knew how to piss you off. I hated him. But Andy saw past that. He saw how fantastic it was to have everybody hate him—what theater it was."

The villainous Nature Boy merely became his newest deity. ("*Oh—he was, in my opinion, the greatest wrestler of all time! He was to wrestling what Muhammad Ali was to boxing, what Elvis Presley was to rock-and-roll music, in my opinion.*") In 1962, only his second year on the big circuit, Rogers was voted by fans the most unpopular wrestler alive—ahead of the despicable Killer Kowalski and the ruthless Crusher Lisowski. He was also nearly unbeatable, which he flamboyantly made known to all as he preened and posed and strutted ("*He invented the strut!*") and demeaned and boasted ("*He invented the term 'I am the greatest!' He invented 'I got the brains!' *") and obliterated all sacred rules of sportsmanship. ("*I once saw Buddy Rogers beat a guy unconscious so they had to carry him off on a stretcher.*

Then Buddy kicked the stretcher over. Buddy Rogers knew ways of ma-nipulating a crowd like no one in the world.") Andy's fierce devotion to the blond champion was boundless; he told everyone who would listen, "Any friend of Buddy's is a friend of mine. Any enemy of his is mine, too." He saw Nature Boy wrestle in person only once, couldn't have been more excited, after which he would forever recall the event as "the saddest night of my life." It was May 17, 1963—he was just completing the eighth grade at Great Neck North Junior High School—and he went to Madison Square Garden in New York, where Rogers was defending his world title against Bruno Sammartino, a towering Italian Goliath. Sammartino pinned Rogers in forty-eight seconds. "It ended with a backbreaker," Andy would grimly remember. "After that Buddy retired. When he stopped wrestling, I stopped watching it for about ten years."

He found other extreme diversion.

The city beckoned, as it will.

The city teemed with possibility most, um, fine.

He had seen enough of it to know.

City = Exciting-exciting weirdwonders.

He never looked up at the soaring metropolis majesty. Instead, he looked down at what splayed and churned and bustled before him— on the streets and under the streets and behind the streets and of the streets. Everything and everyone and every smell and every noise was here and here was where one could be whatever/whoever one wanted to be, could become other things and other people and—

Dhrupick . . .

Dhrupick—the spirit that was Dhrupick—could be loosed here, was born certainly probably to experiment here to discover things here. Manhattan, every stained and pocked crevice of it, every parcel of its soddenspeckled pavement, would be whatever he/they wanted it to be. Here was where he/they would transcend always.

The boil grew and grew on the back of his neck—for a year, he claimed—pulsing at times, festering with pus, and the doctor, when the doctor finally looked at it, called it a cyst. A cyst! Oh! He liked his cyst quite a lot, was fascinated with it, this purpling yellowing bulb, protruding an inch from under his skin and just as wide in circumference, it was much more substantial than all of his lifetime of pimples, pimples which never stopped rising even now on his grown-man face and his grown-man back, welty kinds of acne pimples, even though he was always good at washing and hygiene and everything, since he'd been seeing dermatologists since he was like thirteen. The doctor wanted to lance the cyst right then right there, but he said no, not yet, and invited the doctor to come to his show at the Improvisation on Melrose Avenue and the doctor did come that appointed night and watched as people were urged to line up and step onto the stage for the privilege of touching the cyst, but only after they submitted to washing their hands in the bowl of alcohol solution which Linda had set up where she was dispensing clean towels and maybe four people actually did it—"Not too hard, now. Just gently. No no no! Just gently. Seriously. Really, don't squeeze it or don't touch hard. You can really do damage if you do. Please. Seriously. This is not a joke. Just touch it. Please don't be funny. Anyone else? That it? Thank you. Um, okay"— but the ones who did touch it were friends and agreed to do it because he wanted them to and everyone in the room including and especially the friends who touched the cyst, not to mention all the viewers who later watched it on television during the program An Evening at the Improv, *were really kind of nauseous over the whole thing. He was quite proud of himself, however, since it reminded him of old things and certain people he used to know. The doctor removed the cyst on another day.*

Best thing the city ever gave him, best thing he ever found there, absolutely, was Hubert's Museum & Live Flea Circus. He was ten, maybe, when Grandma Pearl first took him. Grandma Pearl lived in the city for a handful of years after Papu Cy died and she liked to show the delicious first grandchild (her Kid McCoy, she called him) secret places and spectacles to further widen his eyes. Even after she later moved in with her daughter's family on Grassfield Road—about which Andy was especially delighted, although it meant bunking with Michael—she never stopped taking him to amazements that he wanted to see, such as when the Fabian boy played concerts in New Jersey and the awful wrestling men did their nonsense in tri-state arenas and, years earlier, when he wanted to be in the studio audiences of the little television programs like *Howdy Doody* and *Wonderama* that were made in the city. But then came the day that they explored Times Square and she led him along Forty-second Street to the penny arcade between Seventh and Eighth Avenues. At the rear of this clattering arcade was the staircase that descended to the basement that was the subterranean urban sideshow that was Hubert's. Opened in 1925 as a dime museum—parlance for the ten-cent admission price paid to view human curiosities therein (although by this time a ticket cost twenty-five cents per)—Hubert's would rank just a shade below Coney Island as the most important place Andrew Geoffrey Kaufman would ever know. It was a very cheerful sad and strange place—a repository of the forgotten and the vanquished and the phony. It was where old-time acts went to die and the only place where certain godforsaken creatures had a chance to make a living. He loved the sweet spookiness of it all and returned and returned to Hubert's, where the first thing he always saw was himself—many many versions of himself exaggerated/diminished fat-tall-skinny-dwarfed-etcetera—in funhouse mirror reflection at the foot of the concrete stairwell. He enjoyed that part every time, almost felt part of the program. Beyond the mirrors were decrepit posters of long-gone former attractions—Weird! Unusual! Primitive! Siamese Twins Doomed to Stay Joined Together Till Death! The Homeliest Woman in the World! Londy the Giantess! The Great Waldo (who swallowedwhole live mice and other breathing things)!

Anyway, those ones didn't work there anymore, but the ones who did got to know the boy very well. These ones, they worked on little elevated stages that lined the long dark occasionally fluorescent occasionally crimson-lit mostly shadowy mildewy expanse. Princess Wago (in her leopard leotards) he loved and also her pythons and boa constrictors (six-footers) with which she danced and sometimes draped over his shoulders, which was exciting. He struck up happy convoluted chats with Phil Dirks, him with the three eyes and two noses and two mouths, which seemed normal enough to the boy, gave him no pause at all. There was Miss Lydia, who contorted herself pretzelwise, and Susie the Elephant Skin Girl (nice to him always, let him touch her mottled gray flesh) and Professor Heckler and His Trained Fleas (beheld for an extra quarter; fleas juggled and rode a merry-go-round and danced and one kind of kicked this little football and they all fed on the Professor's forearm—blood!) and Sealo the Seal Boy (a man with tiny flippers instead of arms) and Presto the magician who always said during his tricks, "I don't really do this. It just looks like it." (The boy most probably remembered those words always.) One guy who was there not very long sang with a ukelele in a crazy high falsetto voice and was called Larry Love the Human Canary, who later grew curly long hair and called himself Tiny Tim and got famous, which was exciting. Estelline, Refined Sophisticated Lady Sword Swallower, was always pleased to have the boy watch her daintily insert four blades, one after the other, including an antique U.S. Cavalry saber, down her proud gullet, then wipe each with a pristine hanky upon removal. But best of all was a horrid fellow named Hezekiah Trambles who went by the moniker of Congo the Jungle Creep, whose skin was the color of swamp water and whose hair stood/shot upright and who was missing many teeth, who took a special liking to Andy, in his own atrocious way, focusing on him while performing his "African voodoo magic"—trying always to enlist him for onstage decapitation. Congo was a crazy man, seemed so anyway, who leapt vigorously onto sawblades but broke no feet-skin and swallowed lit cigarettes, then swallowed foul liquid which never extinguished the cigarettes which he then spit up still burning. He plucked hair from heads—Andy's certainly—and put it in a slimy bucket and chanted great gibberish over the bucket and pulled out a phony snake and threw it into the small crowds that gathered, once per hour, to behold such wonder. Afterward, Congo and Andy would talk in their own particular not dissimilar friendly awkward manner.

It was perfect down there. And they were in a basement just like him in his basement doing things other people didn't do, which was all very normal and regular really. By the time he was twelve, he began sneaking off into the city on his own or with Jimmy Krieger to visit Hubert's and excavate other urban delights. "We did the whole Truffaut *Day for Night* thing, where we'd skip a day of school and play hooky. We did it about four times between the ages of twelve and fourteen—and that was just with me. Who knows how often he went alone. But Andy would drag me along to show off his friends [at Hubert's]. He'd obviously been going there for a while because he had already made friends with some of these freak people. We would stay there for a long time and the snake lady let us touch her snakes and we'd see all the acts and look at the embryo in a bottle that was supposedly a lamb with three heads. We'd also go down to this record shop in the Times Square subway where you could listen to records on headphones. He liked to play the song 'Louie Louie' over and over to listen for the secret dirty words, which I always thought was funny. Or else he'd listen to a lot of Elvis Presley. That was my earliest recollection of him getting infatuated with Elvis. Then we would go down to Greenwich Village and walk around and look at the oddities—bikers, girls holding hands, beatniks, that sort of thing. We went to all these coffeehouses where the beatniks read their poetry, the most important of which was Cafe Wha? He would listen to this poetry that would give me a headache. I think we had our first espressos there, too. They sometimes beat bongos when they recited the poetry, which really interested him. He liked those hipsters."

(6) Oct. 26, 1963

HE GETS ILLUSIONS THAT HIS FLY IS ALWAYS OPEN

He gets illusions that his fly is always open.

When he goes to work.

When he goes to school.

To him, people will notice.

To him, people will always be looking at him.

He gets illusions that his fly is always open.

When he walks down the street.

When he goes to a dance.

He gets illusions that his fly is always open.

Who gives a damn.

(7) Oct. 27, 1963

WHAT WILL HAPPEN IF

What will happen if I tell my teacher that I hate her?

She will send me to the office. That is all.

And what will happen if I get bad marks in school?

And do not go to college? And do not get a job? And die in
my twenties?

Nothing. I will not feel pain.

What will happen if I *get* good marks in school?

And get praised by my father? And go to a good college?

And make a billion dollars?

I will be part of the camouflaged unhappy competition.

And what will happen if I get bad marks in school?

And get beaten by my father? And don't go to college?

And move down to the Village? *And be happy?*

What will happen if?——What will happen if?——Ask yourself:

What will happen?

It was a godly time when words were god. Such godwords—those
he heard, those he composed—were cadenced in stacatto thuds,
hung on grim ellipses, and were best punctuated with drumskin slaps
or fingersnaps or *dig-can-you-digs*; he dug but madly, oh yes. He
began to dutifully wear black, like all good Beats; at very least,
usually had the little black faux-turtle dickie under his oxford collar.
He made the scene, brought the words he had written (often
during lunch in the Great Neck North High School cafeteria
or during classes that bored him extra madly, a freshman

Ginsberg/Ferlinghetti, mind pointedly pointed elsewhere), brought the bongos, too (not a conga scene), brought the existential questioning therein, brought all to the underground world (down more dark steps) of Cafe Wha? (MacDougal near Bleecker, heart of Village cool), where he insinuated himself onto the afternoon stage—fourteen years of age!—or, more conveniently, to the nearby MacDougal East coffeehouse on Plandome Road in Manhasset, Long Island (suburban scene, not quite as cool but workable).

He was a tall gangly cat with a mouthful of braces a-gleam.

The voice was croaking now, puberty stirring and all.

He needed to spill with a little profundity, since the birthday gigs did not afford such freedom. He needed to deal with the outcast stuff, the loner stuff, the why-can't-the-man-(father)-let-up-on-me stuff. Stanley sometimes drove him to the coffeehouses, picked him up later, sometimes even stayed and listened to the son's poetry (along with the tolerant/bemused hipsters at tables digging as best they could), shook his head with some small incredulity but liked seeing the boy's initiative such as it was—but still.

Hereabouts was when two great novels had smacked him in the face, one about living/surviving life in the beautiful dregs, the other about wandering highways in aimless pursuit of sweet truth—Hubert Selby, Jr.'s *Last Exit to Brooklyn* and Jack Kerouac's *On the Road*, both the godliest of godlyworks. Could he stop reading them? He could not. He read them to tatters, over and over, for years to come. Freak misfit outsider tragic/melancholy/profane books, they inspired him very very madly. He even started noodling with a novel of his own, a feral and violent delirium he would call *The Hollering Mangoo*. But, more urgently, he focused on the short form. And so from October 1963 through May 1964—basically the entire span of ninth grade—he wrote, then performed, thirty-one not-too-terribly-awkward beat poems of desolation, longing, ennui, confusion, and rage. Thus, the epidermal shrugs and *um, fines* unmasked themselves on sheets of innocent notebook paper. . . .

"My hope is like a hollow skull" was the first line of the debut effort, "A Chosen Few: A Love Poem"—with annotation at bottom,

"That phrase is an idea from the program *Hootenanny."* (Television, as ever, fed all inspiration.) He dug deep, then deeper. The fifth poem—"Hi"—explored the banal emptiness of obligatory greetings **(". . . Here comes one that I know, or knew / Should I say hi to him? / Here comes the one that I just met / Should I say hi to her? / . . . *I hate the hi");*** the eighth—"The Faggot"—depicted ostracism he may have known **(". . . He buttons his top button / And minds his own business / Then the popular ones come / With their high pitched voices / And say, 'Look at the faggot!' . . .");** the sixteenth—"Damn Them"—responded to aforementioned popular accusers **(". . . Damn them! / The ones that ruin my existence / The existence I try to live peacefully. . . .");** the nineteenth—"'Tis Amusing"— vengefully elaborated on same theme **(. . . I HATE THOSE DAMNED MORONS! / I will kill them / Kill them all / Let me rise up and / SCREAM / But— / 'Tis amusing. . . .).** Geek pentameter somehow clarified his world with an acuity that he would never again muster. Bongo-riff-voice was honest in ways that he wasn't nor would ever wish to be. In "Eidandrofields"—his second poem—he all but shrieked for compassion/notice **(". . . I AM A HUMAN BEING. . . .")** and concluded with this conundrum of revelation **(". . . Eidandrofields is my den / My place of escape / Where I keep my flowers—yet am I a flower lover? / Where I keep my records— yet am I a music lover? / Where I keep my writing and poetry—yet am I a writer? / I curse people—yet do I hate them?").** Did he yearn to belong somewhere outside of his den? He did very much. "Lonely" arrived twenty-fourth in the poetic oeuvre and said all in these open- ing lines—**"There goes him / There goes her / There they go / I am lonely. . . ."**

The yearnings were suddenly very real.

More than anything else, it seemed, he wanted love.

5

Am I in love? I guess I haven't met the right girl yet, but I will, and I hope it won't be too long, because I get lonesome sometimes. I get lonesome right in the middle of a crowd. I get a feeling that with her, whoever she may be, I won't be lonesome anymore.

—Elvis Presley

By this time, he had fallen in love once, he said. He tried to convince others of this later, much later. When he got himself famous enough to give interviews, it was sometimes all that he could talk about—this particular love, how it had changed everything for him, he said. He would even phone up the *National Enquirer*—which was something he loved to do, much later—and beg the tabloid to convey this seminal tale of hopeful/hapless heartache, which it did without hesitation. (Headline: 'TAXI' STAR'S SECRET: I'VE BEEN IN LOVE 17 YEARS WITH A GIRL I'VE NEVER MET!) He found her in seventh grade, he said. He usually recalled her long dark straight hair and her black leotards and always professed that she was the sole reason he had pursued a limelit life. "I fell in love with this girl in junior high school, but I never got to meet her or talk to her because I was incredibly shy. . . . Every time I would get near her, my knees would shake. But something in my soul felt so close to her soul. I know I'll never feel that way about anyone again. . . . They say Capricorns only fall in love once and I think this is the once. . . . I made note of what classes she was in so I could pass her in the hall. Every day I'd practice things to say to her, but I never had the guts to go up and talk to her. I even thought about tripping over a trash can in front of her so she'd notice me. . . . I decided I'd have to become famous before I'd have the confidence to meet her. So everything I've done for the past seventeen years has been so that I'm worthy of this girl and can go out with her." Then she disappeared, he said, variously. He said (to *New York Newsday*) that just when he began to seriously perform birthday party entertainment—so as to start making himself worthy—"The girl I fell in love with left town, before I met her or could even find out her name." He never knew her name, he said; he knew her name, he said, but was not ready to reveal her name, he said. He said (to the *Enquirer*): "I'm not prepared to name her, but she's a brunette who attended Great Neck North Junior and Senior High School from the seventh to the tenth grades—from 1961 to about 1964. She'll know who she is if she reads this." Which was to say, she knew him, which she never did, he said. She left in 1964, he said, and she left by the end of 1961, he said. He said (to *The Washington Post*) that she moved away after the first semester of seventh grade and he never saw her again. He said (to *The Village Voice*) that once his epic novel-in-progress, *The Huey Williams Story*, was made into a movie, he would dedicate the movie to her, "Then I'm gonna feel worthy enough so that I can actually go out and say her name and put on a real search for her. Then I'll find her and then who knows what'll happen?" He hunched over one tape recorder (*Los Angeles Times*) and said to her directly, "If you are reading this now, you should know that everything I did was for you." Then he added, thinking aloud, "But what if she doesn't like what I [just] said and when I call her she'll say [coldly], 'Oh, hello, Andy, I read what you said and . . .' And gosh, what if her father reads it and says [gruffly], 'Who does he think he is, using my daughter in a . . . ?' But it's so romantic, maybe she'll say, 'Oh Andy, that's so-o-o sweet.' "

Anyway, once she disappeared, he knew that he would find her again, if only he knew who she was, since he knew who she was, if only she had been real, which she was, except she never was, not that there weren't girls just like her who never noticed him, whom he loved from a self-imposed frozen-out distance. Well, she/they would be sorry, he liked to say.

He was watching Elvis get girls all along. Now *there* was confidence! Elvis was getting Ann-Margret in *Viva Las Vegas* right about the time he finished his thirty-first and final beat poem (unlike the others, four words, four lines, untitled—**"I liv / e / to I / ive"**—tough to perform). He was, he knew, the only beatnik to madly dig godly Elvis, whose sneers and lipcurls over brightwhite tooth enamel (no braces) induced chick paroxysms galore, never mind the leg/hip-swivels. He missed no Elvis film, was ever the repeat box office customer, glued himself to the subsequent television broadcasts of each, studied the execution of all Elvisian conquests—*babybaby-baby meet-me-after-the-show-baby*—mimicked the delivery in mirrors, knowing he could never try this in actual life, but liking that he could do it as well as he could, thinking he could maybe do it somehow somewhere besides the den if circumstances were denlike. In the den, he played Elvis albums—would eventually possess forty-three of them and they in turn would possess him—singing along while pounding/seducing conga in lieu of actual girl, wanting actual girl very badly. Hormones flamed, boy ached.

He was a good-looking boy, no question—although tending more and more toward disheveled presentation. He had also been discovering new physical strength and endurance skills in gym class—finished second in cross-country track race (very proud), excelled at swimming, rope skipping, rope climbing, sit-ups, chin-ups (setting GNN Junior High record with thirty-five), and wrestled with alarming vigor. "For the first time in my life I was considered a good athlete." Social skills, however, remained out of grasp. He knew not how to make easy conversation with anyone, certainly not females. When conversation occurred at all, he was never a generalist, always a specialist who spoke passionately about his passions, and only those who shared his passions (if even somewhat) cared to sustain any sort of dialogue with him. "In Great Neck," he later recalled, "there were three groups of kids—the hoods, beatniks, and 'poppies' [as in popular ones]. I was a beatnik, but my parents wanted me to be like the poppies, who were well-adjusted, dressed nicely, and drove nice cars." Jimmy Krieger, for instance, became a poppy, very clean-cut, adept with girls, so much so that he eventually drifted away from Andy, as goes all teen Darwinism. "Andy was not very cool with girls," he would remember. "He wore a lot of white T-shirts or sloppy stuff, didn't care how he looked. To high school girls, he wasn't attractive. They didn't want to know him."

Earlier on, Krieger had orchestrated a couple of innocent prepubescent, prebeatnik "date" nights wherein he and Andy and a friend named Barbara Levy and a girl she knew got dressed up and were parentally ferried to the Copacabana nightclub in the city to see Paul Anka and Frankie Avalon sing. Photographs from such nights evinced painful awkwardness of boy thrust-and-harnessed in suit and tie, hair askew, mouth of metal, eyes agape, uncertain of comportment amid female company, poppy potential nil, but thrilled to be near show business, nonetheless. (Avalon and Anka each posed with him after their shows, slinging an arm around his narrow shoulders.) He seemed to belong elsewhere, on the fringe, which was where he fled and stayed and found fringe friends, lost in ways he was not, slack renegades grinding ambiguous axes, ready for amusement always, as was he, and so he became their amusement—his oddness fascinated them—and they became his audience and things got better and also dangerous and certain girls of existential beatnik bent began to like him precisely for who he wasn't.

So—here was how he won favor and gained entry into the slim fragment of society that would have him: He went where wind blew him, like Kerouac did with Neal Cassady, usually smack into questionable corners. Already, he was solid with his poetry jaunts to the Village (no kid ever did that), and he had stalked Olatunji there as well, paid the giant West African to give him afternoon conga lessons—where and how to put his hands—there at the famed

Village Gate nightery (got to pound drums *with* Olatunji—ohhh!). Mystique was in place, if only others knew. Wind also blew him via his bicycle to the center of Great Neck, to Frederick's malt shop, by the train station on Grace Avenue, in front of which—on the sidewalk, on the curb—disenfranchised youth congregated and grumbled and chortled and wearily posed. (Frederick's was owned by people named Selby, like writer-hero Hubert Selby, Jr., whose first name, Hubert, was like shrinely Hubert's Museum—making-for-a-godly-coincidental-oh!) He carried with him always a canvas knapsack containing a beaten-up copy of Kerouac's *On the Road*—he referred to it like a prayer book, evangelically citing passages—and reams of loose handwritten pages comprising his own novel, *The Hollering Mangoo*, which would be completed by his sixteenth year. Whenever he heard Kerouac invoked around the malt shop or in the park across the street, he brandished his copy of *On the Road* and followed with a fan-flourish of crumpled *Mangoo* pages and an open invitation for anyone to read from them. These loiterers and lollygaggers—they were all *attitude*—could not help but fall prey to his peculiar hubris, except for the ones who urged him to scram and elected to smoke in another direction.

Mangoo, he indicated to the ones intrigued, was a teen angst fantasmagory, a tour de force of rage and horror and self-discovery played in the ominous shadow of an ephemeral bellowing beast that chased main characters throughout various kingdoms and suburbs. It was very very jackkerouackian, he promised. Also, it made no sense in the least whatsoever at all—but he pointed to the good parts, anyway. Like where this girl named Sadie screams the word **fuck** 103 times on page 5 and 189 times on page 6 (presented in seven columns twenty-seven times vertically—nothing else on the page) and also exclaims the word **shit** at the top of her lungs 127 times on page 53; and like where Sadie takes a bludgeon to her mother's left breast **("Here go your tits, baby!")** and keeps hammering **until, finally, it was hanging like an apple on a string and wobbling,** and proceeds to tear it off and throw it **against the walls, the ceiling, and bounced it on the floor;** and like where this boy named Charley is whiplashed unmercifully by his mother until his right eyeball is sliced in half and **blood was spurting out of it** and she keeps cracking the whip and leaving scars everywhere **("All right, Ma! That's enough! Fuck you, Mother!");** and like where the mother of the Mangoo beast attacks the narrator boy by pelting him with clumps of dried vomit **so I hid in a barrel but it was *full of shit* so I was in up to my neck while this crazy mother threw vomit at me—what should I do—duck?—it was a problem . . . but she kept throwing it at me so I ducked and got my face all full of the doody which now I realized was Charley's and it was *his* mother who threw the vomit which hit my face.** Years later, sheepish upon reflection, he said *Mangoo*—"the ultimate fantasies of a sixteen-year-old" whose characters combined "different aspects of myself"—was created during "my obscene period." He had once shown it to his English teacher, he said, and delighted in the memory of almost being expelled as a result.

"I wrote this book," he said, "so people would vomit."

Most probably, he wrote it to purge himself, to sublimate a hostility so corrosive (over feeling dismissal from all quarters) that not even his poetry could plumb such depths. The bile could surface no other way. But to share it—kind of artfully, on paper—with others was to clankclatter his cup against cage bars, to get extreme unexpurgated re-action/attention. (He was, in effect, doing all of the hollering, if inwardly—not the mangoo.) Earlier, he had performed TV playlets in school shrubbery for similar purpose. Now, however, he became a curiosity worth noting—and perhaps a tad too frightening to ignore. Among the first of the Frederick's crowd who paid heed was another beatnik aspirant named Moogie Klingman, who wanted to be Bob Dylan and understood weirdness to be an asset. He saw raw nobility—or was it fine freak madness?—in this popeyed poet with the wild book pages. "His Kerouac fanaticism was Andy's calling card to the beatnik scene in Great Neck—that and *The Hollering Mangoo*," Klingman would recall. "He was kind of an aloof nerdy guy, but people came to be really taken with him because he was so strange. He would pull out these pages, but I don't think he seriously meant for anyone to actually read them. He just meant to impress us that he was weird."

They were close for several months, during which Moogie instructed him in rebel ways—on how to defy parents ("He'd say, 'I've got to be home by six,' and I'd tell him, 'Andy, today you're going to stay and hang out and you're not going home till midnight!' But he'd just say, 'I can't,' and he jumped on his bike and rode home."); on how to develop proper scornful attitudes ("He never said anything bad about anybody, never even talked about anybody, was always being very nice and polite, never jealous or competitive. He was just in his own world."); and, most crucially, on how to make it with girls. They spoke of sex frequently, as in what-will-it-be-like? And as in I-will-have-sex-all-the-time-once-I-ever-actually-have-sex. Finally, it was Moogie who first lured a female into the arena, somewhat, which Andy thought was fine. "I got this girlfriend, a kind of foxy hippie girl named Liz, and we would show Andy how to kiss by kissing in front of him. Tongue kisses, a little petting. He would watch closely and study. I would feel her up and he would stand there taking notes in his mind and say with extreme politeness, 'Oh! Very good, this is how you kiss? Oh, could I see that again? Oh, that's very interesting.' "

The girl he found for himself—not for sex or anything, just to kind of indulge his romantic stirrings, which was a major start—called him from out of nowhere, called looking for him, but she was not looking for him, she was looking for Andy Kaufman, but not him, the other Andy Kaufman of Great Neck, whom he wasn't (who *was* this guy?), with whom she had attended camp, who had neglected to give her his phone number, so she was going through the Great Neck Kaufmans in the phone book, lots and lots of them, asking for Andy Kaufman, and the phone rang on Grassfield Road and Andy Kaufman answered and that was how he found her. This was the summer of 1964, before tenth grade. He would fictionalize this kismet the following spring, writing in the school paper, *Guide Post*, a short story entitled "On the Road Again (Part I)," above which was splashed this self-conceived bio—"About the author: Andy G.

Kaufman has traveled around Greenwich Village and San Francisco with such people as Allen Ginsberg, Gregory Corso, and a few girls. During the summer, he plans to travel across the country with Jack Kerouac, Dean Moriarty, and a few girls."

It is funny how things can come up so suddenly. With me, the thing happened on a Sunday afternoon. . . . I was about to take a bottle of sleeping pills when the phone rang. "Hello." I heard the sweet little voice of a girl about my age.

"Hello . . . I'd like to speak to Geoffrey Andrews."

"Oh, this is he. Who is it?"

"This is Janet Brown."

"Well, this is Geoffrey Andrews, but I don't know any Janet Brown." It turned out she was some girl [not actually named Janet Brown] from Rockville Centre, there was another person named Geoffrey Andrews and she had called me by mistake. . . .

"Well, isn't this something," she said. "Would you please tell me about yourself?"

"What—er—uh—yes—um—what—do you want me to tell you?"

. . . I told her that I wrote poetry, read it in Greenwich Village cafes, and played the bongos in Washington Square Park. That was it. That phone call was God. She dug it, too! She [said she] played her guitar in the Park and she dug poetry. After a few hours of talking we were in the cool. . . . We talked until the sun burned out, and I dug every minute of it. There was just one hangup: She was too embarrassed to give me her real name, address and telephone number. . . .

As story/satire continues, he never hears from her again and so—because she had lied about her name—he quests on bicycle to Rockville Centre, Long Island, with his own name pinned to his jacket, so as to flush her out of hiding, meeting many characters along the way, but not her. Funny thing that did happen was all of above—the providential telephone mistake begetting hourslong conversation mutually dug—but her name was Marilyn Blumberg, which she did not conceal, from Rockville Centre, who played folk guitar and shared his passions for Kerouac and radio humorist Jean

Shepherd and roaming the city affecting hipness ("I thought I was another Joan Baez—dark hair split down the middle, black jeans, black turtleneck, black shoes, very beat, very New York, very very cool."). Before hanging up, they made plans to meet at the New York World's Fair in Flushing Meadows beneath the Unisphere globe sculpture (his idea) directly under the tip of South America—under Tierra del Fuego. She told him to have a flower in his teeth in order to recognize him. "He said, 'I'll do it!' He told me it would be a rose. I'll never forget when I first saw him sitting under there—he had a carnation in his mouth; he said he couldn't find a rose—and I was surprised that he was this tall and lanky, sweet and cute guy. He was a little abashed initially because it had been much easier to be over the top on the phone. But he loosened up over the course of the day. I just couldn't believe I was meeting this guy from the phone."

Once loosened, he led her to the African Pavilion, hearing drums pound as they got nearer, and there amid huts full of antelopes and zebras and birds was Olatunji on congas, representing Nigerian heritage, playing, leaping, suddenly recognizing his pupil—*Ahhnn-deeee!*—which, as per plan, impressed Marilyn ("Andy was very excited to show me that they knew each other."); they spoke with the great drum master for a while, felt almost as though special blessing had been conferred, knew they would see more of each other. They did; usually they would meet at Penn Station, training into town from opposite ends of Long Island—"Mostly, I snuck off to see him," she said—then descend upon Greenwich Village to hang out. They explored coffeehouses and folk clubs and bookstores. "We would just enjoy being kooky together, doing little spontaneous playlets on the streets, little Marcel Marceau mime things, performancy things. He was awfully good at it. Or he might imitate people he saw, but never in a nasty way. He was very very intent on people watching. He always made me laugh. Then we would go to Washington Square Park and sometimes I'd bring my guitar and we'd sing, which was cool." He tried out his Elvisspeak on her, demonstrated for her his ability to lip-synch to the Mighty Mouse theme song (his idea for children's parties, he explained, was to move his mouth only when the voice of

Mighty Mouse declared "Here I come to save the day!"), became many other people for her—sometimes this scared foreign guy with a funny accent—which seemed to be a very big part of just being himself. "He absolutely worked at being very uninhibited that way. But the relationship never got very intense. Mostly, it was about hanging out and talking on the phone. There wasn't anything like intimacy, but Andy was very shy."

He and Michael knew a song, frequently sung by miscreants at summer camp, which went: "Last night I stayed at home and masturbated, it felt so good, I knew it woooould—long strokes, short strokes, knock-it-against-the-wall strokes, slam it, bang it. . . ." Passing each other in the house, one would sing to the other, "Last night I stayed at home," and the other would sing, "And what'dja dooo and what'dja dooo?" Brothers. They smiled secretly and never sang any further.

Meanwhile . . .

The rebellion, such as it would become, coincided with other chaos, with desperation no adolescent son—this one especially— might care to fathom. Stanley Kaufman was in trouble. Grandpa Paul had had it with the bauble empire he began. By the middle of 1965, he walked away, exhausted, no longer his big buoyant carnival self, and left Stanley holding the bag and all there was for Stanley to do was to put KARU-ARKÉ—as the once profitable business was now called—out of its sublime misery. At decade's outset, these girls Audrey Hepburn and Jackie Kennedy—simplicity girls—they had stopped with the elaborate accessorizing, didn't wear the belts or the earrings or the pins, did not *adorn* themselves much at all, and women noticed this, as women will, and they followed suit. Mrs. Kennedy's late husband had already killed the hat industry—the young President never wore them; men noticed; hats were dead overnight—and now the costume jewelry business was similarly plunged into dire spiral. Stanley and his father's partner, Ruderman, cut future loss by pulling the plug in October. Panic reigned on Grassfield Road everywhere but in the downstairs den where Andrew G. Kaufman of the eleventh grade now hosted various visitors of unseemly dishevelment and intent. Vacant-eyed longhairs came and went down there—usually through the outside rear sliding glass door of the otherwise sealed sanctum—issuing upward sounds of larger commotion, cackles, screams, guitar-twangs, drumbeats, soul music, James Brown music, folk music, Elvis music (always accompanied by a chorus of displeased groans). Upstairs, the irritable head-of-household would occasionally accost his son, berate him for his slovenly appearance, the unkempt facial hair, the sorrowful wardrobe selections, the lack of self-respect and self-discipline, the continuance of academic devastation, and the sudden ongoing presence of questionable youths on the premises. His pipe collection, he noted, had vanished from the house. His liquor cabinet—he may or may not have known—was being plundered as well. Was that burning incense he smelled? Correct responses to all criticisms/allegations were demanded. Only the briefest of yelping excuses were proffered—*I thought you wanted me to have friends!* et cetera—upon which son would walk away, upon which father would howl after him or shake his head defeatedly or howl elsewhere. Janice registered it all as familiar din, became very involved in television soap operas, made the best of all circumstances. She also made late night snacks for Andy and his odd crew, which balanced tensions nicely. Because, adding to the tumult, Stanley had immediately decided to make a new go of it, to start his own jewelry business (the only business he knew), but do it all different, get a new partner, aim for a new youth market, lighten things up, address the new tempo of the new times—they would even call the company Tempo so as to declare themselves mod as mod could be, thus bankable. New pressure therefore gripped him, shook whatever equilibrium he still possessed. "I was wetting my pants," he would remember. "I was scared stiff."

* * *

The boy had taken to truancy as means of escape.

Whereas previously he could disappear from reality without leaving the room, he had recently learned to disappear—quite physically—into mad shared adventure, into nocturnal unaccountability, into the gloamy parks of Great Neck and the sensual abyss of Manhattan. He perfected sneaking off as minor artform. Told parents he was somewhere he wasn't and had no intention of being; manufactured alibis and cover-ups and rarely got caught. *He was independent,* his father remembered, not knowing the half of it. He rode the Long Island Railroad like a veteran of suburbanschlep wars. Gregg Sutton, his first and only ally in Elvis appreciation, had moved after sixth grade with his family to the city's Upper East Side, to the ninth floor of a building on Sixty-sixth and Third—three floors below his colorful cousin Glenn Barrett, one year older, susceptible to any entreaty of mayhem. One night in 1964, Sutton answered a light knock at the apartment door. There he stood: "Um, do you remember me, Andy Kaufman from Baker Hill Elementary?" "He had been to Hubert's Museum that night and decided to come over. We had stayed in touch a bit on the phone, so he knew where to find me, but I hadn't seen him since Great Neck. He was talking about Fellini's 8½ and had *The Hollering Mangoo* with him—what a piece of work. I got Glenn to come down, then we went to Central Park that night and sort of fantasized and played. This became a regular thing. We'd go to Central Park, maybe blow a joint or whatever, and just act crazy. You can be anything you want in New York City—it doesn't matter. You can be any way on the street—which became one of Andy's credos. We'd be soldiers or rock stars in the band shell. We'd do characters and get into fake fights. He loved the fake fights. He and Glenn would roll around the lawn in mock knife fights—never-ending knife fights—just to see if anyone watching would try to stop them, which they didn't. It was New York. Johnny Carson would make jokes about how dangerous Central Park was at night. Andy was oblivious. I'd say, 'Andy, there are people in here who really might stab you.' 'Oh, no! They won't stab *me!*' I guess we met the enemy and it was us."

Eventually, Andy beseeched them to return to home turf: "Um, you guys should come out to Great Neck one weekend. You can stay at my house. There's some hip kids there—you'll be a big hit. Ohh, they'll think you're real bohemian beatniks!" By this time, his circle had widened. A couple of other guys, named Doug DeSoto (who, like Moogie, attended Great Neck South) and Gil Gevins, a fellow North attendee, had embraced him and pulled him into a small roguish hippie clique they would come to call F Troop, borrowed from the popular TV situation comedy about bumbling cavalrymen. Sutton and Barrett showed up in town wearing grievous dispositions and little leather caps—Sutton with his guitar, Barrett with his harmonica, a pair of traveling bluesmen immediately suspected to be out-of-town drug pushers. "We looked like hell," said Barrett. They were inducted with little hesitation into the fraternity. F Troop would fast become the stuff of lunatic legend in the precincts, with Andy as sole mascot—mirthful marauders who tried everything many times over. "The five of us were the core of F Troop," said Gevins, "and we were real snobs in a lot of ways. It was a very closed circle, because in our minds we were the hippest, coolest kids who ever lived."

Sutton: "We were thick as thieves. We spent weekends together taking group acid trips, going into the city, hanging out in Great Neck at Andy's house or at Gil's house, going to the park at night, getting stoned, attempting to get girls. Everyone knew us."

Glenn Barrett: "We were the scourge of the town, needless to say."

Moogie Klingman: "F Troop was a bunch of fucking assholes. Andy joined F Troop and didn't bring me with him and they kept me out. I discovered him and brought him on the scene; they formed an exclusionary clique and stole him away. Then, suddenly, they also started stealing our women—they were all gravitating to F Troop. Who gives a fuck about F Troop anyway?"

They did as they wished.

They were hooligans of much panache.

They crashed parties, dropped pants, spilled paint, ruined parties, forged irreputable reputations. They headquartered in Allenwood Park—sometimes Grace Avenue Park—beneath or up in trees, strummed guitars, taunted girls, pawed girls (not Andy; too shy), altered reality.

They consumed copious amounts of marijuana, flirted with acid, went on four-day hash binges. Andy, according to all, ingested with prudence, great moderation. He would remember differently—"Between the ages of sixteen and nineteen, I was smoking marijuana every day. I was also taking [less regularly] DET, LSD, DMT, Dexedrine, all kindsa things."

Gevins would maintain that Andy dropped acid but once, then forced all present to listen to Elvis albums repeatedly. Difficult trip except for one, who played conga in time: "We went nuts. His thing with Elvis was a real pain in the ass." (He once dragged Barrett to a Harlem movie house to see the new Elvis release, *Spinout*, the only two white people in the audience.) Another night, he and Barrett got stoned and, on a dare, rode bicycles through town "buck-naked."

They drank anything they could find in anyone's home, but usually had some older guy named Abe buy them bottles of Thunderbird. Andy liked to call it *red wine*, so as to lend greater dignity to the papersack ferment. He *liked* his red wine: "I was a heavy drinker and it got heavier and heavier until I was like just getting drunk all the time. I look back and think, *Boy, I almost became an alcoholic.*"

Barrett taught him how to smoke cigarettes: "He asked me to show him. He was very proud of that. He always used to introduce me to people as the guy who turned him on to cigarettes. My big claim to fame—now I'm ashamed. But he never really smoked anyway. From day one, Andy was a closet existentialist. He wanted to experiment with everything, wanted to experience all that he could in life."

Their sieges upon Manhattan escalated; they nearly destroyed a Bleecker Street spin-art emporium (squirt paint, rotating canvases; acid, havoc); they played inebriate pirates—lots of *arrgh matey!*—aboard the Staten Island Ferry (promptly ejected at port); they camped out on the remote Point at Central Park Lake; they panhandled in front of the Plaza Hotel, Andy offering tuneless songs for coinage; they slept in a rotting abandoned building on the Lower East Side; they preferred that their nights of rabble never end.

Doug DeSoto played in a band called Fragment of Love that appeared at Central Park music festivals, where they met a sophisticated fifteen-year-old named Ginger Petrochko, who would go-go dance along onstage and quickly become an F Troop fixture. F Troop once came to a party at her family's apartment, brought fireworks, burned holes in kitchen linoleum with sparklers, were thrown out.

Andy always went to Fragment of Love practice jams, never much liked the music, rolled up his jacket like a pillow and took naps on the floor; during breaks, he would awaken, borrow a guitar, and pretend to be Elvis—*thankyou thankyouverrrramuch.*

He began making fateful allusions—casually—would say things— *When I am famous . . . I am going to be famous one day, mark my words. . . .*

He told them that Elvis would personally assure his success.

They never necessarily believed anything he said.

They razzed him about the Elvis hit, "In the Ghetto"—would relentlessly mock the word *ghet-tohhhhhh.* He took umbrage always, would contend, "He's not so bad!" On the other hand, he thrilled to any one of them going off on a temper tantrum. Sutton and Gevins, mostly. He thought it hilarious.

Members preferred not to be alone with him, since he never said much, preferred having somebody else there to cover the silences, which were sometimes elephantine and, well, a little *dull.*

They all loved his eyes, theorized as to what might be behind them.

He wanted them all to think he was crazier than he was; they knew he wasn't as crazy as he wanted them to think; they thought he would either become famous or become a dead wino.

Great Neck police came to know all of them on a first-name basis. Hassling F Troop was de riguer for local law—they were instructed at every turn to empty the contents of their pockets, usually on the hood of a patrol car. Andy would always go last. He would begin methodically—"We'd all stand there thinking, *Please, please, don't have any marijuana in your pockets!*" said Barrett—and continue slowly, reaching, digging deep, front and back, jacket and pants, searching, extracting papers, snot rags, cards, string, gum, comb, keys, coins, dollars, tissue, Elvis pocket calendar, stuffed wallet, copy of *On the Road*, lint as well. "Everything would come out. Even *we* were amazed at the amount of junk he would have in there. But that was Andy—he'd say, 'Oh, wait a minute, I have one more thing,' then again, 'Oh! Here's something else.' He wasn't even a wiseass about it. The cops thought they were being put on. If they were, he never told us."

One night, F Troop gave an impromptu "concert" at the Great Neck home of ancillary member Peter Wassyng, whose parents were out of town. Twenty revelers *paid* for the privilege of witnessing the haphazard spectacle (such was their lure). Andy opened the show, staging a fight with Barrett that began on the roof of the Wassyng house, continued on and down an adjacent tree, from which they rappelled in full tussle to the ground, where Barrett feigned collapse, Andy feigned victory, upon which he picked up a guitar and began playing and singing an exaggerated version of the Animals' hit dirge, "The House of the Rising Sun"—*There izzzz a house in New Orleans....* Then, at the end of the song, he pretended to die—and die—and die. "He died for fifteen minutes," said Gevins. "Like he'd been shot in one place, goes down, gets to his knees, he's shot in another place, he gets up, he's writhing on the ground again, he gets up, goes down . . . then up . . . then down—for *fifteen minutes!* F Troop is in complete hysterics and everybody who paid admission is getting more and more pissed off. It was like a precursor to Andy's whole career in microcosm. It was also the first time—outside of kids' parties—that he'd done anything so crazy in front of an audience."

Another night, they were returning by car—somebody got one—to Great Neck from the city and cops tried to bust them for pot possession on the Fifty-ninth Street Bridge—*where a dirty little face had long ago popped up in Daddy's rearview mirror, surprise!* They beat the rap and repaired to the Kaufman house, where nobody was home, descended to the den to recover from the hassle. "We were bored," said Sutton. "So Andy did his children's act for us for the first time. He gave us a little taste. He had us sing 'The Cow Goes Moo' and do the 'Old MacDonald' lip-synch routine with the phonograph and he did Mighty Mouse, too, and a few other things. It blew my mind. He had us all in stitches. That was the first inkling I had that Andy might have talent. I never realized it before."

Days before his seventeenth birthday, he vanished. He was gone from Grassfield Road, gone without a trace, did not return home at night, left an ambiguous suggestion on the premises that he would be gone for good. No longer would his father need to criticize him, to yell and yellllllllll at him for looking/acting LIKE A BUM!!!!! It was over. "I was his enemy," said Stanley. "All I wanted him to do was to cut his hair!" They did not see eye to eye on much of anything, really. To duly punish his father, the son chose to disappear on the very first day of business for the brand-new Tempo costume jewelry corporation. It was also the first day of the first market week—January 1966—necessarily the most important day of Stanley's new life and future life. "It was make-or-break time," he said. Janice called him at the office and he exploded and alerted his new partner, Tom Tessler, and together the two men canvassed all of New York's train and bus terminals and contacted police and found nothing. "Nothing whatsoever. He was a miserable son of a bitch. He just left us and we didn't hear anything for more than a week. We finally got a call from one of his friends, who said he was in Boston." He came home via rail; Stanley waited at the Grace Avenue train stop, fuming inside his car. "He got in the car and, as we were driving home, we got into an argument right away. With the car moving, he opened the door and jumped out and started running away through the park. I got out and chased after him, screaming, *'You son of a bitch! Get back here!'* I'm cursing, I'm yelling, I'm huffin' and puffin' trying to keep up with him. It was like running after the fox that got away. I thought I was gonna have a heart attack."

They mended. They had to. Grandpa Paul—big bubbly hambone facilitator of magical inspiration, unwitting architect of his eldest grandson's future career—died that April. Patriarchal umbrella (expansive multicolored beach version) was gone. Paul's eldest son and Paul's eldest son's eldest son needed to achieve reckoning, as Paul would have wished. Andy instigated the only way he could: "It was his inspiration to get us back together," said Stanley. "We were on completely different wavelengths and I had to get off my kick with the hair and realize there was more to life than that." Andy handed his father a copy of *On the Road* and asked him to read it. Stanley read it. One weekend morning he knelt beside his bed, where he liked to read (back problems), and "I got to a particular passage and I started to cry because it was so tremendously moving. It related to the conflict between this father and his son. I now understood why Andy wanted me to read this book. At that moment, he walked into the room and he saw me there and he knelt down next to me and we sort of read it together. And we both cried. And we began to understand each other a little better. There was détente and finally a little mutual respect."

Oh! Victory triumph conquest. It happened at last. It happened the way it happened because Margaret had sadly departed family employ—the children were all of responsible size now—leaving free her maid's quarters, the small bedroom beside the den, to be usurped by the wily denmaster himself. The move was logical and obvious. He would now control the entire lower level of the house on Grassfield Road, except for the laundry room. Downward, he lugged all prized possessions, installing his Howdy Doody puppet, his Willie the Clown doll, wrestling magazines and artifacts, chin-up bar, Fabian photos, Presleyana in vast array, congas, broken bongos, stacks of comic books, record collections ever growing, beatnik books, his own poetry and writings, and every oddity his grandparents had ever given him. Plus, now there was extra square footage for F Troop sleeping bags so as to allow for inevitable group crashovers. So—they found this girl on New Year's Eve at Penn Station, a devastating hippie chick, smarter than her years, which were the same as theirs. Her name was Carol. Oh, a most beautiful redhead, very, um, liberal and forward sexually, an alto-

gether new kind of chick, a city chick, to boot. Glenn fell in love with her first, serenaded her on harmonica, and they started doing it in no time. She came to Great Neck a lot and would decide—believing in free love and all—to arbitrarily get it on with each member of the troop. She had not yet completed her mission, since Andy was Andy and he was not easy to engage as such. On the night the world changed, she had been making out with most all of them down in the den until there was only Andy, whom she led into his new bedroom and suggested greater measures. Very very excited but—oh! He told her to wait and rushed out to his friends and said, "Um, okay, what should I do?" "He had zero idea," said Gevins. They sat him down and mapped each movement for him. "We're talking very graphic instructions, all about lubrication and insertion and licking and biting and stroking, step by step." He kept having them repeat what they told him. One more time, from the top. His eyes bulged as he drank in the precious invaluable information. "Now, wait, so first I kiss her? How long do we do that?" After a half hour, he said, "Okay, I got it now." The troop— all of whom had been convulsing throughout—rose up to pat his back encouragingly, told him, "Good luck! Go for it! You can do it!" At ten o'clock the following morning, they would all remember, he emerged from his bedroom with eyes resembling golf balls and he pronounced in an effusive tone they had not heard before, "Today I am a man!"

"In the eleventh grade," he proudly told an interviewing person years later, "I lost my virginity and kissed a girl the same night!"

But he screwed everything up. He always did, every time he got a little too cocky. He noticed this pattern in himself and hated it. He actually came to believe that he was cursed in four-year cycles. "Every four years I'd be successful for a few months. Then that would blow away. [After losing his virginity] it was great. For the next few months, I got really high headed about it and I went out with a lot of girls. Then I got really stuck up . . . and I went too far." He saw certain moments of the seventh and eleventh grades as high points and all periods that intervened or immediately followed were hopeless and dismal (and, um, fine). With this girl Carol, it was the same. They kind of dated and had sex and she openly adored his odd/awkward sweetness, sincerely urged him to be a better him, which she knew he was. She learned to slip down through his foliage-obscured subterranean bedroom window—as many would over time (just for the illicit thrill of it; the back door to the den was ever an option)—and showed him how to do *things,* which he liked very very extremely much. Other hippie girls sensed his new-found power and enticed him as well and what else could he do? After all, the other guys did it, too. But this Carol girl was more special, more interesting—whenever he gave her train fare to and from Manhattan or bought her espresso coffee ice cream, she blithely joked about how he was paying her for *services rendered.* Then he once made a similar crack to her, only a little less playful, not to be mean, not really, which truly made her feel like a prostitute—*he dreamt of prostitutes, couldn't believe such a wonderful thing could exist, and this Carol was able to sort of make him feel like he was paying her for their sex, only in fun, just fooling, but still, oh!*—which she didn't think was funny and she stormed away and he felt like an asshole, then figured he was an ass-hole, and just went ahead and acted like an asshole, and his grades went deeper into the toilet than ever before and he told his father that he wanted to drop out, but his father convinced him he would be less than nothing without a high school diploma, so he stayed on and ded-icated himself, just barely, to the twelfth grade and graduated, just barely, from Great Neck North, 419th in a class of 461 (due to a final 70.6 grade point average, thankfully not the utter basin of D-ness) on June 23, 1967, thereby setting forth in a world he mistakenly thought he knew well, equipped with an IQ of 114 and an inscrutable malevo-lent novel and the ability to entertain children and drug-dazed friends and no exact idea of just how he would become famous other than knowing that he would and then everyone who ever doubted him would feel foolish, very very foolish, please mark his words.

Of course, shrinks had returned to his life. In the last stages of high school, as he traipsed again into fated nadir, they were back, one in Great Neck, another (a black doctor, kind of exotic) in Brooklyn. Same routine. Now they were giving him new sorts of reality tests and he shared his reality as he knew it and it was a reality unsettling to psychological purview. His father, his mother, they saw him smile, just like always, as he left the offices, or as he returned home from such inquests, having given new recitations of conjured otherness, extemporaneously executed—no, really. There was a war on—did he know this? What exactly did he know of Vietnam? *Wasn't it like some restaurant?* Did he believe in his country? *His invisible twin brother was Japanese, so he was conflicted, of course. He could never be angry at somebody Asian/Oriental, unless maybe the chow mein in the restaurant didn't taste right, but these things happen, don't they? It's not their fault, maybe the stoves weren't working the way they should, everybody makes mistakes and stuff, right?* He got his letter, just as all scions of Great Neck upward mobility aimed to get theirs. It was a breeze, for him. The doctor wrote to strenuously suggest that his patient be kept from military service at all costs. "He said I was in a fantasy world since preschool days and I was in a little bubble and I couldn't be broken out of it and if I was in the Army my fantasies would get the better of me and I'd completely lose my mind."

He cherished his 4-F status, thought it quite funny, showed off the doctor's letter to the guys. "I remember it pretty well because it was hilarious," said Gil Gevins. "Everybody wanted to get out of the Vietnam War with a 4-F, which was a permanent deferment, and Andy was so proud to have gotten his. The letter stated something to the effect of the standard thing, 'paranoid schizophrenic with psychotic tendencies.' Then it went on to describe how every teacher from the first grade on had noticed that Andy was kind of strange and detached from the situation. And that he had scored zero on every reality test ever given him, that he lived in a complete fantasy world. And all of this was basically true. That was the funny thing about the letter. That *was* Andy. He *did* live in a fantasy world, but at the same time he knew what was going on! He really was out of his mind, but was always exactly aware of it. He was aware that it was all this kind of game that he played. He knew what he was doing—not all the time, but a lot of the time. He just encouraged people to believe what they wanted."

* * *

"Vait! Vait-vait-vait!

I would like to tell you de story of de three people who was carrying the beegest cannon in the world to Spain! Eet was, eh, two boys and one girl. And they had thees beeeg cannon. You know, eet was feefty feet long! And they carried eet over the mountains and under the valleys. And one day they get to the top of de highest mountain in Spain. So the first boy, he point this cannon toward this castle—you know, to shoot! You know, because he was the boss. You know, so he want to point it. And he turned to the second boy and he say, 'All right! Hand me the cannonball!' And, you know, but de second boy, he say—'Duh, I thought YOU had them!' So, vait-vait-vait, so, listen, vait! So they both—eh—they both turned to de girl, and she say—'Don't look at me!' You know, because, eh, they forgot to bring the cannonball. You know? They have the cannon, but they have no cannonball! They could not shoot! Do you understand? Tenk you veddy much!"

Lost year began in waiting. He wait-wait-waited. He waited to know what to do but could do nothing much—about dreams, future success, certain fame—without proper ammunition. How to begin? The Troop dispersed to colleges and universities and hospitals—returned home only for occasional weekends and holidays—so he was mostly on his own. Further learning did not intrigue him, what school would have him? He applied to no college at all, despite entreaties of his father. He needed to wait and think and drift, basing himself mostly in the Grassfield basement. Elvis kept him company. He spent more time with Elvis than ever before. "I would stay home most of the time and just play his records and imitate him—I adopted him as a character, combed my hair like him, dressed like him, made believe that I was him. For most of the day, every day, for that one year, I worked on my imitation." It was something to do. And then there was the foreigner person he liked who had no name, who spoke in funny timid blinking loops—he had introduced him to kids at school, then to kids at birthday parties, then to strangers on the streets of New York when he wanted to not be himself and beg for handouts. *Eee-bi-da? Eee-bi-da!* ("That's a language I made up myself to confuse other people, and make them feel I'm really speaking a dialect.") Being foreign never felt foreign since he sort of was foreign—he knew—but then, too, certain television people he liked often became foreign, like Sid Caesar, and the man on the Steve Allen program, Bill Dana, who became this other foreign man, José Jimenez, who was Spanish or something. His own foreign man, whom he would call Foreign Man, really belonged to no place, kind of like himself. *Eee-bi-da.*

Lost year required money, so he worked. Previously, he had bussed tables at Chop Meat Charlie's in the middle of town, jerked soda at Frederick's. Now he worked for Jones Taxi of Great Neck, driving businessmen to and from the train station; would sit outside the station waiting each night, big-eyed white boy talking to all of the black cabbies, sharing their bags of hooch, absorbing their sad beautiful tales, listening to their jive jokes and jive music. He drove delivery vans for another black man named Grady Corley—the small black population of Great Neck came to know and like Andy very much—carting groceries and butchered meats around town, making drops at homes of illustrious residents such as talk show oddity Professor Irwin Corey ("The World's Foremost Authority") and comedian Alan King, who lived most luxuriously (like a show business sultan) bayside on the Sound at King's Point. He had become friendly with the comedian's son, Bobby King, a point which Alan King would later not see as coincidental. "To this day, I think Andy Kaufman became friends with my son just so he could get to me. Every once in a while, this crazy kid would come up to deliver meat—and do five minutes. He would insist on seeing me and I'd come down to the kitchen in my underwear. Then he'd start doing takeoffs on movies he had seen on television for me! Very nice kid, but crazy as a loon, you know? Finally, I called the butcher and said, 'Get this kid out of my house!' I mean, it's very difficult to be amused by someone delivering meat."

Bobby King, meanwhile, was dating an Irish-Catholic girl named

Gina Acre, whose sister Gloria had been two classes behind Andy at Great Neck North. Gloria Acre was dark, mystical, stylish, well-read, spiritual, sweet, wise; she had a knack for dispensing advice and insights among disillusioned constituents—"Like Lucy in the *Peanuts* comics with the five-cent psychiatric counseling booth," she liked to say. Andy had once gone to her home, at the urging of a mutual friend named Almus P. Salcius, who told her, "I really think he needs to talk to somebody." Gloria recalled her new patient "sitting on my couch in an Andy way, sort of slouched, his hands on his lap, and not really having much to say except 'Do you want to go to a movie?' That was the beginning."

Lost year was not so bad, really, now with her, void was filled. He bought himself a black limousine sedan with flip seats in the back from the Grace Shipping estate (four hundred dollars) and got a livery cap and drove her everywhere unless he borrowed one of Grady's Econoline vans and drove her everywhere, usually with her sister Gina and Bobby King along for the rides. (Stanley remembered donning the livery cap himself for fun and chauffeuring his son around Great Neck, son imperiously waving through rear tinted windows at gawking pedestrians. Said father, "Once we mended, we were mended. More or less.") He became Elvis for Gloria—"He sang 'Love Me Tender' to me all the time. We couldn't go anywhere if there was an Elvis Presley movie on television"—and played role of boyfriend with greater conviction. They did not say they loved each other—how did people ever do that?—but they did. "It was very intense. It was very all-consuming." Den couch kissing moved down hall to full intimacy behind bedroom door, parents upstairs looking the other way. ("Again, it was almost like the *Peanuts* cartoons—you heard the parents, but you never saw them." She overheard just one screaming match between Andy and Stanley—surprised by the vituperative passion exchanged—whereupon Andy took her and stormed out of the house.) They smoked much pot, drank whatever could be found—Grady sometimes came over with bottles of Champale malt liquor and passed the bounty.

Gina Acre called him Crazy Andy—a sobriquet he had heard

quite plentifully by now—and he led all concerned on addled adventures. On Halloween, deeply stoned, they infiltrated the small cemetery behind All Saints Church and attempted to raise the dead. Gloria accidentally moved a granite slab and unearthed two urns of cremated ash—remains of some eternal couple—and instigated a séance. "We lit candles and held hands in a circle and I began, '*I am a bridge into the unknown. Come to us, Spirits!*' " Whereupon a gang of local greasers pounced and scared them into apoplexy, which was exciting. They once ended up in Professor Corey's kitchen—after some civil rights fundraiser—smoking dope with the wild-haired Professor, his wife, and their son Richard Corey, a rare fellow Elvis enthusiast. "I think it was the Professor's pot," said Gloria. "It was the first time we ever got stoned with actual adults." Said Gina: "Andy worshiped the ground the Professor walked on. Gloria would complain to me, 'Oh, we have to go to the Corey house again!' " He took her to the city—often earning fast cash by chauffeuring in impatient rail commuters—and playacted various street scenes of romantic intrigue. ("He would storm up behind me and say, '*You! I told you I never wanted to see you again! Why are you following me!*' And I'd go right into, '*I'm sorry! I can't stay away! It's impossible! Don't do this to me!*' And people would be turning around, looking.") Gil Gevins had gotten a rattrap apartment on the Lower East Side, near his New York University classes—Andy and others contributed rent toward stayover privileges—and they would call to order impromptu F Troop meetings, which inevitably involved new assaults on Central Park and its unsuspecting populace.

Best of all, they reaped the material benefits of thickness with Bobby King, whose father's splendiferous Gatsby-like estate—with pool and cabana overlooking the rippling Sound—became their crash oasis, especially when the famous comedian was out on the road. They frolicked in the pool—Andy, naked, frequently—and lounged about. Peter Wassyng would remember Andy walking obliviously through the screen door of the King cabana—oh!—"Just spaced out, as usual." Once they left the pool heater on overnight and Alan King, who was to host a party the next day, had to ship in ice blocks to chill the hot-soup chlorinade. They helped themselves to libations from the cabana, drawing endless draughts of beer from bottomless kegs, using always the frosted mugs that were ever cooling. The mugs, more than anything, inspired Andy to achieve something similar in life. *"Frosted beer mugs!"* he kept crowing and would always remember doing so. Gloria heard him vow repeatedly, "Oh, when I get rich and famous, this is what I will have! Frosted beer mugs and a keg for my own self!" On at least two occasions, they rode with Bobby's father in Bobby's father's Rolls-Royce into the city to watch him perform on *The Ed Sullivan Show.* Andy was enthralled with the live broadcast hubbub, the red-lit cameras, the stage directions, the people scurrying, the havoc under the bright lights. It was time for him to do something about it. He heard about a school in Boston—not too picky about high school grade point averages—that specialized in teaching television production. Plus, he liked Boston, had thoroughly explored its oddest corners when he ran away from home. He waited until August 1968 to have his transcripts sent to this television school, this Grahm Junior College—only a two-year program!—and arrived there a few weeks later to start getting famous. Gloria would come visit and they would make a baby.

6

Actually, if one imagines a story called "The Funhouse," or "Lost in the Funhouse" . . . the beginning should recount the events between Ambrose's first sight of the funhouse early in the afternoon and his entering it . . . in the evening. The middle would narrate all relevant events from the time he goes in to the time he loses his way. . . . Then the ending would tell what Ambrose does while he's lost, how he finally finds his way out, and what everybody makes of the experience.

—John Barth,
Lost in the Funhouse

Very famous, after a fashion, living deep but humbly in the Hollywood Hills, he continued all the fictionalizing, after a fashion. Datetimeplace: November 29, 1980, 1:55 P.M. Greenvalley Road. The first book of the epic saga (with three books more to come, at least!), now reached handwritten pages 397–398, which would conclude this portion of the young entertainer's life:

"Come on. All aboard!" called the conductor.

Huey turned and boarded the train. He kept looking back, down at his family, who kept waving at him until he was out of sight. Then he turned forward, remembering with a clear picture the sight of his father and mother with their arms around each other while they had been waving. He wiped a tear from his eyes, and his mouth hung open as he looked around at the scenery that passed and thought about all the past: the family, the amusement park, school, Tiny and the gang, his grandpa, Grandma, the adventures, the loveliness, the trucks, the cabs, and all that he had been through in his life so far. Then he thought about his dream girl and his goals, and all that might lie ahead of him.

He looked upward and sat up straight. Then he closed his mouth and smiled.

Tears did come first, they really did. Now he would start all over again, not knowing anyone really, which was very disconcerting since he had gone from abject loneliness to popular renegade crazy person to abject loneliness all over again. He would be homesick, spectacularly homesick, would feel like Elvis when Elvis went into the Army. He walked around for months, longer even, with the Elvis song "I Feel So Bad" caroming around in his head. He lived on campus and campus was hemmed into Kenmore Square, where he resided in the men's dormitory, Leavitt Hall, 645 Beacon Street, room 629—a few blocks from Fenway Park, where some other men played baseball. So he had no choice but to find new bushes in a nearby park, wedged between college buildings, enclosed by a wrought iron fence, where he could keep himself company. "I would occasionally see Andy after eleven o'clock at night alone in the park and we would speak briefly," recalled fellow Leavitt resident Jonathan Kleiner. "Several times, rather than return a greeting, he would speak in a high-pitched tone, with words that did not seem to be words at all, and certainly not English words. And at times he would not use words at all, but just a collection of sounds, as if he could convey his thoughts or expressions without putting voice to them." *Um, eee-bi-da? Sebella gussh! Sebenye metitemya yaderni nidee terma.* Kleiner, who worked the Leavitt Hall switchboard graveyard shift, would come to withstand strategic advances of same foreign fellow, no longer foreign, latelate at night before switchboard closing—"Andy would be returning to the dorm and would ask me to watch him try out things. He would want the lounge area around the switchboard cubicle darkened, and at one point asked me to look at his pants. He was wearing what appeared to be lime green satin pants with a strip of tape running down the outer seam of both legs. He then proceeded to set up an old phonograph, put on an Elvis Presley record—'Hound Dog,' if I remember correctly—and launch into an impression of Elvis, which included removing the tape to show a dark black stripe down the outer seam of the pants, similar to what would be on a tuxedo. The impression was not very good at first, although he obviously kept working on it."

Funny place, this Grahm Junior College, which had been the Cambridge School of Business—a small secretarial school, really—before an eccentric businessman named Milton Grahm took command in 1950 and slowly began adding broadcast curricula and buying the finest broadcast equipment (Bell and Howell everything) and building extraordinarily professional broadcast studios (two studios for black-and-white transmission, one for color, and one fully operational twenty-four hour stereo radio facility), which beamed closed-circuit signals throughout a stately red-bricked colonial campus that kept growing, as Grahm Junior College, as it was renamed that very year, 1968, advertised its straightforward-hands-on-get-to-work-then-get-out-and-get-a-job-already policies in various trade publications. "Learn by Doing" was the Grahm motto, emblazoned on all seals and stamps, carved into granite and bronze abounding. A steadfast student body of approximately one thousand aspirants weaned on/enthralled by the cultural birth of television itself, with Howdy Doody as their logical progenitor, were not required to be previous academic marvels of any sort as long as each could fork over a most stiff annual tuition of nearly five thousand dollars across two extremely focused years of Learning-by-Doing. Grahm was thus awash in grown children of some privilege, all eager to transmit themselves via frequency and cathode ray into American homes as quickly as humanly possible.

So Andrew G. arrived that autumn to *apply* himself as never before and would soon shock loved ones and self by making the dean's list, while struggling to keep from missing his den and those who had dwelt and buffeted him there. He was known to skulk about forlornly—unless opportunity arose to display familiar oddball hubris. Often, he wandered in late for classes and reprised his penchant for removing layer after layer of clothing, not ever to be funny, and enjoyed the chuckles this would incite, pretending to look hurt by the chuckling, sometimes conjuring wetness in his tear ducts, which was a matter of adroit practice and concentration. "Andy was extremely shy, didn't talk much, was kind of a loner," said instructor Don Erickson, who saw certain sparkle as it was intermittently dispensed. "He only blossomed in the performance courses. In the production courses, on the other hand, he blossomed when he had to be responsible for what he did both in front of and behind the camera. He was always better when it was about him."

Gloria Acre, now of the twelfth grade at Great Neck North, came to see her college man in Boston for a long weekend that October. He got a nice hotel room so as to be worldly, kind of. They romped, consumed wine, some dope, each other, having much sex; hereabouts, she later calculated, sperm found egg. Happily reconnected, quite unaware of what was to be, they took cabs around town, creating larks—at his instruction, for driver's benefit, she became his cold, heartless mistress, said she would not leave her abusive husband for him; he petted her and sobbed and groveled. "You're not worth my time," she told him. Cabbie scolded her for this, said, "Lady, you don't know how good you have it. Obviously, this guy really cares about you." Cabbie told him, "Buddy, I understand. I've seen these kind of women before." Andy was ecstatic, they laughed; he sputtered with his dreams and fears and she listened and believed. "He wanted to make a name for himself. He just knew he was destined for some sort of fame. He knew what he didn't want to be and that was to end up in the gutter like a street person. That was a constant fear." She went home, they stayed in touch, not urgently, not dependently, just nicely.

He was mustachioed now, and the mustache winged full across his face and grazed against great Elvisian sideburns which fed a beard of haphazard intent, and the hair on his head was a frazzled bush of mayhem; he looked like rabble, like a war-protest professional, although he protested nothing, had no feelings about political unrest, had no notions toward social awareness. He drifted past keening sit-ins, past picket-bearing peace-and-loveniks (they were *very* upset, it seemed) from Boston University down the pike, from his own school, from Harvard and everywhere all around him—the world was shrieking with radical ideas and ripping to shreds and numbing itself in cannabis clouds or worse—and, instead of caring along in chorus, he solely concerned himself with self-concern. He felt anxious, knew not why, sensing shadows of destruction threatening large goals that he could not permit to be imperiled. F Troop personnel visited and he and Glenn Barrett jubilantly pretended to kick the shit out of each other in public places and then they all got jumped in front of a dive bar on the wrong side of town and actually had the shit kicked out of them. "I guess this was their bar and these guys just didn't like the way we looked," said Barrett. "I was getting bashed badly in the eye and out of my other eye I caught sight of Andy being held by two guys and another guy starting to pummel him. And Andy was very calmly saying, 'Oh! No, no. I'm gonna get a haircut tomorrow, I promise.' Like he was quietly reasoning with fucking barbarians. He was just being Andy." At Walden Pond, they all dropped acid, except Andy, who tried to keep the rest of them from straying toward harm or oncoming traffic or drowning. Soon after, at the apartment of Peter Wassyng, who attended Boston University, he smoked a joint and said it would be his last joint ever and it actually was.

"That was the last time he ever did any drugs," said Wassyng.

[um, oh]

"The last time I took any drugs of any type was November 20, 1968," he would later recall, proudly, as is the convert's wont. "That was fifteen days before I started meditating. Because when you start Transcendental Meditation, you're asked to refrain from any nonprescription drugs, including marijuana, for fifteen days before you start, so you'll get the experience, the proper experience, without any external influences in the nervous system. Drugs stay in for about fifteen days, they found. So the drugs ended right then and I began learning about enlightenment in early December. Because I went to college to study to be in television and I said to myself: Now what do I want to do with my life? Do I want to keep getting stoned—which I don't really enjoy all that much—or do I want to really do something with my life, you know? I want to be on television. I want to be successful at what I do.

"Now, this meditation, according to what they told me at the meditation center in Boston—what will happen is that it gives you deep rest and it expands your consciousness and gets rid of stress and gets rid of things that are holding you back from accomplishing what you want to accomplish. They didn't say anything about [stopping] alcohol, but what I found was that, as I meditated every day, as time went on, I wanted alcohol less and less, until I just stopped drinking it entirely."

The bliss people, they had caught his eye. They were blissful happy friendlyfriendly people, whereas other people were so angry about war and presidents and things—but the bliss people had *innocence* was what it was. His own innocence, he had begun to think—*that's what it was exactly!*—was not so innocent anymore and, if he was not innocent, then how could people believe him when he said he was just fooling only in fun no really? They would just think he was a jerk but he wasn't a jerk because of his innocence which was getting less and less innocent. Plus, he did better with girls and with friends when he was innocent. "I always had trouble acting naturally, acting like myself. When I did thrive socially, I was at my most naive and innocent. No one had met anybody like me. I was very innocent and lovable—like a little boy. And when I lost my virginity and started going out with a lot of girls, I lost this side of me. For the next two years I tried to recapture it, but you can't go back. Every few years my innocence [had] come back naturally, and I would have a great time again. I was very confused. In college I started meditating . . .

and after that, I didn't have to think about how to act anymore." The bliss people in their TM Center seemed to blink away all bad things and they smiled so hard and so fast at him when they handed him the pamphlets which he took and read and decided to live life as they lived theirs—except that he was never much of a natural smiler per se. Peace Energy Happiness Maharishi—four words spun in an official halo crest encircling the grizzled benevolent face of His Holiness, Maharishi Mahesh Yogi himself—symbolized and defined the Movement, and it *was* a movement, quite new and very old and seriously Eastern, whose credo was just like Learning by Doing because it was all about focus. *Sit comfortably for fifteen to twenty minutes twice a day with the eyes closed and the Transcendental Meditation technique is easy to learn effortless to practice and does not require specific beliefs behavior or lifestyle and is open to all people of all ages cultures religions and one's mind settles down and one experiences a unique state of restful alertness that is Transcendental Consciousness when the body gains a unique state of deep rest releasing accumulated stress and revitalizing the entire nervous system resulting in development of the mind's full creative potential and improvement of health so that one enjoys increasing success and satisfaction in life and exhilaration and bubbling bliss and coherence and positivity.*

Well, nothing would happen overnight, of course, and it didn't, but eventually it did—"Slowly, but surely, I just felt such confidence and so much more strength within me." Now he had found the tool and would always say the tool had saved his life, had spared him from the gutter, had given him the ability to quash all shyness and step up and get on with it. Plus, he liked it because it was kind of like sleep and sleep was among his favorite activities and so he had started taking his energizing enlightening meditation "naps"—that was how he thought of them, as little *naps*—twice a day and sometimes he liked them to last way past twenty minutes and sometimes these *naps*, one or two hours in duration, would drive people crazy because people had to tiptoe around while he took them, which inconvenienced everyone, and oftentimes, much later, the *naps* made him very late and very tardy for important things and cost other people lots of money and engendered much anger and resentment toward him, which was, um, fine.

Meanwhile, Elvis came back! Elvis made his first television special ever and it was called *Elvis* and NBC broadcast it on December 3 at nine o'clock and millions and millions of people tuned in and everyone decided that Elvis was back and would thereafter refer to the program as Elvis's comeback special and one hippie boy in Boston who would begin to meditate two days later and would never stop until he couldn't possibly meditate anymore also (and especially) watched the program, watched with a ferocious intensity and felt a bubbling bliss unrivaled, and kept wondering what everyone meant when they called it a comeback special.

She knew that it was in there and did not believe that it was in there. But her visitor never came, not that month, not the month afterward, and she would get up before school and eat her breakfast which she then promptly vomited, morning after morning, but it could not possibly be true, would not allow herself to think for a moment that it was. She told no one, not her sister, not her best friends, no one, especially not him, because it could not possibly be true. "It was total avoidance," she said, "until the final moment of truth. I knew in my heart of hearts after a period of time, and I just refused to deal with it. I'd always been really sort of tiny—not petite, but small—and I was getting bigger and bigger. Not that much bigger, but bigger. So I started exercising like a mad person. I vitamined myself to death." She took to wearing big Mexican wedding blouses—a fashion statement, nothing more, honestly—which obscured the belly enough as long as she kept dieting and denying as well as undressing and dressing in the bathroom with the door locked. "Obviously, I'd gained weight. People commented, including my parents. In fact, they did try to worm it out of me at one point. They knew something was wrong. I'd just pitch the biggest fit and say, 'Listen, if you don't trust me, we can go to the doctor'—which I wish they'd taken me up on—'and we can deal with this once and for all!' " Her sister Gina would recall, "She got very secretive and really *testy*. There was a point where I thought I was gonna kill her myself!" But she had studied the art of playacting with a remarkable tutor who was lately closing his eyes and reclaiming lost innocence and also learning remedial television by doing, and so she committed thoroughly to this ruse that was all her own. "I was horseback riding at five months, and camping. The bathing suits had those blousy overtops, so I was covered." Her senior year of high school continued on as such, marching delicately toward graduation in drastic covert performance.

The bliss people—why did even *they* sometimes call themselves *bliss-ninnies*?—noted his progress and dedication most approvingly. On February 10, 1969, he began at their urging a six-month course in something called Yoga Asanas, which was really a regimen of posture exercises to limber the body to better greet the deep silence that would keep him from ending up in the gutter. Among other skills, asanas helped enable a small mastery of the lotus position, which was the preferred position if one was truly serious about moving toward enlightenment, which, in his case, also meant toward show business fame. His instructor—a mentor, really—in this phase was Prudence Farrow, who had returned to Boston after her rather famous trip to India the previous year. Prudence, whose mother was Jane in the old Tarzan movies (oh!), had gone there, as most people knew, with her younger actress-sister Mia, whose surprising marriage to Frank Sinatra had just broken up, and they had studied and meditated with the Maharishi and all four Beatles atop a mountain. (John Lennon found her devotion to TM training so adorable there that he wrote a song about her, right there, called "Dear Prudence.") Anyway, she quickly saw something of herself in Andy—"He was kind of spaced out and stuff"—and recognized his need for the meditating life. "He had gone through the sixties, like a lot of us, with those drugs and all the questioning, which created havoc especially in someone so young. He was going through that kind of damage and he didn't have parameters. He was walking around without checks and balances. He was disconnected. For Andy, meditation began to give him a connection inside—a self-ease—that he desperately needed."

She gave him his course booklet of exercise illustrations and told him that the Maharishi himself would want him to practice the asanas once per day, figuring that this would get his attention, which it did. Her association with the Beatles, meanwhile, piqued no interest in him because he cared nothing about the Beatles, but he had just received a very very important piece of information and he scribbled the information on the inside cover of the asanas booklet— "Elvis Presley, 3764 Highway 51 South, Memphis, Tennessee 38116." He had found Graceland. He knew that it was only a matter of time before he also found the god who dwelt therein. His various pieties were now coalescing in his impressionable brainfloat and so he began to write his second novel—*God*, he titled it, although sometimes he called it *G*d*, and later, *Gosh*—which was nothing if not a Presleyan iconography, an homage laced with biblical subtext, Zen teachings, beat rhythms, and more amusement park rides. Also, its 147 pages were best not to be read—utter nonsense to the eye—but to be performed, quite elaborately, in recitation (lots of sound effects and dialects), which only he could and would attempt.

God—he later believed it might have made a "nice little cartoon"—showcased the divine ascent of a beer-guzzling truck driver named Larry Prescott who was very much Elvis Presley. Larry gets himself famous by going on national television and performing "Hound Dog" while gyrating uncontrollably—**AH JUS' CAIN'T HE'P IT! AH JUS' GOTTA MOVE!!!!! And the knees just started a-wiggling. And the hips started wiggling. Round and round went his knees, and he *moved*, and baby, I mean he *really moved*! And through the sweat of his brow, a contented smile broke out all across his face as he sang: WEEEEEEEELLLLLLLL THEY SAID A-YOU WERE HAH CLACE BUT DAT WAS JUST A LAH. . . .** (TV censors, of course, immediately insist that the cameras pan no lower than his waist.) Larry's star soars and he invests in a theme park called Heaven, built once the Atlantic Ocean has been drained to make room for it, none of which seems to thrill God Himself who later angrily performs "Hound Dog" as well—**"You ain't heard nothin' yet!"**—despite lower back pain. Other featured characters include a floating boy named Tinctured Puncture and a floating girl named Gina, who giggles throughout **(Tee-hee-hee Tee-hee-hee),** and Queen Silga and King Fluke of Alegadonia (the King likes to declare, as had Nature Boy Buddy Rogers, **"I am *The* Greatest!"**) and Larry's manager Manny Mackelblatt, whose moxie bears some resemblance to that of Elvis impresario Colonel Tom Parker. The author, meanwhile, practiced his dramatizations of *God* for bemused cohorts and patient Grahm faculty members over months and months to come—during which several events of note transpired—finally debuting the work on December 1 in the living room of a women's dormitory at neighboring Simmons College. Four days later, *The Simmons News* school paper published a review—his first one ever!—under the rather reserved headline ANDY KAUFMAN PERFORMS "GOD" WITH EXPRESSIVE DELIVERY. Among observations therein: "[This] non-literal novel is comparable to an abstract expressionist painting. . . . Kaufman [has] created a fragmented funhouse fantasy. . . . [His] versatile improvisations carried the audience through incoherent passages until parallel events became interwoven. His expressive delivery complete with sound effects and gestures did not lag during the two-hour reading; nor did his voice crack under the strain of five-minute tee-heeing and hummmmmmming. Kaufman's vitality controlled the event and the myriad assortment of voices talking, gurgling and singing."

Of course, he had reached that moment after traversing a road paved with varying triumphs and fateful turns. In his Grahm classwork, he had been putting forth fine and broad performances before cameras and microphones (all real, none imaginary), for which at times he could not believe such a thing could be happening to him although he knew it was going to happen in constant continuum once he was famous no really. Radio held little intrigue for him, but he took a requisite course in which, among other tasks, he wrote and recorded commercials for products, legitimate and fake, suited to his own unique obsessions. (For the Elvis film *Speedway*—"Yessir, Elvis really socks it to 'em in his newest role, as Chad Taylor! He sings, he swings! See him sneer, see him fight, see him kiss the girls!" For the acne salve Blem-Stik—"Now, everybody, take your Blem-Stik and smear it on your face! Yessir, now look at your face! Or feel your face, or something like that! And how do you like that?! The pimples are all gone!") He became a stalwart among TV thespians in the innovative live-tape class productions conceived by Don Erickson, climbing into whichever personas were requested of him—he would somberly sing Jacques Brel dirges or issue grandiloquent soliloquies or pantomime street loon histrionics in sync to Top Forty hits. He inhabited several deceased lamenters who populated the ghostly town of Spoon River, Illinois, in *Spoon River Anthology*—a failed Broadway show based on a collection of woebegone poems by Edgar Lee Masters, which Erickson adapted for a class television project. He played a dead laughing guy and some dead old guys and a dead mystical guy and one dead extremely angry guy who spouted scorn through pursed and smacking lips that flapped and pouted under his thick-droop mustache (this was a very good look for a mean bastard, he thought)—"*You saw me as only a rundown man with matted hair and a beard and ragged clothing!*" he bitterly groused. "*Sometimes a man's life turns into a cancer—after being bruised and continually bruised until it swells into a purplish mass like growths on stalks of corn!!*"

But his crowning achievement came when Erickson instructed each student to invent a dramatic interpretation of the exquisitely tortured pop aria "MacArthur Park" that had been a major radio hit for the actor Richard Harris. Erickson would recall, "Each of the students would go alone into the studio with two cameras and a couple of spotlights on them, and the rest of the class and I were in the control room, where we would tape this stuff. Everyone had given a very good dramatic reading of the song, but no one was prepared for what Andy would bring. He sat down and buried his head in his hands, leaned over forward, and when he came up he was an anguished eighty-year-old Jewish man dripping Yiddish dialect." *Someone left their cake out in the rain? Oyyy, I don't think that I can take it . . . Cuz it took so lawwnnnngggg to bake it?* "We were laughing so hard—I actually fell on the floor and was gasping for air. I had him repeat it just so I could see it again all the way through. It was just so fucking funny. For that alone I gave him an A in the course. I mean, the boy was incredible."

He had plans that summer. He went back to Great Neck and showed his family "MacArthur Park"—only after demonstrating how the other kids had done their flowery renditions—and Stanley and Janice and Michael and Carol convulsed accordingly and Stanley and Janice could not get over the excellent grades he brought home with him and he beamed because they beamed and his father declared, half-jokingly, most encouragingly, over and over again, because it was a credo from his own days at school, "You shall be heard!" Also, Andy reported to them about his meditating and about how it had made him a better person and he urged them all to try learning and Carol and Michael and Janice began giving it some serious thought and Stanley rolled his eyes. Meanwhile, right away, he busied himself driving his limousine into the city (he had discovered a lucrative ploy of waiting outside the swank Four Seasons restaurant and grabbing big spenders who emerged after dinner and required a semiplush lift to destinations various) and sometimes he stuck his head into this unique kind of nightclub called The Improvisation (just to see what it was like) where people went onstage and got no pay and started breaking into show business (singers and comedians mostly; six years earlier, he had walked in and offered to do his birthday routine and was chased off before he could display his talent and told to come back once he had reached legal age) and he also worked again delivering for Grady and also did a little cab driving around Great Neck, so he tucked away money throughout June because he had big plans. He had an uncle in Hollywood who wasn't

a blood uncle but was best friends with Daddy's brother Jackie—
Uncle Jackie was his only real uncle—and so Sam Denoff, who grew
up five doors down from the Kaufmans in Brooklyn and went on to
become a tremendously successful comedy writer, had long been
known around the family as Uncle Sammy. Among many great jobs
in his wonderful career, Uncle Sammy wrote for Steve Allen's program in the early sixties—even back then Andy would call and ask
him questions galore (who *was* this José Jimenez?)—and then, with
his partner Bill Persky, he wrote some of the most famous episodes
of *The Dick Van Dyke Show* and, by this time, all the great comedians knew exactly who Uncle Sammy was. Anyway, Andy had decided that this was the summer he would go see what Hollywood was
all about and he would go stay with Uncle Sammy and also with
Uncle Sammy's mother, Aunt Esther, who was best friends with
Grandma Lillie and then also there was Gregg Sutton, who now
lived in Los Angeles and attended UCLA and was trying to get
started in the music business—so there were plenty of places to
sleep. He would go west for several weeks starting in July and this
was the plan because, at the very end of July, Elvis Presley—who
hadn't really performed any live concerts since the 1950s—would
open a monthlong engagement, two shows a night, at the
International Hotel in Las Vegas, Nevada—which was not very far
from Los Angeles (a mere bus ride or easy hitchhike, he figured)—
and the penultimate plan, of course, was to go find Elvis and to show
Elvis the novel he wrote about him and there really was no sense in
trying to deter him from this goal because it would happen because
it had to happen.

Gloria called him not long before he left. Now in her eighth
month—her stomach bulge still remarkably small thus fairly imperceptible beneath billowy frocks—she knew that she would give birth
to this child whose prenatal existence was yet unknown to everyone
but her. (She took her diploma onstage at graduation, perfectly con-
cealed beneath ceremonial robes.) She had no notion or desire to
have him marry her, knew he could be no kind of responsible husband and father, was unsure that even she could be a care-giving

mother, but her belief in God and in life was such that she would have to bring the baby to term and face the consequences. She realized, however, that if there was one person she should tell, it was him. "It was nighttime. He came over to my house and we walked over to the park. We were sitting on the swings and nobody else was there. I said, 'I have to tell you this. I'm pregnant. I don't know what else to say.' His eyes got wide and he looked at me and then he said. 'What are we going to do?' "

Tears came as they will in futility. It was, of course, unbelievable as certain momentous true things tend to be. He kissed her and held her and she said that it was good that he was going to California. She said, "Well, I'm glad you're going away because you shouldn't be here. My father will kill you when this comes out." Her parents had always liked him—they were always charmed and amused by his crazy extrapolations, even brought him along on family trips to the Jersey Shore—but this was real life most real and most life shattering and her father most certainly would have killed him or done something awful and it was going to be insane enough without that happening, so she said he should go find what he was looking for and not to worry. He felt terrified and relieved all at once. She sent him on his way; he went. Everything would be, um, fine.

He told no one, not a single soul. He went west and brought *God* with him and also his conga drum (maybe he would break into big-time show business while visiting) and saw the sights and goofed around with Sutton and drove Sutton's roommates crazy when he stayed with them in Beachwood Canyon. "Andy had given up pot and we were all big pot smokers. So he'd say, 'Can you put that out?' We'd all be riding somewhere in a Volkswagen and they'd close the windows and start smoking pot, just to torture him. He'd be in the backseat and insist on opening the front window and sticking his head out so that he'd have the last laugh. They couldn't stand him but Andy was so self-absorbed, he didn't have the time to notice or to hate somebody back. He didn't realize when people were bad-vibing him. It was his world and we were all scenery." Sutton had formed a rhythm-and-blues band called Yes Indeed and Andy went along with them to a private gig at a home in Brentwood at which a woman rode in on an elephant and, at one point during the Yes Indeed set, he elected to wander up onto the stage and became Elvis and he sang "I Feel So Bad" and all of the jaded Hollywood partygoers stopped cold and watched. Said Sutton, "He just stole the show."

The daughter arrived just before 6 A.M. on July 19 and she arrived amid hysteria, not the mother's hysteria, but that of the mother's parents and also that of the father's parents, who had been notified of the stunning blessed event by the mother's parents just after 6 A.M. on July 19. The day before—when nobody knew anything yet—Gloria was out paddleboating with friends and later that night went to a party and, while dancing, realized that her legs were moving farther and farther apart and knew labor had begun and went home and had her parents take her to the emergency room of North Shore Hospital, where the Acres finally learned that their daughter was not only pregnant but about to deliver a baby. The doctors noted Gloria's size and first thought she was six months pregnant and about to abort until an attendant spotted a head crowning and concluded that an actual birth was under way. It was a girl—"Very white, very tiny, and she had this little fuzzy brown hair," Gina Acre said—and Gloria decided to call her Laurel ("for victory"). The child was whisked to the nursery—her eighteen-year-old mother was discouraged from holding her, for fear of bonding, for fear of whatever was going to occur next. The Acres immediately and angrily phoned the Kaufmans; Stanley and Janice rushed to the hospital, apoplectic, astonished—"It was a shocker," Stanley would remember—and pledged all financial assistance with hospital bills et cetera on behalf of their son, whose exact whereabouts they knew not. They visited with Gloria—Janice told her, "Andy can marry you!" and her mother yelped, "Waitaminute! She's already made *one* mistake!"—but they did not see the baby. "We were told not to," said Stanley. "And we didn't." And their hearts felt leaden and their blood boiled, so furious were they with Andy and they would apprise him of such in no uncertain terms if and when they heard from him out there on his cockamamie trip. And it was decided that Catholic Charities would oversee adoption procedures, but only after Gloria made sure the child was baptized. And later the next day the phone rang in her hospital room and it was Andy—who had learned of events in no uncertain terms—calling from Disneyland which, said Gloria, "was so appropriate." "It was like 'Hi!' 'Hi!' I mean, it was okay. He was terribly sweet." Two weeks later, she was permitted to see the baby at an interim foster home, was finally allowed to hold her, and shortly thereafter was able to have her baptized—Laurel Rachel Acre, a name the child would not know as her own—at St. Bernard's Church in Levittown. Laurel wore the same baptismal gown that Gloria and Gina and most everyone in their family had worn. They snapped photographs on the lawn in front of the church and the adoption people took the child immediately afterward and she was gone and on every July 19 for years to come Gloria would plunge into a deep blue wrenching funk. Andy, meanwhile, would wonder on odd occasion what might be happening in the life of this other life to whom he had helped give life. He always wondered—when he wasn't thinking about other things.

Vegas beckoned. He waited until Elvis got there. To kill time, he went north to San Francisco to visit his second cousin, Rebecca Lawrence, a social worker who lived with her husband, Steve Tobias, in the Mission District. By this time, he was known to all perimeters of the Kaufman family as the most unusual/colorful specimen ever to emerge from their gene pool. At every family Passover seder, for instance, he would famously disappear from the dinner table, run around to the front door, reappear clad in linens and wearing a long false beard, then wordlessly reenter to take the ceremonial seat saved for the Hebrew prophet Elijah, so as to sip Elijah's unsipped wine and entertain relatives. (*Fun with religion!*) Thus, Rebecca and Steve anticipated his visit by setting up their brand-new reel-to-reel tape recorder to capture whatever whims he cared to unveil. The first order of business was to read from *God*, of course, and then he read aloud various surreal dreams that he had transcribed (shrinks had encouraged him to do this—the only professional advice he ever heeded—and, besides, he planned to rewrite some of the dreams as short stories). The last dream that he recited had not been transcribed, however, and he told it extemporaneously and it was a remarkable fear-of-failure dream about a boy named Jack. Very much like him, Jack wished to become a famous entertainer (he had enacted pretend shows near the school playground for imaginary audiences et cetera) and Jack had a well-connected uncle who one day arranges an audition for him with important producers and, on his way to the audition, Jack is corrupted by a gang of guys who pick him up hitchhiking and ply him with drink and dope. Jack finally arrives for the audition in a showroom, three hours late and stoned, and he goes onstage to face the restless crowd that had been waiting and waiting and getting angrier and angrier—whereupon Jack suddenly elects to spew mindless bile toward all present: "I need this like a hole in the head! Fuck all of you, you stupid no-good dirty bastards! I hate all of you—especially *you*, Uncle! Thanks for nothing!" Then, as he leaves the stage, the audience erupts into enormous cheers and Jack is a big success.

"Wow," said Steve Tobias afterward, while the tape spooled forth. "So that's how you get applause."

"Yep," said Andy, sounding most pleased with himself. "By waiting."

Steve and Rebecca then began to quiz him about the performances he had been giving at various Boston coffeehouses—really three random spring nights in which he had incongruously taken the stage between folksinging acts and performed as Elvis (wearing the iridescent lime green suit that F Troop member Doug DeSoto had given him, over a gold turtleneck sweater). "When I have the Elvis Presley suit on," he told them, "I feel like Elvis Presley." Steve asked: "You mean you really believe you're Elvis Presley?" Andy: "Yeah, I *become* Elvis Presley. People probably think I don't like Elvis Presley or they think I'm goofing on him and stuff, because it's kind of funny and they laugh when I do it. Like I jump into the audience and touch the girls and they scream sometimes, not all the time. But I like them to. But I don't do anything to be funny."

Not to be funny, he then became Elvis for his second cousin and her husband, borrowing Rebecca's guitar and turning up the collar of his jacket and slicking back his hair ("This isn't my costume, so I won't be able to do it as well as I can"), and he strummed the only four chords he knew as best as he could and sang an impassioned "Blue Suede Shoes" and a mournful "Are You Lonesome Tonight" and then Rebecca requested "Love Me Tender" and, speaking in his Memphian drawl, he said, "Ah've been singing 'Love Me Tender' ever since Ah wuzz a little boy. And Ah love that song. It means a lot to me. Ah get real serious and hope that Ah cain finish it, because Ah have never been able to. And Ah'd appreciate it if you-all didn't laugh." And he began to sing and he sang half of the song at which point he began to weep and he kept singing through loud convulsing sobs until the sobs overtook the words and dissolved into full-on blubbering. Steve and Rebecca applauded and, composing himself instantly, thus alarmingly, he answered, "Thank you, thankyouverrrmuch."

He returned briefly to Los Angeles, where Sutton took him to a costume sale at the MGM lot in Culver City and they bought a hot pink suit which they thought might have been from *The Wizard of Oz* but probably not, which he would wear to meet Elvis—or to at least get Elvis's attention. He moved to Uncle Sammy's house, where he asked to hear as many show business stories as Uncle Sammy could bear to tell, and then he moved to Aunt Esther's house, where she couldn't understand why this boy with his *farkuckte* meditating needed to sit like a lox behind a door and let such nice hot meals that she made for him get so cold. Anyway, it was Aunt Esther who told him to take an all-night bus to Las Vegas so that he shouldn't have to waste money on a hotel room for an extra night and he followed her advice and carried his pink suit with him on the bus and arrived the next morning at the International Hotel, which was crawling with Elvis fans from everywhere in the world, but not one of them, he believed, was as ardent or as clever as he. A plan was necessary and he had not much money but he did manage to pay to see one of Elvis's shows unless he didn't see Elvis perform at all because so many versions of the story would be told that no one, not anyone, would ever know exactly for sure what happened and even he would change things around in tellings and retellings to the point wherein discrepancies would abound so that several variations of actuality could well have been possible. But he had to wait and wait if he was to succeed in confronting Elvis. He had to bide time around the hotel at which he may or may not have ever gotten a room because he was in Las Vegas for four long days or else just over a day, during which time he waited and plotted. It was then, during just such a waiting period, that he stumbled into a lounge late one/that night at the International/someplace else and discovered an entertainer with whom his life and reputation would later become so inextricably intertwined as to bring great confusion/damage to his/their career/careers. The name of the man singing in this lounge was Tony Clifton, but perhaps not—but the name of the man singing in this lounge was Tony Clifton, but perhaps not. Tony Clifton sang like a cement mixer and wore a garish peach embroidered tuxedo and a scrubbrush mustache and gaudy rings on fat fingers and shades that obscured rheumy eyes below which bags hung like hogs in hammocks. He had a way about him—or so Andy Kaufman thought/imagined. "He made quite an impression on me," he said years hence when it was necessary to become defensive about Tony Clifton. "His first line was, 'I'm in Vegas—they got a lot of cool chicks here, you know what I mean?' He was awful. He threw a drink on a girl and tore her date's jacket, pushed people around. He got into fights with people; he bragged. He was so extreme that it really impressed me." What he knew then or didn't know until a short while thereafter was that he would want to imitate Tony Clifton as part of his show business act which he would debut in all of its grandeur sooner than later and then maybe when he got famous enough he could help the real Tony Clifton also become famous and then they could do things together but mostly separately and it would be wonderful/horrible.

So he put on his pink suit. He had figured out a way to meet Elvis and it was going to happen in the kitchen through which Elvis had to pass before and after performances en route to and from his palatial suite upstairs. In the course of days/hours—maybe, perhaps—he had somewhat befriended a security employee who came to pity/tolerate him and who was impressed that this harmless wide-eyed college boy had written a book about Elvis with such a nice religious title and so—very much on the QT—the security guy explained to him the logistics of Elvis's movements throughout the hotel. They hatched a plan, after the security guy's palm had or hadn't been properly/pathetically greased (twenty dollars or five dollars or nothing at all, per whichever version): During Elvis's midnight show, he would be allowed to secret himself in a shadowy alcove along the kitchen corridor. There he would have to wait until Elvis and his men came bustling by after the performance and then he could step forward and proffer his greeting. And so he did just as he was instructed. Stashed in the darkened corner where he quavered, while the distant cacophony of Elvis and band and backup vocalists bounced along kitchen tiles, he began to quietly repeat over and over a sacred Buddhist chant that he had been told would make all dreams come true and, if ever there had been a situation to employ such mystical optimism, this was that—

Namu Myoho Renge Kyo . . .

Namu Myoho Renge Kyo . . .

Namu Myoho Renge Kyo . . .

He said it a hundred times and another hundred times and another and then the music stopped and thunderous applause and hooting wafted down the corridors and then that trailed off and then hurried voices and laughing voices got nearer and clearer and, as the voices were finally almost upon him, he stepped forth, glowing pink, gripping his *God*, clearing his throat. And Elvis's men—Joe and Sonny and Red et al.—stopped suddenly and moved toward him and this other voice (OH!) said something like *waitaminute waitaminute fellas* and the eyes had never been this big ever before and he said something like *mister presley i wrote this book about you and it's called god* and—well, time all but stops in such crucibles of dreams—Elvis Presley regarded the oddity before him and *what the hell* came toward it and looked at the pile of pages in its hands and heard something it said about God impersonating him or some damned thing and his lip curled slyly and he rested his hand on the oddity's shoulder and said something like *well now that's very good that's very good* and he shook its hand and was precisely heard to remark, *Man, this guy's got a weird mind!* And then Elvis Presley strode off and Elvis's men looked back over their shoulders as they moved on and they were hyuckhyucking and then they were all gone.

And he was very very extremely very very pleased with the compliments that he had received from Elvis Presley Greatest Performer Who Ever Lived who had seen his book and shaken his hand and this was a most extremely buoyant moment for Andrew G. Kaufman who decided that heavenly benediction had been bestowed and that nothing would ever stop him—"And the next day I was all over Las Vegas playing slot machines. All I had was five dollars, but I put in pennies and nickels, trying to win money. Just twenty dollars was all I wanted, so I could go see Elvis Presley again. To make a long story short, I lost the five dollars."

7

He who hesitates is sometimes saved.

—James Thurber,
Fables for Our Time

Ever so enthused by wondrous occurrence, somewhat familiarized
with places he had not known before but would know well later—the
conquering hero returned home long enough to face that which he
had missed while away. Gloria had him meet her at a girlfriend's
house (neutral territory) and she showed him the photographs from
the lawn of the church where Laurel—well, *the baby* . . . well, *their*
baby . . . but not really theirs anymore—had lain and cooed for the
camera. "He just looked at the pictures and his eyes got really big and
he said something like, 'Wow, that's her? God, it's really hard to believe. . . .' He asked me all about it, what had happened, how I was.
And, I mean, I was still in crisis over it. But he knew that." He really
knew not what to say to her, but was as tender as he had ever been,
if not more so. He had reveled for so long in creating awkwardnesses
of his own merry design and this awkwardness was his as well but it
was also hers and it was profound and there was nothing really to
revel in and nothing really to say. All that he could do was hold her
hand and hold her and then, sweetly as could be, say goodbye and

then go back to Boston and focus attention elsewhere and he did just that.

Big movement now. No time to be wasted. Momentum was all and all would now have to come quickly and blur into wild masses of experience and accomplishment so that he could get to where he needed to go. Already, he had shorn the facial hair because it just got in the way of destiny and also incited acne. So he picked up where he left off. He left off in the spring with ideas flying and mechanisms in position. Al's Place was a coffeehouse in a basement—he was very keen on basements—in a dormitory right across Beacon Street and Al was Al Parinello, an enterprising student who ran the casual venue and booked the talent, and Al had withstood repeated entreaties from Andy, who begged and begged for stage time. Finally if warily, Al allowed an opportunity for this peculiar relentless fellow whose only claim to craft were birthday routines and funny accents and an Elvis impression. There was an available night on the schedule and Al told him, "Okay we can make something happen this Friday. I can pay you five dollars." And Al would recall that Andy said, "Oh!" "He didn't expect the money part. But the result of all this made for one of those rare moments in life—because, from the minute he went up onto that stage, Andy was literally a star. I believe he opened with his Foreign Man character, hopeless and inept, all pidgin English, and there was nervous tittering in the audience. And he did Mighty Mouse with the phonograph—and I was astonished by his timing, absolutely impeccable. Then he had the conga, which he started banging in sync with this crying jag—he had started crying as the Foreign Man because he lost his place and said he was ashamed, but he turned this into a conga symphony banging to the beat of these big gulping sobs. The audience was going crazy. And then the way he closed was absolutely sensational because it was Elvis—and it was incredible because the coeds were *screaming!* I'm saying they were emotionally involved with this impression to the point of screaming! I can still hear the screams. I remember looking around, thinking to myself, *Something very important is happening here. . . ."*

Elsewhere, *Uncle Andy's Fun House* was happening and this was his dream culmination of all birthday acumen and sensibility and he had already gotten class credit for it in April when it was first written up as a prospectus for a fifteen-minute television show that was then shot with Grahm cameras with Uncle Andy himself producing and starring as a manchild leading children played by other students— "dopeheads who sat on the studio floor while he read to them from a rocking chair," one dour witness recalled—through a wonderworld of happily didactic tomfoolery. Oh, but the *Fun House* had great promise—he often envisioned spending his entire future there, or someplace like it, with children, with puppets, with games and songs, like Buffalo Bob. Even the theme song he wrote for the show borrowed the melody of "It's Howdy Doody Time"—

It's Uncle Andy Time
It's Uncle Andy Time
An-dy and Bee Bop, too
say Boo-Bee-Doo to you;
Let's give a rousing cheer
'Cause Uncle Andy's here
It's time to start the show
So kids let's go!

That fall, he convinced the Grahm faculty to let him broadcast the show semiweekly in living color over the campus closed-circuit station, WCSB-TV (for Cambridge School of Business), and he foraged through Boston day schools to recruit wee peanut-gallery members and designed a set with big happy faces slapped on the walls and inflated many balloons and set up a puppet theater where Mr. Bee Bop, a beatnik puppet, dispensed with cool proverbs. Al Parinello came aboard as puppeteer and occasional sideshow barker (there were freak puppets) and also played the role of Mr. Pumpkin, who wore an orange slightly crushed cardboard refrigerator box—"my head was the stem"—and did as he was told. (For a public relations course project, Parinello designed an *Uncle Andy's Fun House* press kit which included a two-page biography of the star—"ANDY KAUFMAN, CHILD IDOL: The name Andy Kaufman may not mean much to you, but to some lucky kids who have had the pleasure of seeing him perform, the name Andy Kaufman is Godlike. . . .") Uncle Andy, meanwhile, had greatly benefited from studying with the meditating bliss people because on camera he was very very blissful and very innocent as he urged children to "dance crazy" and drink vast quantities of chocolate milk and brush teeth in rhythm to songs like "That's Amore" and "T-R-O-U-B-L-E" and "Don't Let the Stars Get in Your Eyes" and peers and instructors alike could barely believe that he had not ingested various pharmaceuticals in order to perform as such. Said Don Erickson, "We just didn't think anybody normal could be this abnormal."

Another weekly WCSB-TV program of note was *The Grahm Spotlight*, whose host and creator, a student named Burt Dubrow, fancied his forum as a wisenheimer *Tonight Show* wherein guests paraded through while Dubrow wryly presided behind a desk and skewered school administration. "One day I got a knock on my door and it's Andy," Dubrow would remember. "He said, 'I've been watching what you're doing and I'd love to come on.' He was very—I wouldn't say *shy*, but . . . *innocent*." He was also purposeful and Dubrow needed to fill air time and it soon became their routine to meet in Dubrow's dorm room the night before each Thursday *Spotlight* broadcast and work out just what Andy would do next to unhinge Dubrow on live closed-circuit television. Elvis came first and then the meek wide-eyed Foreign fellow turned up as a regular foil and began to say *tenk you veddy much* so often that it became his signature and there was also the Mighty Mouse lip-synching phonograph bit plus "Old MacDonald," and "Pop Goes the Weasel" (he assumed the voice of a stentorian father singing the song in nonsense rhymes with a precocious daughter, as the record spun and scratched beside him). "One week we worked out the following: Andy would come out after I introduced him *as Andy*, which was kind of rare. He was usually somebody else. And he would do a terrible stand-up comedy routine, just horrible unfunny jokes like 'Why did the chicken cross the road?' So he did this and, of course, nobody in the studio audience was laughing. One joke was worse than the next. Finally, Andy looked up with those eyes and got very upset with the audience— 'Look, all I'm trying to do is make a living while going to college and help pay for my tuition and you people don't have the *decency* to laugh at me! I don't know what you want, but I'm *trying* and *trying* here, but you!—you don't care if you ruin everything for me!' And he began to cry and get hysterical and there was this question in everyone's mind—Was he or was he not sincere? Finally, after crying crying crying, he reached into his pocket and pulled out a gun! Then he put the gun to his head and just as he was going to shoot himself, I ran over and tackled him to the ground and—commercial! And then when the show returned, we just sat at the desk talking as though the gun incident never happened—we never mentioned it in any way. Which was the whole idea. People asked me for days afterward if I knew he was going to try to kill himself on live television. And I just said, 'Of course not!' He saw this as a remarkable triumph."

And so the Grahm Junior College experience continued apace in just this fashion, with performances coming whenever and wherever possible, as he seized any spotlight afforded him: He worked regularly at Al's Place honing his material and also tried other local coffeehouses and meanwhile kept producing the *Fun House* even though it was often difficult to get children to come to the studio (milk and cookies and chocolate cake always helped) and he remained a fixture on Dubrow's program and then, after the first reading of *God* in the women's dormitory, there were more and more readings of *God* and his parents and sister attended one such reading and claimed to like it very much even though it made no sense and then a group of black performance students asked him to do Elvis in their Soul Time Review, which was an interracial first—"They said I would be the, uh, comedy relief and the token white buffoon. They thought it was really gonna bomb. But then they liked it!" So he moved forward and maybe it was because things had been going so well that he began to expect another downturn because the downturns always came about a month after his birthday during such productive periods whereupon he would plunge and lose his way again. It was a curse that he believed in, so he meditated hard to stave off the plunge, then learned not long after his twenty-first birthday that he would not have enough credit hours to graduate on time because he had been so consumed with building his future in show business that classwork had fallen aside. To complete his associate's degree in broadcasting he would have to stay in Boston through the summer and fall of 1970—about which he felt disconsolate and his father felt bitterly disappointed, what with tuition squandered due to apparent lack of academic diligence ("plain laziness," said Stanley), all of which meant that his show business career would have to wait a bit longer.

Fortunately, the Transcendental Meditation people were there to stoke his confidence and help him maintain his innocence and provide evenings of enlightened discourse. It was after one such evening—which had buoyed him somewhat—that he led a group of fellow bliss devotees to a Harvard Square ice cream parlor and, as they waited on line, which was very long, he was no longer him but became the other one with the vague Mediterranean heritage and the hopeless demeanor and at last it was his turn to place his order and it began—*Ehhh . . . I would like to have de ice cream but you have so many of de ice cream kinds how do I know vich vun ees good? Can you tell me vich vun ees good to order? Maybe I try taste each of de ice cream please?* "The people behind the counter were trying to be very nice because they thought this foreign person needed help," said Phil Goldberg, a TM friend who watched with astonishment. "Then they started getting impatient because he wouldn't make up his mind. He began to taste every flavor, one after the other, and the line was getting longer and longer, and people were starting to say things and getting more exasperated. I'm thinking, *Enough, Andy— cool it or someone's gonna hit you or something.* But at the same time

I was amazed by his persistence and conviction." *I know! I will have de mocha cheep, with de mocha and de cheep!* "Mocha chip was, of course, the only flavor they didn't have." *No, but-but I vant de mocha cheep! You know? De mochacheep?* "And he never stopped, for twenty minutes, took it to the absolute brink where someone was about to jump on him, and then finally—" *Ehh, all right . . . I will have . . . ehhhhhhhh . . . de vaneella! Tenk you veddy much.* "—he chose vanilla. That was it. We left and laughed. And that was the first time a lot of us realized that he was serious about becoming a comedian."

That July, he met the Maharishi at last—and, apparently, in the nick of time. He had gone to Poland Springs, Maine, on what would be the first of many many TM course retreats that he required himself to attend. His dedication to the replenishing deep silences and the quest for enlightenment/innocence had, of course, fully overtaken him. (It kept his eyes from taking on the hard glint of cynicism, he thought, which he disliked in other eyes, especially in the eyes of certain show business people on television; it kept his eyes lolling in space, which felt right, felt like who he thought he was. He knew all about his eyes.) At this particular retreat, as was custom, His Holiness had come to share his divine wisdom with followers who had convened to absorb his teachings and step forth to ask questions at a microphone set before them. Andy sat among the flock with a question burning in his gut, but could not bring himself to ask it because it was a complicated question and a personal one and it wasn't even really a question but a confession all about the plunge he felt enveloping him and so he went back to his room and began composing a letter to the Maharishi on some Grahm stationery he had brought along on the retreat.

Dear Maharishi,

I realize that you are a busy man and probably don't think about people's personal problems very much, but I have one which I would like to tell you about. Please listen. . . . I will have to begin with a short "life story": My life has been going in definite 4 year cycles. . . . It

seems that every 4 years, a few months are lived happily, then in around February things begin to drop and get worse and in that summer things are terrible and remain so for a few years until the good part comes around again in another 4 years. Things start picking up around the year before the good year. . . . The good part of the good year lasts only a few months. (I am referring to things in my mind and feelings.) . . . I began meditating in December 1968 and was due for a "good frame of mind" period in fall 1969. Things started climbing and the summer of 1969 was very nice and the fall and early winter were very good and I kept remembering that according to the pattern, things would go bad, but I didn't think it would happen this time because I was meditating. However, in February, everything fell apart and things got progressively worse. . . . Now I feel terrible. I think I'm more unsociable now than when I didn't meditate.

He stopped there and never finished the letter and never said anything to anyone about the things-in-his-mind-and-feelings, possibly because when he read the pathetic nature of what he had written he may have realized that it was his job—not that of Maharishi or anyone else—to address that which dogged him and to take responsibility and get on with it. Maharishi, who sat there waving his flower as he issued positive profundities, would have certainly told him as much. The point of life was, after all, to be happy and light and therefore success would follow. There was, as all meditators knew, no room for dark thinking. His father had told him that he would be heard—*You shall be heard!*—and Elvis Presley had admired his mind and there was nothing to do but to clear it of bad things-and-feelings. And so he got through his summer and through his autumn and stopped eating red meat (interfered with destiny, he felt) and completed his curriculum and performed stagecraft with renewed conviction to his future. (In November, he wrote a letter to his family and added in a postscript, **"Dad, thanks for the advice about keeping a stiff upper lip. Afterwards I wrote a story about a guy who kept a stiff upper lip. The**

advice made me feel good." He also wrote that his mother's sweet potato recipe had turned out well.) Boston felt more and more like home to him, largely because of the tether of TM; he had grown so proficient at meditation principles that he was now invited to become an instructor, which was very exciting. Teacher training and indoctrination would be overseen by the Maharishi in Majorca, Spain, beginning in February and continuing through May. He would go—at some expense—because it was what he needed to do and, by this time, no one except him could fathom the paths of his dreams.

Jan. 12/13, 1971

Dear Dad,

Tonite I worked unloading a truck full of boxes filled with books. I made $5.00 for 45 minutes of work. It really felt good doing real labor like that. It reminded me of when I used to work for Grady. I kind of forgot what work like that was like, all these years at Grahm.

The reason I'm writing you this letter is because there are a few things I've been wanting to tell you but I've found it hard to say them. I've been meaning to say thank you for quite a while but I guess it sounds awkward. Anyway, I really do appreciate all the things that you've done for me and I want you to know it. I'm aware that I've put you through many hard times.

I want you to know that in all seriousness I do plan to become a very accomplished performer. Ever since I was very small I've fantasized about it. Do you remember the "shows" I used to put on in my room? This is a very definite goal of mine. After all, look at the actual experience I've had: 12 years of entertaining at children's parties. The first step, Grahm Junior College, is finished. I apologize for it taking so long and don't blame you for being a little bothered about it. As far as procrastinating, you're right. I've always been lazy and a procrastinator. My methods for attaining my goal might seem a little unusual to you. I consider myself an unusual performer. I must, if I am to make

it. My next step (going to Majorca) may seem wrong, like another procrastination. Meditation has helped me a great deal. I am extremely
pleased with it and sincerely feel that I would have not been able to
do as well in my performing without it. The next step toward pursuing
my goal is to go to this meditation course. Please rest assured that it
is not another procrastination. It is an essential part of my career. One
day, I shall be an extremely accomplished performer.

I must say, after our talk that night when you said that from graduation I'm on my own, I was left with a scary feeling. I guess it's normal. However, there is a certain element of excitement also. I'm on
my way ("I shall be heard") and I welcome any suggestions that you
might have. Thank you for everything.

Love, Andy

*His Holiness sat before them and wore his robes and held his flower
and regarded his flock knowing these were those who would go forth
with his wisdom and bring others to him and to the light. They had
been in this beautiful place across the sea for just over three months,
learning together, plumbing their quiet spots for sustenance, searching
for truths and asking questions at the microphone which recorded all of
this advanced-training congress. And so it was on May 5 that the one
who wished to eventually entertain in an extremely accomplished manner stepped forward to hemhaw and inquire about what it was that he
would do in life and divine the spiritual methods and the meanings of
what was to be. Because the Maharishi had never before been deposed
on the workings of show business, his governors decided to take the resulting exchange and archive it under the heading of Maharishi on the
Value of Entertainment—although the inquisitor would not be named
in the records. Among TM scholars, however, the exchange would become minor legend precisely because of who it was that asked the questions. He began:*

"Um . . . what is the value of entertainment? Is there a good value
of entertainment—like comedy, tragedy, literature, television, and

going to the movies and nightclubs? Also, if everybody was enlightened, would there be any need for entertainment?"

The holy one, ever mystical, thus somewhat inscrutable, replied that there would always be such a need in a changing world of relativity. Entertainment, he continued, should have an energizing value. Any entertainment that does not revitalize our mind and body, he said, is not entertainment. And anything that is derogatory to energy or intelligence or vitality, he also said, is not entertainment but something opposite. Maharishi went on to suggest that Knowers of Reality—his term for TM teachers—should also avoid keeping late hours in which to be entertained, since it may tire them and inhibit the experience of Being. Good night's rest, very important.

The inquisitor then wondered whether people in an enlightened world could still go to movies and watch television and there is some beseeching and some desperation in his voice. The Maharishi replied that there would still be room for such, but only happy programs would exist, never sad ones.

"There won't be any sad programs? There won't be any need for tragedy?"

Sad programs are not entertaining, he was told. The purpose of entertainment was to enliven life, to create delight, to instill more vigor and energy and intelligence!

"Any more programs where the hero dies at the end?"

The bliss people laughed nervously and the Maharishi seemed perplexed and the inquisitor knew well that if Elvis had not died at the end of Love Me Tender *he could not have sung from the clouds before the closing credits, which would have made the movie not so great. He and Michael once watched* Lassie Come Home *on television in Great Neck and, throughout the film, they took turns leaving the room to cry, then took turns teasing each other about it, which was a happy brotherly memory for both of them.*

"I like to watch programs that make you want to cry at the end. Will there still be programs like that?"

Mass nervous bliss laughter again. (Such persistence, this inquisitor!) Maharishi told him that as society became more positive, there would be more comedies and fewer tragedies. Then the inquisitor mentioned the sort of comedian who does darker things, unpleasant things, yet funny things, and the Maharishi said that such a comedian has a low level of consciousness and could clearly benefit from a little elevation.

"I wonder if a crazy man—"

They laughed—never had an inquisitor inquisited quite like this— while Maharishi interrupted to say that crazy men tend to be unreasonable and not the best examples of positivity.

"No no, a crazy man, a crazy man, somebody, for instance . . . he isn't exactly crazy . . . like some of the old comedians who were looked on as odd. But they were naturally that way and that was their career. . . . What I'd like to know is if a comedian who is, let's say, naturally kind of an oddball, looked upon as an oddball, and he's a comedian because of that, because people laugh at his oddness, but he *likes* it and everything—"

Maharishi responded that people don't like oddness, that it was not the oddness that creates delight for people, but rather something in between two extreme oddnesses—a field of silence—that creates a thrill. . . .

[—this was what he had come for, this part, this would tell him everything that mattered and he would learn to do everything just as it was being explained—maybe he had been doing it this way all along; it seemed like he had—but now it became a little clearer to him, so he listened hard as the holy one parsed the ephemeral wisdom—]

Oddness, according to his holiness, was simply a tool with which to create contrasts for an audience. He offered an analogy for the inquisitor—the comedian's craft, he said, was akin to building two walls side by side and leaving a space in between. The mere presence of those two walls then creates a contrast based on an awareness of the space. And by building such contrasting walls of oddnesses, the comedian is implicitly calling attention to the length and the depth of the silent space that connects the two. And within that space, said Maharishi, lies the harmony that thrills the soul and appeals to the heart!

[—um—]

The comedian, said Maharishi with beatific patience, must first say one thing and then say another thing and these two things will usually

*contrast—but what makes the contrast so evident is the journey in be-
tween, which is the journey through a field of silence. And it is the experience of this journey—from, perhaps, the gross to the subtle—that
creates delight. The silence, then, is the very impulse of life!*

[—actually, he was confused about the walls and needed that part
repeated and crystallized—which was that if a comedian does one
unexpected thing and waits before he does another unexpected thing
then he will receive a better sort of laughter, which was not unlike
what Uncle Sammy had always said about things called Set-Ups and
Punchlines, but Uncle Sammy had never dwelled on the part about
Silences and certainly Silences were something that he (Andy) personally had great ability to produce, having heard his share of them
during a life of creating Oddnesses, so this was all most inspiring—]

*So then the Maharishi went on about this phenomenon and then
the inquisitor inquired about whether the comedian makes this all happen consciously and he was told that the comedian must be conscious
of building the walls but the silences are for the audiences to locate.
Still, there was one dire and personal consideration/worry to finally
clarify here—*

"So if a crazy man who everybody laughed at because he was crazy
started meditating, then he'd be a better entertainer?"

*If he likes to be an entertainer, Maharishi replied, then he will be
better.*

"He won't become more serious and not be crazy anymore, will
he?"

[—because that would not be very good at this point—]

*Maharishi replied that if seriousness will entertain the environment,
then he will be necessarily serious. If lack of seriousness is required, he
will embody this lack as well. Whatever way he wishes to work, he will
remain an entertainer, in the largest sense, to his environment. He will
feed others with life, create thrills of joyfulness in their hearts. Through
Transcendental Meditation, his holiness said, the entertainer is able to
radiate more of life and this—he emphasized— is the purpose of an entertainer.*

[—so then he would be, um, fine—]

*   *   *

He arrived for national consumption three years later and the how
of his arrival—on something called *Dean Martin's Comedyworld*
(happy-happy-program!)—was certainly predicated on the teachings
in Spain. It was also the product of blithe tedium, penniless persistence, and iron will. But, upon arrival, his silences would be majestic and deafening, thus thrilling. (It was unheard of to be as unheard
as he permitted himself to be—the brazen manipulative awkwardness
of it!) And his walls would be impossibly fortified with constructs of
quicksilver—shuffled personae, sly juxtapositions, imbalances never
imagined by other mortals. He would still be considered a crazy man,
no less crazy for having found enlightenment. He was crazy and also
more wise about his craziness. He worked onstage as no one ever had
before; he never told the truth; his material asked no one to relate
(and inadvertently made fun of those peers whose material did); he
most often heard the appraisal *original*, sometimes in a bad way, then
more and more in a very extremely good way. This Dean Martin program on which he would debut—and on which Dean Martin never
appeared—was a temporary summertime replacement for the very
popular NBC-TV Dean Martin program on which Dean Martin actually did appear. Both shows, however, were produced by Greg
Garrison, who conceived *Comedyworld* to be an ambitious cavalcade
of comic enterprise, old and new, featuring classic film clips, bits of
some recent British nonsense called *Monty Python's Flying Circus*,
interview montages with very famous comedians and, more saliently,
a wellspring of fresh material from young stand-up performers—"the
kids of today who will be the stars of tomorrow!"—who were videotaped at various nightclubs around the United States. (The show
would pluck from the vine such smartass punks as Jay Leno, Jimmie
Walker, Freddie Prinze, et al.) Garrison had smelled a boom coming—*suddenly kids wanted to be comics instead of rock singers!*—so he
went to New York in April 1974 to audition talent and it was at the
Improvisation on West Forty-fourth Street that he first saw the foreign
kid do the Mighty Mouse—"He just knocked me out. I said, 'Put him

on the show.' They said, 'Well, he's never done television.' I said, 'He's done enough. Put him on!' " He went on, in fact, twice—on the first and third installments of the program, broadcast June 6 and 20—and he appeared each time immediately after snippets from Charlie Chaplin films, *Modern Times* and *The Great Dictator*, respectively. (His was deemed the only performance material feathery and innocent enough to complement the golden swoons of Chaplin.) For the first shot, taped at the Improv on April 26, he was introduced to viewers—almost with a disclaimer—by "Roving Comedy Correspondent" Nipsey Russell—"Our most recent immigrant to *Comedyworld* has just passed through customs at the Improvisation. . . . He's just here from a little island in the Caribbean, and possibly you won't understand him too well. But let's give a listen to Andy Kaufman!"

As was by now obligatory—and as it would be for at least the next four years—he entered as Foreign Man (never mind that his actual name gave whiff of Long Island; somehow he *was* an immigrant of varying nonspecific origin). Thus he shambled out in front of the legendary brick wall wearing one of the two Foreign Man uniforms that would never be replaced—tatty ill-fitting blue-olive-tan checked sport coat (formerly Stanley's, as was the pale pink jacket he sometimes opted to wear) over blue oxford shirt over black turtleneck with gray flood pants and white socks and brown loafers. Hair was slicked into an oily wave. Arms were rigid at sides, danglefingers ever tapping at air as though he were vertically typing invisible words. (With the finger movements, he innately counted his rhythms—his memory banks were wired to his digits, a small secret he rarely shared and barely understood himself.) Fear screamed in cerulean blue eyes. Pinched uncertain adenoidal voice quavered and—right there on very same network air which Howdy Doody breathed, sort of—"I . . . *I am very nervous because ees my first time on TV. So, you know, last night ees very hard to go to sleep. . . .*" Point here was to engender empathy by being, well, deeply pathetic—so very bad and so very sweet; so desperate to be in show business, thus so desperate for love. There ensued what he privately called Bombing, and Foreign Man had always Bombed with a pure and pristine magnificence that built the first wall of oddness that led to the next wall of proficiency (odder still) and all that occurred betwixt was plain tragic fumphering. So he launched into the already long-employed misbegotten tale of the two boys and the one girl who hauled a cannon over the mountains of Spain and discovered that no one had a cannonball to fire at the castle (*"Don't look at meeee."*) and the requisite audience discomfiture came as ever. Then he attempted just one *eemetation*, that of *de President Neexon*, droopfaced and rigid, shooting both fists skyward into victory Vs—receiving laughs before opening his mouth—*"vait-vait until I give you de punch!"* Then, with voice unchanged—*"Let me make one thing perfectly clear . . . um, I am de President of de United States, make no mistake about that! Tenk you veddy much!"* Wordlessly, he next walked over to his phonograph, dropped the needle on the turntable, and Mighty Mouse played and he precisely lip-synched only to the rodent tenor's infrequent seven-word braggadocio—*Here I come to save the day!*—absorbing all intervening moments of chorus by standing and fidgeting, eyes darting, pouring himself a glass of water, sipping the water, waiting through silences most cavernous and impressive, clearly incapable of saving any sort of day but then again . . . *maybe*. And then the record ended and cheers came like they always had and he bowed repeatedly.

The next day, he drove to the Playboy Club Resort in Great Gorge, New Jersey, where he performed poolside under spring sunshine for the *Comedyworld* cameras again as Foreign Man. (He had to place his guitar case and prop valise and tape recorder—the act always required serious *lugging*—on a chaise lounge behind him. Congas, as ever, stood to his left.) This time Comedy Correspondent Barbara Feldon read the cue-carded introduction—". . . I can't think of a single performer I'd rather be watching than this absolutely *adorable* young man from the Caribbean Islands. . . ." Then more gentle Bombing ensued—*"Tenk you veddy much I am veddy happy to be here tonight, er, today, but you know there is vun thing I don't like about thees place ees too much traffic. You know today I had to come on de highway there was so much traffic eet took me an hour and a half to get here. But talk about de terrible things, my wife, take my wife please take her. No, no, I am only fooling I love my wife but she don't know how to cook. . . . Her cooking ees so bad ees terrible. . . ."* He began his eemetations—Nixon again and Ed Sullivan (*"Tonight we have de r-r-r-r-r-really beeg show!"*) and then he segued into that which was by this time the signature opposite wall of the Foreign Man repertoire except only now a larger population would begin to know it and once it was known it would become expected and once it was expected it would become a burden that defeated the elements of surprise and incongruity that he cherished. But that would come later because now he was brand new, a bright oddity possessed of rehearsed naïveté and true charm making a small but significant step forward from the swirl of obscurity, and so he said, *"And now last but not to be de least I would like to eemetate de Elveece Presley!"*

For Elvis, he wore hidden layers, like he used to wear to school not to be funny. He turned his back to the audience, as dictated by professional impressionist law (*must-make-metamorphosis-mysterious!*), and bent over the chaise to switch on the tape that played the momentous recorded opening strains of "Also Sprach Zarathustra" which would swell into the raucous chords of "See See Rider" (all lifted directly from an actual Elvis Las Vegas concert album), during which he shed his checked coat and his oxford shirt to reveal a yellow silk blouse which he then covered with a teal tuxedo jacket and, still facing aft, he combed back his hair in pompadourian fashion, strapped on his guitar, swiveled to the music, then peeked out over his shoulder to display the perfectly cocky sneersmile that belonged only to Elvis Presley. He spun forward and *was* Elvis, prowling the pool patio with mock lascivious intent, slack babyface cheeks jiggling, sinewy legs jangling, and then the recorded intro music stopped as he stood fully transformed at the microphone and the audience applauded—and just before he would now speak in the voice of Elvis Presley, no longer Foreign Man at all, and say *"Thank you thankyouverrrmuch!"* and continue his Elvisian patter and launch into sublime replication of some familiar Elvis hit and radiate crackling ions throughout, after which he would throw articles of his costume into the audience and heave winded breaths while trying to

regain composure and then finally speak in the voice of Foreign
Man, no longer Elvis Presley at all, and say *"Tenk you veddy much!"*
and meekly ask for his clothes back, one of Greg Garrison's videotape
editors abruptly cut elsewhere because of broadcast time constraints.
He would not know this until he watched the program in June, thus
realizing that he had been left at the microphone hanging—stranded
mid-feat in the silence that preceded the true tricks that were his
unique currency. And he was heartily disappointed, which was fine
no really, because at least it happened on network television, on his
second appearance on network television in *two weeks* no less, and he
would have another chance soon enough because things were really
only starting now and it had taken him so long to get this far.

And so, back in 1971, Maharishi had regarded the boy in Spain as
a puzzlement what with all of the crazyman talk and thereby discouraged bliss hierarchy from indoctrinating him just yet as a teacher.
"People there thought Andy was very unstable, found his behavior
kind of peculiar, asking the Maharishi about *humor*," said Don Snow,
a training cohort who had been made a teacher on the Majorca trip.
"It's considered very disruptive to have somebody who's emotionally
unstable on these advanced-training courses." Andy, however, dis-
agreed with this assessment and sought out His Holiness two months
later in Massachusetts and pleaded his case and was then given status
as a teacher. He had not returned to Great Neck after Majorca and
would only make periodic visits home until autumn of 1972, when he
would reclaim the den as headquarters and borrow family cars to hawk
his act in the city and elsewhere. Until that time, he hired on at the
Student International Meditation Society (SIMS) in Cambridge,
where he did clerical work and dispensed mantra and initiated new-
comers to enlightenment and also performed at TM parties as well as
at Al's Place and was allowed to return to Grahm to make a sample
tape of *Uncle Andy's Fun House* to send off to television stations but
the taping was disastrous—he was disorganized and then he accidentally smeared chocolate cake on the white cyclorama studio partition,

which incensed student director Marc Summers, who would later host game shows and who then threw his headset at Andy in disgust. "I told him how unprofessional he was and then I was out the door!" said Summers. "I thought this guy should probably be in a mental institution somewhere." Jimmy Krieger of Great Neck was now Jim Krieger of Boston University, where he studied film and made student films for which he recruited his childhood friend as star and they were artful little sixteen-millimeter films smartly shot in grainy black-and-white. Among roles he essayed in the Krieger cinematic oeuvre were a flower thief loosed upon Copley Square, a hapless fellow evicted with his young wife from a tenement and forced to wander Cambridge in bathrobes, Elvis Presley musically lamenting a leak in the roof of an apartment, and a fully frocked priest engaged in passionate necking with a nun on various public park lawns as Bostonians gawked in horror. Of the young woman who wore the nun's habit, Krieger recalled: "Andy really loved this girl, was crazy about her. But she was serious about becoming an actress and wanted nothing to do with him. And he would constantly say, 'She's gonna regret it. I'm gonna be very famous one day and she's gonna regret not knowing me!' " By all accounts, he would say this about many women. He once led Parinello and a group of guys down to a bus terminal where he promised to make irresistible moves on each girl that alighted. They watched from a distance as he moved toward girl after girl, issuing strange noises from the corner of his mouth—*schkk-schkk,* as one might urge a horse to giddyup—then asking, "Hey, baby, you doing anything today?" *Schkk-schkk.* "One by one, these girls would tell him, 'Get away from me! Get away from me!' " said Parinello. "Then he started getting hit with pocketbooks and handbags. He just looked at us and vowed, 'Okay, I'll get the *next* one!' " Later he said that these women, too, would all be sorry one day.

He was a confirmed nomad at this point, cared little where he slept, had no place of his own, crashed either with Krieger in nearby Somerville or wherever a bliss person had an empty couch—vagabondism suited him and always would, even when very or somewhat famous. As long as he could meditate for two hours per morning in complete silence—"He didn't want a pin to drop," said Krieger—and again at night and could prepare his newfound macro-biotic diet (brown rice and raw beans and similar flavorless purities) and could stow one daily carton of Häagen-Dazs ice cream in a freezer (could not sleep without first devouring a full pint), he was fine. Meanwhile, his professional devotions continued to burn brightly. That November, he had dragged Peter Wassyng to see Elvis perform at the Boston Garden—"We sat there in the balcony and it was like watching someone worship Jesus!"—and the following June in New York he dragged his sister to Madison Square Garden for an-other Elvis concert, after which he made her run with him all the way across town to the Plaza Hotel, where he mistakenly believed Elvis was staying. The very next week, he became Elvis again, albeit in a completely different fashion than ever before. Quite momen-tously, it was for a *real* television program on Chicago's powerhouse ABC affiliate, WLS-TV, where Burt Dubrow was now producer of the talk show *Kennedy-at-Nite*, hosted by popular broadcaster Bob Kennedy. Elvis had just played the Chicago Stadium and, to capital-ize on lingering local frenzy, Dubrow had flown in his former Grahm foil to actually be interviewed as though he *were* Elvis. For *thirty* tele-vised minutes! Kennedy, who had spent time with him before the show, quickly gave away the conceit in his introduction—"It's almost more like talking to Elvis than, frankly, talking to a fellow by the name of Andy Kaufman. . . ." Andy had brought along piles of per-sonal Elvis memorabilia to display on camera and wore a white tuxedo jacket and allowed his hair to be teased into a minor bouffant. What he was not allowed to do, however, was to actually sing as Elvis. Instead, he was directed to lip-synch along with Presley records and, as he did so (committing several flubs, since this was not what he re-ally did in his act), he was half the Elvis that he had ever been. Confined as such, he still acquitted himself nicely during interview segments, employing a relaxed drawl and many sly lipcurls, while im-provising his way through the mind of his hero. Only when a caller to the program asked how he maintained such a sexy body did two lives blur—"Well, ah tell-you-what—ah do yoga every day. . . . It's called Transcendental Meditation. Ah started a few years ago and found it to be a verrrbig help to me. . . . Helps to keep me young. Makes me feel better and it's the easiest thang in the world to do." (Elvis Presley, for the record, was a yoga enthusiast, but had no truck with Transcendental Meditation. That, he believed, was the province of the Beatles.) Nevertheless, Andy saw the experience as a suitably untraditional local television debut.

Two other notable strides had been made in the first half of 1972: In February, he was hired—by dint of a blind referral—to actually perform as the opening act for a Temptations concert in Northampton, Massachusetts. The predominantly black audience was, according to his subsequent reports, completely offput by Foreign Man and made it vociferously known and so he wept and wept onstage and pulled out his large cap gun and walked off into the wings and fired the gun into a microphone and thudded to the floor and the room went silent and the Temptations sang extra hard that night to make up for it. Then, in late May, one of his television idols, Steve Allen, came to perform with the Boston Pops Orchestra; Allen's comic cohort Louis Nye was also on the bill, and Andy discovered that both men were staying at the nearby Sheraton Hotel. Because Uncle Sammy had written for Steve Allen, Andy believed this entitled him to a meeting in which to seek advice from the innovative television host. So he went to the hotel and used the house phone and—"A young fellow with a teenager's [he was, in fact, twenty-three] unsteady voice was calling," Allen would later recount in his book, *Funny People*. " 'Mr. Allen,' he said, 'I'm Sam Denoff's nephew . . . I was wondering if I could come see you.' " Allen finally relented, since he saw no way out of it, and invited him to his room, where Nye was lounging. "He impressed both Louis and me as socially awkward, incredibly ill at ease, a bit awestruck, and somewhat offbeat. To this day I don't know whether there was the slightest element of put-on in our first conversation, though I doubt it." He stammered out an explanation of his accomplishments and dreams and Allen, to the best of his recollection, told him to keep doing what he was doing but to try doing it in some of these new audition-style showcase nightclubs, like the Improvisation in New York or any such place in Los Angeles, so as to be closer to talent scouts. That, of course, was something he already knew and he would be doing just that within months, exhibiting relentless drive, foisting himself in deft foreign disguise upon unwitting club owners, never making the approach as a scion of Great Neck, never being who he was, always being who he wasn't, hoping that which forced audiences to indulge him with pity would work as well on the gatekeepers of certain spotlit stages.

Steve Allen, who would come to know Foreign Man well just a few years after that urgent hotel meeting, later turned his professorial eye to the character: "There is more to Foreign Man than just a heavily accented speech pattern that sounds funny to native American ears, such as Bill Dana's José Jimenez," he would write. "Foreign Man is also a creature suffering from cultural shock, future shock. His attitudes are hopelessly out of synchronization with those common in the time and place in which he has landed. He simply does not understand the American sense of humor, but thinks he does. He is so confident in this regard, in fact, that he's willing to get up in front of nightclub audiences and try to do what Henny Youngman, Milton Berle, or Bob Hope does." Indeed, Foreign Man was designed to brim with oblivious bravado. He was both tool and secret weapon, the irresistible career emissary dispatched to do the bidding of Andy Kaufman. He would be the foot in every important doorway. And, one way or another, he would always shove Andy Kaufman across every threshold.

He left Boston and returned home and, by September, the foreign kid began turning up on curbs outside of clubs, starting with clubs on Long Island, and the first sort of club there that permitted him onstage was a strip joint and he fumbled his way through eemetations before introducing the next naked dancing lady, then came back out to complain about his wife's cooking before another naked lady shimmied forth—and he was not well received but the ladies felt sorry for him and were very nice, which was exciting, but ultimately not very helpful. Then he auditioned for a popular Roslyn music club not adverse to comical acts, called My Father's Place and, as with Al's Place, his material glistened from the start and there was a standing ovation after his first set. "I felt like a comedian," he later said, as though the notion had not previously occurred to him. "It was coming in rhythms, this laughter." He returned again and again and became a dependable mainstay (give or take more than a few nights of wavering reception, the apogee of which was the night a hurled beer bottle bounced off his forehead) and frequently emceed for songwriter showcase nights. He began to experiment further and to perfect the complete arc of Foreign Man's transformation into Elvis—"Anytime there was an Elvis Presley movie on television, day or night, he ran to the nearest TV set in the place," said Eppie Epstein, who owned the club. Whenever possible, he led audiences into old and new coves of whimsy or deceit. At the congas, he would invoke the room to repeat the following nonsensical sounds—*oh-wah* and *ta-ta* and *foooo* and *lie-am*—and have them keep repeating with him as he quickened the conga beats until everyone realized they were shouting *Oh what a fool I am!* Richard Hersh, who helped manage My Father's Place, would recall, "The audience loved it because they *were* fooled, they played right into his hands—and then he had their attention." To quell serious stagefright—"He was very nervous before going onstage. It was like being bar mitzvahed every night, okay?" said Hersh—Andy began requesting time to meditate in silence for fifteen-minute periods before and after performing. "It was a very significant part of his theatrical presentation, almost to the point of mystique," said Epstein. "He would come offstage and become a monk. You [couldn't] see him—he'd be meditating. [Afterward he'd blankly say], '*Um, hi . . . how are you? Oh, thank you . . .*' Like a different person."

He made occasional forays into the city, got onstage downtown during amateur nights at the Bitter End, continuing his rounds until late December, when he returned to California for another long advanced-training TM retreat in Santa Barbara. There, he entertained meditators as Elvis and put out word that he was looking for a place to stay for a few weeks afterward down in Los Angeles. A young

TM teacher named Linda Mitchell, who aspired to classical guitar virtuosity (which was kind of like show business), offered her parents' guest house in Encino, where many transient bliss people had been welcome. His two primary orders of business were to see if he could (a) get onstage at a new club on Sunset Boulevard called the Comedy Store, which he'd been hearing much about, and (b) get a chance to appear on the television quiz show *The Dating Game*, not necessarily to meet girls (although he enjoyed that possibility) but to insert Foreign Man into a very different cultural reality. "He wanted to do the show as Foreign Man," Mitchell recalled, "and they just didn't want Foreign Man." Day after day, however, he stormed the production office unwilling to accept defeat and was finally auditioned on camera and was amusing enough to secure an *okay-we'll-think-about-it*, which he took less lightly than the producers may have. (He called them every day for the remainder of his visit, just to see if a decision had been reached, which it had not.) Uncle Sammy, meanwhile, knew the veteran comic Sammy Shore and his wife Mitzi Shore, who owned the Comedy Store, where every nascent American purveyor of stand-up entertainment had begun to make pilgrimage in hopes of being discovered. Sam Denoff would remember: "I called Mitzi and said, 'Listen, I have this guy, I'm not sure what he does.' She told us to come over and we hung around backstage and then he went out and started to do one of his crazy foreign things with the audience. And, Jesus Christ, the people went *whaaaa?* And I couldn't even look over at Mitzi, because I didn't know what the hell she would think. He was unpolished, but he had this idea that he was gonna send the world up." Mitzi Shore wasn't sure what she thought either, but she noted that he held some unusual sway over the crowd, which was not the easiest thing to do in West Hollywood, where the rather jaded clientele generally resisted such silliness as chanting gibberish along with a boy beating a drum.

Back in Great Neck that February, the mission escalated. Fortified by chutzpah tested in Los Angeles, he would now audition in places that had previously only intimidated him. On his behalf, Eppie Epstein put in a call to Budd Friedman, the powerful star-making owner of the Improvisation. Friedman's memory: "Eppie said, 'You've got to see this guy!' And that's all he said. And for some reason I believed him." Friedman told Epstein to send him in for open-mike night the following Monday, the twelfth. Meanwhile, Andy knew that regular Thursday afternoon auditions were held at a brand-new Upper East Side showcase club called Catch a Rising Star. So he loaded his various prop cases into his father's car on February 8 and drove to the club, where he schlepped everything through the door, mystifying the talent coordinator Conan Berkeley and the house pianist Eddie Rabin. Then Rabin encountered him primping alone in the men's room—"This strange guy asked me, *'Are you de piano player? I will be singing de Elveece? You know de Elveece?'* And I thought, well, I guess he's the real thing. I mean, there was no reason to put on a foreign accent for me alone in the men's room. Then he went out and did the act and I realized I'd been had." At which point, Berkeley, who was greatly impressed by the audition, would remember saying to him, "Can you come back and perform tonight?" And he went back into the Foreign Man and said, *"Oh! Yesss, I will be back yesss!"* Berkeley told Catch owner Rick Newman to specifically watch for this immigrant person that night, so Newman and his friend, the prominent young comic David Brenner, stood in the back of the room and witnessed Bombing as they had never understood bombing before. "He started speaking in a language that I'd never heard, that David had never heard," said Newman. "Then he began crying." And the conga-crying—"He never said a word of English for his first eight minutes!" said Newman—moved toward eemetations toward Elveece—"and then we lost it, just fell off our chairs!" The audience, meanwhile, was either ecstatic (per memories of Newman and Berkeley) or enraged (per Brenner); afterward he tottered to the rear, where Newman professed glee and gave insightful praise, inviting him back all weekend and whenever he wished to be seen, and where Brenner counseled him after such a dismal showing—"I said, 'You know, you can't go by what that audience did to you tonight. Don't listen to them. Not only are you funny, you've got something no one else has.' I mean, he was a comedic con artist and that night he was breaking down barriers that nobody knew ever existed!"

He jubilantly drove back to Grassfield Road sometime before dawn and wrote a note to his family while preparing his ice cream: **Feb. 8 [really 9], 1973, Dear Mommy, Daddy, and Carol** [Michael was now a Business major at Penn], **I had a very prosperous day today. I auditioned at a niteclub of the type which I attended with Uncle Sammy in L.A. and was asked to perform tonite. The man who runs the show really understood my act much more than anyone else I've met in this business . . . and I've been asked to return this Friday and Saturday nites. Tonite's show went well and Jackie Mason was in the audience. So it was a good day. And Mon. nite I am at the Improvisation and Wed. nite I audition at Dangerfield's. So every-thing is going well. Thank you very much.** (He had now begun clos-ing all family correspondence with Foreign Man's signature stamp of gratitude.) And that morning, while he slept, his parents scrawled at the bottom of the note, "Great! There's nothing we like better than to see you have things go your way—Loads of good luck." They also told him to use the car as he needed it, which he did. The note that he left them the following night reported further onstage prosperity and news that people from *The Dating Game* had called and wanted him to be on the program in two weeks, but he had told them that that probably wouldn't work out, so they had suggested he call them collect before his next trip—**So I made it after all!** On Sunday, he performed again at Catch and wrote afterward, **Boy, tonite was excit-ing. I met Doc Pomus, who wrote many many Elvis Presley songs and some Fabian songs and many more. He liked my act very much.** It was almost as though Elvis had been watching him, he thought. He also reported that both Rodney Dangerfield (whose nearby Upper East Side club would audition him on Wednesday) and Jackie Mason were there watching him as well.

Then, on Monday night, he walked into the all-important Improv, where Greg Garrison would find him fourteen months hence and put him on the Dean Martin summer comedy show, which would be the break that preceded all other breaks that propelled him to where he needed to go. And Silver Friedman, wife of Budd Friedman, and possessor of certain mystical visionary powers, would remember his first steps into the club—"He was in a total state of discovery always. Everything he would look at, it was just as though he was seeing it for the first time. And so he stood there in the doorway, looking all around him—I mean, I don't want to seem like too much of a witch—but I remember seeing a basement ceiling over his head, a low ceiling, and I saw carpeting and drums and him in this rec room . . . a den. He gave off a very strong energy. Then later we found out about him practicing in his Long Island basement all those years and I went *oooooo!*" And Budd Friedman would remember greeting him—"I said, 'Where you from, kid?' *'An island in the Caspian Sea.'* Okay. So he went onstage and the people were sort of laughing—I didn't know what to make of him. Until he did his Elvis and I just fell on the floor. Who knew there were no islands in the Caspian Sea?" And that night he wrote—**Dear Mommy, Daddy, and Carol. They liked me at the Improvisation and I can come back, so I'll probably be doing two shows a night—one at the Improvisation, and one at Catch a Rising Star. Thank you verr-rry much.**

8

To crack a nut is truly no feat, so no one would ever dare to collect an audience in order to entertain it with nut-cracking. But if all the same one does do that and succeeds in entertaining the public, then it cannot be a matter of simple nut-cracking.

—Franz Kafka,
A Hunger Artist

Like never before, this was their time. Those possessed of youth and hubris who stood alone with microphones, telling clubdrunks about their mothers fathers wivesgirlfriendsboyfriends lovetroubles neuroses ethnicities fears, sharing their Observations about life dating commercials hygiene pets fashion fastfood toiletseats politics movies doctorslawyers agentsshrinks conveniencestores hotelrooms airlinemeals sexdrugsandrockandroll—it was their time to say *notice me* and it began a rush, then an onslaught, wherein more and more of them kept coming forth to display their singular/similar attitudes. And if it were not for this being their time, it could not have also been his time, even though he did not do what they did. He was theater whereas they told jokes—but he belonged with them; there was nowhere else to put him. It was the only context in which he made sense, not that he made sense, not that he ever tried. So the others, the joke people, they always stood in the back of the room, whatever room, to watch what he would do next. To them, he was spectacle and mascot, not a peer; scant few of them could ever manage what might resemble normal conversation with him. He would not/could not drink beer with them or talk sports or chicks or news of the day with them; after his sets, he busied himself with the club's supply of ice cream or chocolate cake, sometimes asking mommyish waitresses to spoon it into his mouth ("I had to feed him as if he were in a highchair," said Zane Busby, who willingly indulged him at Catch. "Like *here-comes-the airplane-open-the-hangar-doorrrrr!*"). But they all watched him work—Robert Klein (revered elder statesman of young comics); Gabe Kaplan (bound for television sitcom); Jimmie Walker (also bound, who observed, "The foreign thing always amazed me because sometimes he actually communicated without speaking English. . . . People responded and you'd go, 'My God! How is this working?!' "); Freddie Prinze (also bound); Richard Lewis (chief intellectual neurotic, who observed, "Andy was almost like Ionesco doing stand-up"); Richard Belzer (emceed at Catch, often helped lug Andy's props into the club basement before shows, who observed, "I couldn't believe the courage. Either consciously or unconsciously, Andy was challenging and educating audiences, stretching their imaginations. . . . He made other performers more daring—he had that effect. . . . He was a performance artist before the term existed"); and Jay Leno (attitudinal iron man, who observed, "Most of us thought he was very funny, but we worried that no one else would get him. We even felt sort of sorry for him. . . . He just behaved strangely, in order to get a reaction of any kind, even hostile. There were nights at Catch a Rising Star when he would lie onstage in a sleeping bag"). No comic ever wanted to take the stage once he departed from it, for he never left an audience the way he had found it—the room would be transformed, rendered giddy or dizzy or dumbstruck or irate. "It didn't take very long to realize as a young comedian that Andy Kaufman closed the show," said Lewis. "You couldn't follow him unless you just ran around the room setting furniture on fire. I think he tried that, too. He was devastating in every sense, great but sometimes completely insane." Of course, they all believed him to be crazier than they were; he believed it was just the reverse—but only whenever he gave it, or them, thought, which was not usually, not to be aloof no really.

So *The New York Times* came to take his photograph onstage at the Improvisation in May 1974—about a month after he taped his Dean Martin appearances and about a month before the appearances aired. He was wearing a feathered Indian headdress (his unspoken homage to wrestler Chief Jay Strongbow; he often wore it to and from the club, even on subway trains) and a yellow T-shirt with silkscreened palm trees swaying across his chest which was the sublayer of all other layers and it was the layer he wore when performing at conga the various "folk songs" from his home island of Caspiar to celebrate seasonal harvest. (One such song, "Aba-Dabbi," was performed in native gibberish to the tune of "Alouette"—with perplexed audience sing-along always attendant.) And then the photograph was published in the esteemed newspaper of record on May 28—which could not have been more exciting—since his likeness was featured among pictures of legendary comics Mort Sahl and Shelley Berman and contemporaries David Brenner and Freddie Prinze. But the photos were assembled around a package of stories about the dark and craven lives of comedians, emblazoned with such headlines as IT'S NOT A LAUGHING MATTER, BEING A COMIC THESE DAYS and DESPITE GAINS HERE, IT'S TOUGH TO EARN A LIVING and PSYCHOLOGIST FINDS FUNNY MEN ARE SAD MEN. And the caption beneath his photograph mistakenly identified him as "Howard Itzkowitz, a young unknown trying out at The Improvisation." And this was his debut in *The New York Times.* Moreover, he was mentioned in none of the articles therein—although he was rather pleased to have been excluded from the one about a dispiriting survey of fifty-five nationally known comics conducted by a psychologist who pinpointed a common thread of childhood trauma in all of the subjects. Meanwhile, the psychologist—one Dr. Samuel S. Janus—was described in the first paragraph as a former "song-and-dance man on the Catskills borscht circuit." (Oh!) *Song-and-dance-man!* Well, there was the solution! Never, ever had Andrew G. Kaufman considered himself to be a comedian. And from that moment forward he would traverse great lengths to correct anyone who ever accused him of such. "I never claim to be a funny man, a comedian, or even a talented man," he would say always thereafter. "I'm just going up there and having fun. And if people want to join me, and watch me, have fun with me, then that's . . . um, fine." And he would conclude always, "What I am is a *song-and-dance man!*" He thought it sounded jauntier. Anyway, *The New York Times* said that he wasn't Howard Itzkowitz in a correction printed two days later.

There had been this meditation girl whom he had met not long before leaving Boston and about whom he was crazy. Her name was Kathy Utman—she was a roommate of Prudence Farrow's—and her spritely air and small mellifluous voice enchanted him completely. He had never met such a blissful being—even among all of the other blissful ones. Diminutive, childlike, she seemed to sprinkle love petals wherever she stepped; he often compared her to a pixie named Piccoli from some story he knew—"He said I was like this little fairy-tale pixie person who came to earth and her job was to make people love each other more and to especially teach all the little boys how to love," she would recall, giggling. He also said that she reminded him of Little Eva from *Uncle Tom's Cabin* and sent her the book with all of the Little Eva parts marked up. He wrote her fanciful, delirious letters—signed them *I could just eat you up* or *MBFUA!!!* ("He said that was the sound of a kiss.") She was a cloud; she loved him back like a cloud might love, couldn't fully commit because she knew he couldn't either really—"I was a little bit careful," she said. But they would play together—when on park lawns he insisted they run in slow motion toward each other with open arms flapping—and she would come to New York early on to see his act at the Bitter End et al. and they maintained an understanding that she, as a cloud, would sweetly hover nearby throughout his life, which she in fact did, more or less, even when she married other guys and in between those marriages as well. "He always said we would live together when we were old. He also said that he heard bells whenever he stood near me."

For this reason, Elayne called her Kathy Bells, not in a bad way, although maybe in an arch-bemused way, as would be her way. But then

Elayne was different, like no one else had been or would be—"I was twenty-one years old . . . street-smart, cynical, and a tough cookie." He met Elayne Boosler not long after Budd Friedman had welcomed him to the performing fraternity of the Improv, where she was a hostess when not slipping onstage to sing, for her dream was to sing herself to riches. The night they connected he had just led the audience—in a bunny hop/conga line—out of the club and onto Ninth Avenue and around the block and back into the club. "I had to seat the whole damn audience again." He was wearing a sweatshirt that said I LOVE GRANDMA— which was a new alternate sublayer. She told him, "You're crazy." He replied, not as Foreign Man, "Thank you very much"—and took her to a restaurant in Chinatown for breakfast, where "with a cool move" she signaled a waiter to bring them water, which he later told her was the reason he fell in love with her. She, meanwhile, loved his beautiful big blue eyes and the way he looked so strikingly handsome from behind.

She was brass like he never knew. She was also game and they be-came characters together—"I happily discovered that whoever he be-came, I had just the girl for him." At Coney Island, she was the bitchy gum-snapping moll to his Tony Piccinini, "an overconfident, inept Romeo" who loudly promised to win giant stuffed animals for her, drawing large and larger crowds that watched him fail and fail until she stormed off while he called after her, "Sweetheart! Baby! Don't do me like this—I love ya!!" He took her to Times Square porn parlors, where she would pruriently stare over men's shoulders and *ahem* until the places were emptied. She would accompany Foreign Man to wrestling matches at Madison Square Garden, where he entertained their seating section whenever a behemoth took a questionable fall— *"Look at dat! Dat guy is so good, he knock de other guy down weethout even haffing to touch him!"* They perfected a volatility that was some-times real and often not and few witnesses ever knew the difference. Silver Friedman watched one nasty imbroglio unfold late one night on the pavement outside of the Improv—"We heard some shouting and the next thing we knew she was hitting him with her purse. And he was shoving her. Then he grabbed her purse and whacked her with it. And they're haranguing like two cats and didn't care who saw it. It was hysterical. But it was a lover's spat and they were very involved in it. I *think* it was real. It lasted about six minutes."

On nights when he didn't have to return his father's car to Great Neck, he stayed in her Greenwich Village apartment; Sunday mornings in bed he would read her the funny papers while eating ice cream. She studied his act and understood every nuance—"To listen to your own silence is an amazing secret of comedy," she would observe (without ever having met Maharishi), "and most people are not brave enough to do that. But he could stand there the longest with nothing perceptible happening, and yet so much happened." Whenever she sang at the Improv, however, he left the room; as such, he convinced her to become a comedienne. She had, after all, attitude to spare and had assisted him most splendidly with a character that he had begun developing who wasn't him or Foreign Man but a guy very much like the foul lounge singer he maybe/memorably saw in Las Vegas—Tony Clifton was his name, although nobody in New York knew of him, so he decided to call his character Tony Clifton. (He privately admitted that Richard Belzer, the acidic emcee at Catch who bore no resemblance except in stage demeanor, also partly inspired the character.) Which meant that he abused everyone from the stage while warbling badly while dressed in a dark coat and clip-on bow tie (for now) and wore a little grease paint mustache while singling out some schlub down in front and berating him until this noisy hostess chickie got fed up and bounded onto the stage and climbed on his back and started whaling on him while he insulted her and told her to knock it off with the women's lib jazz and said she oughta go back into the kitchen and raise babies like all chickies were meant to do whereupon she slugged him and he fell and begged for mercy until she left the stage in triumph and he started in again about how she should go back to the kitchen/babies and she moved toward him again and he said he was just kidding and everyone was furious and he would flee as hissing filled room as per busted steam pipe. Anyway, she *was* funny—could actually make him laugh (nobody else did really)—and so he counseled and coached her (quite incongruously) on how to *relate* to au-

diences and break that fourth wall and "come down off the stage";
one night, in desperation, she offered gum to an audience and heard
better laughter and she knew she was onto something. No one really
understood their relationship, the yin and yang of it, the fire and ice
cream of it, although Silver Friedman would note, "I think he released the child in her." And everyone saw his influence when she
took to arriving onstage while humming "The Way We Were"—just
as Barbra Streisand did at the very beginning of the hit record—except Elayne never sang a word and kept humming and hummed the
entire song; it got big, if unusual, laughs.

And they were together, more or less, until he had to leave for
California a couple of years later and often he taped their conversations
before and afterward, because he had recently begun taping conversations with everyone—street people, cab drivers, old people—and he
gave her one tape they made together on which he lectured to her
about the semiotics of a performer's fortitude in the face of defeat and
she would poignantly play a piece of that lecture (which was a piece of
him) near the end of one of her HBO stand-up comedy specials many
years hence when she was famous and there was his voice, insistent
and helpful—". . . You're on a railroad train, you go through a tunnel.
The tunnel is dark but you're still going forward. Just remember that.
But if you're not gonna get up onstage for one night, because you're discouraged or something, then the train's gonna stop. You're still in the
tunnel, but the train's gonna stop. [So] you [have to] just keep going. . . . It's gonna take a lot of times going onstage before you can
come out of the tunnel and things get bright again. But you keep going
onstage—go forward! Every night, you go onstage."

Every night, he went onstage and most nights received no pay other
than spotlight and, with luck, applause—for this was policy at the
Improv and at Catch a Rising Star, although Rick Newman graciously
permitted performers to order from the menu, which in Andy's case
meant dessert, preferably chocolate. And because he went onstage
every night on as many stages as would have him, he was pitifully

broke most of the time and was forced to consider a life in the theater and began filling up his daybook that spring of 1974 with times and locales of open casting-call auditions for chorus members and male lead singers and male dancers (he *was*, after all, a song-and-dance man) for such Broadway and road-company and dinner-theater productions as *Grease* and *Pippin* and *Kiss Me Kate* and *South Pacific* and *I Do, I Do*—and he was, of course, uniformly dismissed as hopeless in each instance. He also failed at an Equity chorus call for *The Music Man*, even though he was every bit the blithe and sly con man that Professor Harold Hill was—had even been deeply *inspired* by Professor Hill as played by the actor Robert Preston; had even taught himself *two years earlier* all five parts of Act One, Scene One, the convoluted multivoiced "Cash for the Merchandise" number, in which the traveling salesmen in the train car natter on in oddball synchopation about their desperate racket. (He had practiced *all five parts* with congas and thought he might at least put the piece in his act one day.) Meanwhile, Foreign Man was now getting so much exposure in the clubs that he needed fresh inept material to provide further journeys into the pathos, so he came up with new, um, jokes—like the one about a little boy named Jesus—*not the same Jesus that live in de church, you know*—whose mother sends him to the market for a quart of milk and a pound of butter but Jesus *he say but Mommy I don't know how to go to de market and she say don't worry just follow de people* but it was Sunday *so de people was going into de church so* Jesus followed them into the church *and he see de man on his stage go, "Oh Jesus! What do you want?" (So, vait-vait until de punch!) So de little boy he say, "A dozen eggs and a pound of butter—" (Oh, oh no I am sorry.) He say, "A quart of milk and a pound of butter!" (You know, because he thought that de church was de market, and that de man was talking to him, you know, because de man say Jesus and de little boy his name was Jesus. Do you understand?) Tenk you veddy much.* And then there was the one about the four men on *de aeroplane and it was going to, um, sink,* so the men needed to get out and so the first man, from Texas, jumps and, as he does, he says "Remember the Alamo!" And the next man, from France, jumps and says "Vive la France!" So *eet was only a man from England and a man from New York. So de man from England push out de man from New York. And as he push him, he say . . . eehh, something dat was very funny, but I don't remember what eet was. But but eet was very funny. Tenk you veddy much!*

On May 23 (2:00 A.M.), he had begun to diagram on five-by-eight index cards many strange and ambitious new ideas for the act, first inventorying the plethora of people who lived within him and his various plans for each—**BRITISH MAN (reads book, is interrupted by dissatisfied audience, continues reading, is humiliated, closes book); TONY CLIFTON (raps, "funny" stories, sings Charlie Brown, women's lib argument, threatened by husband, punched down by lady); LAUGHING MAN (comes out, laughs, tries to speak, raps about kids these days, takes encores & begs off); FOREIGN MAN (tells jokes, stories, Mighty Mouse, Conga Drums, retires from show business > Crying—OR becomes Elvis); BLISS NINNY (talks nice—I love you all, etc., repeat after me: *Hello trees,* etc., *Oohhh*); DUMB MAN; PRESIDENT (?); SLEEPING MAN (?); BORED ANGRY MAN; NEBBISH MAN (funny pathetic voice); PARANOID COMEDIAN; SOUTHERN MAN (cowboy country singer); DRUNK (?); WRESTLERS; CRYING MAN; NERVOUS MAN (wears earplugs, can't stand noise); CRAB (cigar-smoking, thick-lipped grouch); THE TELEVISION (have a TV character pop out of screen and become live—maybe the bad guy).** This last would require greater technical advancement than had been developed by 1974, especially for nightclub stages—but a mad visionary appeared to be at work. And for the next three weeks, in the hours just before sunrise, he drew up plot-twist scenarios that placed these people onstage, one after the other, and sometimes all at once, and sometimes all of them coming through the television screen, and sometimes getting into wrestling matches with each other, or appearing on a mock *Dating Game,* and there would be **Applause & Reaction** signs that lit up (at inappropriate times so as to goad audiences) and an anticlimax **wherein character unresolved yet forgotten (possibly disliked by audience) returns to be resolved,** or else there could also even be an onstage **Tornado changing everyone's lives in the middle (or maybe end).**

Certain people inside him had been showing up in clubs by now—

not with him or anywhere near him, because he wasn't there when they were, which came to be understood when they did not respond to conspiratorial winks or *hey Andys*. Tony Clifton was making himself known, as was British Man, whose clipped accent faltered as often as his starched readings of *The Great Gatsby*—British Man was, for reasons unknown, a proponent of Great American Literature. "He would start by reading all the copyright information and small print in the front of the book," said Rick Newman. "The crowd would seem amused at first, then as he kept reading and got two pages into the first chapter, some people would get up to leave. But he wanted that." A protracted negotiation with the audience ever ensued, during which a rattled British Man always tried to press on through the indignation— "Everyone would go *booooo boooooo*," he later explained. "And I'd say, 'Now, look! If you're not quiet, I will have to close the book and forget about the whole thing!' And there would be cheers. Um, you know, I would just do it for their reactions." (Years afterward, a false legend circulated that he had read the entire book to an audience in Fairfield, Iowa—home of Maharishi International University—because the Midwestern bliss people were simply too polite to leave. In fact, he rarely finished the first chapter anywhere, much less two pages. But he liked telling that story.) Sometimes, if he disliked an audience—"like when they would be so terrible and rude and I felt no satisfaction performing my regular act for them"—he would open the book and begin reading in his own voice. At Catch, he once sent Sleeping Man forth to try it—"He took the book, the microphone and a flashlight with him into his sleeping bag," said Newman, "then read it while zipped up inside. It looked like a talking sandbag onstage."

Meanwhile, he had begun cross-breeding Laughing Man with Bliss Ninny (adding a dash of Clifton) to create Nathan Richards, perhaps the happiest and most unctuous entertainer ever to tread boards. Dennis Raimondi, a TM follower who had become a close friend through Kathy Utman, observed Richards in early club development—"He was the kind of guy who bounced onto the stage and just gushed: *'Hey, ho ho ho how ya doin' it's great to be here you're such a beautiful audience you are beautiful people and I'd like to sing for you because you're just so special to me. . . .'* He would just be, you know, a little bit too blissful. And he'd wander through the audience and sing to them—*'I have often walked down this street beforrre thank you thank you'*—and kiss the women, most of whom just pushed him away. And he'd say, *'Come on, you love it and you know it, baby!'* Then after the song he'd say, *'Gosh, I'd love to stay and sing for you all night, but I have another gig.'* Then he'd run offstage to no actual applause, then come back and say, *'All right, I'll do another song just because—'* He would do that like ten times. Some people were ready to throw dynamite at him. Then again, other people actually believed he was for real and *enjoyed* him. Once, we were out in front of Catch a Rising Star afterward and a lady came up to tell him, 'Nathan, you really have a beautiful voice!' And Andy looked at me after she left and said, 'Sometimes I think they'll *never* understand what I'm doing.' "

There were those who did and some of them would provide new avenues of pursuit. A New York businessman named Jim Walsh, who had launched various entrepreneurial ventures with football star Joe Namath, took a particular shine to him one night at Catch—"I thought what he was doing was creative genius and told him so"— then informally offered himself up as a quasi-manager. They had brainstormed frequently since early winter (usually in macrobiotic restaurants as dictated by Andy) and Walsh placed calls that eventually led to little bookings at little events around town and thereabouts, including a quick stint refereeing a hamburger-eating contest at a midtown Burger King, all of which meant a couple hundred dollars here and there—plus Eppie Epstein always found ways to throw him small change at My Father's Place. So he was amassing some meager proof for his family that he was making headway. Then, as the airing of his Dean Martin shots approached (for which he received two five-hundred-dollar checks), he met the comedy team of Albrecht and Zmuda, who were Chris Albrecht and Bob Zmuda, a pair of young out-of-work actors fresh from Carnegie-Mellon in Pittsburgh who had come to the big city to starve. They had been scraping by on the fringes of outer

Off-Off-Broadway before hooking up with the owner of a failing mid-town dinner-theater called the Little Hippodrome, where they initially hired on to do carpenter labor and waiter work. As business grew more dire, Albrecht was made a floor manager and Zmuda became a chef and, as their paychecks bounced regularly, they were given license to live on the premises and, whenever opportune, pass themselves off as co-owners of the place. And so, that May, when Zmuda quite accidentally stumbled into the Improv—and experienced the epiphany of stand-up comedy, which he instantly saw as the future—he let it be known that he and his partner were not only theatrical impresarios but also budding comedians (neglecting to mention that they had no act). "I figured this was our only shot at becoming real operators, if you know what I mean," he would recall. So he fed Budd Friedman this enterprising line of canard and somehow secured stage time for their new act—Albrecht and Zmuda, Comedy from A to Z—which boasted much visual hokum, as written up with great haste by Zmuda. Among their bits was a sideshow lampoon: "I would swallow a sword onstage and bleed everywhere—people thought I was actually bleeding. It was pure gross-out kind of material." Andy saw and liked this gag very much, as did Foreign Man, whom Zmuda enthusiastically approached after the first time he watched Foreign Man work, whereupon Foreign Man complained about haffing a bad back and asked Zmuda if he would *please-tenk-you* load his props back into his car for him—which was the first of hundreds of times Zmuda would do just that—and then, according to Zmuda, as the car pulled away, Andy (not Foreign Man) was heard to holler into the night, "*Sucker!*" Thus was begat a most significant bond of brotherly humbug.

Zmuda, for his part, was a keen student of grandiose imposterism and artful fakery. An affable native of Chicago's Northwest Side Polish community, he had cut his teeth as part of a local guerrilla street theater troupe whose finest stunt had ensemble members positioned along a Chicago Transit Authority bus route, where they would board a bus in small clusters at each stop, then begin gagging and wheezing along the way until the bus was full of passengers complaining of toxic fumes, forcing the driver to abandon his route and call for emergency assistance. They did this repeatedly. He enthralled Andy with such tales and other ones from his brief tour of duty as assistant to the legendary renegade screenwriter Norman Wexler (*Joe, Serpico*), whose supposed eccentric furies and quixotic adventures had makings of further inspiration for Tony Clifton. "Andy's eyes would just bug out when I told him this crazy stuff," he recalled. Zmuda and Albrecht had, meanwhile, instituted a cabaret policy at the Little Hippodrome and began recruiting acts from the Improv. By mid-June, Jim Walsh had hatched a deal through them to stake Andy as the headliner of a nightly showcase to run the length of summer—with handbills hailing him thusly: FROM THE DEAN MARTIN COMEDY HOUR, NEW YORK'S MOST HILARIOUS ENTERTAINER. The late night showcase—which followed a musical revue staged earlier in the evening—also featured several complementary acts, including Walsh's only other client, a chanteuse named Tina Kaplan, and the antic stylings of Comedy from A to Z. "Sometimes there'd be no more than twenty people in the audience," said Walsh, "but they were wonderful people like Marlo Thomas and the playwright Herb Gardner. And they would bring their friends to see Andy over and over again."

And then *The New York Times*, in the person of critic Richard F. Shepard, came to witness both ends of the bill and, on July 11, a review was published under the headline SONGS AND A NEW COMEDIAN MAKE LIVELY CABARET. Praising the entire evening of entertainment, Shepard singled out "a new and brilliantly funny comic performer named Andy Kaufman," declaring him "the star here," whose work "defies categorization. He is more in the Sid Caesar tradition of prepared material rather than in the stand-up mode. He gives you no quotable lines, very few describable schticks, yet he leaves you laughing, loud and hard. He enters, speaking with a peculiar accent that could be Spanish, Greek, whatever, but it's none of them. . . . He imitates Elvis Presley, does a bravura performance with vocal of a 'folk song' from an island in the Caspian Sea; it's hilarious. . . . His manner is one of complete non-self-confidence. He falters, retraces his steps, and it is in this facade of uneasiness, marked by awkward yet eloquent gestures, that his talent for the comic shines."

And then, one night shortly thereafter, Dustin Hoffman with his friend Murray Schisgal, the writer, and their wives happened to wander down East Fifty-sixth Street and into the doors of the Hippodrome just as a fellow with a peculiar accent walked onto the stage, and Hoffman, focusing an unparalleled actor's eagle eye on the performance, was intrigued to notice that the fellow was very extremely nervous—"His hands were moving down by his sides, almost like he's playing an invisible piano, and he's wearing a suit that looked badly shrunk. I thought it must have been an amateur night. And, in the first ten minutes of his act, half of what was originally a half-full audience got up and walked out. At first blush, I thought, *Oh, this poor bastard.* And then suddenly he made that swing—right from poor bastard to genius. I'd never seen anybody do a bad act on purpose before. But he was so good that he appeared to be literally summoning up beads of sweat on his forehead, drenching himself in the embarrassment and being affected emotionally by the fact that they weren't laughing. People had their heads down, as if the guy had lost his bowels or thrown up onstage—you had to look away, but you couldn't. It was like watching a nervous breakdown in slow motion—and it was rhythmic! It had nuance and poetry and it killed me! I had never seen anything like it before. He was like a beautiful dandelion, so fragile that he might just blow away in the wind. Then he cried and worked the crying into the conga drums—*oh God!* The technique, with the originality and imagination of it! He was *fearless!*"

Hoffman led his party backstage afterward to offer congratulations—"I remember being surprised at how big he was. When he did that character he was like the size of Woody Allen, and then you meet him and he's a Goliath. And I remember how sweet and shy he was." Murray Schisgal would recall, "He was very polite but also absolutely ebullient. He looked like the happiest guy in the world because Dusty came back to see him. He was really just floating." Hoffman, in fact, was equally thrilled and began sending friends to the show and dragging others back with him and, on July 31, the syndicated columnist Earl Wilson reported, "Dustin Hoffman was at the Little

Hippodrome for the fourth time to see zany comic Andy Kaufman, described by one viewer as an anti-comic."

One of the friends Hoffman sent forth to behold the spectacle was Woody Allen himself, who would remember, "I thought he was quite good, quite amazing in certain places—the Mighty Mouse thing and the Elvis Presley come to mind. What he did, he did in a talented way, no question. He came over to me afterward and asked if he could have a chat with me one afternoon. He was awfully nice, so I had him come to [my manager] Jack Rollins's office. And I chatted with him for a while, but most of his questions were odd because— I'll never forget this—somewhere he had gotten the impression that I was a Transcendental Meditationist. He had heard that I pilgrim-aged to India every year. And I said that nothing could be further from the truth. I have respect for it, but I have no interest in it what-soever. And he was explaining to me that he was very, very interested in Eastern religion and Eastern philosophy. Which was, uh, nice. Then we talked about show business for a little bit and that was it. But I found him quite amusing and, you know, very unusual."

His first impact upon popular consciousness, the moment he was born unto universal memory, would come fifteen months hence and he would then seem to have materialized from nowhere, inexplicably, like a wraith. By then, he had rehearsed his craft for twenty-six of the twenty-six years he had thus far lived. When it happened, as it hap-pened, he did not utter a word, he was silent, the fingers would twitch at his sides and his eyes would strobe and he would sip the water and wipe his mouth, as the Terrytooners exalted the mouse by way of the phonograph and he would wait for his three opportunities to step for-ward and heroically move his lips and it was just as it had been since he invented this particular exercise for little birthday children, but re-ally for himself, when he was no more than fourteen. But now it would seem to glisten like new (unless someone had viewed his club work or glimpsed the Dean Martin debut). And every other sly transgression he would attempt before cameras from that point forward would seem

Stanley and Janice
Kaufman on their
wedding day -
June 5, 1945

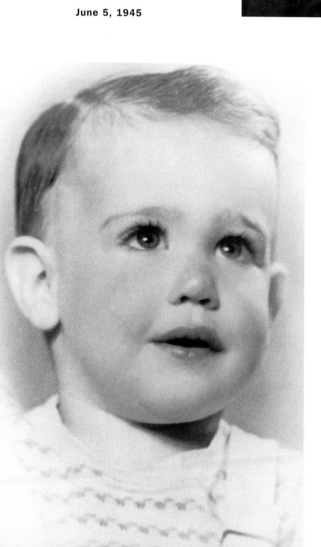

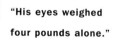

"His eyes weighed
four pounds alone."

Andy with younger brother Michael and sister Carol on Bar Mitzvah day

Showing

off his

early

Elvis

moves

STAR-
STRUCK
AT THE
COPA

Frankie Avalon
and Andy

Andy, Paul Anka, Barbara Levy, and Jimmy Krieger

Andy
entertains
the kids in
1963

Flower child

With the family
dog, Snoopy

Lounging at F-Troop headquarters
in Greenwich Village circa 1967

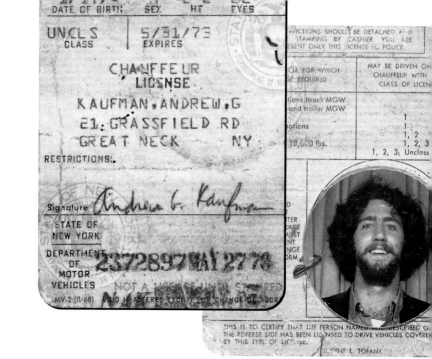

The motley crew: Andy (far right) does his best James Dean

UNCLE

ANDY'S

FUNHOUSE

Courtesy of Al Parinello

ndy's Fun House

~~interspersing~~

"~~nc~~le Andy Time"
It's Uncle Andy Time
" " " "
An dy + Bee Bop, too
say Boo Bee doo to you
Let's give a ~~noisy~~ cheer
cause Uncle Andy's here
It's time to start, so plan
So kids let's go

"~~nc~~le Andy"

Uncle Andy Show

1. Song - Everyone Says
2. Interview Kids
3. Toothbrush brushing - music
4. Mr. Bee Bop - proverbs for the day
5. Mr. Bee Bop and Uncle Andy duet - I Taut I
   Puddy - Tat
6. Magic
7. Song - Pachalafaka
8. Cartoon - Oswald Rabbit
9. Dance Crazy
10. Eat Lunch - Chocolate Milk
11. Mr. Bee Bop and Uncle Andy - Comedy Skit
12. Follow Leader Hula.

WCSB TV

equally new, when in fact not much of it was, because the ideas had gestated in adolescence, then grew as he grew. And so the birth on record would be remembered as October 11, 1975—which was a Saturday night, which was the first Saturday night that NBC broadcast a radical live ninety-minute comedy and music insurrection that would change the way comedy and music would thereafter be experienced on television. Especially comedy. *Saturday Night*, unforgivingly beamed live as it unfolded from Rockefeller Center in New York (same building where Howdy Doody had worked), would come to be known as *Saturday Night Live* and it was designed for a new generation—edgily produced-written-and-performed by young turks for an audience of same—and its first years would become hallowed in retrospect, would be remembered as golden and culturally important and unmatchable in quality. Thus, all that transpired in its inaugural broadcast would be the stuff of time capsules, although no one could have guessed this when it happened. But there it was, all fairly indelible—the opening moments in which John Belushi played a befuddled immigrant (oh!) learning to speak English from writer Michael O'Donoghue by repeating, *"I would like to feed yur fingerteeps to de wolverines,"* before both collapsed in death; Chevy Chase's first mock "Weekend Update" newscast; the first sketch involving costumed Killer Bees; guest host George Carlin's first monologue (of three that he delivered during the show); fake commercials for Tryopenin aspirin and superabsorbant Mini-Pads; the short film by Albert Brooks; the offbeat playlet featuring new mutant Muppets created by Jim Henson; songs from Billy Preston and Janis Ian; the filmed drive-around-New-York segment in which pedestrians were bade to "Show Us Your Guns" and did; the nascent and grungily irreverent ensemble work of the Not Ready for Prime Time Players, who were Belushi, Chase, Dan Aykroyd, Garrett Morris, Gilda Radner, Jane Curtin, and Laraine Newman; and the novelty act, as it was called, which appeared toward the latter moments of the show's first half hour, in which a nervous man dropped a needle onto a phonograph and stood there waiting and received much laughter and applause and left.

To get to that night, more people had to keep discovering him and he would keep doing what he did and had done—all of which happened as haphazardly as fate would decree. Quirky events along the path would accrue the heft of legend. Foreign Man would ditheringly appear on local television, making his hometown debut on *The Joe Franklin Show*, and the venerable Franklin would be rendered more disoriented than even Foreign Man. Not long thereafter, he was bumped at the last minute from *Midday Live with Bill Boggs* due to breaking news, then turned Cliftonian in his indignation and ranted at producers and refused to leave the studio premises until security came to handcuff him and escort him to pavement, about which he was inordinately pleased. On Columbus Day 1974, he gave Foreign Man a name—he wrote in his daybook **my name: Baji Kimran**—not that he ever told anyone, because he obviously needed to be Andy Kaufman in order to become famous. Later that month, Walsh booked him for a week at the Bijou in Philadelphia, where he opened for a young songwriter named Barry Manilow who was building heat around a new record called "Mandy" and Manilow would take the stage each night to find it strewn with debris which the audience had hurled at the opening act—"They just *hated* his guts," Manilow said. "My whole job that week was to try to bring them back from the edge of revolution." Andy also began a long association with a club called Pips in the Sheepshead Bay section of Brooklyn, where he was actually paid and additionally got to consume all the ice cream he wished (preferably hot fudge sundaes in beer mugs for better mixology)—and where he regularly dragged the waitresses and Seth Schultz, son of the owner George Schultz, to Coney Island at two in the morning so they could ride the Cyclone with him. "He always made us ride in the last car of the Cyclone because he said it provided the full-whiplash effect," said Schultz. In November, Walsh sent him to Fort Lauderdale to open for the Supremes (minus Diana Ross) at a nightclub owned by his friend Bobby Van and, after his first set on the first night, the manager of the Supremes forbade him to step onstage again. Walsh spoke with Andy on the phone afterward and told him, "Look, Florida is the wrong audience for you, I made a mistake in letting you go down there, but—since you're there anyhow—when that Bobby Van

comes into your dressing room, I want you to do Crying Man." (Van
called Walsh forty-five minutes later and said, "Oh, Jim, I feel terrible!
Poor guy's having a nervous breakdown in his dressing room and
won't stop crying.") There would be odd gigs in private men's clubs
and at the Continental Baths (whose largely gay male audience wore
only towels or less) and at the Mr. Olympia Contest and at restaurants
and niteries throughout the tristate area, in addition to dutiful nightly
stops at Catch and the Improv, where the Friedmans had also hired
him to emcee a weekly Sunday showcase of children performers.
Silver Friedman remembered him arriving twenty-five minutes late
on the second Sunday of the series and her saying to him, "Andy, next
time you're late, at least call us! We didn't even know if you were coming!" And his eyes turned black and he countered, *"Don't yell!"* "It was
like my little reproach had stabbed him," she said, "and suddenly he
almost looked *menacing,* to the point where if I'd said another word
he would have either walked out or killed me. Anger, I realized, was
a very big issue for him deep down in there somewhere."

By winter's end, he and Walsh drifted apart as casually as they had
come together, with no hard feelings, although Walsh had grown
concerned over Andy's mental well-being—"He had come up to my
office on Lexington Avenue and he started talking about what he really wanted to do, which was to play Carnegie Hall and then take the
audience the next day over to a deli to have milk and cookies. And
then he said that when he became *really* successful, what he most
wanted to do was to buy the Atlantic Ocean and drain it and build a
city there. And this was now bordering on . . . I mean, if this guy's serious we've got some problems here."

Meanwhile, NBC had hired a bright young producer named Dick
Ebersol from ABC Sports and saddled him with the task of creating
a new live late-night comedy-variety program to replace the Saturday
repeats of *The Tonight Show Starring Johnny Carson.* The show—
whose content was still a mystery to all, including Ebersol—was to be
up and running in Studio 8H of Rockefeller Center by the fall of
1975. So, in the holiday dusk of 1974, Ebersol began cruising New
York clubs for talent and it was at Catch a Rising Star that he spied

his first real quarry—"The first image I had of Andy will never go away—it was Mighty Mouse. I thought it was the damnedest thing I'd ever seen. It was like stepping into a whole other world—and I had no idea how many other worlds that I would ultimately go to with him." Ebersol instantly befriended Andy, started riding regularly with him from Catch to the Improv, watched him spoon up the various parfait layers of his act, breakfasted with him and Elayne, all the while talking and talking about this new show which Andy would absolutely have to be part of. Around the same time, Ebersol convinced a young Canadian exile of rich comedic pedigree, Lorne Michaels, to come build and produce the show with him. Ebersol said of Michaels and their mission, "Our minds met in that the one thing we wanted to do was to take the language of young people and make it the language of television. We both had this philosophy that television was always at least ten years behind what was actually happening. Television was very risk aversive." By March 1975, seven months before their debut, he informed his new partner of the first risk he wished to put forth—"I told Lorne that I had one guest booked for the first show—Andy Kaufman. Lorne had no idea who he was." Michaels then went to Catch with talent scout John Head to see for himself, then went ten or fifteen times more, and was ever mesmerized—"It was as beautiful a thing as you could witness," he would recall. "Aside from being funny, he wasn't enmeshed in the show business of it—show business being that it was simply an act. There seemed to be some other commitment, something very pure and more personal about what he was doing. And it was simply arresting."

Also that March, a wily filmmaker named Larry Cohen came to the Improv in search of someone with a "certain crazy look" who could infiltrate the upcoming St. Patrick's Day Parade in police uniform—marching in line with actual NYPD cops, as though he were a member of the force—then appear to go berserk firing a phony gun at random, then pretend to be shot down, then fall to the ground, mouthing the words "God told me to," and play dead. He quickly spotted a worthy candidate onstage and Andy said he would very much like to do it. He had, he said, some experience at wielding fake guns and pretending to die. Cohen's project was to be a made-for-television detective movie called *God Told Me To*, wherein various New Yorkers believe they hear the voice of God asking for bloodshed and they comply in accordance. ("Strangely enough," Cohen would say, "this was before the Son of Sam murders, but Andy bore an amazing likeness to David Berkowitz, the real guy who heard voices and killed people.") Cohen told him where to show up on the day of the parade, whereupon a police uniform would be provided for him. Cohen asked, "So, what size jacket do you wear?" "I don't know." "Well, what size shirt do you wear?" "Um, I don't know." "Shoe size?" "I don't know." Cohen said, "You're a grown man. How can you not know what size clothes you wear?" Andy said, "I wear my father's old clothes."

A uniform awaited in any case on St. Patrick's Day and he donned it—"And we left him alone for a few minutes while I went to organize the crew and then I came back to find him walking around as a policeman and he was goading all these Irishmen behind barricades on the sidewalk, all of them half drunk already. He had his police cap on backwards and he was making faces at them, deliberately provoking everybody. They wanted to jump over the barricades and just beat the shit out of him. So I start pulling them away, shouting, 'Get back! He's an actor! He's not a cop!'" Anyway, he stepped into the parade and fell in with marching cops who knew nothing of what was happening (since Cohen had gotten no permit to film) and he pantomimed his killing spree and dropped dead as though riddled with bullets as cameras rolled and police marched onward. "The funny part," said Cohen, "was that there must have been five thousand cops on the street and yet nobody bothered us because they just assumed that if we were doing this, we must have had permission from *somebody*. Otherwise, who would go out in the middle of five thousand police officers and start firing a weapon? It was an exercise in sheer audacity. Andy, of course, thought this was absolutely the greatest thing he'd ever done!"

Having secured his first professional acting credit—which would amount to four minutes of eventual screen time—he was summoned in April to Philadelphia, where his Grahm cohort Burt Dubrow now worked on the staff of the nationally syndicated *Mike Douglas Show*. Just as with the Elvis scheme in Chicago, Dubrow had cooked up another plot. The show's producers had made a running gag of tormenting Robert Goulet whenever he guested with Douglas and now Goulet was set to appear again and Dubrow believed that Laughing Man, posed as a boom-microphone operator, would properly devastate the singer. So Laughing Man was in position as Goulet was asked to sing "The Nearness of You" to the wives of four hockey players and so he began to sing and Laughing Man could be heard shrieking in hyena fashion and Goulet stopped and said "What is *he* laughing at?" and Mike Douglas approached Laughing Man who gulpingly indicated that someone in the control booth was saying funny things into his headset and Douglas scolded him and Goulet started singing again and the shrieking also started again as viewers now watched the boom operator convulse in seizures, then sprawl across the stage gasping idiotically, ruining the song, forcing a commercial break, pleasing everyone except Robert Goulet fans and four hockey wives. Certain redemption came in the final segment of the show, however, which had Douglas and guests—Goulet and the blind guitarist José Feliciano and David Brenner—perched on a line of stools and there, on the farthest stool, was Laughing Man. Douglas and Feliciano and Goulet casually sang a couple of songs and everyone swayed to the music and then Douglas said, "We're gonna hear from Andy Kaufman, who was our Laugher earlier in the show—Andy, what are you going to do?" And Foreign Man said he would *eemetate, ehh, de Elveece Presley*, then got up with back to cameras, combed hair, sneered over shoulder, turned and performed "Jailhouse Rock" while Feliciano sang backup and Goulet's jaw dropped and Brenner snapped fingers proudly (knowing what he already knew) and Douglas sputtered at finish, "That's incredible!" And it had been as though no one else was really there except him, as though these actual famous entertainer people who writhed happily on stools were invisible to him. It had been as though he was playing to old bedroom walls where only the cameras really mattered.

*　*　*

Deep silence was necessary before what was to come and that summer he went to Switzerland, to a tiny resort town called Thyon-sur-Sion, and he would meditate there for two months with the others, then wander parts of Bavaria with Dennis Raimondi before what was to come. Maharishi would not be in attendance until later, which was fine, because there would be endless hours to pass with good bliss buddies Dennis and Phil Goldberg and Dean Sluyter, who would listen to him talk about his passions in his inimitably innocent way. They heard about wrestling—Elayne would send him wrestling magazines so as to keep him informed—and about his Huey Williams book, which was still forming itself in notes and drafts. "His favorite topics," Sluyter said, however, "were how many Swiss chocolate candy bars he'd eaten each day and how many times he had masturbated. In both cases, if he was to be believed, it counted out to be about a dozen." Then Maharishi finally showed up and Andy—who had been hearing a great deal about the value of celibacy and how expending sexual energy outside of marriage was depleting to good meditators, which was alarming since he liked sex very extremely much—decided to go to the microphone and ask His Holiness once and for all, in no uncertain terms, if this was true. And he used words like semen and sperm and spilling and penis and ejaculation and Maharishi had previously preferred to skirt this indelicate issue and he tried now to change the subject but Andy did not relent. Said Goldberg, "No one had ever been impertinent enough to persist in this line of questioning, but Andy was truly curious and meant no harm. And he was forcing Maharishi into a yes-or-no circumstance. A lot of people were muttering for him to stop and others of us thought, Go ahead! Someone's finally got the balls to ask about it!" And so Maharishi sighed lengthily and, as there was no way out, traversed the subject more didactically than he had ever before and basically said that, yes, once the energy in the semen was wasted it was gone forever, which was not great news for Andy, who knew he would have to make up for such drainage in other ways. But everyone would remember this exchange every bit as vividly as the *crazyman inquisition. And Foreign Man, meanwhile, took daily walks to the village, where he taught little Swiss children the language of Caspiar and he would lead them around in their lederhosen and they would chant* eee-bi-da eee-bi-da yak-ta-bay eee-bi-da *and sing "Aba-Dabbi." Then they would all eat chocolate. And when it was time to fly home, his suitcase was too heavy, which meant paying a tariff, so he stood at the ticket counter in Zurich and began taking clothes out of his suitcase as airline people and Dennis Raimondi watched. "He put on three pairs of pants, four sweaters, and three jackets to wear on the flight," said Raimondi. "And he never broke a sweat all the way home."*

Lorne Michaels put him on camera and taped an obligatory audition, not that it mattered, because he was firmly understood to be part of the birth-march of *Saturday Night*, but everyone else had to do it as well, so he recited "MacArthur Park" not as an old Jew but as himself, which wasn't really very funny which he never tried to be anyway. He sat with a forearm propped on a desktop at 30 Rockefeller Center and spoke the lyrics twice, pouring it on just a tad in the second rendering (with dramatic closing-of-eyes in anguished places), and Lorne thanked him and said, "You want to do something else?" And he said, "Um, okay," then looked down, then looked up and became dew-dripping mushmouthed hillbilly and drawled, "*Fasterna-speedn-bullet-mo-pahrfulna-loc'motive-abletuh-leap-tawl-buildnsna-sanglebown—Look upna sky, it'sa birrrd, it'sa playyyun, nope, it's Suprmayn, yeeppppp, Suuuprmayn-strayunge-vizzter-frum-enuthr-planet-who-cameta-Earth-withpahrsnabilitiesfarbeeyon'thoza-mortal-meyen—*" And when he was finished a smattering of applause echoed in the room and he smiled shyly and got up and left.

He became a fixture around the show's seventeenth-floor production offices in the weeks before the October premiere. He did not fraternize as much as lurk. Relatively few staff or cast members knew who he was or what he was or what he was supposed to do—although John Belushi had become an early true believer after having seen the

conga-crying in clubs. Anne Beatts, a newly recruited writer, first encountered him slumping in Lorne's antechamber—"I thought, *Oh,
man, is this the kind of person they're hiring? I don't know if I want to
be a part of this!* He was so twitchy and weird and had bad skin. He
looked very nerdy and geeky. I had severe doubts about the show
from the beginning and my initial impression of Andy was the first of
them." Very late on the Friday night before the broadcast, however,
her opinion changed when she saw him rehearse, which he almost
didn't because the rehearsals dragged on interminably and he had yet
to perform a run-through of Mighty Mouse for the crew and finally
he said he had to leave. "And it was like—'Wait, you can't leave!'"
Beatts would recall. "And he said, 'No, I have to go if I'm going to
make the last train back to Great Neck.' Lorne told him, 'No, Andy,
we *need* you here.' So he said, 'Well, I guess I could get my mother
to come pick me up. . . .'"

On October 11, he meditated twice, locking himself in the office
of head writer Herb Sargent—once before dress rehearsal and again
before the live broadcast. Both times he taped a note on the door—
Please do not disturb me while I meditate, Andy Kaufman. All around
him, panic and mayhem swirled as would become customary
Saturday Night crucible. Then all panic escalated after the dress rehearsal, which went desperately over the ninety-minute limit.
"There was a lot of weeping and wailing and fierce argument,"
Michaels would recall. "We had to make cuts and one of the choices
was to cut Andy. And that was the one thing I wasn't going to do.
Andy was sacrosanct. More than any one thing in that first show, he
represented the spirit of what we were trying to do. Not only was it—
in the language of the time—a *hip* act, but the very hippest aspect
was that he only lip-synched the part of Mighty Mouse. That was the
essence of avant-garde." Said Ebersol, "We put him on in the first
half hour because we felt it was a killer. And it killed. The audience
went nuts. When the show was over, the commercial parodies and
Andy were the only things that people talked about. And he knew at
that moment that that was it for the piece. Mighty Mouse had killed
night after night for years in the clubs—but now television had eaten

it up and it wasn't going to be a surprise anymore." Nevertheless, he was pleased enough with himself that night to consume as much ice cream as could be found in midtown Manhattan.

The following week's show was built around the reunion of singers Paul Simon and Art Garfunkel, which left little room for much more than cursory sketches. But he was brought back most purposefully for the third and fourth broadcasts to lend presence and continuity. On October 25, again in the first half hour, guest host Rob Reiner introduced him (whereas stentorian announcer Don Pardo had done so in voice-over the first time) and he wore exactly what he had worn before—Foreign Man's checked sport coat, white jeans, black dickie, pink shirt—and he stood next to the phonograph again and moved his mouth to "Pop Goes the Weasel," mirthfully evincing the larger vocal role of playful father to antic daughter. But his own voice, once again, was never heard. Then, on November 3, Candice Bergen— who had beheld his act more than once at the Improv—announced, "Boys and girls, this is a man I love very much. The word *genius* comes to mind, but I'll let you decide for yourselves." And here was Foreign Man at last, more tentative than ever, as pitch-perfect Bombing began with the cannonball story moving into his eemetation of de Archie Bunker—*Ehh, you stupid you are so stupid everybody ees stupid, ehh, get out of my chair, Meathead, de dingbat get into de kitchen making de food, ehh everybody is so stupid, tenk you veddy much*—at which point he lost his place and fell into a chasm of silent squirming, then in feeble effort to cover he offered to dance and sing and did (*la-la-laaa!*). Next, most historically in the realm of live television, he uttered the words *ehh could we stop de tape?* Then—*I think we should turn off de TV. . . . I don't know if you are laughing at me or weeth me . . . but I am trying to do my best but I forgot what I was going to do. . . .* And so, of course, he blithered and wept, emitting the rhythmic yelping breaths that brought his hands to the conga which he beat into manna which was, um, exquisite.

And within that four-week span of live broadcast reckoning, he had become more dependable than most anything else on the program and he remained a mystery but was also now a mystery of burgeoning fame, which was the plan all along. "I got to know him in the way that I get to know pretty much everyone I worked with on the show," Michaels said. "Because of the pressure, there's a kind of unavoidable intimacy. He had this real enthusiasm for what he was doing and he was very gentle. We never really talked at length—he'd just sort of tell me what he would do. Even before the show went on the air, we'd gotten to a place of trust. If he was enthusiastic about something he wanted to do, I didn't have to know much more. Within the club of the world I lived in, he was the edge—probably more than anybody else I can think of in comedy. There were lots of people doing variations on Lenny Bruce or doing what Richard Pryor had done, but here was a guy coming out of a completely original place. And you had to stand back and simply respect that."

And it was during those weeks and then in the months to come (then years thereafter) that he dwelt transparently amongst *Saturday Night Live* rabble, a separate and benign entity who came and did and scored and left—without sharing the secret of himself with more than a few of them. "I probably never spoke more than two words to him," said Beatts, and the same was true throughout the ranks. But there was one notable exception toward the beginning and that was Chevy Chase, the first breakout star in the cast, who projected something akin to likable smugness ("I'm Chevy Chase and you're not!") and prep school suavity, which were traits diametrically opposite to any possessed by Andy. But Chase, who also became a head writer, had moved into Herb Sargent's seventeenth-floor office, which had a couch, and with the couch came the meditator who had already claimed the room as his deep-silence sanctum. "There were times when I'd walk in and he'd just be lying on the couch or doing some kind of yoga thing, or not," said Chase. "But I was so self-confident and sort of disarming—basically I just didn't give a shit—that I had no compunctions about simply facing the obvious with him. And I think the fact that I truly didn't give a shit made him comfortable to just be Andy. He knew there was no foolin' me—so we were able to talk about things. I remember engaging him in conversations about his method of preparation, his general health and well-being, his san-ity, his acne. I asked him if he knew that he was funny and if he took pleasure in the responses he got to his work. Because he never really appeared to enjoy anything. And he said, yes, that he truly enjoyed the responses. He was always testing onstage, searching—is this funny or is it not funny or is it just odd? And did he care if it was funny? You know what? He did care. I once asked him, 'Do you know how brilliant you are?' And he turned shy again. He said he didn't know if anyone 'got it'—if they laughed at him or with him. But I think it meant something to him that I asked. I was sort of the cat's pajamas at the time and he respected that. But he also looked at what I was doing as rather pedestrian, I think, considering where he was headed.

"What's interesting is that with those doors closed, we actually chuckled a lot, we had real laughs. Then he would step out of the office and become the quiet wide-eyed guy again. But those eyes were like the eyes of a tiger. They were always looking around for fresh prey."

9

Constantly risking absurdity / and death / whenever he performs above the heads / of his audience / the poet like an acrobat climbs on rime / to a high wire of his own making. . . .

Lawrence Ferlinghetti,
from the poem "Constantly Risking Absurdity"

Rarefied wind blew west, as it will, because west is where certain sorts of dreams go to flourish or to corrupt themselves or to die. He had been west and knew he would go again but knew not when or how. And so it happpened that Carl Reiner dropped into Catch a Rising Star with his wife, Estelle, in early October, before *Saturday Night* and Mighty Mouse expedited matters of renown. Reiner, by this time, was understood to be a comedic Midas whose deft touch helped gild the legends of Sid Caesar, of Mel Brooks's Two-Thousand-Year-Old Man, and of sitcom archetypes Rob and Laura Petrie (he created *The Dick Van Dyke Show*, about the secret life of a comedy writer, in his own image); soon he would direct the films of a former Disneyland boy-magician named Steve Martin, whose own burgeoning career in stand-up comedy had already begun to incite a national stampede among young club jokesmiths. (Martin's unprecedented enormity made him comedy's first rock star—further inspiring a generation of enterprising or envious wisenheimers.) And so the Reiners experienced the bafflement that was Foreign Man with keen wonder—

"Seeing him for the first time and not knowing what to expect was a wonderful thing," Reiner would recall. "It was altogether new. We didn't know what he was getting at. But we knew *he* knew those jokes were bad. Nobody could be that dumb. We quickly realized we were watching something very unusual and historic in comedy theater." Then, of course, came the Crying, then de Elveece, then Reiner took him aside out on Second Avenue and pledged to help him, told him to call next time he came to the West Coast. (Dennis Raimondi, who witnessed the encounter, remembered Andy turning to him after Reiner walked away and saying, "I never go to the Coast. What's he talking about?") Reiner, meanwhile, would remember nothing about that conversation other than the wavering countenance he addressed—"When I talked to him, I saw outer space all over his face. His spacey face. His eyes weren't zeroed in; they were everywhere else, as though he was thinking, *Why am I talking to this man?*" And days later Reiner was back in California, lunching with his nephew/manager George Shapiro and Dick Van Dyke in the NBC Burbank commissary, where he re-created beat for beat this new act he'd seen at Catch a Rising Star. Shapiro would say of his uncle's enthusiasm, "He has absolute ear-recall and so he became Foreign Man and did everything Andy had done, to the letter. He said, 'This guy's got the most unique, unusual, crazy act I've ever seen. George, you've gotta help him!'" Shapiro allowed that he wasn't sure that he wished to manage such an odd specimen, but said he would help him as best he could. And Van Dyke, who had been engaged in early development talks with NBC to do some new kind of variety show, absorbed all this and was heard to muse, "I wonder how we could use a fella like that."

Confluence of fates began interlinking at an accelerated clip, for Carl Reiner's son, Rob Reiner, then went to see this Foreign Man in New York at his father's insistence and heard the eemetation of de Archie Bunker telling de Meathead to get out of de chair and, since Rob Reiner actually played de Meathead on the sitcom *All in the Family,* and since he was scheduled to host one of the first *Saturday Night* broadcasts, he was dutifully impressed and told Andy, who, in turn, declared that he wanted Rob Reiner to be the first person to introduce him on the show, which caused certain havoc and embarrassment in that Lorne Michaels wanted Andy on the first show and Rob Reiner was slated to host the third, on which he could then introduce him again, never mind that Andy was very upset about the whole thing. Meanwhile, there was the Uncle Sammy Denoff connection, which Carl Reiner discovered when he next began to re-create the act for Uncle Sammy, who had cowritten countless episodes of *The Dick Van Dyke Show* and whose manager was Uncle Carl's nephew George Shapiro, and he stopped Carl Reiner in mid-sentence and said, "I *know* that kid! He considers me his uncle!" Also: In New York, Carl Reiner had given George Shapiro's phone number as well as his own to Andy and one day in early November George picked up the phone and heard, "*Ummmm . . .*" and it was Andy calling to say that he was coming out to Los Angeles after his third appearance on *Saturday Night*—not one installment of which George had seen, since people in his crowd had dismissed the program as "a poor imitation of Sid Caesar's *Your Show of Shows*" (on which Carl Reiner had become famous)—and this was all getting awfully providential. Andy told him that Budd Friedman was flying him out to work at the new West Hollywood Improv. Friedman, at that time, was eager to display the wares of his New York bumper crop in order to compete with Mitzi Shore's lock on local talent at her Comedy Store on Sunset Boulevard. Shapiro agreed without hesitation to come see Andy when he hit town and hung up and none of this was news to him since Budd Friedman had called him earlier that day to say there was this strange guy from the New York club that he was bringing out and this guy needed a manager and George ought to come see him work. "All of a sudden," said Shapiro, "there was no escaping this person named Andy Kaufman."

Shapiro, for his part, was new to the management business, but a veteran of the agency business, where he had risen through the ranks of the New York William Morris office, starting out in the mail-room—the William Morris mailroom being the fabled bottom-rung incubator of innumerable future sharks and moguls. From there, he floated through the company as a temporary secretary, sometimes helping out visiting agents or agency clients, which was how he found himself answering phones for Colonel Tom Parker, Elvis's manager, whenever the Colonel came through town. "The Colonel always lectured to me—'*Everything is money,*' he told me. '*Everything depends on money. It's all money. How much money did we make today?*'" He apprenticed under various agents involved in various television projects and programs, which was how he found himself backstage at *The Ed Sullivan Show* when Elvis made his first appearance. "Elvis was the first person to ever call me *sir*. No one ever called me *sir*. I'm from the Bronx. They don't use that term in the Bronx." Shapiro was then and ever an exuberant little wiry guy with quixotic ideas, a born nurturer; he climbed onward, was brought to California in 1961, handling deals for Steve Allen's short-lived ABC-TV variety show, where he introduced Allen's head writer Bill Dana (a.k.a. José Jimenez) to the writing team of clients Sam Denoff and Bill Persky, for whom he also got jobs on *The Dick Van Dyke Show* staff. He then oversaw Denoff and Persky's creation of the sitcom *That Girl*, starring Marlo Thomas, discovered Jim Nabors, who became Gomer Pyle, brokered much show business in general, and —perhaps most significantly—brought into the William Morris fold a no-nonsense deal-maker named Howard West, whom Shapiro had known since the third grade at P.S. 80 in the Bronx. And in 1974, when Shapiro struck out on his own to form a management company, it was West whom he lured to become his partner, so as to form Shapiro/West and Associates—a prototypical good cop/bad cop cooperative, wherein George coddled the talent and Howard drew blood from the buyers of talent. Their small client list a year hence included Uncle Carl and comic actor Marty Feldman and comedienne Ruth Buzzi and the animator who created Scooby-Doo and Uncle Sammy and some other writers and now George went to the Improv on Melrose Avenue to see the kid from New York with the Bombing and the Crying and de Elveece and—since heavens and lineage had dictated this—he was floored. "He just totally floored me." Then he brought Howard West to see their future client. "I knew I wanted to sign him. I told Howard, 'This guy—I get excited just sitting and watching him!' So Howard came—Howard is kind of a buttoned-down businessman—and he just stared at me." West would recall: "I didn't hate it. Some of the material was very clever, smart, funny. But you look at some of the other material and say, *Are you kidding me?* That's the reaction I had—a mixed bag. I mean, Andy had a set of balls."

All of which was to say that Andy landed safely in California and the oiled machinery of momentum awaited him there and it engulfed him and he took to it completely and—though he would return to New York at every opportunity and always believe New York was where he belonged—California had claimed him and California would now decide what to do with him. He would submit as best he could and it would still be nothing if not a roiling artistic struggle, which would become apparent soon enough, but not too soon because now it was time to truly start becoming famous.

So George expressed excitement, which was exciting, and became his manager before the year was out, focusing mostly on what they could do in the new year, and George had lots of ideas and was very, um, excitably excited about how things would work. Budd Friedman, meanwhile, had put him up in a small transient-hotel bungalow a few blocks from the club, off of Melrose, because he needed to showcase his New York import for several weeks, and that was where Little Wendy found him or where he found Little Wendy, who was Wendy Polland, a comical songwriter, whom he decided to name Little Wendy because her manner was sweet and loopy and befuddled and also because she was very short and had the voice of a precocious child. Andy had gotten her phone number from a TM person because he didn't know many people in Los Angeles and the TM person had seen Wendy perform her songs at retreats and thought she could maybe work with Andy onstage somehow. And so she came over and didn't want to take off her coat because she thought she was fat and she kept apologizing for herself— "He just loved that I hated myself, basically. Also, he liked that I had this 'innocence'—not that I was innocent, but I made sure to be just as light and as pure as possible around him, because that was soooooo important to him." *She sort of fell in love with him right away was what happened, but he was oblivious of course and just wanted her to hang around with him, and so he called her every day and she came over and watched him eat breakfast while he watched* Father Knows Best *on television*—"And he would just well up with tears every single day while he watched it. He would really cry." *They drove everywhere in her Volkswagen, which he also borrowed a lot, and went to Fellini movies and Luis Buñuel movies and Charlie Chaplin movies and by then she had become an onstage accomplice for him, usually pretending that she was his little sister and she would shake maracas and sing little songs with him like "Banana Boat" and "The Ballad of Davy Crockett" and "Sioux City Sue," thoroughly perplexing/charming Improv audiences. But that came well after her unusual debut at the club which happened the very first day they met at the bungalow where, per her memory, he asked her,* " 'Have you ever had a very terrible experience?' And I said, 'Yeah.' And he said, 'Something really awful?' And I said, 'Yeah.' And he said, 'Would you like to go onstage and talk about it?' And I said, 'Sure.' So that night he went to Budd and told him that I would go on ahead of him and I went up and talked about how this other fellow had dumped me because he wanted a tiger in bed and then I happened to go to his house and there was this girl who was everything I should have been and I was so depressed, I went home and took a bottle of Empirin with codeine and tried to kill myself and then I had to go to the emergency room and they gave me this stuff that made me gag and gag and gag—all these pathetic details. And then I got off and Andy went up right after me and he told a pathetic story about how he had become an alcoholic and his wife and kids had left him and he was now living in the street and asked the audience for spare change and who knows what else. Then he went up to Budd afterward and said, 'What did you think?' And Budd said, 'I don't have time for this.' "

Early on, he would also bring Wendy to a benefit for Cedars-Sinai Medical Center at the Beverly Hilton Hotel, where Carl Reiner was

being honored as Man of the Year and they did something at the dais
before a room full of doctors in tuxedos and wives in evening gowns and
George was there and so was Norman Lear and Rob Reiner and others
and whatever they did—a song or something, nobody would remem-
ber—it was awful and the room was silent and Carl Reiner sat morti-
fied throughout— "Nobody laughed," *he said.* I don't know what the
hell it was. I wanted to crawl under the table as it was happening. I
had to avert my eyes. Nobody can describe it because everyone was
afraid to look. If people weren't in tuxedos, they might have hit him."
And Andy knew that he had died at the Cedars-Sinai event, that he
and Wendy had bombed most horrifically, so afterward as they were
heading for the elevators among the crowd of doctors et cetera who had
hated him, he told her to play along with him and they got into an el-
evator with the disapproving people— "And he started beaming very
happily and said, 'We were *fantastic*! Did you see that audience!
They *loved* us! We really killed!' And he kept on that way while everyone around us just glared, you know?"

He was not always Foreign Man, he was saying without saying, by
becoming other selves, trying darkness, trying surprises. But they
loved the Foreign Man—these industry people in the West, they
loved his *newness* and his *freshness* and his *cuteness*, never knowing
what he knew, which was that Foreign Man was only a small part of
his repertory company and he worried (just a little) that they only
wanted that part.

They only wanted that part.

George quickly started selling Foreign Man with notable success,
had right away gotten him a shot on a prime-time ABC-TV variety
special hosted by game show moderator Monty Hall, which aired in
mid-January, wherein Foreign Man played a doorman inviting Hall
into a tiny vacant nightclub in which Foreign Man was also the head-
waiter, the emcee (*Ladies and gentlemen, presenting in de night-*
club—Andy!), the talent (de cannonball story), and the orchestra that
followed (*I am walking down de Swanee River la la la. . . .*). A week

later, on January 23, Foreign Man debuted on *The Tonight Show*, largely because Steve Allen was substituting for Johnny Carson and Allen had been to the Improv to witness with delight the career progress of this strange fellow from the Boston hotel room. By way of introduction, he cleaved carefully to the conceit that was now becoming modus operandi, that Foreign Man could not be named Andy Kaufman, that he required special explanation in order to maintain his ruse. So Allen first spoke of the Improv as a place where *anyone* can get stage time and—"I happened to be there recently when a fellow—not really a performer—a fellow from the kitchen—a busboy or whatever—came up onstage, and he was quite entertaining, and I thought you might like to meet him. His name is just Andy. Would you give him a warm welcome and we'll see what happens. Here he is—from the kitchen!" And what followed was de traffic and de cooking and de little boy named Jesus and de Archie Bunker and then he lost his place and started over with de traffic and de cooking, then *but right now I will like to do for you de music record* and he closed with Mighty Mouse which was met with bemused good cheer but not with the frisson of discovery that had charged through Studio 8H in New York three months earlier on *Saturday Night*, which worried him (just a little), and yet he had now been on *The Tonight Show* and that was ever its own greatest reward.

Happily, he was back in New York that February, where on the last Saturday of the month he returned to *Saturday Night,* appearing toward the middle of the broadcast after host Jill Clayburgh had selected four unwitting audience members to climb onstage and participate in the television debut of Old MacDonald. He wore a dark coat and tie with sneakers and a straw farmer's hat and voicelessly (again) pushed and pulled the genuinely stagestruck/giddy foils to and from the dead microphone where they gobble-gobbled and oink-oinked and viewers connected with their helpless giggling pantomimes and his bouncy letter-perfect control and it was all very pure and exciting, a manipulation that became instantly unforgettable. (He later explained the universal response to this particular feat— "There are no punchlines in it or in anything I do. It's more like you're laughing at Old MacDonald because it's a concept, because these grown people are playing a game with me, and we're having fun together, which I guess is funny. But I don't expect anyone to laugh.") And, again, he had left an artful imprint on the upstart comedy program—again, with a birthday party bit forged in his Great Neck den—which would now have to resonate for a while, since he would not return to *Saturday Night* until the following January, since Foreign Man was needed in California, where the importance and impact of *Saturday Night* would remain in question for some time to come.

He waited while George hatched new plans for him, which meant much work at the Improv, where comic actor Harvey Korman became enamored of Andy and of Jay Leno and brought his friend Johnny Carson in to see them and this of course was not unlike bringing the mountain to Muhammad, if not more so, because Johnny Carson was king, unimpeachably such, and could shift the course of an entertainer's life by dispensing one wink and pressing his thumb to forefinger which meant okay-penultimate, which meant fortune and/or sitcom would follow most certainly. (It had worked that way already for New York club alums Freddie Prinze and Gabe Kaplan, who respectively starred in hit shows *Chico and the Man* and *Welcome Back, Kotter.*) Andy, of course, knew this and was oblivious to this and having Carson there was, um, fine. And Johnny watched and laughed at both men—the one with the big jaw who would years later take his desk and the one with the foreign accent who futzed and banged drums—and told Budd Friedman, "Yes, they're funny, but they don't have six minutes." Friedman would remember, "Ironically, Jay did ten minutes and Andy did like fourteen"—but what Carson meant was six isolated minutes of imperviously packaged punchlines that would work on *The Tonight Show.* "Johnny wanted more jokes, less attitude," said Leno, who was dejected, but Andy was less so since he had already appeared on Carson's program, albeit sans Carson. Anyway, George soon lured comedy writer-producers Bob Einstein and Allan Blye to the club, knowing that they were in the process of creating an inventive variety series for Dick

Van Dyke to be part of NBC's fall television schedule. They decided without pause that Foreign Man had great possibilities and envisioned him in a running gag wherein he would interrupt and annoy Van Dyke week after week with eemetations and jokes and music records and so they invited him to come perform his material for the star and writing staff and somehow he felt compelled to read aloud from *The Great Gatsby* at the outset of the meeting, which came at the end of a long day, which had the writers and Van Dyke shooting baleful daggers at the two producers throughout the recitation. "I thought the guys were going to kill Andy first and then kill us," said Blye. "Dick thought we had lost our minds," said Einstein. But nobody left (though there was some movement toward doing so) and Foreign Man set aside the reading in order to weep and to play congas and to exude innocence and Van Dyke began to laugh—"Why I laughed I don't know," he would remember. "He was strangely psychological. He liked to lead you one way and then suddenly turn the tables around and make you angry. And then vice versa."

George nailed down a deal to have him appear in all thirteen episodes the network had ordered of *Van Dyke and Company*, which debuted September 20 and left the air due to low ratings on December 30 and won an Emmy award in the category of variety programming nonetheless. Tapings commenced in late summer and he was introduced in the first episode as pink-jacketed Mr. Andy, finalist in a Fonzie look-alike contest, placing second behind a strapping African-American fellow, about which he protested to Van Dyke—*But he don't even look like de Fonzie! I think you don't like me you make fun of me because I am from another country!* And to appease him Van Dyke grudgingly allowed him to *do a song or a joke so I can be on de television* and every week thereafter he returned during moments most inopportune—*but-but you said I could come back*—to vex Van Dyke, who would angrily relent to each transgression, often humiliated in the presence of such guest stars as John Denver and Carl Reiner and Chevy Chase and Lucille Ball, who declared, "I know who this young man is—I've seen him on your show many times and I think he's just sensational," before she too stormed off in a mock huff. And after each prickly on-air negotiation with Van Dyke, Mr. Andy the Foreign Man proceeded to expend his complete inventory of surefire bits, performing Mighty Mouse and Old MacDonald and Pop Goes the Weasel and a record of a clucking operatic chicken and all Caspian folk songs and two numbers in which he led a faux-tribal percussion consortium called the Bay City Street Conga Band while singing the Disney anthem "It's a Small World" and, on another week, the novelty tune "I Go Mad When I Hear a Yodel" (throughout which he yodeled to conga beats) and he also did three Elveece transformations and countless eemetations and Bombings and Cryings and all of his jokes with de punches—and he arguably became the most popular element of the show. One week guest Freddie Prinze surprised Van Dyke by donning the pink jacket and lugging out the phonograph and saying *Tenk you veddy much I would like to do for you some eemetations*, which further evinced the character's happy saturation upon the audience. But he knew that he was corrupting his material by lending it to a context not of his own design, diluting the emotional comic-drama of each piece just to rankle the star who was gamely pretending to lose control of his own show. Einstein was forced to constantly assuage him—"You had to spend time with Andy to convince him to take what he did and put it in a form that made sense to the show. There had to be a reason for him to come out and interrupt Dick, rather than just introduce him as a stand-alone player. And we needed Dick to participate in some of his material, which no one had ever done before. So Andy was very concerned."

Therefore, most of his off-camera hours on taping days were spent in the quieter corridors of NBC's Burbank headquarters, where he sat on a pink blanket and meditated. Van Dyke would vividly recall the instance of a heated exchange with staff members outside their studio during which "we looked down and there was Andy on his blanket in the middle of the hall meditating. We didn't disturb him at all. He never blinked an eye or seemed to even know we were there. But he was extremely shy, very polite, very respectful. He very rarely said anything unless he was spoken to."

✻ ✻ ✻

Clifton was called upon to obfuscate the sweet-chirping-tenking-dithering-whirlwind of it all which showed no sign of slowing. The little innocent fellow was once again pushing doors open, the largest doors he had ever known, and this was fine but also terrifying because he wanted to display more of his secret people and nobody wanted anything inside of him but the cute one—George said he would have to let Foreign Man establish him and keep on establishing him because not everybody watched every program on which he appeared and there were plenty of forums to repeat his bits and stars were only made on their ability to deliver and deliver with familiar consistent material—and it just didn't feel right. But it had to be right. He meditated in the deep silences to quell the fears and really what did he have to fear? Becoming famous? But still Clifton was needed—at the Improv, at least, certainly—but Clifton was never far and had already been screaming at rude and boisterous neighbors from the veranda of the Bay Street apartment he had taken in Santa Monica with a TM friend named Andy Dickerman. "He would be yelling things like, *'Hey, I got some chickies here and I need some quiet so put a sock in it over there already because I'm a good friend of Frank Sinatra's and know some people you don't wanna know if you know what I mean!'*" said Dickerman. "He did it even when the situation didn't really require it, when people weren't all that noisy. I think he was just practicing his stuff." And Clifton was back at the club with a vengeance while Foreign Man made hay on television, and California crowds truly loathed him. Said Budd Friedman, "I became an expert on body language from behind because I'd watch the men's shoulders to see if they were going to attack Andy, or Tony, onstage. I'd come up behind them and go, 'No no no, it's only a joke!'"

And, of course, there was no Andy when there was Clifton, which became an increasing irritant to comics who had dwelt in trenches with him long enough to feel deserving of conspiracy rights. Freddie Prinze entered the club one night, saw Clifton, said, "Hey, Andy"— and Clifton lurched for him and said, *"That's Clifton, punk! It's Tony*

Clifton! It's guys like me who made it possible for young punks like you to get on television! You should have some respect! It's Tony Clifton!" And he poked and poked at Prinze's chest while he harangued until Prinze grabbed Clifton's wrist and threw him face-first against the wall and wrenched the wrist upward and upward into his vertebrae and pounded Clifton's head against the plaster, and another voice desperately emerged from Clifton's mouth, screaming, "It's Andy! It's Andy! I'm Andy, okay?!" Jay Leno would also greet Andy every time he saw Clifton, who always sputtered back, *"I don't know who Andy is, punk!"* Leno finally tried a different tack—"I decided to appeal to him in a way that would provoke any comedian: I told him that somebody stole his act. I said, 'Hey, Tony, when you see Andy, tell him I saw a guy last night at another club doing the whole Tony Clifton bit! Same mean-spirited bad singing—everything! It was unbelievable.' Suddenly, Tony's eyes turned into Andy's eyes, and they were full of panic. Then I heard Andy Kaufman say, 'What guy? Where did you see this?' I cracked up—'Aha! Gotcha, Andy!'"

Clifton found a regular Los Angeles foil—which meant someone to play poor sympathetic schlub whom he could call up onstage to insult and douse with a glass of water, thus incite audience venom— in the person of Mel Sherer, a rotund (*Hey, fatso, c'mere*) comedy writer for Rich Little and Jimmie Walker who shared Andy's surrealist bent, which was established upon their first meeting at the Improv. Andy said *hello* and Mel said *hello* and Andy said *hello* and Mel said *hello* and Andy said *hello* and Mel said *hello* and Andy said more *hello*s and Mel paused and said more *hello*s and then Andy said *hello?* and Mel paused even longer and said *goodbye* and walked away and they started working together the next day, which meant Andy would go to Mel's apartment and bounce ideas off him. One day as they worked, Mel's phone rang and Andy answered the phone as Clifton and it was a woman friend of Mel's from the East Coast who was coming to visit and Clifton kept her on the phone and poured on the charm (such as it was) and invited her to his place in Santa Monica and she accepted and he rushed home to greet her as Clifton, clad in a bathrobe, and told her he was taking her to the beach and he changed into a suit and tie and he grabbed some towels and they went to the beach, which was empty—all of which Andy later told Sherer—"And he said they had to find the perfect spot on the beach, so he made her move the towels at least fifty times and he was still fully dressed in his suit. Finally, they settled a spot under the lifeguard tower and he said, 'Okay, let's go now,' and they left—and she just went along with it for some reason. They went back to his place and he said, 'Do you know anything about the Belva Tessel?' And she said no. He said, 'Well, it's a Swiss massage thing and you do it in the shower. You wanna see what it's like?' And she said okay and they took off their clothes and got in the shower and he just started making up this massage technique. Finally, of course, they ended up having sex, which was the point. The next day, she called me and said, 'I really liked your friend Tony.'"

And his boyhood yearnings for women and their supple flesh had grown exponentially in California (along with his early television renown) and he dated as many women he could attract with his innocence and his awkward lovability and, though he preferred being some form of himself as he won their affections, there were instances (he said) in which he spent nights or weekends of carnality without shedding the cloak of Foreign Man. He squired various TM women or actresses, taking them to see late showings of *The Texas Chainsaw Massacre* (which he loved) and to vegetarian restaurants and to Chinese restaurants and to Duke's coffee shop for chocolate cake and to Disneyland and Knott's Berry Farm to repeatedly ride the roller coasters—and, because he didn't have a car, Little Wendy usually chauffeured obligingly. "As soon as he started going out with a woman, he would say, 'Now, don't get serious!'" she would recall. "Some of them got really insulted. He also liked to tell them that he was really special and that he couldn't have a serious relationship because he had so many big plans. He once told me that *this much tongue*—like a half inch—makes all the difference. In other words, once he put that extra half inch into a kiss, it changed the whole dynamic of the relationship. He *hated* that he needed to be with women, because he didn't like the mind games they played with him. Which I guess was sort of ironic, wasn't it?"

Cindy Williams, the actress who had just begun acquiring fame as Shirley in the ABC-TV sitcom *Laverne and Shirley*, met him at the Improv that autumn and had already been smitten with his work on *Saturday Night*. "From the moment I first saw him [on the program], I just wanted to be a part of whatever that mirthful wonderful magic was that he did," she would recall. And he was not opposed to letting her peek behind his facades (because, after all, she was getting famous too and was very extremely pretty) and they began a casual mirthful affair over the course of weeks that grew into an easy friendship and she would drive him to the Improv and he would meditate in her car and sometimes he would get into Clifton character at her home before going to the club, which never thrilled her. "I couldn't *stand* Tony Clifton," she said. "He'd say, 'Once I'm this character, I'm not going to come out of it.' There was a tinge of scariness about that. I couldn't find the delineation and he wouldn't betray it. I'd threaten him—'You either stop being Tony right now or I'm not giving you a ride or I won't go grocery shopping with you! That's it!' I hated it." She would pull his hair and once punched him in the stomach to make him stop. "He could get a lot more out of me if he'd be Elvis. His private Elvis made me melt—it just superimposed itself over him. I'd say, 'Let Elvis try to seduce me.'" But he brought her to the club on New Year's Eve to heckle Clifton—"Oh! And I want you to do it with your French accent," he instructed, "and when you jump on Tony's back, you should bite his ear"—and she did as told and shrieked from her table "in this terrible French accent" and called him a *muzz-aire fuck-aire* and pounced and bit and was so grotesquely shrill that the audience hated her more than they hated him. "When it was over, Budd Friedman took us aside and said, 'Out! Both of you! Out, now!'" Shortly thereafter in New York, he enlisted her to go-go dance behind him at Catch a Rising Star while he sang "Oklahoma"—whose execution he had recently perfected by performing it while bouncing up and down and throwing his fist into the air slightly ahead of and behind the relentless beat, which elicited laughter that had/had not surprised him. Anyway, the supplementary effect of a go-go dancing television actress—"doing the jerk and the hitchhike"—seemed to overwhelm the crowd. "They were," she said, "like, stunned."

So they wanted Foreign Man so they got him. *Van Dyke and Company* was gone, but he was not and, throughout 1977, the ingratiaton crusade marshaled itself across the landscape without mercy, beginning by way of bombardment. He returned to Philadelphia to appear with Mike Douglas and cohost Bernadette Peters on January 12 and Douglas introduced him to viewers with reference to the Van Dyke show as "a visitor in our country" and he sat down, still draped in his makeup bib, and indicated that he had seen the horror film *Carrie* the night before—*thees little girl nobody like her and at de end they make fun of her and but then she kill everybody*—and he read aloud from a children's Dick and Jane book, as Douglas helped him with difficult words like *funny*, then discussed his way with women, telling Peters, *If I went with you I would open de door*, and he performed Mighty Mouse. Three nights later, he was back at last on *Saturday Night*, now well into its second season, and announced after eemetations of President Carter (*Hello I am Meester Carter President of de United States*) and of his Aunt Esther (*You come eento de house right now*) that he would do de Elveece, which he had never done on the program, the mere mention of which drew approving hoots and yays from the audience, which was an altogether new phenomenon (nightclubs notwithstanding). He wore the sleek new rhinestone-studded black jumpsuit with vast white winged collar that had been designed for the Van Dyke appearances and he sang "Love Me" and "Blue Suede Shoes" and summoned to the performance an altogether taut electric precision rarely deployed in earlier outings and George said it was his best televised Elvis ever and would always maintain that opinion. And the following Monday, his second appearance on the daytime talk show *Dinah!* aired, wherein he was oddly introduced by Dinah Shore as Andy *Kup*man visitor-from-another-country (she greeted him on the first occasion by gasping, "My, you have such startling blue eyes!" to which he replied *tenk you veddy much*). For this appearance, taped a month earlier in Las Vegas, he unseated Marvin Hamlisch at the piano, where Dinah gathered with Bob Hope and Sammy Davis, Jr., and performed a "love song" (*Give me a keess keess keess, vy do you do me like thees thees thees?*) and made smooching noises into the microphone during which Dinah and Hope and Sammy exchanged wary glances before he became de Elveece, which forced Sammy to bend over, as was his inclination, to convulse gleefully.

And that Friday—because certain walls had tumbled, thanks to Van Dyke—Johnny Carson welcomed him onto *The Tonight Show*, noting, "This is the first time we've really met," and indulged him with a kindly measured patience usually reserved for minors or the elderly. But there he sat beside the king of the night and Grandma Pearl watched in New York and Grandma Lillie watched in Florida and Stanley and Janice watched in Great Neck and, if there had been any lingering doubt about their boy and his eccentric dreams, it vanished in this seismic moment. No showcase in America—it would be forever understood—mattered more than this showcase when Carson presided over his own program. And so he had meditated long and hard in his dressing room (with Do Not Disturb warning posted on door) before he stepped out to bask in the evanescent shimmer of great opportunity. And he was flawlessly flawed as necessity demanded. Carson asked, "Where are you from originally?"

FM: *From Caspiar. Eet's an island.*

JC: Caspiar?

FM: *Caspiar.*

[One audience member applauds as though zealous with native pride. Carson casts a surprised withering eye toward the assemblage.]

JC: *That's* a first in show business!

Which provoked a large laugh among all, perplexing Foreign Man, who clearly perplexed Carson, especially when he did not drop character during the commercial break, before which the geography of Caspiar was explained and after which came discussion of his quest for American citizenship and reading skills—he demonstrated again with a Dick and Jane recitation as Carson helped him with the word *funny*. Then he performed jokes and eemetations, losing his place with de Ed Sullivan, starting over again before chanting a cappella the Caspian harvest song and Carson said, "That's very good, Andy. Very, very amusing. You'll have to come back with us again sometime." And after the taping, Carson stuck his head into Andy's dressing room and said, "You're very funny, kid. I don't understand how you do it, but you're very funny." And Foreign Man responded *tenk you veddy much.* And Carson shook his head and winked anyway.

A week later Freddie Prinze shot himself in the head and died within forty-eight hours and fellow comedians grieved and Andy did not want to think about it and chose not to attend the funeral—where fellow comedians flocked—because he did not want to think about it. He had by this time become a boarder in a big house above the Sunset Strip owned by actress Joanna Frank, sister of rising television writer Steven Bochco, and he took a bedroom next to Joanna's and people came and went—TM people predominantly, since Joanna was one as well—and Joanna's ex-paramour Richard Beymer, the actor who played Tony in the film *West Side Story*, lived in the basement. Joanna Frank experienced Andy as an uncommunicative narcissist unwilling to give more than passing nods; she fully engaged his interest only once, when he quizzed her about a cleansing diet she had begun—"He was fascinated with the way the bowel movements happened and what came out." She would remember another conversation—a soliloquy, really—in which he told her, "I always knew that I wanted to be in the entertainment field. And what I was looking for was a place where no one else was doing what I was gonna do. I didn't want competition. I knew that I really couldn't compete. I had to find something that was not being done." Ultimately, she could not find humanity behind his eyes—"I don't think Andy's heart was very developed at all. His mind was developed and he was crafty. He had this total single-pointedness, this obsession with himself, with his work—he didn't have any off-moments like normal people do, when you're just a person. He was always *on,* he was always doing

The Andy Kaufman Show no matter where he was. And he was always using people for his end result." So he would have Mel and
Little Wendy come over to the house, because he wanted to try something completely new, he wanted in fact to mount his own talk show
at the Improv, in which he could do what he most desired and experiment with personae, and he convinced George to make a deal
with Budd Friedman to let him take over the club for three succes-
sive Saturday nights, beginning at two-thirty in the morning, and perform a faux broadcast for club patrons only, and the show would be
called Midnight Snacks (since it would be nearly midnight in Hawaii
and parts of Alaska, which was the pretend target viewership).
Richard Beymer, who was a fledgling filmmaker among other avoca-
tions since his acting career had somewhat stalled, agreed to videotape the shows as well as loose rehearsals at the house and Joanna
agreed to be a guest on one show and Mel would direct and aspiring
comedy writers Merrill Markoe and Cheryl Garn asked if they could
help and were made "producers." Said Markoe, "I certainly wasn't
writing for him—nobody could write for Andy Kaufman. You could
suggest. But he had to just ad-lib and do his own thing." Everyone
would receive one dollar as payment for their participation, since
George said that would compensate for all binding rights to the material just in case anything of value grew out of the exercise.

Midnight Snacks began on the last Saturday in February and concluded its run on the second Saturday in March and played to packed
predawn crowds and Foreign Man would do twenty minutes at the
start until Andy blinked him away and stated in his own voice, "Ladies
and gentleman—so far everything I've done for you, really, I'm only
fooling. This is really me." And during false commercial breaks, he
purposely turned monstrous and snappishly Cliftonian (minus disguise) and berated Mel Sherer—"This is Mel, our floor director. Hey,
Mel, why don't you bend down and show everybody your bald spot!
Come on, get down there and kiss my feet! Get down on your knees,
Mel!"—and Mel would sheepishly acquiesce until the break ended
and Andy would resume blissful unctuousness at his interviewing
desk, which was noticeably several inches above the guest chairs

which were peopled with his revolving platoon of plants whom he either ignored or forced to wrestle with each other (Markoe and another woman grappled, much to his delight, in the second show) or humiliated or openly flirted with or instructed to take naps. "You know," guest Joanna Frank told him onstage, "in all the time I've known you, this is the first time I've ever really been able to sit and talk with you. I just feel like you ignore me all the time. It's like your eyes get all glazed over and you twitch your nose whenever I look at you." (He squirmed and barely defended himself and later said that he liked this exchange a great deal.) He also introduced a segment called Has-Been Corner during which he cheerily questioned alleged show business failures so obscure as to be believable—"How did you know it was all over for you?"—the first two of which were made-up characters but, on the third show, Richard Beymer consented to withstand the embarrassment. "Well, tell me," said Andy, "how does it feel to be up in front of lights after fifteen years of doing nothing?" And Beymer replied, "You're really sick, you know? You come out here and do jokes at other people's expenses! I'm *not* a has-been!" And as the finale of each show, Andy beckoned his cast to link arms onstage and sway to and fro and sing Fabian's "This Friendly World" with him (just like he had envisioned as a boy) and, when the singing had stopped and business was done, he would turn nasty again and pat Mel's stomach and say, "Hey, what are ya growin' in there? Kiss my feet, Mel!" And it was a secret to no one who knew him (as well as he could be known) that he cherished the old Elia Kazan film, *A Face in the Crowd*, in which Andy Griffith played the beloved broadcast entertainer Lonesome Rhodes who shucked-and-grinned in public and was a loathsome horror in private—and he really wanted extremely badly to star in a remake of the film once he was really extremely successful.

Foreign Man returned to *The Tonight Show* two nights before the second Midnight Snacks infraction and told Carson about it—*we have good time lots of fun and I sit at desk like you*—and also discussed his love life—*I have girlfriend but I cannot say her name because her boyfriend may get mad.* Then he went forth to display his Elveece for the first time on the program—reprising the songs he performed on *Saturday Night*—

upon completion of which he said, per custom, *tenk you veddy much* and Carson applauded with unmasked glee and cackled loudly and wiped a laugh-tear from his eye and that was the final canonization necessary to market the franchise. Mid-March, he traveled as the opening act for Sonny and Cher—now divorced but still working together—going to Honolulu (where the *Advertiser* reviewer, who referred to him as Al, wrote "I still can't figure out if Kaufman is for real, or simply a bad joke") and to San Francisco (where the *Chronicle* reviewer used words like *originality* and *hilarity* and advised readers, "Note the name"). Then he returned to Los Angeles to become the franchise.

George Shapiro and Howard West had sold him to the American Broadcasting Company with some ingenuity, and with a caveat, in that he would be the delightful Foreign Man on the network as and when needed, first in a sitcom pilot already developed to suit him and then as a guest performer on six variety specials hosted by other people (guaranteeing him $30,000 inside of one year at $5,000 per appearance whether or not he was utilized)—but, more importantly, he would be supplied a budget of $110,000 to create and produce a late-night special for himself, plus an additional $25,000 to write his own sitcom pilot. And the economics of it all meant nothing to him and he told George to call Stanley and give him the financial details, then and ever after, because he just wanted to focus on the work. On March 29 he fulfilled his first obligation and taped the pilot for a "futuristic" sitcom called *Stick Around,* in which Foreign Man was an android household servant (named Andy) employed by a most annoying family-of-tomorrow and it was an odorous endeavor beyond redemption, which the network instantly realized, opting not to turn it into a series, although the executives had liked his work as the robot. *Robot . . . oh . . . he would be a robot again . . . later . . . in three years . . . it would be a very bad thing . . . very very extremely bad thing . . . and the makeup he would wear . . . taking hours and hours to apply . . . he would look like lacquered fruit and, oh, the smell . . . and they said it would almost be like an art film . . . George even thought so . . . but . . . oh. . . .* Foreign Man then did de Redd Foxx variety special and was very funny interrupting de nightclub sketch and somehow ABC had no other variety specials for him to infiltrate for the remainder of the contract year and so there was thirty grand for a day's work, not that he understood, though George and Howard and Stanley did. And, in June, Foreign Man went with George to the production offices of the game show *The Hollywood Squares* hoping to secure a celebrity square for him to occupy and the producers were amused at the outset of the visit but grew less so as the mask did not drop and minutes passed and the pidgin-dither continued and producer Jay Redack said finally, "Well, lookit—*shit*—we're getting no place. Time is valuable here and so if you're gonna fuck around . . ." And Foreign Man was truly stunned by the outburst and George yanked him out of the meeting then sent Andy back in and Andy was perfectly congenial but said nothing of what had just transpired and got his square and George whispered to Redack afterward, "That's the first time I ever saw him break character like that!" And Foreign Man taped a week of shows for them, although he was never asked to return.

Uncle Andy's Fun House was what he wanted to call the ninety-minute special whose rehearsals would begin July 12 with taping to commence three days later at KTTV studios—but the *uncle* part seemed a bit presumptuous at this point, so it would be called *Andy's Fun House* but the network would advertise it as *The Andy Kaufman Special* but the advertising part would come much later because network entertainment president Fred Silverman was much too terrified to actually broadcast it any time during his term of office. (It would be, according to Silverman, "too avant-garde" with its oddball pacing and sly/dry moments of dead/awkward air and it would frighten dim-witted viewers, who were the viewers he seemed to prize most.) Many weeks earlier, and twentysomesuch years earlier, Andy had started writing the show. But Mel would now help him, too, and where was Bob? *Baaab? Baaaaaaab?* Back in New York, Bob Zmuda had become the preferred Clifton stooge (*You're Polish!? Hey, look at Polish here! How many Polish does it take to screw in a lightbulb, Baaaaab?*), *especially* after the Little Hippodrome went belly-up and Zmuda hired on as a bartender at the Improv, where he was ever available for plant hijinks. (His comedy partner Chris Albrecht, meanwhile, became house manager at the Improv after Budd went west.) Andy had always told Zmuda that once he became famous he would want Zmuda to write for him because Zmuda was a prankster after his own heart and had big fanciful foolish dangerous dark *ideas* and was an expert, like Andy, at altering truth and embellishing truth and disregarding truth—he said "gotcha" a lot—and he was a very sweet guy and it was a shame that he didn't meditate. "Bob is comedy *personified*," Andy liked to say. But Zmuda had disappeared from New York and George finally found him that spring working as a short-order cook in San Diego, where he had fled with his girlfriend to rethink show business. "Kid," George told him, "your ship just came in!" And so they plotted in late spring—Andy, Bob, Mel, George—and conceived a structure not unlike that of the Midnight Snacks shows in which Andy would preside at a desk even higher than before and turn Cliftonian when the cameras appeared to be off and abuse floor director Zmuda and he would reprise the Has-Been Corner with a cohort named Gail Slobodkin, who had been a child actor on Broadway in *The Sound of Music* ("Did you lose a lot of friends?"), and he would interview Cindy Williams, asking her if she had any hobbies or diseases or if she had ever been under the care of a psychiatrist and whether she was Laverne or Shirley and what her costar Penny Marshall was really like, then force her to sing "Mack the Knife" against her will. (Originally, she had rehearsed a monologue from Edward Albee's *Zoo Story* which ended with her pulling a knife and stabbing him to death on the air—but then how would he finish the show?)

Foreign Man was, of course, required to open the show, sitting quietly in a stuffed chair near a television set on which the program was to be broadcast, and blink into the camera and welcome viewers and tell them that ABC gave him one hundred thousand dollars for the special *and they told me take thees money and you can do anything you want weeth it . . . so I went on vacation weeth de money . . . I spent all de money, now I don't have any of de money left . . .* and that basically there was no special . . . *eet's not joke, I will just sit here for ninety meenutes . . .* and softly hum to himself to kill some time before leaning forward to say *now that we have lost the audience and only my friends are there, now we can watch my special.* Then Foreign Man began describing the special as he watched the television set on which Foreign Man walked onto the stage and did de act and transformed into de Elveece who wore a new and most extravagant white studded jumpsuit designed at a cost of approximately $3,500 for the show by Bill Belew, who had designed most of Elvis's costumes—and this costume was made from the very same material Belew had once used for Elvis, plus the same gems and studs, which was exciting. ("Andy asked me a million questions about Elvis," said Belew. "You could tell there was a very *pure* and *sincere* esteem, sort of an awe.") After singing "Treat Me Nice" and tenking the studio audience, he said everything that he had done so far had been fooling and this was the real him. And later he would have the audience (whom he addressed as *boys and girls* throughout) sing "The Cow Goes Moo" with him and demonstrate for them how to prepare an ice cream snack and again he would sing "It's a Small World" with the Van Dyke conga players (whose name had become the B Street Conga Band) and he and Little Wendy would sing "Banana Boat" and Nathan Richards would perform "Tie a Yellow Ribbon" (which would be edited from the show) and Tony Clifton would summon from the audience Miss Jones, his former elementary school teacher, and confront her—"*You useta tell me that I was never going to amount to anything! You always useta ridicule me in front of the class! Well, I kinda amounted to something, wouldn't you say? Wouldn't you say, huh?! How much money you makin'?*" (And this, too, would be cut.) And, in the end, all participants would lock arms and sway and sing "This Friendly World."

But the emotional zenith of the project was the appearance of special guest Howdy Doody, who was the *real original* Howdy Doody, although a second newer Doody called Photo Doody (because he photographed well) would be brought in also and it was Burt Dubrow from Grahm who made all of this happen. Andy knew Dubrow was pals with Buffalo Bob Smith, who of course was Howdy's best pal. So Andy called Dubrow and said, "You gotta do me a favor. You gotta get me Howdy." And Dubrow convinced Buffalo Bob to play along, which meant Buffalo Bob flew in to record Howdy's voice, which kept dislodging itself into phlegmy coughing spasms during the sound recording session, which frightened Andy—especially when Buffalo Bob gagged at one point and blurted, "Could I have a drink of water? My fuckin' throat is killin' me!" "Andy was mortified," Zmuda would recall. "And he wanted to get the hell out of there. This whole imaginary world he loved was being destroyed right before his eyes." And there would be the story of another scare when Andy thought he was about to meet Howdy for the first time prior to rehearsals and was so excited that he couldn't sleep the night before and then he kept asking crew people who had seen Howdy, "What's he like? What's he like?" and then he nervously approached the puppet which was not a puppet to him at all and he suddenly screamed, "That's not Howdy! That's a phony! That's Photo Doody!" And he ran to his dressing room and locked the door through which people heard sobbing and objects crashing and . . . Well, Zmuda always liked telling that story. According to Dubrow, who heard it directly from original Howdy puppeteer Pady Blackwood, who was there to operate Howdy for the special, Andy announced to all present at the outset, "Please don't show me Howdy. The first time I want to see Howdy is when we're taping." So he rehearsed with Photo Doody until the moment when cameras rolled, which was when he at last met his childhood hero, "the first star that I was ever aware of in my whole life," and there they were together in tender union with Andy not simply talking to the puppet, but delicately *relating* with it and sharing the most elemental part of his soul in the process—"Howdy, I just want you to know I've looked forward to meeting you and being able to talk with you like this all my life. And I'm finally able to and I just want you to know that I, um, love you and I can't get over what's happening right now at this moment. I can't believe it. I've wanted to do this my whole life and I wish we could talk for eight hours. I just have so much that I'd like to tell you. There's just so much to say. . . ." And his eyes seemed to mist over during much of their long, earnest exchange in which Howdy spoke of living in a box for seventeen years ("Wow," said Andy, "isn't it boring?") and thanked Andy for his countless warm sentiments and explained that Buffalo Bob couldn't be there tonight because he had some other show to do—which Andy privately believed was just as well. And at the very close of the special, Foreign Man, in his review of all that had transpired, noted, *To have de Howdy Doody . . . oh! dat was touching you know because then you think you have Howdy Doody and eet's going to be funny but eet's really serious I think eet was brilliant and Has-Been Corner, eh, dat ees bad taste, went a little too far . . . but you know lots of show ees very stupid but lots of eet was very good. . . .*

Mel would remember the coughing, how Andy coughed a lot during the rehearsals and the tapings. "He said it was nothing, just a little cold or something. But it wasn't going away and it didn't go away. I said, 'Andy, you've got to go to the doctor.' He said, 'I don't really go to doctors—I go to holistic practitioners.' He fought me and fought me on this." Anyway, he had always coughed. Everyone knew he always coughed. It was like a habit kind of. And the Crying never really helped matters—with all the bleating esophageal contractions, which were sort of brutal, so as to make the loud rhythmic *eeeeeeeppppp-eeeeeeeppppp*s that took him to the drums. But it was, of course, nothing. Everyone knew. It was, um, just a habit.

Fred Silverman said *noooooooooooooo way* would ABC broadcast that thing, even in late night, and so it just sat there and this became desperately depressing to all involved but to none more than Andy, who could not understand the concerns. "I don't know," he said. "It's not political or dirty. I tell people at the beginning to shut off their sets, but that cannot be the reason. . . . Everything I do is very innocent, very G-rated. My special could be shown on Saturday morning and appreciated by little kids. . . . Everybody tells me the Howdy

Doody piece is too long. But I loved it. Howdy Doody is my friend."
But it was, they/Silverman said, too off-the-wall and too far-out and
too whatever else and George eventually took it to NBC and Lorne
Michaels wanted to run it in the *Saturday Night Live* time slot and it
was all but a done deal when suddenly Fred Silverman became entertainment president of NBC and said *noooooooooooooo way* would
NBC broadcast that thing. But by this time he was Latka on ABC and
the new entertainment president there, Tony Thomopoulis, decided
to just put it on the air, almost without warning, at eleven-thirty on
Tuesday, August 28, 1979—and more than two years had elapsed
since it was made—and it actually slightly outrated *The Tonight Show*
on NBC. And the critics who wrote about it seemed to mostly admire
it although lots of them also seemed a little worried about Andy. Janet
Maslin in *The New York Times* called it "a generally crisp, often very
funny program that in no way endangers Mr. Kaufman's comic elu-
siveness. When any of the several characters Mr. Kaufman imper-
sonates here suddenly proclaims himself 'the real me,' rest assured
that he is lying." But then Marvin Kitman in *Newsday* called the
Howdy segment "embarrassingly private" and said the show was "vin-
tage 1977 Kaufman, before he started to turn." (*Oh!*) But then Kay
Gardella in the *New York Daily News* called him "a comedian whose
star is rising faster than his comedy repertoire. . . . You get the uneasy
feeling when you're watching him that he's going to run out of gas
before the show ends. . . . What he needs is more material." But then
Howard Rosenberg in the *Los Angeles Times* said it was "absurdity
carried sometimes to the point of brilliance, sometimes to the point
of tedium. . . . Watching this for a while, it becomes obvious . . . Andy
Kaufman should be wearing a straitjacket." But, of course, they were
saying those things more than two years later.

Elvis would die twelve days after this—which was Andy's August
4 appearance with Johnny Carson which would be his final appearance with Johnny Carson—which was the first time that he was the
real him on *The Tonight Show*. Carson could not seem to connect

at all with the real him. "It's a little difficult to explain what Andy does," Carson said by way of introduction. "He will do it when he comes out." So he came out with eemetations and Elveece and threw pieces of the new white costume into the crowd until he got down to the I LOVE GRANDMA sweatshirt (which Pearl and Lillie separately kvelled about, *Wearing it, can you imagine, in front of Johnny like this?*) and then his eyes became vacant and wandered into and around the cosmos and he sat and talked (hesitantly) with Carson who mentioned the night Harvey Korman first brought him to see Andy (neglecting to share his initial appraisal) and then Carson asked if that foreign character made him feel more secure (since this real him character did not seem so secure since Carson was having to pry spontaneity and remedial discourse out of him) and Andy said, "Well, sometimes." (Panel chatter with comedians was never so damned stymied as this was.) And, after a little more genial awkwardness, Carson seemed most eager to send him over to his conga drums for a harvest song after which he was gone. Mercifully. Carson later relayed to his producers, not in an ambiguous way, that maybe Andy would be better off visiting with guest hosts in the future.

And then Elvis died.

Kathy Utman—whose voice produced bells in Andy's head and who was put on Earth to spread love—was ending a marriage and had moved to Los Angeles where she hovered near, as was their implicit spiritual arrangement, and she often drove him places. And on August 16 they were in her car heading to the airport because he was leaving for New York and it was a lugubrious day, thick and dark and wet, and they were taking the shortcut down La Cienga Boulevard— "It was really raining hard, which isn't so common in L.A. Andy was driving and then we heard it over the news on the radio. First we didn't believe it and then we were crying. It was a moment that sticks in my mind so clear and so sad. And we kept driving. And he kept looking at me through his tears and saying, 'It's not true. It can't be true. It's not true. It couldn't be true.' It was just so sad to him."

And California rain kept pouring down.

* * *

The man and lady who adopted her never called her Laurel, of course, but named her Maria—Maria Bellu (kind of like Priscilla Presley's maiden name and also kind of like Elvis's costumer)—and she was a happy little eight-year-old who knew she had another mommy and another daddy somewhere about whom she was certainly curious and she lived not so far from Great Neck, in Roslyn, and she had large wonderous eyes, everyone thought.

The father she never knew, meanwhile, would talk about her, not terribly often, but often enough, to very few people, and some of them imagined that he was simply in character, some character, some character that required a specific paternal history, but he said that he was glad that he had brought a child into the world but wished he hadn't made the mistake under such youthful circumstances. And he hoped she was okay. He told Mel that maybe when he got really really famous he could find a way to get in touch with her. Mel told him (or told that character) that he would have made a very interesting father.

The real him thing continued and he deployed it as almost a passive-aggressive strike against the show business pigeonholing that had been subsuming him. (The real him, of course, was not the real real him, except in voice and eye movement; the real real him was the existential puppeteer who decided what would happen whenever people were looking.) Late that summer at the Improv, he taped the Second Annual Young Comedians Special for the cable network Home Box Office and he sent the real him to the stage after the prop comic Gallagher had bludgeoned a watermelon with a sledgehammer and later on he sent Tony Clifton to the stage before a manic new improvisational artist named Robin Williams closed the show. But first, the real him enthusiastically stepped forth and said, "Thank you very much. Right now I'd like to do a comedy routine. [At the mere notion of which the audience laughed savvily.] Up to now, every time I've appeared someplace I always do that Foreign Man character that I do.

And I'd like to branch out, you know, do myself. So . . . so, you know the baseball season is with us and this reminds me, last year I was in New York in the baseball season and I went to Shea Stadium one night to watch the Mets play. And these two old ladies were walking in the stadium, they were carrying their own liquor and they were drinking throughout the game. By the middle of the game they were so drunk they couldn't see the scoreboard. So they made up their own score and this was what they came up with—bottom of the fifth and the bags were loaded. [Mild bemused laughter from crowd] But . . . but you know, speaking about baseball and sports . . ." The material, of course, got even less coherent and less amusing and his real eyes darted and he finally paused at great length and he heaved the sighs of crisis as people laughed. Then: ". . . Um, I don't understand one thing . . . no, seriously . . . Why is everyone going *boo* when I tell some of the jokes and then when I don't want you to laugh, you're laugh-ing, like right now? I don't understand. . . . [Real eyes now grew wet as he became more disconsolate.] Ladies and gentlemen, thank you. I think I . . . it's not working, so . . . I think . . . thank you and I'm sorry and there's other acts and so I really shouldn't have done this. . . ." And, after further apology and stalking offstage in shame, he returned and Conga-Cried his way into various harvest songs (doing slick gib-berish audience patter in between—as though he were Foreign Man's more uninhibited brother, Conga Man, working the Borscht Belt) then left to exuberant applause and walked to the corridor at the rear of the club where he pushed a hand into the faces of everyone stand-ing there.

Clifton emerged later in his black suit and clip-on bow tie with the greasy mustache and hair waxed down and he held a cigarette and clumsily opened with "Tie a Yellow Ribbon" as though it were a gift—*"What's so funny? I'm not up here for my health, all right?"*— then began his attack—*"Ya know, I'm not useta playing small places like this. I'm doing it as a favor! So if you wanna be a good audience, I'll sing for you, I'll tell you some stories, we'll have some fun. You wanna be a bad audience, I'll walk right outta here!"* As ever, all such threats were met with much applause and, as ever, Clifton persisted—brought up audience members, including Mel and Bob, to join him in the syncopation chestnut, "If You're Happy and You Know It Clap Your Hands," which fell to ruins when Zmuda got the glass of water dumped on his head and later a female heckler took bait—"*What are you, women's lib? I'll push your face right in your drink!*"—and jumped Clifton, who ended his set declaring, "*I just want to say—If I could make one person happy tonight, it's all been worth it.*" (Mel and Bob waited in the corridor afterward and physically assaulted him on camera as final punctuation.)

And Robin Williams finished the event, having to follow the mayhem that was Andy, whom he had gotten to know somewhat through Elayne Boosler (the three of them had gone to see Chief Jay Strongbow wrestle at Madison Square Garden—"He loved the good-versus-evil phenomenon," Williams recalled, "that people believed enough to hate the supposed bad guys up there"). And on this night, and the few others that he found himself following Andy to a stage, he was fascinated to encounter the condition of the crowd in aftermath. "It was like walking into a vortex. The audience all looked like deer in front of a Peterbilt semitrailer. They had that stunned expression, where the mouth drops all the way down to the table like in the Tex Avery cartoons. Andy once ate a meal onstage, saying nothing while he ate and the audience stared at him. And Clifton was the extreme—the ultimate nasty side of show business, the dark side—Jersey meets Vegas. Andy toyed and toyed with every possible facet of human reaction. Like a Fisher-Price Laser—be careful how you play with it."

Deck shuffled accordingly, with deeper purpose. Real him was introduced October 15 by host Hugh Hefner on the *Saturday Night* stage (emblazoned with large Playboy rabbit symbol) and, bouncily, he stepped out to execute "Oklahoma" and sat at piano to lead audience in "The Cow Goes Moo" and stood to become Elvis—without explanation or segue—and performed "I Need Your Love Tonight," which was his very first favorite Elvis song and this was his unspoken tribute to his dead hero and, afterward, he made sure to get the phone number of the Playboy Mansion from Hefner's people and Hefner would remember him as being "an unusual cat." A week later Clifton opened several shows for him at the Comedy Store—Mel had long urged the idea upon him of hiring Clifton for just this purpose. (Zmuda rudimentarily sculpted putty onto Clifton's cheeks, jowls, nose, chin so as to better obscure certain realities that lurked beneath. Also a black roadkill toupee was thatched to his head.) And, as a second opening act, the local services of Michel Bernath's Beginning Tap class were enlisted, which filled the stage with a dozen multiaged hoofers whose heart exceeded talent but spread good cheer in any case. **(Very unusual opening act, but that is something that excites me about Andy,** said Shapiro, later recalling the moment in his audio-diaries. **Of course, he tries things that were never tried before.)** Lily Tomlin was in one audience and, she later confessed, had worked her way through a bottle of champage, with which Clifton did not sit well, so she heckled him and Clifton told her to go to the kitchen and make the babies. She persisted during Andy's portion of the show, protesting when he bade Little Wendy to sing "Davy Crockett" with him—"*Misuse of women!*" she screamed—and also hollered when he recited his Jewish-dialect version of "MacArthur Park"—"*You're a great artist; you don't need approval!*" "By which he was duly mystified," reported *Rolling Stone*, whose correspondent spoke with him afterward. (Tomlin finally stormed out.) The show business bible *Variety*, meanwhile, most ebulliently reviewed the show, which ran across consecutive weekends into November—"The guy's original, and he's dynamite. . . . During the course of his two hours or so onstage, Kaufman assumes at least three distinct characters, segueing from one to another smoothly and believably; it's just as though he were three or four different performers." The review also described Clifton as "what must be the strongest example of black humor to have played the generally giggly Comedy Store; the kind of act that those who aren't totally revolted will want to return to with unsuspecting friends in tow. . . . It isn't for everybody, but what that's hard-hitting and innovative is?"

Visibly buoyant, he took the *Saturday Night* stage again December 10 wearing the blue floral Hawaiian shirt of Conga Man and slapped drums while performing his bravura imaginary tribal rant—in which he essayed the parts, in spectacular profundos and squealing glissandos, of a villain casting doom upon a helpless maiden—then continued on to banter with the audience in glib-gibberish, pulled a mortified woman onstage and attempted to levitate her (finally yanking her up by the hair), and concluded with the "Aba-Dabbi" singalong that portended a dancing jag during which he feigned an abdominal seizure. And never once throughout the appearance did he utter a discernible English syllable. Back in Los Angeles on the third day of 1978, he taped the bit all over again for an ABC special celebrating the history of *Variety* on which host Alan King called him "a young man I happened to have discovered." (In his kitchen?) Whereupon George, with the brokering assistance of star-agent Marty Klein of APA, dispatched him to the Pacific Northwest on his first college tour (for which Zmuda was permanently installed as road manager and F Troop musical eminence Gregg Sutton, who had also played the Comedy Store gig, came aboard as bandleader). He then appeared in Chicago with the rock-and-roll nostalgia act Sha Na Na before returning for a *Tonight Show* spot on Monday, February 20. Steve Martin, also a client of Marty Klein, was substituting for Carson on this night. By now sanctified as the white-suited white-headed comedic demigod of a generation—his powers were such that, in 1973, he led a college audience into a McDonald's [oh!] requesting six hundred hamburgers, then at the last minute changed the order to a single bag of french fries—Martin had been introduced to Andy by Klein at the Comedy Store engagement. "It wasn't the typical backstage meeting," he would recall. "He was inpenetrable with eyes wide open, definitely in his own world. And he was allegedly being himself at the moment, so I sort of realized that he was weird."

And so Martin introduced him to the Burbank studio audience and he went directly to his drums and reprised every beat and *eebida* of his Conga man transmogrification, complete with female levitation and singalong, to equal success. "I remember observing at the time," said

Martin, who beheld all of this from Carson's desk, "that it was a classic example of anticomedy. In anticomedy, one of the most difficult things to accomplish is—once you state the premise which is funny and they laugh—you have to keep it going. That's what he managed to do for eight minutes, maybe longer. And it was funny all the way through. To me, that was the miracle. He managed to sustain it by being funny *internally* after the premise was stated. Once you go out there and start with the gibberish and they go, *Oh, it's gonna be the gibberish thing*, then you have to come up with the humor and the jokes to keep it going. That's what I thought was amazing about it—sustaining that in absolute gibberish which was known only to him but accepted by us."

But what followed when he joined Martin at the desk—where he was greeted by fellow guests Kenny Rogers, Elke Sommer and Steve Allen who proffered the word "funny" as they shook hands—was an exchange that traversed the craft of his multiplicities in an altogether new manner. Martin, upon congratulating him on the performance, began, "That character with the, uh—I don't know what kind of character it is exactly or where it's from."

AK: What, which one?

SM: The one out there that you did.

AK: Oh, no—that's really me.

SM: Ahhh. And then—

AK: The Foreign Man, you mean? That's another character.

SM: Mmmm-hmmm. So that was really you out there. And then what are you doing right now?

AK: Right now? This is really me.

SM: Oh. [Audience laughter] And then—now, what about the Foreign Man?

AK: No, that's not—that's just a character I do.

SM: Oh, I see. [Laughter] So there's two real yous, and then there's a character.

AK: Well, there's some others also—there's other real mes—but Foreign Man isn't one of 'em.

SM: I see. Where did you originate that character, the Foreign Man?

AK: In New York. [*Well, who would understand de Boston?*] I used to perform at a place called the Improvisation. . . . And I would go onstage and my act began with my Elvis Presley imitation. [Applause— *tenk you, well, who would understand de Boston?*] So then people would say: 'What is this? He thinks he's Elvis Presley!' So I—I wanted to come up with something like, innocent, so that people would like me—and then I could imitate Elvis Presley. . . . because people thought it was off-the-wall to do Elvis Presley. So I made up the character for that. [*Um, de Boston de Great Neck no really.*] And, um, I would come onstage, I'd say, *Ehh, tenk you veddy much* [Laughter, applause, *Vait-vait, oh they love thees character they don't stop de clapping*] *I am happy to be here but, ehh, ees too much traffic today took me an hour and a half to get here.* And everybody would go, 'Oh noooo . . .' Because the audience, they really believed it was true, so they would go, 'Oh no—this guy just got off the boat, he's gonna starve, he's gonna starve.' But then one person would start going [stifled giggle], you know, embarrassed. But they didn't want me to hear them laugh. So I'd hear like one person *almost* laugh and I'd go *Vait-vait until I fineesh* and they just couldn't help it—they had to laugh. So once they started laughing, I'd make like I thought they were laughing with me when, really, they were laughing at me. And the whole thing would—

SM: You actually went out to *deceive* in a sense.

AK: Yes, so they would all get embarrassed. And then—

SM: That's an interesting point of view—to *embarrass* the audience!

Three years later he would elaborate on this theory to a reporter person—"People used to be embarrassed when they saw [Foreign Man]; they'd look away, and out of that embarrassment they would start laughing. . . . Nowadays someone would see that and say, 'Oh, isn't that great—a comical foreign immigrant who tells inept jokes. What a funny *premise*.' They would see the outer—a 'funny premise'—but they would miss the whole *point*, the whole *depth* of where it came from. And where it *came* from—the drama, the sadness—is what makes it funny."

Anyway, the audience in Burbank that night laughed with-Martin-at-him and, also anyway, this was as much unmasked truth as anyone needed to consider at present, if ever.

　　He conceived another one whom he felt was as lovable as the one they all loved a little too much. So he and Zmuda wrote a pilot script for a series about this other sort of hapless fellow and this fellow's friend. ABC had promised him money as part of his deal to write such a script anyway and since they didn't like the special maybe they would consider this and so he and Zmuda wrote through most of that January and completed their final draft on February 1 for a show called Fingers and Knuckles. *The episode, entitled "Easy Come, Easy Go" (also an Elvis movie) introduced this pair of good-hearted New York street performers—one of whom (Fingers, a.k.a. Zmuda) was a savvy city-hardened operator and the other (Knuckles, a.k.a. Andy) was a sympathetic idiot whom, Andy said, had "just gotten off the bus from the Midwest." (Privately, he believed Knuckles had incurred brain damage in an auto accident, though that would not be part of the script.) But they were inseparable and often said to each other, "You can't have fingers without knuckles," and in the story Knuckles was sent to the store to buy groceries (and not cupcakes, his staff of life) and mistakenly received the wrong bag of groceries belonging to their neighbor lady Mrs. Willowbee and her winning lotto ticket was in the bag and a mean guy then tried to rob them but they subdued him and Mrs. Willowbee gave them a reward with which Knuckles acquired a mountain of cupcakes. ABC hated it. And Andy would lament long thereafter, "Knuckles is my prime creation. That's one character they will not allow on nationwide TV. . . . When they read the script and saw the Knuckles character they said, "Look, I mean, face it—this character can't make it from here to the* elevator.' *And we said, 'Yeah, that's right.' I mean, neither could Lou Costello or Stan Laurel, none of those guys could make it to the elevator. . . . But this one guy actually said to me what I think is one of the classic lines ever by a network executive. He said, 'But this is like Laurel and Hardy or something; we want something good like*

Laverne and Shirley!' *I mean, do you realize what that—? In a nut-shell, that's . . . Boy."*

Two nights after the visit with Steve Martin, Clifton returned for a three-night engagement as Andy's opening act at the Comedy Store. "Mr. Clifton requests that all cigarettes and tobacco smoke be extinguished before he will perform for you tonight," Zmuda announced to the house from backstage, whereupon customers grumbled and snuffed accordingly, whereupon the spackle-faced Clifton (eventually) stepped forth dragging fitfully on a cigarette—and fresh new hostility was minted. Four pedigreed comedy writer-producers, all former brain-trust alums of *The Mary Tyler Moore Show*, were present for one such performance, specifically to assess the potential of Foreign Man as part of a new ensemble situation comedy they had been given carte blanche from ABC to put directly onto the network air, no pilot script necessary. Their names were James L. Brooks, Ed. Weinberger, Stan Daniels and Dave Davis—all brainy TV golden boys of the highest order—and they watched Clifton and enjoyed Clifton, and George Shapiro, who knew exactly why they were there, whispered to Weinberger and Brooks, "You guys can't acknowledge this to Andy, but *he's* Tony Clifton." "And that," Brooks would recall "just blew our minds. Because we all thought of ourselves as pretty sophisticated in the realm of comedy theater—but *Jesus!*" "It never occurred to us," said Weinberger, "because we were there to see Andy." They didn't know and now they knew—and several months later they would wish they never had, but then again . . . "Clifton just upped the game for us," said Brooks. They loved all that Andy did and told him so afterward and said they would like to work Foreign Man into their yet-unwritten show as an immigrant garage mechanic for a New York taxi company and Andy looked at George and George said it sounded fantastic and that they should call with more details and Andy asked them, "Um, so you *liked* Tony?" And they looked at each other knowingly and said that indeed they had.

He would headline at the rather grand proscenium which was Town Hall in New York on March 4, a booking designed to connote certain importance, since it was the first time he would give a major concert on home turf. As ever when he returned to the metropolitan area, he headquartered himself in his den on Grassfield Road and, on the evening of March 2, he played the auditorium of Great Neck North High School, the alma mater from which he had escaped eleven years earlier—and, very secretly, very privately, he saw this as his *revenge* and he had always dreamed of this revenge, of returning to *show them* because he always knew he would show them and they had always laughed at his dreams, at his declarations of destiny; they had always dismissed and punished and ostracized him and he knew they would by sorry and he would make them sorry and so that was what he was now prepared to do. Of course, only some of the teachers were left and not many of them came to the auditorium which was crammed with students who knew he was sort of famous (certainly many of them had seen him on television). He kept Clifton away and did his own bidding and the students whooped throughout, especially whenever he said *tenk you veddy much*; the school paper reported, "They were screaming like crazy, 'Do it, Andy!' or 'You're the greatest!'" And the girls squealed for Elvis—"One girl even ran up to kiss him and Andy replied, 'I'll see you after the show, honey!'" And the boy from the paper asked him afterward if he had been a loud kid in school and he replied, "Are you kidding? I was the one voted Least Likely to Turn Out This Way." And he spoke fondly of cameras in bedroom walls and cameras in playground woods and the doppelganger boy, Alfred Samuels, and the mysterious man he had seen in Memphis when he was five who wasn't Elvis Presley no really and he noticed that everything at the school now looked much smaller to him.

Snow dumped on the city two nights later, which did nothing to thin the ranks of the capacity crowd at Town Hall, where Clifton slithered from the wings a half hour late and commenced the event. The Kaufman family proudly witnessed (although Stanley and Janice hated every second of Clifton's affront); battalions of friends and industry people were there as well. Lorne Michaels brought a small contingent of *Saturday Night* colleagues and this was to be his first significant encounter with Clifton. "It was, of course, horrible—an indulgent conceptual joke. The bad-lounge-singer notion was not terra incognita for most of us—Jo Stafford had done it as Darlene Edwards and Chuck Grodin had done one called Huck Saxony. But Andy did his brilliantly, so everyone was patient. But it was during intermission that he pulled one of the coolest moves I'd ever seen. He had left his body-pack microphone turned on in the dressing room and suddenly you heard Tony Clifton ranting to his managers about having just performed for the worst fucking audience that he'd ever been in front of. There were no more than about twenty people still in their seats—out of the eight-hundred-plus, most of whom had gone to the lobby—and we listened to this wonderful secret harangue. It was brilliant." *Variety* saw the concert as a portent of career transcendency— "This audience was way ahead of him, pleading for certain of his w.k. [well known] pieces, like 'Mighty Mouse,' 'Thank you very much,' etc. . . . There is no denying that some of the things he does are nothing short of comedic genius. [His Elvis Presley] is often so real as to be frightening. Kaufman may not be for everyone, but he has a strong cult now and, as he hones and builds support, he could become a major comedy force." The review mitigated its enthusiasm only in the matter of Clifton's performance—"too long and trying."

Which was what Uncle Sammy Denoff tried to tell him backstage afterward–before the whole family went out for Chinese food. ("What else would Jews do?") "So Andy said, 'How do you think it went, Uncle Sam?' I said, 'I think it went pretty well. But you have to rethink this whole Tony Clifton thing, because you're turning off the audience. They're not laughing at the character. The idea is to make them laugh, but it's too obnoxious.' He said, 'You're absolutely right, you're absolutely right! I'm not gonna have him back on the show. I told him he's finished!'

"So I said, 'Yeah, okay, okay . . . but I'm serious, Andy. No kidding.

Rethink it, because there's a way to do that and make it funny.' He said, 'No, you're right—he's finished. We had a big fight and I told him he was through.' I said, 'Andy! What are you—come on! Look who you're talking to here!' And he wouldn't back off and this went on for about ten more minutes until I finally said 'Pass.'"

10

I liken what I do sometimes to a life game, an adventure in absurdity, an adult fairy tale in which I engage people emotionally and intellectually. . . . I like to think people will learn something from my hijinks; that they will become a little more cautious. . . . Because the next time around, their hoaxer might truly be diabolical and rob them of things far more important and meaningful.
—Alan Abel,
The Confessions of a Hoaxer

There now awaited the imprimatur of legacy-in-shorthand. He would soon become . . . a name of a character in a thing. And thus, in all aftermath, he would most often be fuzzily remembered as having been . . . a name of a character in a thing. The name would be—give or take a letter—exactly that of a potato pancake; the character would be his but not his any longer; the thing would live on in flickers of recollection as something that had been quite good, a television series that most people had meant to watch more than they did. And this was to be his legacy-in-shorthand, that which in years to come would inform occasional blank expressions that greeted mention of his name—*ohh himmmmmmm of coursssssse*. He would know this sooner than later and it was, um, fine and also discouraging because of all else that he was and that he would do. He sensed/feared the imminent cultural shackling of it from the get-go. So he wavered at the idea of committing himself to the enterprise. *(Can't we just put Foreign Man in a trunk for a while, like Howdy?)* George, however, explained that it would be foolish not to take advantage of such a lofty opportunity— *this was going to be a very classy show without doubt; these were Mary Tyler Moore guys for God's sake*—and the money he would earn would only afford him freedom to pursue other dreams. So negotiations between Ed Weinberger and Shapiro took wing shortly after the Comedy Store encounter. The producers were to begin writing their first episode in April and they had already decided that the series would be called *Taxi*—inspired by a September 1975 *New York* magazine article, "Night-Shifting for the Hip Fleet" by Mark Jacobson, about an eccentric cab company in Greenwich Village—and among first priorities was to sign Andy to the cast. "Andy was reluctant to do the series," Weinberger said. "I mean, he wanted to do it, but didn't want to work every week; he had these other things he wanted to do." Concessions were made from the start and would continue to be made over the next five years, but first they would have to deal with the initial thirteen episodes ordered by the network. He would agree to appear in no more than eight of them—and in only one of those as a featured player; he would perform in the rest as a background novelty who blithered betwixt plot points involving the other seven principal cast members.

But there would be one more demand—"It was the deal-breaker as far as Andy was concerned," said Shapiro. "Without this, he wanted nothing to do with the show." Weinberger took Shapiro's call and listened: "George said that Andy now insisted that in at least two of the five shows that he didn't work on, we would have to hire the acting services of Tony Clifton. If we wanted Foreign Man, we had to take Clifton. I laughed. George laughed. We took Clifton. I mean, what the hell."

One week after Town Hall, here at last was British Man on the live Saturday Night broadcast, bedecked in effete plumage (black waistcoat and tie and tails and peach ruffled shirt), pacing behind host Art Garfunkel, who introduced Andy Kaufman. British Man then bent over his phonograph and tested the needle on the record of marching music which began to play, but he removed the needle and, in his thin and brisk accent, greeted the audience, which he complimented on the many bright smiling happy faces therein and starchily proceeded to inform — "They told me that since there were only about twenty or twenty-five minutes left in the show tonight, since I've been on several times before, they said that they trust me, the producers and the people who run the show said they trust me very much and that they would let me do *anything* I want and I could have the rest of the time, if it takes that long. So I was wondering what to do, what could I do to fill up this twenty, twenty-five minutes — could I sing a song? Do a dance? Then I thought, well, you know, before I've been on the show and I've done characters like the little foreign man, the foreign immigrant who goes *tenk you veddy much I am veddy happy to be here,* you know, and then I've done this American character — *Hi, I'm Andy! and hello how are you oh the cow goes moooo.* . . . But I thought instead of doing that, why don't I just come out and be straight with you and be myself. Then I thought, well, what should I do, what should I do? I was at a loss. And so I saw this book . . . and it reminded me of when I was in school, when this literature teacher gave it to me to read, said it was the greatest American novel ever written. I take issue with that — I don't believe that it is. But what I'd like to do tonight is to read it to you and then perhaps you could point out some subtleties that I might have missed — in case, if we have time to follow for discussion. It's called *The Great Gatsby* by F. Scott Fitzgerald and here it is — 'Chapter One . . . ' "

Audience coughing spasms began at outset of fourth sentence. Derision gained in surliness by last word on page, which visibly perturbed B.M. — "Now look, let's keep it down please! Because we have a long way to go and I am pressed for time!" *— then by top of second page groans of exquisite agony tore through studio —* " . . . 'Only Gatsby, the man who gives his name to this book, was exempt. . . .' Now look! If I hear one more word I'm going to close the book and forget about the whole thing!" *— and they cheered, and B.M. walked off, then walked back, resumed reading as insurrection mounted, to* *which he responded in lecture*—"I think what we need nowadays is more discipline! You know, when I was your age I used to have to walk seven miles to school! Spare the rod and spoil the child is what I say! Good half-round in the woodshed would do some of you very good!"—*Lorne Michaels now approached and whispered into his ear and retreated*—"What?! Well, I have been asked to leave, ladies and gentlemen! And I resent it!"—*and his indignation rose and he indicated that, after the reading, he had planned to reward them by playing a music record, which the audience seemed to want now, so he said that he would play it*—*after he had finished reading*—*and he reopened the book and was met with screams and after further futile negotiation he stalked over to the phonograph and set down the needle and waited through protracted hisses and skips until the sound of his voice issued forth*—"'. . . Only Gatsby, who gives his name to this book, was exempt . . .'"—*and he stood beside the phonograph and prissily gloated.*

These were now heady times, headier than ever, flush with the empowerment of conquest after conquest, such as they were, which were uniquely compliant to his vision, such as it was. He was *gotten*, was what he was. The right people *understood* him or *believed* they understood him—or at least pretended to, so as to impress their sophistication upon others. He kept hearing that word *genius* and also *brilliant* and George would hug him hard and Bob would hug him hard and everyone was rather giddy and he knew there was nothing that he could not do. Drain the Atlantic Ocean? But of course. One day, for certain; it was something he had always wanted to oversee. Or play Carnegie Hall? Um . . . yes! Maybe George could make some calls. They were all likening him to these other people named Pirandello and Ernie Kovacs ("I never saw Ernie Kovacs, but I understand that's a compliment") and Ionesco and something called Dada ("People keep mentioning that name to me. . . . I've been told my work is Dada and I don't want to know that it is") and, meanwhile, George kept saying the word *exciting* and everything truly was exciting and the ice cream was always cold and the chocolate was always thick and the roller coasters were always fast and the women were—*well* . . .

He wrestled one on his last birthday at the surprise party that Little Wendy threw at his apartment. (He had moved to La Cienega Towers, a high-rise just below Sunset where he rode the elevators with Elliott Gould, and Kathy Utman had become his mostly platonic roommate/housekeeper and Wendy had become his personal assistant, whose duties included ordering subscriptions to every female-wrestling magazine in existence, plus all other professional wrestling publications.) Bob, meanwhile, had arranged the birthday wrestling match because it was something Andy had always wanted to do. (Zmuda had seen his private collection of eight-millimeter films featuring bikini-clad women tangling with one another—the sheer sexual electricity of which—*oh!*) So it was that Gail Slobodkin—late of Has-Been Corner—and her singer friend Marilyn Rubin (on whom Andy nursed a deep crush) were called upon to wrestle each other in swimwear at the January party and he would then wrestle the victor who was Marilyn and it was all very playful except that he was very very excited by all of the rubbing between his body and hers and she stayed after the others went home that night and then he wrestled her soon thereafter onstage at an Improv event in front of people like Bette Midler and Raquel Welch and others who were appalled, none more than Marilyn herself, who lost (just barely). "A lot of people thought it was self-indulgent and terrible and everything," he said. "But I didn't care. It was a fantasy come true."

Which was to say, he believed that with all new hubris came *entitlement*—and, most of all, he believed that he was entitled to disregard. So he would now aim to seize any opportunity to disregard structure, expectation, rules. It would be part of his art—the disregarding—and it would be calculated always, never done in slipshod fashion, never executed without purpose or means to an end. And he would make all effort to become *known* for it—since, if he was known for it, then George would have less mess to clean up afterward. George could just shrug and say, "Well, that's Andy," and that would always be enough. And Zmuda had this credo that he kept imposing—"Kaufman," he would urge, "the system was made to bend, the system was made to bend, the system was made to bend"—and Andy knew that anyway because he had been bending it all along. But he and Bob together expanded his playground exponentially, removed any boundaries that might forestall whatever delicious theater-of-life escapades they elected to hatch. They would scheme always now, the two of them. Nothing much would remain very extremely sacred. Of this renegade partnership, not that it was ever to be an equal one, George had patiently observed, "Their mental age is somewhere between twelve and fifteen. When they are really sophisticated, they reach the fifteen-year-old level." And this was evident once they left New York after the *Saturday Night* extrapolations of British Man and flew to Columbus, Ohio, where Burt Dubrow was producing a local teen talk show called *Bananaz,* on which Bob was introduced as Dr. Robert Zmuda, filibustering author of a new book on the little-known science of *psychogenesis,* whose stiff windbaggery was interrupted by Andy's arrival in the studio which effectively quashed any wavering interest in Dr. Zmuda, who became increasingly ruffled and eventually lunged for Andy—*"Don't you touch me! I think that you are a phony! You are not a doctor! That man is not a doctor!"* And the teens in the audience sat mystified and the host was wholly bewildered and Dr. Zmuda was noisily ejected while Andy played congas and the show ended. After which, Andy and Bob were beside themselves. Dubrow, meanwhile, would answer to management.

In fun only fooling no really:

He was this other one for Mike Douglas in Philadelphia a few days later. He came out and sang the song "Confidence," which Elvis had sung in the film *Clambake,* but he sang it as himself and clumsily strummed along on his guitar *(With a C and an O and an N and an F and an I and a D and an ENCE! Put'em all together and what have you got . . .)* and then he led the audience in "The Cow Goes Moo" but upon sitting down at the panel with Mike and Carol Channing and Robert Goulet (again) his articulation grew huskily middle-European with a decided arrogance and suddenly he was a new self altogether who spoke of being influenced by a children's television host called Captain Jack and— *"And I thought, This is a good man for me to do. All right, I will develop this man, this character, and so I call it my American character, Andy. . . . This is not something that I want to talk about, really. Because I want people to think that it's my real voice. But because this show is interested in truth, I am talking this way. But I hope that people will just forget it, you know."* And so a program of blithe chatter fell into his stony abyss of awkwardness. Brows furrowed as he had hoped. Finally, if tentatively, Douglas asked, "Where are you from, Andy?" *"What difference does it make where a man is from? I have traveled! I was raised throughout Europe, Africa, and different countries. But what difference does it make?"* And the point of it all was to demonstrate that this was the real Foreign Man— that by merely pitching his voice into a higher nasal range, he could instill this haughty Euro-locution with gentle innocence, which was what people most enjoyed, which had brought him success in show business, even though he was now confessing to being an unlikable fraud.

Before he resumed his American character and moved to a set of cymbals on which he accompanied his own otherwise a cappella rendition of "You'll Never Walk Alone" from *Carousel*—received with muted shock—he was forced to allow Mike Douglas to disrupt his excellent flight of new disregard. Douglas, in actual sincerity, wished to pass along information that Andy had never heard before and it was perhaps the most important information that he had ever heard in any of his lives. "I wanted to tell Andy something that has nothing to do with comedy or anything," said Douglas. "I was recently with a man named Jerry Weintraub, who handles, among others, John Denver, Neil Diamond, Bob Dylan, Frank Sinatra. He also booked Elvis Presley on all of his engagements before he passed away. And he told me that Elvis told *him* that of all the people who did impressions of him—of Elvis—he enjoyed *you* the most. And I thought you'd like to know that. . . ."

*   *   *

(Oh!)

And he was in the midst of being an asshole when he heard this.

And he didn't break asshole character even as he heard this.

And he seemed to be completely unaffected by hearing this, even though the audience applauded most rousingly—they were proud of him!—and so did Carol Channing and Goulet. But he could only momentarily glaze in a fashion that no one but his intimates would recognize as a chink approximating humanness/humility/happiness before telling everyone that it would be better if they forgot that he was this new self and believed that he was really his American self because the song would work better if they forgot the other—"Please make believe," he said—and it was very extremely poetic that he sang "You'll Never Walk Alone" at that particular moment (since the lyrics were about triumphantly walking through the storm and holding your head up high and not being afraid of the dark et cetera which was all very metaphorical), although this would not occur to him, because that sort of thing never really did.

(Well, he certainly knew that Elvis had recorded the song eleven years earlier and it was released as a single on Easter of 1968 and it didn't do very well, but it sounded really inspiring when sung only with battering cymbal accompaniment the way he was doing it now. Also, he tried to sing it with soaring gospel inflections just the way Elvis had.)

*   *   *

It began in earnest on April Fool's night in Tucson, Arizona, whereupon they had discussed the possibility of trying this before, but now—because they were on the road and it would offer new means to interact with women—they decided that the time was right. He wanted to rub against a body onstage, he told Bob. About an hour into the act, the gauntlet was thrown. "We decided to offer five hundred dollars—make it really big, so as to get the women up there," he said. He had adopted Clifton's appraisal of the feminine species to goad them toward entwining with his body. They were, he hectored, only good for raising the babies and washing the carrots and peeling the potatoes and such. He would wear white long johns with black shorts pulled over them, since Bob told him he should never do it bare-chested, what with the acne on his back which Bob said was disgusting. Anyway, he picked one—they *hated* him, the ones who had come onstage for the money and the challenge—and he pinned her certainly but while they were rubbing he told her to come backstage after the show. And it would always work this way.

Only one of the characters would be a career cab driver and the others would be different things but they drove cabs to make ends meet—there would be a boxer and an actor and a transplanted country bumpkin and an art gallery receptionist (the only female)—and then there would be the dispatcher who was a little rat. Also, there would be the mechanic who always wore coveralls and spoke in his own indiscernible language and was relentlessly innocent and adorable. . . .

He purified himself in every way. The diet, of course, was full of mulches and grains and weeds and sprouts and broths and curds and juices and herbs—all of which certainly balanced and purged the chunks and mounds and nuggets and bowls of chawwklitt . . . he called it chawwwwwwwkkklitttttttt and his eyes would dance at the sight or mention of it. He washed his hands rather obsessively, too. The more famous he became, the more people wanted to shake hands with him (he was never very good at this, kind of a limp grasp) and he would never touch food if someone had touched his hands, so sometimes in restaurants where people would come over to greet him repeatedly, he would have to keep getting up from the table and going to the bathroom to rewash his hands before he could eat again. And always in restaurants he dipped his utensils in his glass of water and rubbed them vigorously with his napkin before deigning to eat with them. He tried to will his bowel movements never long after eating; he sat and waited for results no matter the duration of digestion. (People got annoyed about this.) He took lots of vitamins before meals (like Mommy taught him) and he would line up the pills in careful meticulous rows then consume them in special order. He did this with almonds and cashews as well—lined them up, ten at a time, and ate them accordingly. (Nuts were sort of sacred.) He liked order just like Daddy did, really. He liked things to be exactly where they were supposed to be. He would scream if somebody moved his pen. He used a different toothbrush for every day of the week except Sunday. He did not like anyone to come into contact with his beddings unless the person was unclothed—the female person, of course—because clothes carried contaminants. (He said this but his motives were clear enough.) Sex was a problem because he loved it with an ardor unmatched—he and Bob sniffed for it on the road like desperate bloodhounds—but he felt that it darkened his spirit and tainted his innocence. To combat the creeping impurity of his powerful urges, he sometimes sent Foreign Man to prostitutes in West Hollywood—there was this storefront setup on Santa Monica Boulevard near Crescent Heights that he knew well. He once even had Little Wendy drive him there and go in with him while Foreign Man negotiated—this was a very pure idea, he thought—then she waited to drive him home afterward and Wendy would remember that the prostitute was not amused in the least by Foreign Man and he emerged worried for his enlightened soul in any case—"We went back to his apartment and he lit incense and did a little TM puja ceremony to cleanse his spiritual self." Anyway, he had scheduled to go on a long Age of Enlightenment Governor Training Course in San Jacinto,

California—from April through much of June. And there he would rekindle his purity and become an actual Governor in the TM hierarchy and he would learn yogic flying, which was kind of like levitating, but more like hopping while seated in lotus position, and it created the most positive energy waves imaginable, and he needed to be positive since he was going to begin work on this television series immediately after the Fourth of July, and he was not at all thrilled about it.

From the start, he kept his distance. He showed up at Paramount on the fifth of July for the first read-through of the first script of the first episode and the actors—they were a lively collegial bunch making with the nervous well-meaning jokey backslapping camaraderie of nascent team endeavor—couldn't get a fix on him. They pumped his fishy palm and searched in vain for connective light in his eyes and gathered the full spectrum of his social grace—*um oh hi fine very good thank you*—which was further strained by the fact that he wore headphones that first day and seemed to be listening to something on a portable tape machine. (Danny DeVito, who was cast in the role of the Napoleonic cab dispatcher, Louie DiPalma, was the only one who ventured to ask what he was listening to and Andy passed him the headphones and DeVito heard tribal chanting.) Foreign Man had been named Latka Gravas by the consortium of Brooks-Weinberger-Daniels-Davis because they, as producers/creators, thought it would be funny and yet not unbelievable. And so it was and he accepted this without any greater qualm than the overriding qualm of having taken this job to begin with. (George said he would get $10,000 for every episode in which he deigned to appear and the money would increase if the series continued.) Latka, meanwhile, was conceived to be something akin to the grease-monkey mascot of the Sunshine Cab Company garage, the concrete crucible of *Taxi* from which all witty twenty-two-minute morality plays sprung forth. His specific heritage would remain unidentified—he would refer to his country frequently without giving it name or locus. He would appear in the first episode, "Like Father, Like Daughter," at the top of the second act, trundling down the garage staircase to ask Alex Rieger—the patriarchal career cabbie played by Judd Hirsch—for help with English lessons. And his arrival was scripted in such a way as to merely navigate him:

LATKA GRAVAS ENTERS. HE IS DRESSED IN COVERALLS WITH A MONKEY WRENCH STICKING OUT OF HIS BACK POCKET. HE IS SWEET AND INNOCENT LOOKING. HE GOES TO ALEX.
WE HEAR LOUIE'S VOICE.

LOUIE
Latka, where are you going? Don't hang around the drivers, I need you to fix a cab on the third level.
LATKA TURNS.

LATKA
(IN HIS OWN LANGUAGE, WHICH SOUNDS LIKE A CROSS BE-TWEEN TURKISH, LATVIAN, AND GIBBERISH. HE SAYS SOMETHING THAT MEANS ROUGHLY: "LET A GUY HAVE A MINUTE, WILL YOU?")

And thus was established the foreignness and the cuteness and the spunk—whereupon Latka moved to Alex who was using the pay phone and Alex said it was not a good time to work on the English lessons (LATKA STARTS TO WALK AWAY DEJECTED. *DEJECTED* ISN'T THE WORD—HE HAS TAKEN VULNERABLE TOO FAR), then Alex reconsidered and Latka eagerly read aloud from his phrasebook " *'Lesson twelve: tenk you chambermaid for your excellent serveece, I am glad I don't re-quire medical asseestance'* " and then he shuffled to a bench to sit be-side new driver Elaine Nardo (played by Marilu Henner) on whose shoulder he innocently rested his head (THIS GIVES HER PAUSE, BUT HE IS SO SWEET . . . THEN . . . LIKE A LOCKSMITH PICKING A LOCK, HE BEGINS SLOWLY PULLING THE ZIPPER OF HER BLOUSE DOWN), and, shocked, she pushed him away and he said, "*No bed?*" and she firmly replied, "No bed." And this would be the debut of Latka Gravas, as

"Here I come to save the day."

With Dick Van Dyke, 1976

With the B Street Conga Band

The Kaufman family celebrates Thanksgiving (1979) at Kutsher's in the Catskills. *l. to r. (standing)* Bob Zmuda with friend, Carol, Stanley, Janice, Andy, Michael *(seated)* Grandma Pearl, Grandma Lillie and Gregg Sutton.

With Tony Danza, Judd Hirsch, Marilu Henner and Jeff Conaway on the set of *Taxi*

Photograph by Bill Knoedelseder

Getting tossed

off the set of *Taxi*

A couple of swine

Tony upstaging Andy at Carnegie Hall

TONY CLIFTON

Photograph by Elizabeth Wolynski

Backstage with Robin Williams at Carnegie Hall

Andy takes the Carnegie Hall audience out for milk and cookies.

THE INTER-GENDER WRESTLING CHAMPION OF THE WORLD

Photograph by Marcia Reed

"I've got the brains!"

Those remarkable, dazzling eyes. Daughter Maria with her late father.

All photos courtesy of Shapiro/West

seen in the series premiere Tuesday, September 12 at 9:30 P.M. (Eastern Standard Time) over the ABC television network which still had no interest in broadcasting his special and now here he was again not only as Foreign Man but as Foreign Man reborn according to the whim of others who had relieved him of the character's creative custody and who would dictate the character's inner life and motivation and destiny. Foreign Man was no longer his, but theirs. It was part of the package.

Resigned to this reality, he did what was required of him as best as he could from the remove he required himself to maintain. The producers, meanwhile, respectfully gave him leeway the other actors quickly began to resent. He came late for rehearsals, when he elected to come to rehearsals, which he would soon stop doing altogether, because he didn't need rehearsals because he had a photographic memory and always knew his lines cold. When present, he regularly disappeared to meditate for long stretches, often in his car, where production assistants would be sent to retrieve him. Everyone was made to wait for him and then he would wander back to rejoin the enterprise and pretend not to notice all the glowering. "I defended him strong to the cast," said Jim Brooks, "but the cast did not like the way he monkeyed with them. They were really furious. It would bubble up. I remember defending him by always saying, 'But he's an artist.' And they would respond, 'An artist doesn't piss on other artists!' " Jeff Conaway, who played the role of struggling actor Bobby Wheeler, came to openly hate his guts—"I didn't see the big deal about this guy. The producers were obviously crazy about him. I thought he was like a José Jimenez ripoff." Tony Danza, who played boxer Tony Banta, had the same initial misgivings—"I always liked to say that he wouldn't have lasted long in my neighborhood. He was *so* bizarre— I wanted to know who this guy was and he would give you nothing. Sometimes he wouldn't even acknowledge you to your face; he'd look right *through* you." Danza once greeted one of his late arrivals by accosting him with a fire extinguisher—"I figured I'd shoot him, get him aggravated, and maybe we could have it out, you know? I could say, 'Why don't you just join in with us here!' So I take the fire extinguisher and start spraying him near the dressing rooms. And he just stands there. He doesn't say a word. And I continue to shoot and just empty the thing. And now I'm the maddest guy in the world—*because he never even reacts!* I didn't get *any* reaction. It drove me nuts. Jim Brooks had to take me aside later and tell me, 'Hey, Tony, no soaking the actors.' "

He kept his walls erect always. On Friday nights, when the show would be filmed before a live audience in bleachers, he sealed himself inside of Latka, interacted with cast and crew only as Latka, took notes from the producers and from director James Burrows and afterward told them *tenk you veddy much.* Marilu Henner would recall, "If someone in the audience asked him to do Elvis Presley, he'd do Latka doing Elvis Presley: *You ain't nutting but a hound dog.* Andy was nowhere to be found."

Amid the new sitcom lifestyle, he started work late that summer as a part-time busboy at the Posh Bagel on Santa Monica Boulevard. He reported for duty only on Monday nights at eleven, whereupon he donned his apron and began pouring coffee and carting trays until closing. He had not bussed tables since his employment at Chop Meat Charlie's in Great Neck when he was sixteen—but he had been eager to return to just this sort of solid finite labor. It was, he believed, part of his roots. Plus, he could do funny things in the course of a shift not to be funny no really. The Posh Bagel hired him on the recommendation of this girl Beverly Cholakian who was a part-time hostess there and whom he had met five years earlier in New York when she was a Revlon model before she moved to Los Angeles to become an actress and got cast as one of the incidental high school kids on *Welcome Back, Kotter* and that was when she began a kind of tortured and volatile affair with Andy, whom she loved deeply (sometimes, per him, a bit too deeply). (He did not want the games of love, just the fruit, and she played the games, which made him yell a lot, and she would call him a big baby and storm off and then they would mend and play until it happened again, and again, and again, but she was very beautiful and he could not stop himself from wanting to be with her, even though his brother Michael had now come to Los Angeles for a long visit and he tried to urge Michael to date her in his stead, but that never quite took, and he did love her, in his way, but that did not stop him from lusting in every other direction, like when he flirted endlessly with a pretty Posh Bagel customer and Beverly interrupted them and said something to ruin his chances and, as Beverly would remember, "Andy went beserk and screamed, 'How could you do that to me! I could have gotten laid!' I mean, can you believe that? He had never talked to me like that before. So I ran to the back of the deli and locked myself in a room while he kept screaming. Then we saw him drive off in a rage, swerving and screeching like a madman." And, of course, they mended again, for a while again, since she wanted to marry him and all.) Anyway, he was what he liked to call an *overzealous* busboy, in that he liked to remove people's food before they had finished eating it and often before they had even touched it. "They would get very upset!" said Beverly. "They would want the food replaced. Many times I'd have to say to him, 'Okay, you've done enough tonight—you can leave now.'" And Gregg Sutton would remember dropping by to say hello on a night when the actor Richard Gere was seated in a back booth with a beautiful woman—"And Andy wouldn't leave them alone. He kept coming by and asking, 'Would you like more coffee?' Over and over and over again. Gere said, 'Quit bugging me!' But Andy comes over again anyway and starts pouring the coffee while looking away, like somebody had called him, and the coffee starts overflowing all over the table and Richard Gere is flipping out in his Armani suit. If he knows who Andy is, he doesn't care at this point. He's screaming, '*What are you doing, you stupid idiot!*' And Andy's saying oh-gosh-I'm-sorry and trying to clean up but only making it worse, pushing the coffee all over them. It was hilarious." And then some reporters found out he was working as a busboy and he would tell them that he did it "because it keeps me in touch with people. Because no matter how famous I may become from show business, I always hope that I could keep my head out of the clouds and remain, you know, just a regular human being. I'm just a human being. And working as a bus-boy reminds me of this."

August ended and Little Wendy quit because she was sick of being Little, of being diminutive in his eyes, thus patronized, and of having to go along with his weird whims at weird hours and withstand his er-ratic cruelties, so they had this big eruption in front of a restaurant in Chinatown, and they shoved each other back and forth and she told him to go fuck himself in a new voice that wasn't at all Little and he told her the same thing and she stomped away. (Such adrenaline he felt! He wondered why he liked confrontation so much.) So he sought a new assistant in his old TM friend Linda Mitchell, the classical gui-tarist in whose parents' guest house he had stayed when he came to Los Angeles and tried to get Foreign Man onto The Dating Game, *and as it turned out—right now, more than five years later—he was actually on his way over to do* The Dating Game *as Foreign Man at last, so he called Linda and told her to meet him and Beverly there. He would be Baji Kimran (which was the previously unspoken name he had created for Foreign Man four years earlier) who was Bachelor Number Three and some people in the audience recognized him and screamed for him to do Elvis but he gave no acknowledgment because the Bachelorette, whose name was Patrice Burke, who would be asking the questions of the three potential mystery dates, had no clue as to who he was, not that she saw him, because she would ask her questions from behind a separating wall with host Jim Lange presiding. And she asked him the first question—"Bachelor Number Three, it's the holiday season and I'm Santa. You're on my lap. Little boy, take it away." And he said: "Vhat? Vait a minute! Vait. I don't know vhat she look like. Could I see vhat she look like?" And Lange told him no, that was part of the game—"But I don't know who she ees!"—then he said she didn't sound like Santee Claus but finally said that he would ask her for "ehhh, a television and eh, eh, record player . . . and food." Anyway, she finally chose Bachelor Number One over the protests of Baji Kimran—"You mean I did not vin? No, I von, I von! But I answered all de questions* de right way! No! I did not lose!"—and he came out to meet her with tears in his eyes and, in truth, he was very angry about losing and Beverly was angry that he was angry and Linda would start work within the week.

New York *magazine*, meanwhile, had sent writer Janet Coleman out to do a major profile of him that would be published the week *Taxi* premiered and this article would be entitled "Don't Laugh at Andy Kaufman." So he invited Coleman up to the La Cienega Towers and Kathy Utman served snacks—Coleman wrote, "We were having this menu: four pints (two chocolate) of Häagen-Dazs ice cream, a box of cookies (chocolate chip), a box of cookies (chocolate-covered mint), two double boxes of Mallomars, a bag of Lidos, a jar of Ovaltine, a can of Quik, and milk." Andy said, "I don't usually have this much chocolate. I'm trying to cut down." Then he told her about his life and about his dream of hosting a talk show where celebrities only discussed the weather and he showed her his novels—God *and* The Hollering Mangoo *and the beginnings of* The Huey Williams Story, *which he saw being made into "a four-hour epic, like* Ben Hur"—*and he spoke of his influences (Fellini, whose* 8 1/2 *he had seen "between thirty and fifty times," and Hubert Selby, Jr., and Kerouac and Steve Allen and Abbott and Costello on television only) and of his personal disdain for Tony Clifton. Coleman wrote that he "would ask me several times to refrain from even mentioning someone so unsavory as Tony Clifton in this piece" and that "he was sorry he had ever hired the guy" for the Comedy Store gigs. And she wrote that George Shapiro told her that Clifton "would be better and very soon advised to consider retiring from show business altogether." But she also wrote very incisively of Andy's work: "He manipulates the audience the way the bullfighter would taunt the bull, maddening them with artfully calculated veronicas until they boo him off the stage, then cajoling them back in for the laugh, i.e., the 'kill' in comedy. He is simply not afraid to die."

The tenth episode of *Taxi* was the one that they agreed would feature guest actor Tony Clifton, who would play Louie DiPalma's

card-shark brother Nicky from Las Vegas. The episode was titled
"Brother Rat" but would be changed to "A Full House for
Christmas" by the time it was broadcast in December and, by then,
all traces of Clifton would be long gone except in the memories of
those who had witnessed the debacle of its genesis. Rehearsals
would commence Monday, October 2—three weeks after *Taxi* had
debuted to glowing notices from critics who reveled in the program's emotional texture and intelligence. "There has never before
been a sitcom written with the dramatic depth of this one," Frank
Rich declared in *Time*, adding that "*Saturday Night Live* Regular
Andy Kaufman brings a saving sweetness to the garage mechanic
who speaks his own variety of fractured English." Dean of TV critics Marvin Kitman enthused in *Newsday*, "What an inspiration it
was to make Andy Kaufman a regular on a sitcom. It's something to
look forward to every Tuesday night. The whole country will be
doing their Latka Gravas imitations by next month." After the series
premiere, Andy had briefly returned to the road, performing a college engagement in Macomb, Illinois (his contract now carried a
new rider stipulating that he would/must wrestle female audience
members no matter what anyone said or thought), followed by two
shows at the Park West Theater in Chicago. While away, he had
Michael oversee the purchase of a brand-new Chrysler Cordoba
and this would be his first new car ever, a big-sprawling-cabin-
cruiser-of-a-car—long and wide and white with sunroof and blue
interiors including, certainly, the fine Corinthian leather upholstery. **Andy did ask me through his brother if I felt it was too os-
tentatious,** George reported in the taped diaries of his special
client's career progress which he began privately recording two
weeks earlier. **It's a nice car, it's sporty, and it's not like driving a
Rolls-Royce or a Mercedes or a Cadillac. I think he should have a
car that he is going to enjoy. He's worked hard, he's paid his dues,
he earned it. So why not, right?** Anyway, before Clifton befell *Taxi*,
Andy returned to Paramount Stage 25 to film two more episodes,
including his first prominently featured show, "Paper Marriage," in
which Latka foils immigration officials seeking to deport him by

marrying, in name only, a prostitute (oh!) whom Alex Rieger hired
to save him. (Upon learning there would be no conjugal wedding
night after the ceremony, Latka laments, *"Boy, America ees a tough
town."*)

On Thursday, September 28, scripts of the "Brother Rat" show—
which had been written solely to facilitate the Tony Clifton contract—were distributed among the cast and all of them wondered
who this Tony Clifton was and why he was playing this role. George
had gotten a call later that day, he reported, from *Taxi* casting director Rhonda Young, who was on the set when the questions first arose:
**The full cast was sitting around the table and Judd Hirsch asked,
"Who is Tony Clifton?" And Rhonda said, "He's a good actor, he's
like Danny DeVito's character—he's a mean and coarse kind of a
guy, a real rat. That's why he got the role." After the meeting was
over, Rhonda went over to nudge Andy and said, "Hey, I did good,
didn't I?" As if to say, "I covered up pretty good, didn't I?" And Andy
said to Rhonda, "Oh, no, the real Tony Clifton is going to be here.
I only imitated Tony Clifton. I know you came into the Comedy
Store and saw that performance, but I'm not going to be here. I'm
going away for three weeks. Next week, the real Tony Clifton is
going to be here to play that part."** And no one would be especially
fooled because Ed. Weinberger—who had been sworn to secrecy by
Shapiro—soon began taking the actors aside, according to Randall
Carver (who played yokel cabbie John Burns), to tell each of them
"that Andy wasn't going to be in the next episode, but this lounge
singer from Las Vegas who might *resemble* Andy, but *wasn't* Andy,
would be there instead. And we all kind of scratched our heads."
Thus the word spread and the concerns simmered. Danza: " 'Don't
talk to him as if he's Andy'—that's what we were told—'buy in!' "
Henner: "We heard, 'It's Andy but it isn't Andy—just play along.' "
Conaway: "I said, 'You gotta be kidding! Everything's always revolving around this guy, because he's always making us wait for him!
And now you're saying we have to talk to him as somebody else?' I
was the last one to agree to go along with it." (Weinberger would recall telling them nothing more than a new actor had been hired to

appear in the next show and their patience would be most appreciated.)

Clifton, meanwhile, required greater measures of obfuscation. Now, more than ever, Andy could be nowhere in plain sight. Zmuda arranged to employ the talents of makeup artist Ken Chase, who had done memorable work for the television mini-series *Roots*, and Chase would design new and appalling facial prosthetics contoured to transform one enigma into another. They went the week before — Andy and Bob and Linda Mitchell — to Chase's home studio in Tarzana, where a cast was made of Andy's head. "He meditated in his car for one hour before he came in to let me take the cast," Chase said. "Then the girl would hold his hand and count out loud while the impression cream was hardening. He was very eccentric." Foam-latex applications were then created to approximate ruddy cheeks and fleshy jowls and bulbous nose — "Our intent," said Chase, "was to make him as physically obnoxious as possible. The cleft in the chin was my idea. Something about a cleft on a guy like that seemed particularly repulsive." Chase also supplied ungainly sideburns and a cheap toupee ("purposefully obvious") and a big "Burt Reynolds" mustache and Linda had gotten the unspeakable salmon-hued embroidered tuxedo with black lapels and piping ("*That* was a *find*," she said, having plucked it from the racks of "a cheesy men's store on Sunset") and also the turquoise ruffled shirt which was to be worn over padding to barrel out the gut. And so they would report to Chase's home each morning before Clifton and entourage headed for the set and the application process would take just over two hours — "Before he would let me make him up, he'd blow his nose twenty, thirty, forty times. Very kooky. And the minute the makeup was completed, his personality changed. Andy didn't exist anymore."

Because Clifton refused to occupy Andy's dressing room, an enormous Winnebago trailer (with fully stocked bar) had been procured by Weinberger and, by most accounts, two bona fide call girls — very tall and blond and accommodating — were separately hired to dawdle with Clifton for the length of the week. (Weinberger maintained that they were extras, not pros.) Also, Linda Mitchell, a brunette, would become Clifton's brassy blond-wigged secretary Ginger Sax; Zmuda would be his zoot-suited handler Bugsy Meyer. They would arrive at the Paramount gates in a rented pink Cadillac. Monday was to be the first table-reading of the script—in which the brothers DiPalma stage a poker game to decide which of them would entertain their mother for the holidays—and that morning the actors all gathered to begin business. **Tony Clifton came to work five minutes early,** Shapiro reported, **and he complained about the other people when they came in late.** (Which was meant to further divert suspicion away from Andy.) And so there they all sat, gawking at him, stifling laughter, stifling irritation, as he hid behind sunglasses and below latex and they saw that the orangey-spongey makeup stopped at his ears and it was Conaway sitting beside him who first smelled the remarkable B.O.—or was it cologne? or urine? or whiskey? or all?—and Clifton lit up his Camels and swigged from his pint of Jack Daniel's and they knew Andy never drank or smoked. But Clifton actually *tried* to be congenial and made much reference to Las Vegas and bleated his dialogue as abrasively as possible ("*Louie, you know Ma—sometimes she's saaaaad, sometimes she's glaaaaaad!*"), altering it beyond anything recognizably written on the page. Mostly, however, he smelled really really awful. "You wanted to take a bath after you'd been in the room with him," Henner said. "He was just sickening, always going '*Hey, pretty lady, how ya doin', baby!*' He kept coming on to me, which Andy never did." In fact, he chased whatever "chickaroonies" materialized before him, offering free trips to Vegas and intimate tours of his Winnebago and it was soon eminently clear that Clifton was in no way capable of acting any part other than that of himself.

"His reading was terrible," said Weinberger. "And the cast was looking at me and I just saw that this was gonna be a bitch. Then Tuesday we had a run-through and that was a disaster. This was not acting. He did not mesh, not even remotely. So I realized that I had to get rid of him. It was too early in the life of the show to make an episode you couldn't air. So at the end of the day I called George and said, 'Look, I have to fire him.' He said, 'Well, you know, Andy's gonna be devastated.' I said, 'I have no choice, you know?' So he said, 'Well, you have to explain it to him.' He told me Andy could walk, might leave the show and take both Tony Clifton and Latka with him. So I called Tony in his Winnebago and asked if Andy could come up to the office and I think it was Andy who then came up and sat on my couch and I was very tentative because I didn't want to offend or lose Andy. But I said, 'I have to tell you: Tony Clifton is not an actor. You know, he's a *lounge performer*. He is just too big for this room; he overpowers this whole episode. He doesn't fit the way we need him to fit. He can't do it.'

"And I was very relieved and surprised when he very quickly said, 'I agree with you. But what're you gonna do?' And I said, 'Well, I have to fire him.' I'm very careful to say *him* and not *you*. And Andy agreed—as always, he was very deferential and polite and soft-spoken, but he said, 'Okay, but would you do me a favor? Would you fire him tomorrow, but not because he's a bad actor? Could you fire him because he's late and comes in drunk or something? I'll have Tony come in late after lunch and then you fire him in front of everybody and say you had to hire another actor because he didn't show up.' And I said, 'Yes, I could do that.' And I saw that this would be theater for him. He was already putting his little script together."

Ed. Weinberger called me just now to tell me how he's going to fire Tony Clifton. From what I understand, he's going to do this in front of the entire cast and crew tomorrow. And it's going to be part of—let's say—"theatre of life," which is what Andy loves. They are going to put on a total scene and a reporter from the *Los Angeles Times*, Bill Knoedelseder, will also be there tomorrow [because he has been writing a piece about Andy]. This whole situation is one of the most bizarre things I have ever witnessed. Really very bizarre. And exciting and interesting and crazy. I'm going to be there tomorrow for the firing.

* * *

Today is October 4—it's Wednesday morning. I found out through the casting director Rhonda Young that they have already hired an actor to take over Tony Clifton's part today. His name is Richard Foranjy. And he was told to report at 2:30. I think I have the *Times* reporter who was supposed to interview Tony coming at 2:30 and the rest of the cast is also coming at 2:30. And I'll be there at 2:30.

Ginger Sax was dispatched to buy gifts for the cast and producers which would be personally distributed by Clifton and his two blond hookers after lunch on Wednesday. Cards would be attached bearing uncommonly warm sentiments—"It's a pleasure working with you. I'm proud to be a member of the cast of *Taxi*. P.S. Let's all break a leg on Friday. Love, Tony 'Nick' Clifton." The gifts were little remote-control battery-operated toy dogs that walked and barked and wagged their tails and each actor would receive one and begin to play with his/her dog which Ginger had already installed with batteries and they all seemed sort of touched by the gesture and certainly amused except for Conaway who would take his yapping dog and smash it against a wall and, meanwhile, they would all wonder why there were at least fifty people sitting in the bleachers after lunch since this was just a Wednesday rehearsal and usually only crew and staff members were present for such routine business. Tony Danza, however, knew something was going to happen because he brought a home-movie camera with him and told the technicians to light the stage when Clifton walked in. And George, of course, sensing history, brought his portable tape recorder so that he might describe the action beheld from his seat in the bleachers. And he had urged the L.A. *Times* reporter Bill Knoedelseder to bring a camera in case any photo opportunities arose. And Weinberger—quite aware of his role in the imminent mayhem—had instructed crew members to call his office the minute Clifton arrived on Stage 25.

*   *   *

It's 2:30 P.M. and I'm sitting up here with Rhonda Young, the famous casting director, and Ginger Sax, Tony Clifton's secretary/as-
sistant. Ginger is a very pretty lady with blond curly hair and a very
sexy green gown—just very classy, someone that Tony Clifton
would approve of, obviously.

[Clifton entered here with his flanks.] Tony is now giving out gifts
to all the members of the cast. Danny DeVito has a big smile on his
face as he is opening up his gift. Judd Hirsch said, "Something's tick-
ing in here." Randy Carver has a big smile on his face. [Much laughter could be heard.] There are a lot of little stuffed animals running
around the reading table now—there's a little Scotty dog, a whole
bunch of different dogs. They are adorable! It's absolutely adorable.
Tony came out with these two young ladies who were in the trailer
with him—a blonde and another blonde. The blondes are completely
breaking up; everyone is breaking up. Tony Danza has a movie camera—he's taking pictures of all the animals. This is sensational.
Clifton is walking around in his peach tuxedo with black velvet collar and blue shirt. He just said, "Let's get back to work!" And the director Jim Burrows said, "I have to talk to Ed. Weinberger about a
script change." Clifton just said that he rented a place and invited
the whole cast to a party there after filming on Friday. He's really
being very friendly right now to the cast.

Weinberger just walked on the set—the executive producer and
spokesman for the producing team. Tony just handed Weinberger a
very nice gift and Ed. immediately handed it off to the executive in
charge of production, Ron Frazier, who put it on the cab in the
garage set. Now they are having a conference in the corner of the
stage, away from everybody.

[Weinberger would recall, "I came on the stage, which was clut-
tered with all these little mechanical things tottering around. Clifton
actually had the same walk as these toys did, which I'll never forget.
He was taking swigs from a pint of whiskey and saying that he just
rewrote the script of the show during lunch. He told me that he wrote

parts for the two girls he had with him. But I had to play my role as irate producer—'Tony, I warned you about this! You're late! I've hired another actor, so get off the stage—you're fired!' I thought it would be over. It wasn't. He wouldn't leave. He waved the script in my face and said, 'Here, read my changes!' And I ripped the script out of his hands and threw it away. He then held out his liquor—'Here, have a drink!' Everybody was now watching us and I was getting slowly pissed because he was betraying our agreement. But he just walked away from me."]

Now Tony is walking back to center stage and he's singing, "Let's get this show on the road, let's go!" He sits down at the table and tells the two girls, "Come on, sit on my lap." Each girl is sitting on a knee in the middle of the stage. Ron Frazier went over and is talking to him and Tony said, "Getcha hands off me! Getcha hands off me! Who the hell are you?" [No one had touched him yet.] Ed. Weinberger is calling me, as [Tony's] manager, onto the stage. I'm now walking down there to get him out. All sorts of commotion—Tony's yelling "I'm calling the cops! Getcha hands off me! I'm calling the cops!"

George's tape would now capture various screams from various players and yet it could not wholly contain the breadth of emotional forensics that engulfed the stage. Voices of order implored that valuable time was being squandered and that there was an actual show to work on. Voices of exasperation huffed into corners. Rages steeped or blew. Conaway had already moved toward Clifton once—"I wanted to hit him," he would remember. "And Jim Burrows grabbed me and said, 'No, Jeff, you should leave now. Let Judd handle it.' I said, 'I'm gonna kill him!' He said, 'That's why you have to leave!' "—then he retreated. Danza kept filming everything and Hirsch watched until he could watch no longer. "I felt responsible for the show," he said later, "and I thought I better help get rid of this guy." And Weinberger was telling Clifton to leave with George, and Clifton hollered, "Where's the director! Let's get to work! I am waiting for everybody!" And finally security was called and three Paramount cops arrived and they knew nothing about any theater-of-life bullshit and therefore lunged very seriously for Clifton who yelled, *"I got a contract here, I got a contract!"* Whereupon Hirsch announced to no one in particular, "He wants a psychodrama? I'll give him a psychodrama!" And his eyes flared with a menace that no one had seen before and he stalked toward Clifton and bellowed, *"You think you are the only one here!? I've got a contract with a whole lot more shows than you got! Get off this set!"* And he began throttling Clifton while the guards yanked at the foul tuxedo and Clifton yelped, *"Getcha hands off me!"* And everyone applauded except for George who shouted, "Don't hurt him! He's a talented man! He's talented!" And the guards and Hirsch dragged Clifton to the doors and he screamed, *"Fuck you! I will be back one day when I play Vegas! None of you will get in when I play! I'll be a big star! You wait and see! You wait and see! Getcha hands off me—I'm going back in there! I am not going to put up with this crap!"* And he was out of the building and Knoedelseder was snapping his newspaper photographs throughout and Hirsch left the security men to complete their task outside and he would recall, "I had no idea what was going to happen after that because the true body I was shoving off the stage was Andy Kaufman. Then I started to realize that I wasn't throwing out Andy Kaufman; I was throwing out Tony Clifton, which was a phantom, a fiction—a fiction with a real body. And how Andy Kaufman comes back and becomes Andy Kaufman again was no mystery to him—only to the rest of us."

And so: Guards roughed him all the way to the studio gate with George scurrying behind decrying the violence while reporter Knoedelseder endured harassment because security wanted to take his camera which he had dutifully kept shooting until Bugsy Meyer strode forth, feigning higher authority, and confiscated the camera and ran with the camera in the opposite direction to another edge of the Paramount lot and handed it off to an accomplice who sped away to safety because Andy wanted those photographs protected and later had George get copies of the negatives from Knoedelseder whose camera was quietly returned after the incident. Meanwhile, Ginger

Sax had collected Clifton in the pink getaway vehicle and deposited him down the block at Nickodel's coffee shop, where he immediately used the pay phone to call Weinberger in his office. "My secretary said Andy Kaufman was on the line, so I picked up and he said, 'Ed., is anybody there listening?' I said, 'No, just you and me.' He said, 'I'm calling from a phone booth and I just wanted to say that you were brilliant!' And I said thank you and he said he would see me in a couple of weeks when Latka returned and that was the end of the conversation." Clifton, however, was banned from ever setting foot on Paramount property again which was, um, fine.

So now I'm driving home, feeling pretty good about the day. We got away with a crazy thing. Why we did it, I don't know. It's Andy's craziness. It was nourishing Andy's insanity. And I was supporting it and so was Ed. Weinberger. . . . Andy called me when I got back to the office after this incredible escapade and he was totally exhilarated. He was thrilled. He said, "Wasn't it great! Wasn't it fantastic! I think this is fantastic! It was a part I always wanted to play! It gave realness, a validity to Tony Clifton's character and I think this is going to be good for his career. I think he's going to get other jobs." And he was as high as a kite. So I allowed him to be high. I told him one thing, which I felt was very true: What he went out to accomplish, he did. He really acted out a role he wanted to play. As crazy as his goal was, he did reach it. And that's okay with him and that's okay with me. . . .

Incidentally, I was told that Andy Kaufman is scoring tremendously as the character Latka Gravas on *Taxi*. They have a rating system for likability and he's going through the roof. . . .

The triumph was such that nobody cared except him and also Bob and, although George was happy for his client, George could live without this *tsouris* to be sure—and mostly everybody who witnessed it wanted to forget it (at least for the time being). Army Archerd, the columnist for *Variety*, got wind and thought about running an item, but Ed. told him that Clifton had a serious drinking problem and the less said about it the better. And Andy wanted to take out an ad in the trades to trumpet Tony's mistreatment at the hands of Paramount and *Taxi* personnel, but Ed. told George that the less said about it the better. And Danny DeVito would say, most diplomatically, "There were some bad feelings toward . . . *Tony*. We all felt it was a big waste of time. It was a very strange game." Knoedelseder, meanwhile, met Clifton two nights later—on the very night the "Brother Rat" episode was filmed without him—for a private deposition in Clifton's room at the Sunset 400 Motel in Hollywood. (Andy had checked in the night before to call Knoedelseder, as Clifton, and arrange the interview.) For the occasion, Clifton's face had once again been shellacked by Ken Chase. And Knoedelseder found him in the dank smoky motel room where Sinatra music played and closed-circuit porno flickered on the television and skin magazines were splayed across the rumpled bed littered with empty whiskey bottles. (Bob was supposed to have had two more hookers there but couldn't convince any to play along at the offering price.) Then, after visiting for a while amid the grim detritus, Knoedelseder took Clifton to a bar across the street, where Clifton drank much Jack Daniel's—Knoedelseder tasted it to make sure it was the real thing—while abusing the female bartender and then he legitimately picked up a Hollywood waif who had wandered in and, eventually, Knoedelseder deposited the lounge singer and the girl back at the motel and fled. When his *Los Angeles Times* piece ran two months later—THE IDENTITY CRISES OF ANDY KAUFMAN—there would be no mention of this night with Clifton, although the *Taxi* imbroglio was covered in a small sidebar that featured one photograph of Clifton being thrown off the set.

And, one week after the firing, on a flight to a college engagement in Albany, Bob let it slip to Andy that all of the actors at *Taxi* had been told early on that Andy was playing Clifton and were urged to just go along with it and this news crushed him and he felt betrayed and became enraged and he called Linda Mitchell to scream and then he called George who calmed him somewhat before he could scream very much. And when he returned to Paramount a week after this, Tony Danza had brought in a projector to show the movies he had shot of Clifton's final day and everyone gathered in a room above the stage to watch—"And we're laughing—you know, laughing at ourselves and at him and at the whole nightmare of it. And then Andy walks in and he stands there staring at the screen. And everybody sort of nervously takes this mass gulp. Finally the movie runs out—and there are a few beats of silence afterward. Maybe too many beats. And then he clears his throat and says, 'Gee, who was that asshole?' And with that, he turns and leaves the room. End of story."

He kept telling George Carnegie-Hall-Carnegie-Hall-Carnegie-Hall and George kept saying I'm-trying-I'm-trying which he was and finally, rather suddenly, definite headway was made—with the help of Marty Klein and the team of other agents at APA who found a New York concert promoter named Ron Delsener who thought it sounded like fun—and a date for the following spring was mentioned and it now looked very extremely likely . . . oh!

George's partner, Howard West, had a dream that month. He dreamt that he throttled Tony Clifton, that he took Clifton by his profane fictitious throat and shook him senseless. Andy had recently tried to teach Howard to levitate from the carpet of the Shapiro/West offices in Beverly Hills. Andy liked to waste Howard's time like that; Howard thought Andy was cute but also fucking nuts. Whenever possible, Andy would eagerly discuss his levitation skills of which he actually possessed none but still. He told people at *Taxi* that he had levitated eight feet in his dressing room. They told him that if anyone could do such a thing, it would be him. A woman friend of George's also had a dream that month and, in her dream, Clifton completely overtook Andy and there was no more Andy and Andy was gone forever. George was mostly impressed that Andy found his way into people's subconsciouses.

* * *

*He finished a two-hour college show in Tampa and told the audi-
ence, "I want to thank each and every one of you." Then he walked
down off of the stage and shook hands with each and every one of them.
It took the better part of another hour to do this. He said "Thank you"
every time.*

At the end of October, George said this into his tape recorder—
Andy told me that he really hates performing on *Taxi.* **He is very
frustrated by the limitations that he endures playing one character.
He wants to do variety shows; he wants to create his own shows
and his own characters. We agreed, he and I, that he will do only
the fourteen shows contracted and no more.** By now, ABC had ex-
tended the series to a full twenty-two shows per season; the producers
would work around Andy's newest disregard; they would agree to the
same demands the following season—and other demands—and said
they would hire a stand-in to perform his rehearsal duties during the
week. He would show up only on Tuesdays for initial run-throughs
and then on Fridays for final dress rehearsal and filming. "You really
didn't have to rehearse with Andy," said Jim Burrows, who directed
most episodes. "Andy knew what he did and he never once missed a
line on camera—which was, of course, remarkable."

Friday nights after filming, the *Taxi* people threw great parties
which he would almost never attend. "I just come in, do my job and
leave," he told the tabloid *National Enquirer* in a story titled ANDY
KAUFMAN: I'M NOT A PART OF THE "TAXI" TEAM. (He had no misgivings
about trucking with yellowish press because those reporters always
printed exactly what he wanted them to print.) "I don't drink or
smoke. I don't go roller-skating or do any of the things those people
do. They're very nice people, but I don't socialize with them. I'm not
a part of the team." Then, in another interview shortly thereafter, he
declared, "*Taxi* is just a commercial for me. It's a means, not an end.
I purposely keep my part real small. I am more interested in my

books and big concerts. *Taxi* is good only in that it is a way of me doing those things. It advertises me to the public."

And, of course, they had to resent him and they also had to respect him and no one could argue that his performances were less than golden. The show, meanwhile, kept garnering serious acclaim, would go on to win the Emmy award for Outstanding Comedy Series during its first three years on the air. And he did not care in the least. "Jesus, you know, *every week* he got big laughs," said Jim Brooks. "He heard an audience really *laugh* at him. And then there were the reviews! But he was *not* seducible. Because if you're gonna get *seduced*, you get seduced a little by that! This was *intelligentsia*, the highest kind of respect. This was not slumming. And he didn't traffic in it at all! He stood outside of it."

Clifton opened for Rodney Dangerfield at the Comedy Store on December 1 and 2. He was twenty minutes late on the second night because the parking attendant wouldn't let him leave the Cordoba on the lot. Dangerfield fumed backstage—"He's fucking with me! He's fucking with me!" Clifton finally burst in through the backstage door hyperventilating—"*You know what he did to me?! You know what he told me!? He said I'm not the star of the show and I can't park here!*" Dangerfield instantly lashed into him—"Andy, what the fuck are you doing? We gotta start the show!" And Dangerfield would recall, "So he talks to me like Tony Clifton—'*I'm sorry, Rodney, I couldn't help it, it was that guy in the parking lot!*' And I say, 'Oh, stop that will you, for crying out loud!' And even though I was angry and kept hollering at him, he stayed in character, he wouldn't break it! '*Ehhh, don't worry, Rodney, it'll be all right!*' " And Clifton went onstage after the no-smoking announcement and sang "You Light Up My Life" and smoked while he sang it—Rodney thought that was a terrific touch—and, after the show on both nights, he stood in the lobby selling xeroxed photographs of himself for twenty-five cents apiece and, at one point, Steve Martin approached him and requested that he sign one "to Steve" and

Clifton began signing and asked, *"What's your last name, Steve?"* And he was told it was Martin and he finished signing and said, *"That'll be a dollar."*

The reviews were not kind. *Variety* noted that this had been "the first time [Clifton has] performed for someone other than his alter ego, comedian Andy Kaufman . . . it's an act that is beginning to get a little stale." And *The Hollywood Reporter*, meanwhile, lifted the veil further, openly referring to Clifton as Andy in disguise—"Kaufman, on for almost an hour, never got anywhere." Andy phoned both reviewers after reading what they had written and strenuously complained about having his name linked with Clifton's. "I treat the situation like a magician and I don't appreciate being called Tony Clifton's alter ego," he told the *Variety* critic, who signed his review "Pollack." Then he angrily asked the *Reporter* critic Don Safran, "Who told you that I was Tony Clifton?" Safran allowed that many people had averred as much. Andy told him, "I don't mind you giving *me* a bad review for *my* work, but to put my name in a review of a Tony Clifton performance is unreasonable and unfair!" He went on to admit that he had played Clifton before at the Comedy Store, but this time it had been the *real* Tony Clifton onstage and, moreover, he said that the real Tony Clifton would soon appear onstage *with* him on December 16 and 17 at the Huntington Hartford Theater in Hollywood and that Safran should come to see for himself and Safran said he would very much like to witness that miracle and Andy felt better afterward.

Six days before the first Huntington Hartford show, Bill Knoedelseder's piece appeared in the Sunday Calendar section of the L.A. Times *and Andy was quoted further on the matter that was plaguing him so unfairly and he couldn't understand why people had to keep talking about this travesty—"I am not Tony Clifton," he said. "We are two distinct personalities. I'm not like that. I never meant for it to get out of hand like this." And his real feelings were on the mournful agitated order of try-to-help-a-guy-out-and-look-what-happens. Clifton was—well, gosh, he hated to use such words, even inside of the private whistling curved corridors of his head—but Clifton was a bastard, he was a fucking bastard, he was a motherfucking goddamned sonofabitching fucking bastard was exactly what he was. But he looked forward to working with him again soon.*

The milk-and-cookies idea had possessed him since college and he used to talk about it in New York—four years earlier, he had told Jim Walsh about wanting to take the audience out for milk and cookies after he debuted at Carnegie Hall and Walsh recognized a worrisome grandiose madness in both notions—but in recent months, as various mad dreams found tether, he had been repeatedly telling George and Bob about it and Bob suggested the idea of getting school buses to transport the audience. (He did, after all, consider his audiences to be as childlike as he—and thus what better way to move large groups of children?) He loved the school bus idea very much and eventually it was all that he could talk about because he wanted to try it out at the Huntington Hartford and even George thought that he was **totally obsessed** with this fairly foolish notion which would certainly be an unnecessary expenditure but probably worth exploring if only to indulge his client—I **felt that we might as well do it, get it out of the way and move on to other things,** he privately dictated with customary measured patience. Anyway, they secured the Olde Spaghetti Factory, an enormous theme restaurant a few blocks away from the theater on Vine, as the destination where the milk and cookies—courtesy of Adohr Farms dairy products and Famous Amos (of chocolate chip renown)—would be served and Bob commandeered ten buses to do the shuttling. And everything about this engagement was understood to be the actual precursor to the Carnegie Hall show, now scheduled for April 26, in that the Huntington Hartford was a beautiful historic legitimate theater, a jewel box of cornices and filigrees and velvety splendor with seating capacity exceeding one thousand. Both shows at the theater were sold out weeks in advance (with top single-ticket pricing set at eight dollars and fifty

cents per) and, along with scores of big names and movers in the industry, his own mommy and daddy and sister and brother were going
to be present for this spectacle—and it *would* be a spectacle because
he envisioned mounting the greatest finale in the history of show
business, a finale so grand that people would never believe such ideas
could occur to a person and then become reality or become something sort of *resembling* a reality. Well, it would *seem* real—no really.

So, in the week prior to opening night, he mustered renewed
dedication to his stagecraft—he trained, he skipped rope, he did a
hundred push-ups at a time, and, most astonishing, he never once
arrived late for rehearsals. (On the road, it had become routine for
him to miss his music rehearsal call-times by two hours minimum.)
Now he hummed with adrenaline, he was very alive and willing to
try big things, also upsetting things. Gregg Sutton, who would as
ever conduct the band, watched Clifton chart darker straits than
ever when it was decided to give the character newfound three-
dimensionality—a wife and a daughter, who would be played by
prim blond actress Patty Michaels and her own cherubic blond
daughter Wendy (whose name was pure coincidence, as Little
Wendy Polland remained estranged from Andy). Clifton would
bring them out early in his opening segment to demonstrate that
they were the reason he needed to work so hard and he would recite
to his stoic wife Patty a long hoary chestnut called "This Is a Wife"
(*She's magic with a dish towel in her hands / Romance running a vac-
uum cleaner / Charm with a smudge of cake dough on her nose / This
is a wife!*). Then he and daughter Wendy Clifton would sweetly sing
a special song that they had always sung together at home and
Wendy would mess up the lyrics and Clifton would turn on her.
"Zmuda pushed Kaufman to take Clifton further," Sutton would recall. "When the kid missed a lyric, Bob showed him how he should
give her a little slap in the face and snap at her—*Pay attention,
dammit!* Bob kept giving the girl these little example slaps and Andy
was laughing this stupid mortified laugh. He said, 'Bob, I can't do
that!' And Zmuda said, 'You've gotta, Kaufman! This is Clifton!'
And, in a way, he was right. It was hysterical. And the kid didn't seem

to mind, although she would pretend to cry onstage, which was perfect." (Director John Landis, who attended opening night, found this piece of audacity amazing—"The audience was *electric!* They were *horror-struck!* People walked out.") Linda Mitchell resumed the platinum role of Ginger Sax and worked the lobby before the show both nights selling fresh xeroxed photos of Clifton standing in his fetid Sunset 400 Motel room. (Knoedelseder had provided the original.) At the bottom of each picture was her handwritten message to customers—"Your very own take-home photo. P.S. This photo may also be crushed and thrown at Tony."

Pouring rain drenched opening night but stopped no one from coming and the seats filled and the people waited . . . and waited . . . while deafening roller-rink organ music pummeled their eardrums . . . and finally Clifton appeared and was eventually pelted with xerox paper and left not soon enough (even George said **Clifton was on too long, strutting around, for my purposes**) and Andy bounced out to "Oklahoma" and the show kept building in usual fashion—although, as with birthday party children, he showed them cartoons such as *Thomas Jefferski*—and he told them that if they were good he would have special treats for them later and he wrestled/rubbed a woman from the audience, pinning her one second before the three-minute bell, whereupon a bald-headed mammoth goon bounded onto the stage screaming, *"Why don't you pick on a man, you skinny little geek!"* And this was professional Hollywood stuntman Jay York and he crushed Andy's larynx in a headlock and twisted Andy's fingers and lifted Andy by the neck and threw him all over the stage and Andy screamed, *"George! George! Help!"* and they had been rehearsing this all week, but Andy had neglected to mention such to his family, and suddenly Janice started screaming from her seat, *"George! George! Help him! George!"* And Judd Hirsch, who was sitting with Janice and Stanley and Carol, would recall, "I'm looking at his mother and his father, who are clawing the arms of their chairs, thinking that their son is going to be injured. His mother grabs my wrist—she doesn't even know me—and says, *'Oh my God, he's gonna get killed!'* I'm now truly fooled because I thought she was part of the act. I'm thinking I'm in a room with another act sitting beside me playing his family. I thought, How did he find these people who look like him? He created the illusion that anything could happen in that auditorium. And, in truth, he was even fooling them!" But then Zmuda, in referee stripes, passed a large prop can of spinach to Andy, who pretended to swallow its contents and freed himself from York, and Sutton had the band strike up "Popeye the Sailor Man" and Andy smugly strutted and began to toss York around the stage until York begged for mercy.

Then later, after Foreign Man (who told the audience *"Tenk you veddy much ladies and gentlemen so far everytheeng I have done for you tonight really I am only foolink thees ees de real me"*) became de Elveece, and after Andy led the audience in a singalong of "This Friendly World," he explained that he wasn't Clifton and demonstrated his own version of Clifton, without disguise, singing "Carolina in the Morning" and then had the real Clifton come out to sing it with him and his brother Michael stepped forth wearing Ken Chase's makeup and Clifton's gaudy apparel and replicated the adenoidal Clifton voice with much swagger. Then Clifton took a bow and Clifton's wife and daughter took a bow and so did Jay York and then Andy announced, "And now direct from Radio City Music Hall in New York—the Rockettes!" And thirteen costumed high-kicking women who were not the Rockettes danced out. And then Andy said, "Ladies and gentlemen, the Mormon Tabernacle Choir!" And the curtain lifted and one hundred fifty black gospel singers in robes who were most certainly not the Mormon Tabernacle Choir raised their voices to the heavens and the audience was ecstatic and they stood applauding endlessly and then Santa Claus, who was Mel Sherer, whom Clifton had assaulted earlier, flew down from the rafters in a sled and styrofoam snowflakes fell everywhere and Andy told the audience that ten buses were waiting in front of the theater to take everyone for cookies and milk. "When he walked us into the street and there were these buses, it was the damnedest thing I'd ever seen in my life," said Dick Ebersol, who had put him on *Saturday Night Live* three years earlier and now beheld the utter scope of the absurdity that he had wrought.

At the Olde Spaghetti Factory, Andy and his family and George and Bob and Linda Mitchell and others doled out the cookies and milk and Andy worked the room and received platitudes and promises of greater career opportunity and veiled movie offers and female entreaties galore. "Of all the times in Andy's life," said Ebersol, "that night was the happiest I ever saw him, wandering from table to table with a big smile on his face. You could tell that he felt that he had put one over on the world. It was a night that he didn't want to end. When we got on the buses to go back to the theater, you could tell that he didn't want us to leave." And Janice told George that she was simply kvelling over her son—Janice Kaufman is just a lovely lady. Everybody that meets her says, "But you're so normal!" When they meet Andy's mother and father, they say the same thing, "They are regular people—what happened?" His parents are so proud of him and feel wonderful about what he's accomplished. Janice said one thing that is really interesting and important. I mentioned that Andy had such a good time onstage tonight and she said, "One thing about that boy—he seems to always do what's fun for him. He enjoys himself in whatever he's been doing in show business and that's a wonderful blessing for him."

He awoke the next morning feeling deathly, his brain aflame with a 105-degree fever, and he could not move—but he would not cancel the show that night and somehow got himself to the theater and George found him slumped in his dressing room wearing Clifton's face and clothes and George helped him button the ruffled turquoise shirt and he wearily told George, "I can't even keep my eyes open. How am I going to do it?" And George said, "I have the feeling that when you get out onstage and the spotlight hits you and you pick up the mike, you're going to get an extra charge of energy, like an outside force coming in and giving you strength. I truly believe this. Go out there and have fun and it's going to be okay." And, by the time it was over, he had gotten his second standing ovation in two nights and Robin Williams had helped serve milk and cookies afterward and he had lost nearly twenty thousand dollars mounting this two-night extravaganza but George said it was worth it and he would earn it all back a hundredfold and, for days to come, George's phone did not stop ringing with congratulations and new offers and John Landis said that he wanted to make a documentary about Tony Clifton.

"Take this from someone who was not formerly a fan of Andy Kaufman—he's got the hottest act going this side of the Himalayas," wrote critic Susan Birnbaum in the lead of her *Hollywood Reporter* review. "An evening with Kaufman is the looniest, funniest, most wonderful way to enjoy yourself." And this would be the only glowing published assessment of the Huntington Hartford program, because other critics were now beginning to display concern and doubt. The critic "Kirk." began his *Variety* review by soberly pointing out that repeated television appearances tend to destroy the potency of otherwise foolproof comedic material—"What may have taken months or even years to perfect can be made obsolete in three minutes of airtime. Which is exactly what has happened to Andy Kaufman. In many ways, in fact, Kaufman may suffer more from TV's appetite . . . [since he] creates a series of characters which depend, at least in part, on audience unfamiliarity with Kaufman as Kaufman to succeed. When the audience knows the character is only a character, and also knows the payoff, the laughter takes on a different form. It becomes participatory and anticipatory, rather than reactionary." Which was to say, so much for Foreign Man and Elveece and Conga Man and Andy himselves and, Kirk. continued, "If TV has hurt Kaufman's portion of the show, the print media, especially locally, has simply destroyed the effectiveness of the opening segment, when Kaufman assumes the character of obnoxious Vegas-type lounge singer Tony Clifton. . . . It's time for Kaufman to come up with a new Clifton." Lawrence Christon, in the *Los Angeles Times,* was a bit kinder and described

Andy as "a sweet-faced, fresh and eager young man with the barest patina of post-pubescent acne around the mouth." Christon also declared him "a master of the put-on," then added, "One problem with the show is that the audience has gotten hip to him quickly— it seems that media burn is happening faster than ever. . . . Kaufman is going to have to come up with fresher material. What is at the heart of his act is the most liberating element of comedy, however: the sense of the unpredictable, even of danger." Anyway, both Kirk and Christon seemed to enjoy the milk-and-cookies part very much. They said it reminded them of something Steve Martin had done.

One week later, on Christmas Eve, he entered Cedars-Sinai Medical Center largely because on that day Bob came over to Andy's new little rented house at 2519 Greenvalley Road in Laurel Canyon and told him that he looked yellow and it turned out that it was infectious hepatitis which was why only three days earlier he had just barely been able to film a big Taxi episode about Alex Reiger dating Latka's mother. Andy's family had been there to watch and Janice could tell that he had never really recovered from what befell him before the last Huntington Hartford show which doctors now theorized might have had something to do with tainted shellfish. He stayed in the hospital through New Year's during which time he had a horrible fight with Beverly who had been taking care of him but he turned cruel again and then she threatened to steal his car and everything out of his house and he got even more cruel and alleged that she only wanted to be near him because he was such a big star which he felt bad about later. George told Andy that he hadn't progressed much beyond the mentality of a fifteen-year-old in his dealings with women. George also said that Howard had just closed a deal for Andy to make $75,000 for three weeks' work playing a wild-eyed televangelist named Armageddon T. Thunderbird in the Marty (also wild-eyed) Feldman movie, In God We Tru$t (or Gimme That Prime Time Religion), a strange title nobody liked but still. Feldman had sent

Andy the script just before he turned yellow and enclosed a beseech-
ing letter which read in part, "Dear Andy: You and I have never
worked together. This situation is intolerable and it must cease im-
mediately.... You do not lack invention. I would be foolish not to
profit from your invention, and so, I would welcome your (Fuck! I
hate this word) input. If you do not play Armageddon T.
Thunderbird, then please consider this letter a suicide note." Except
for the swear word, Andy was very touched. He recuperated at home
for a couple more weeks, during which time he went through his fan
mail and if the mail was from a girl and if the girl had enclosed a
photograph of herself and if she looked reasonably attractive and if
she had written down her phone number, he called the girl and
arranged to meet her the next time he performed in her area and
maybe they could wrestle. He made several dozen of these calls and
hundreds more in the months and years to come and would get laid
very extremely often because of this. Sometimes he would tell George
to book him in areas where certain such girls especially intrigued
him. Also, he turned thirty on January 17 and told George and
Beverly and anyone who asked that he was not ready to be with just
one woman and that he wanted to continue his houndsmanship in-
definitely since now it was easier to get action and everything.

Then Jeff Conaway hit him. This was after the Golden Globe
Awards ceremony which was held January 27 at the Beverly Hilton
Hotel and Andy came late to the ceremony even though he had
been nominated for Best Supporting Actor in a Comedy Series (as
were Conaway and Danny DeVito) and, by the time he arrived, the
award in his category had already been presented to Norman Fell of
Three's Company, which didn't matter at all to Andy who showed up
only to be polite. But the *Taxi* people—who were excited to have
won the Best Comedy Series award (right in the middle of their first
season, no less)—begged him to come to a private celebration afterward at Trader Vic's, also in the hotel, but he didn't want to go but
they made him so he went. He sat at the end of the long table com-

mandeered by the group and noticed that bits of food were landing on him as if thrown and he looked up and saw Conaway smiling devilishly and Conaway said, "How you doing, Andy?" And Andy said that he was um fine, then went over to visit with Judd Hirsch, who was sitting across from Conaway, and Conaway, who was a little drunk, decided to further engage Andy at that moment. "I thought maybe if I talked to the guy, I could break the ice and get to know him, you know?" he would recall. So, according to what Andy told George immediately afterward, Conaway said, **"Andy, let me ask you a question. Do you have any respect for us?"** Andy said, **"Of course I do, Jeff. I respect everybody in this cast."** And Jeff said, **"Well, you don't show it. You don't show up to rehearsals at all, you don't come through for us, you don't seem to give a damn about us."** And, per Conaway's memory, Andy "got right in my face, like spitting in my face, and screamed, '*I don't give a fuck about any of you!*'" And, according to what Andy told George, Andy said nothing of the sort but turned to walk away and **when Andy started to leave, Jeff said, "Your work habits stink!" Andy then explained that there were other things in his career and Jeff said, "What career?" And Andy answered, "I've had a career for ten years." And Jeff said, "What do you do in your fucking career?" Andy said he does nightclubs and concerts and Jeff Conaway said, "Your career is nothing! I've been in this business for nineteen years!" Andy started leaving again and Jeff actually pulled him down.** Per Conaway: "I didn't think about it, I just hit him. *Boom!* Square in the jaw. And I got up and hit him again. And he went down on the table and I jumped on top of him. And the drinks and food were flying everywhere. And I'm pounding him and screaming like a drunken Irishman. This was like months of frustration coming out. I figured that he dared me by saying he didn't give a fuck about us, but in a million years I'm sure he never thought I was gonna belt him." Per Andy, per George: **He started to swing and Andy told me that Tony Danza and a few of the other guys held him back. Conaway was screaming, "I want to kill him! That goddamned guy is never at work! I want to kill him!"**

Anyway, he left and Conaway called him at home a few days later and apologized and said that he had been drunk and way out of line and Andy told him that it was okay and that he knew Conaway was drunk and thus not in control of himself and Andy suggested they get together soon to talk it out. And Conaway was flabbergasted by his benevolence—"He was so forgiving and so understanding. And he apologized, too, for provoking me. I thought, *This guy's amazing! What a guy!* And so after that we got friendly."

To get to Carnegie Hall:

That February, Foreign Man taped a Cher special called *Cher and Other Fantasies* and he played Adam in the Garden of Eden and Cher played the serpent with the apple and also Eve but Eve as a New Jersey harridan in cat-rimmed eyeglasses. A week later in New York, on February 24, he was himself again, as such, on *Saturday Night Live*, where he performed "I Go Mad When I Hear a Yodel" with the B Street Conga Band, as he had done on the Van Dyke show, and he was as good as ever although there was not much laughter from the audience which was understandably rendered agog (arty juxtaposition et cetera). Lorne Michaels, meanwhile, had begun to detect some change taking place which became more and more apparent with Zmuda now fastened to his side. "With success, there were now people around him that seemed opportunistic. I hadn't much liked Zmuda, perhaps wrongly, for that reason. After Andy went out to California, I also think he felt this pressure to get more astringent in what he did on our show, so that his stand-up had less of a desire to please, because he was doing that professionally on *Taxi*. Suddenly, he wasn't getting laughs and didn't mind. Andy, who had been this benign artistic presence and had happily done two or three minutes at a time on the early shows, now wanted to do six or seven minutes. The feeling around *Saturday Night*—particularly as the cast's popularity heated up, and particularly with John Belushi— was, *Why was he still considered untouchable?* It wasn't that anybody—John included, and maybe even John most of all—ever questioned him while it was still in this *innocent* thing, for lack of a better word. But it got a little slick, a little more West Coast, a little more show business. It was now less innocent and I was surprised."

And then he toured again and his touring life, especially on college hustings, had now become a cockeyed caravan bent on fleshly pursuit and serial idiocy. He missed planes constantly and would only step on a plane with right foot first (superstition) and, once on the plane, he and Bob improvised altitudinous hijinks—he would weep uncontrollably or feign panic attacks and Bob would slap him loudly or chastise him loudly and it was great fun for an audience of two, meaning themselves and/or each other. He liked to carry a toy gun in his suitcase and, on March 14, American Airlines caught sight of it in the X-ray detector and guards pounced on him and he tried to explain that he always carried his toy gun, for ten years he had carried his toy gun, and they roughed him up anyway and he missed that plane as well. And Bob, of course, found him to be a complete pain in the ass on the road, no matter that he loved him like a brother, and came to abhor playing the role of caretaker, shepherding him to engagements, feeding him phony rehearsal times and phony departure times (two or more hours earlier than they were actual, because he would always be at least two hours late for such irritants), then keeping him company at asinine day-parts and night-parts and dawn-parts, having to check under his hotel beds and peek into his hotel closets to make sure that the boogeyman was not lurking therein, and never being able to go get properly loaded, since "Koughman"—as Bob liked to call him—would not indulge in anything stronger than chocolate. And so Bob learned ways to ditch him, to shove him off on other poor bastards and this was most easily achieved in college scenarios because there was always some kid in charge of getting them to and from wherever the hell they were supposed to go.

Best/worst/standard example in ditch-Koughman history: March 21, 1979; York College; York, Pennsylvania; poor bastard—kid named Terry Cooney, age twenty, soon-to-be-amazed. The show went well; Andy wrestled mannish girl, won, not his type, wanted other options; back to Ramada Inn, Cooney driving Andy, Bob, in his own Ford Pinto; at Ramada, Bob handed Cooney twenty dollars and said, "Take Andy out to get something to eat." (Ditch was thus completed.) They drove, Cooney, Andy, no Bob, to three places, in each of which Andy questioned management as to whether the fish was fried or broiled; he wanted broiled; it was always fried; he settled for a Bob's Big Boy; ordered himself fried fish and two chocolate shakes (Cooney: "I'll never forget that he had *two* chocolate shakes"); he accidentally-no-really spit some shake on their waitress ("The woman was horrified, she was fuming"); then it was okay because somebody recognized him as Latka; back in Pinto, Cooney asked, "Back to Ramada?" Andy said no; said, "Let's do something"—as in females. They drove to another nearby college, to Lancaster F&M, to a frat party Cooney knew of; on the way, Andy rifled through Cooney's glove box; Cooney worked college security, kept handcuffs stashed in box, just in case ("I couldn't see what he's doing and the next thing I know I heard *click-click*"); and now they were handcuffed ("I said, 'Oh God, Andy! I don't have the key! It's back in York, thirty minutes away, on my dresser!'"). They went to the frat party handcuffed; they danced with women handcuffed; women threw themselves at Andy and they felt up the women handcuffed ("Wherever Andy's hand went, my hand followed. I was living vicariously through Andy—two guys' hands, one girl at a time"). By 4 A.M., they returned to the car; Andy wanted food again; they entered an all-night joint handcuffed; at the table they hid connected hands under napkin ("I'm turning different shades of red"); they both ordered food that required knife and fork; they took turns with utensils ("We were constantly borrowing each other's hands to cut things"). It was nearing 6 A.M.; Andy was not tired; Cooney said his roommate's ski club was having a sunrise breakfast party before early skiing at nearby Round Top mountain; they went and nobody wanted to ski because Andy had come; a girl there professed love for him, urgent love, very extremely, and invited him to her sorority house; Andy, Cooney went handcuffed to sorority house at 9 A.M. ("At one point I was sitting in the hallway with my arm stuck inside the girl's bedroom door and that was when my hand had the best time of its life"). They had sex with the girl handcuffed, with Cooney outside the door, with Andy en flagrante inside the door ("I just used my imagination because I was trying the best I could to be a gentleman while handcuffed to this maniac"). Finally, they returned to Cooney's apartment and detached themselves and then Andy jumped on top of the bed of another Cooney roommate and bounced until the roommate awoke and thought the world was ending. Near eleven, twelve hours after their special nocturne began, Cooney deposited Andy back at the Ramada Inn where Bob awaited, refreshed. A friend of Cooney's later that day asked him what Andy was like. "And I said, 'That's the problem. He had different personalities all through the night. I didn't know which was the real him.'"

He wanted one of the tall blond hookers that dallied with Clifton at Taxi . . . the one who was originally from Denmark . . . whose name was Anna . . . he wanted Anna to come to New York for Carnegie Hall. . . . Andy told George that she was beautiful and very nice and good at sex. . . . When Andy had had sex with her before — as when he had sex with most hookers — he had asked people to look into his eyes afterward. . . . He had asked Kathy Utman or Linda Mitchell or Wendy before she quit to look very deeply into his eyes and he would say, "Did I lose my innocence?" and usually they said he didn't but sometimes his pupils were kind of opague . . . not as full of light as at other times. . . . (He had this ongoing argument with Linda — he thought prostitutes were the wisest women in the world because they understood men; Linda would always disagree. "He would call me in the middle of the night sometimes and start the argument all over again," she said. "He couldn't stand me to disagree.") Anna said she would fly to New York on Thursday, April 26, which was the day of the night of the concert, and would stay with him until Sunday. . . . Andy sent George to her apartment a week before the show and George gave her her plane tickets and hotel information

*and two hundred dollars for her first night of sexual service with Andy
and confirmed Andy's proposal that she would get another three hundred if she spent the rest of the time with him and George was also
impressed by her sweetness and saw nothing wrong with any of this
because there was nothing wrong because Andy never made it sound
very wrong. . . . Anyway, at Carnegie Hall, she would watch the concert perched in the gilded filigreed honor box above the stage, seated
next to Stanley and Janice who also thought she seemed like quite a
pleasant young lady. . . .*

There would be twenty school buses to accommodate the 2,800
people who would come and this was a problem because to have
twenty buses idling beside Carnegie Hall after ten o'clock on a
Thursday night conjured the promise of midtown traffic tangles
most horrendous. So it was decided that he should give special pa-
tronage to local law enforcement which was why on Sunday night
he had appeared at a swank Shubert Theater benefit to help provide
bulletproof vests for the New York Police Department. He did three
numbers (two were Elvis ones), and he performed on a bill that included the likes of Robin Williams, Lauren Bacall, Marlo Thomas,
Chita Rivera, and Sarah Jessica Parker, the twelve-year-old star of
the Broadway musical *Annie*, who noticed (as only a twelve-year-old
might) that both Williams and Andy were awkward and sweaty and
skittish offstage. Of Andy, she recalled, "He didn't seem like a confident man. And his eyes were so, you know, *wet*." Gregg Sutton,
who accompanied him on bass guitar that night and who would conduct the orchestra on Thursday, watched the effete theater crowd
display pronounced disinterest in Andy—"They didn't get him. It
started to make us feel a little nervous about Carnegie Hall."
Meanwhile, *Good Morning America* correspondent Joel Siegel
brought a camera crew to 21 Grassfield Road in Great Neck, where
Andy led a tour of the cradle of dreams that was the Kaufman basement and introduced Janice to the camera people and the viewer
people—"This is my mom. Her name's Mommy. And she's very em-

barrassed, aren't you, Mommy?" Janice *(pinkening)*: "Yes, I am."
Siegel: "How do you react to the things you see Andy do on television?" Janice: "I love it. I love it all. I'm one of his best fans." (Of
course, the wrestling and the Tony Clifton business she could do
without, but this wasn't the time for mentioning that.) Andy then
told Siegel about the little girl in seventh grade with whom he fell
in love but never met and said that everything that he had done for
the last fifteen years was to earn her attention, especially Carnegie
Hall—"It's only so I can get more confident and become more famous so I can meet this girl." Siegel: "You're telling me the truth,
right?" Andy: "Um, yeah."

It would all be the same as before only different and bigger and
more unwieldy and not as well paced and cameras would film it and
the film would be broadcast in a severely truncated fashion on the
cable network Showtime three months later (when it would still look
unwieldy), but everyone who was in the auditorium that night would
never forget what they experienced and, later, what they ate. Because
this was New York, because this was Carnegie Hall, his campaign of
disregard was both magnified and sanctified and was thus made instant media legend. He would always consider it to be his greatest
professional triumph, edging out his two other greatest triumphs—
his network special that the network still wouldn't air and the Clifton
holocaust at *Taxi*. (Only one other event would enter this hallowed
private arena of conquest and that event would actually take place in
an arena and he would be the only one who considered it a triumph
since it would telegraph to the masses without ambiguity that he was
not who they thought he was, not that anyone ever thought they
knew anyway.) As with opening night at the Huntington Hartford, it
was raining again, albeit lightly. Celebrities were there again—Andy
Warhol in row one; Dick Cavett, Penny Marshall, Rob Reiner, Jerry
Stiller, Anne Meara, et cetera. (Also present, down in front, were F
Troop stalwarts Gil Gevins and Glenn Barrett and Ginger
Petrochko.) The program would begin—as it had been eccentrically

advertised—at the stroke of three minutes past eight o'clock; Zmuda in referee garb would lead the audience in a sixty-second countdown to evince such.

Ten minutes before eight-oh-three, Clifton stalked about the back-stage corridors, very unhappily—he was to begin the proceedings by singing the national anthem, then recite the wife soliloquy (this time minus presence of wife or child), then sing just a little more and refuse to leave the stage. Chuck Braverman, who was producing the Showtime version of the concert, sat outside the theater in the technical truck and told his sound man to switch on Clifton's wireless microphone to make sure it worked. "So he turned it on and we heard Tony Clifton privately telling Zmuda what an asshole Andy Kaufman was—how he couldn't stand him and that he didn't want to go on, that he wanted more money and more credit—just ranting and raving and screaming. And neither he nor Zmuda had any idea that I was doing a mike check at that point! Everybody in the truck just sort of froze and looked at each other and collectively thought, *Uh-ohhh, what are we in for tonight?*"

One minute before eight-oh-three, an elderly woman who was a man who was Robin Williams who was disguised as an elderly woman who was supposed to be Andy's grandmother wordlessly tottered from the wings and settled most visibly into a plump easy chair at stage right where she would remain—a docile silent specter—for the next three hours of exposition. As George would report in his exuberant postmortem, **He sat there the whole show, reacted as a little old lady would react, sometimes laughing, sometimes nodding, and also nodding off. She acted as though she were falling asleep a few times.**

Eight-oh-three: Gregg Sutton, maestro, who wore black tie and tails as did each member of his twelve-piece ad hoc ensemble, lifted his baton. There commenced a remarkable ten-minute overture that he had arranged for this occasion, an orchestral suite that portended all that would follow—Mighty-Mouse-The-Impossible-Dream-Popeye-the-Sailor-Man-MacArthur-Park-The-Cow-Goes-Moo-Oklahoma-Love-Me-Tender-Jailhouse-Rock-This-Friendly-World-

Carolina-in-the-Morning. "It was high-class insanity," he said. (He had intended to conduct in white gloves but had to forfeit them to Robin Williams so as to conceal giveaway hairy hands.) Clifton then emerged and began his attack—as he performed "The Star-Spangled Banner" a montage of images were projected on a large movie screen behind him, including rippling flags, jet flyovers, missile detonations, goose-stepping Nazis, and Hitler himself.

He did it beautifully, said George. **For Tony Clifton. People seemed to enjoy it.** Before being removed from the stage (and this was his most abbreviated appearance ever), Clifton introduced his "protégés"—the Love Family, a legitimate ensemble of eight brothers and sisters, ages three to fifteen, whose five-part harmonizing was actually very big in Venezuela (Andy had stumbled upon them in Los Angeles on the Venice Beach Boardwalk). And so the Love Family took the spotlight and earnestly launched into sugary medleys from *Hair* and *The Sound of Music* while moving about in sprightly/awkward geometric choreography. And the audience—sensing put-on—rebelled by the second number and booed them to tears which were real (actual real tears! oh!); the Loves, now crushed, left the stage which had now been spattered with debris. **It was very sad and uncalled for and really cruel,** said George, who also noted, **I felt they were on too long.** Sutton said, "For the first time in history, the audience wanted more Clifton! It was a very hip crowd."

Andy took over and did what he had done before again—with certain alterations. "Um," he said early on, "when I was starting in show business, my grandmother—we used to talk a lot and she said, 'Why are you wasting your time?' And I said, 'Grandma, one day I'm gonna be playing Carnegie Hall.' She said, 'Oh, come on!' I said, 'Yup. Grandma, I promise you—I'll be in Carnegie Hall and when that day comes, I'm gonna give you the best seat in the house!' So, anyway, there's my grandma over there." And he pointed to the man on the stage who was not his grandmother and said, "See? I told you! I told you this would happen, right?" And he then promised the audience an evening of surprises and cartoons and games and prizes and big-name stars and treats. ("Everybody say *milk*. Okay, now everybody say *cookies.* Okay, very good!") And he brought out an actual street person named Grant "Bliss" Bowman whom Andy had discovered two New Year's Eves ago in Times Square singing a blissful Happy New Year song at the top of his lungs, which Bowman now blissfully reprised, and re-reprised, and re-re-reprised. (Zmuda and Sutton were dispatched earlier in the week to find Bowman on his favorite corner where they lured him with an offer of one hundred dollars payable after the show; Bowman would not listen to their entreaties until he received—on the spot—a bottle of port, which now protruded from his back pocket. "He wanted the kind that didn't have a cork," said Sutton.) Then, Andy showed a forties-vintage Hopalong Cassidy one-reeler that Grandpa Paul had given him long ago, wherein dancing girls wearing horse heads affixed to their waists gamboled to the tune of "I've Got Spurs That Jingle Jangle Jingle"—after which he brought out the only surviving dancer no really named Eleanor Cody Gould with whom he chatted for a while. (Her: "I knew Tom Mix!" Him: "Did you know Will Rogers?" Her: "Oh, no—and I always wanted to!" Him: "How did you feel when his plane crashed?") Then he made her ride a stick pony as he borrowed Sutton's baton and led the orchestra in a dizzying rendition of the song from the film, whose tempo he accelerated until she collapsed of a heart attack and was pronounced dead and was covered with a jacket and she lay in state . . . for a long disturbing silent interlude . . . until Andy returned wearing an Indian headdress and performed a sacred tribal dance and she snapped back to life—and it worked just as they had rehearsed earlier in the hotel suite. **A couple of people walked out,** George reported. **Two people in front of me walked out during that segment. They didn't appreciate that type of humor. But most of the audience enjoyed it.**

Business as usual followed—an arduous draw at wrestling (his eleventh undefeated match!); the vengeful return of Jay York (thwarted again by spinach); a most powerful and arresting Elvis (who went into the audience to serenade Gil Gevins's mother); the Andy-and-Clifton duet (his brother, Michael, again donned the veneer); the revelation of

Robin Williams; the Rockettes who were not the Rockettes; the Mormon Tabernacle Choir who were the Borough of Manhattan Community College Choir (many black members, all belting "Carolina in the Morning"); Santa Claus; the prolonged standing ovation; and the announcement—"Thank you. This is the first half of my act. And for the second half . . . you've all been very good—you really have—and I'd like to take you all out for milk and cookies now!"

And, in his terrycloth bathrobe, he led them out into the drizzle and the buses had to make repeated trips to and from the New York School of Printing, whose large cafeteria had been furnished with a sea of toddler's tables and chairs, where mini-bags of Famous Amos and half-pints of Cream-O-Land were consumed as clowns and magicians and jugglers performed, while in the school auditorium a quintet of off-duty cops crooned soul music and were then followed by a Hindu street mystic named Man-Sun who charmed a snake and hypnotized a rabbit and reclined on broken glass. "It was P. T. Barnum meets Jung, you know?" said Robin Williams. "People who were heavily into hardcore drugs were going, 'Oh, this is nice!' This wasn't party till you puke—this was *milk and cookies*! It was Howdy Buddha time."

And Andy worked the assemblage again, elated to be sure, and agreed to a rematch challenge from his wrestling partner that night, a towering comedienne named Deborah Croce whom he did not know and whom he again could not beat nor could she beat him. And amid the circus, Stanley and Janice beamed and Stanley told a reporter, "I think that behind all the frivolity and all the craziness, there is a very, very serious man." Stanley would understand this point even more profoundly when he learned how much money it had cost his son to produce this night of debit—the union laborers alone were greased an extra ten thousand dollars in cash just to load in the equipment at Carnegie Hall. Andy would erroneously claim that the losses again hovered near twenty thousand, although Stanley knew better: "He took a bath."

*   *   *

It ended at three in the morning and he had announced to those who remained that the show would continue at one o'clock the following afternoon on the Staten Island Ferry and it did and three hundred or so people were waiting when he and Zmuda and Sutton arrived a half hour late in a cab and he bought them all ice cream cones and he wrestled Deborah Croce again to a draw and he performed "MacArthur Park" and led a singalong to "Mighty Mouse" (which was the only time in history that he sang the entire lyric) and attempted to begin a round of "Ninety-nine Bottles of Beer on the Wall" (nobody wanted to play along) and told all present that in 1982 he hoped to have enough money to transport an audience around the world. Then, at five o'clock, he returned with seven people to the temporary offices George had set up at the Sheraton City Squire Hotel and told George, "These are the last ones." And he gave them cookies and milk and went back to his hotel, the Lombardi, where he meditated and then spent the next two nights having sex with Anna the nice hooker.

11

They call me a madman now. That would be a distinct rise in my social position were it not that they still regard me as being ridiculous as ever. But that does not make me angry any more. They are all dear to me now even while they laugh at me—yes, even then they are for some reason particularly dear to me. I shouldn't have minded laughing with them—not at myself, of course, but because I love them—had I not felt so sad as I looked at them. I feel sad because they do not know the truth, whereas I know it. Oh, how hard it is to be the only man to know the truth!

—Fyodor Dostoyevsky,
The Dream of a Ridiculous Man

George called him an extremist. And he was that. And he became that even more so. He became an extremely extreme extremist. And this would cause much undoing, wherein excess would breed ruin, wherein appetite for whim would devour him. He would sate and sate himself until poison seeped inside—and, although he did not feel it there and could not know it was there, it was there. The eyeglow became red-rimmed and bloodshot and it flickered and dimmed. Fewer and fewer were fooled and fewer still would care to be. Innocence was more elusive than ever. Innocence had become a game of chase and he would have to chase harder to win and he would often bore of that chase and maybe he couldn't win now, anyway. He had tasted conquest but there was never enough and his idea of conquest did not tend to resemble that of others. Already every one of his heartdreams and boydreams and camera-in-wall-dreams had, more or less, come true—so he had to conjure new ones and these new ones inspired other new ones, larger ones, and the larger they were, the darker they seemed to everyone but him. Now more than ever—for reasons he did not try to comprehend—speed was essential. Thus darkness fell in quick serial thuds and it was, um, fun.

Movies had become the business of primary concern, the next logical career step—as exemplified by the successful crossovers of contemporaries like Chevy Chase (*Foul Play*), John Belushi (*National Lampoon's Animal House*), and Steve Martin (*The Jerk*). And so three weeks after Carnegie Hall, he began rehearsals in Los Angeles for his role as the corrupt megalomaniacal televangelist Armageddon T. Thunderbird in the Marty Feldman religious satire *In God We Tru$t*. But he had actually started practicing well before that. He had worked the shimmering rants of Thunderbird into his act, slipping into a white bouffant wig during various March college and club dates, and invoked the wrath of the Lord before congregants who had come to see him do Elvis. In New York, he had stood under an umbrella in front of Carnegie Hall, disguised in the wig plus Groucho Marx nose and mustache, clutching a hotel Bible and screaming at passersby—"I know why it's raining! It's raining because the Lord is crying! And he wants you all to buy umbrellas!" He then pointed to a poster advertising his forthcoming concert and declared, "This man should not be allowed onstage! He has no talent; he's an impostor! He should not be allowed in Carnegie Hall; I-I-I-I-I-I-I-I should be in Carnegie Hall!" ("Most people thought I was a crazy umbrella salesman.") He flew to London following the concert and positioned himself every afternoon for a week on a soapbox at Speaker's Corner in Hyde Park and told British pedestrians that he was God and argued to unify time zones around the world so it wouldn't be necessary to always have to change the hands of His watch when traveling. Then he returned to the back lot of Universal Studios to complete his grandiloquent acting assignment—"He never appeared on the set as Andy," said Feldman, who both wrote and directed the film. "He arrived fully charactered as Thunderbird and never once left him." And during the shoot, he became friendly with Richard Pryor, who played the role of God. Pryor would sit in Andy's trailer, where Andy often recited from his novel-in-progress (which he was inordinately fond of doing when virtually anyone was within earshot) and one day Linda Mitchell encountered Pryor stepping from the trailer—"He came up to me and he seemed a little stoned and he had tears in his eyes. He put his arms around me and said, 'Linda, he's a *genius!* He makes us all look like nothing!' I said, 'What are you talking about?' Richard said, 'He's been reading his book to me.' I said, 'God, you *are* stoned!' Then I thought, maybe I'm missing something, because I thought *Richard* was a genius." (In the publicity notes Feldman prepared for the film's release, the book would now be characterized as such: "Titled *The Huey Williams Story,* Andy describes it as a fictional biography of a neighbor he once had who would stand watering his lawn. That is all he knew about his neighbor. The neighbor's name has been changed in the novel. And the fact that he watered the lawn has been eliminated lest the neighbor recognize himself.") Feldman, who took a professorial shine to his young charge, would later mordantly note, "In Andy, there is something underneath the playfulness—a sense of danger, a kind of genial anger, as if the way we wearily come to see the world is simply insufficient."

Not long thereafter, George secured an office suite at Universal for Andy and Zmuda as part of a deal made to realize *The Tony Clifton Story* as a major motion picture. Universal had optioned an outline written by the pair after an unpleasant altercation in February, when the idea for the film was conceived by a comedian named Ed Bluestone, who, like Andy, was a Marty Klein client at APA. Andy had loved Bluestone's idea—in which Clifton would fall from Vegas lounge greatness, then lose his wife to another singer, whereupon

Clifton would marry his own manager (a man), whom he then married many more times before he died at the end of the movie. (Andy would have played both Clifton and the unctuous performer Nathan Richards.) Bluestone pitched the story to Universal and to Paramount—with Andy and George and Zmuda and various agents in attendance—and both studios were deeply interested in having Bluestone commence writing, which displeased Zmuda, who insisted that he cowrite the film with Bluestone, which Andy believed was fair since Zmuda had certainly contributed to Clifton's character development. But Bluestone adamantly refused to work with Zmuda and, since Clifton was Andy's intellectual property, Bluestone was summarily removed from the project (about which he was furious), thus forcing Zmuda and Andy to invent an entirely new Clifton story, which they immediately began to brainstorm. On March 9, they were at the Playboy Hotel and Resort in Lake Geneva, Wisconsin, where George had flown in to listen to the story line that they had cooked up. The three of them sat around a table in Andy's suite and George turned on his tape recorder and Andy insisted that they all smoke cigars while he and Bob enacted the story, because they had been smoking cigars throughout the writing process because that was what they thought real screenwriters did. (George said: "Suppose I tell you that Neil Simon doesn't write with cigars." Bob responded: "He's a completely different kind of writer than we are. This is *our* way of doing it.") Anyway, they performed the essence of the movie for George and George thought it was a little confusing but a very good start and, when the first draft was completed in August, most of the elements had remained and others had been added. This draft—which the studio executives would find too dark largely because Andy, playing himself, was the despicable villain of the script and Clifton was the good-hearted hero—would quietly circulate throughout smarter quarters of Hollywood for years to come because it was eventually understood to be something of a comic masterpiece, a mind-bending house-of-mirrors tour in which identities sublimated other identities and tricks were played upon other tricks and real life interchanged itself with fiction and vice versa.

Meanwhile, the executives who had tried to shepherd the script toward workability—Thom Mount, Sean Daniel, Bruce Berman—would years later still feel varying pangs of remorse over the fact that the many rewrite demands had pushed the concept so far away from its miraculous original premise as to render it toothless and then finally dead.

"It was completely brilliant—and unreleasable. Perfect. Just what I needed," said Mount, who ran the film division for Universal. "It could have been a little less brilliant. We took a position that it was too dark in its ending, and it was. It had a sucker-punch, bait-and-switch sensibility that Andy loved, but would have been difficult for an audience to deal with because there was nothing in it to consistently trust." Daniel, who was second in command, would add, "I have to say that the phrase *ahead of its time* genuinely applied here. I believe that had it come twenty years later Tony Clifton, as a persona and as a movie, would have been a giant hit, tapping into a much bigger culture of cynicism." Ultimately, it was Universal president Ned Tannen who pulled the plug (after expending nearly two years of patience with the project and, in the meantime, having hired Andy to play a robot in a film that would embarrass everyone involved with it). And even Tannen would harbor chagrin in hindsight. "It's funny that it stuck in his brain," mused Daniel, "because in later years I was sitting with Ned when *The Tony Clifton Story* came up in conversation and he said, apropos of nothing, 'You know, *that's* the one we should have made.'"

They initially wanted the film to be made in Stinkavision, so that whenever Clifton sprayed on a certain repulsive cologne to entice chickaroonies (it was called Purple Passion), theaters would be engulfed in the stench. They believed the natural antecedents to their film were *King Kong* and *The Hunchback of Notre Dame.* "You see, this man on the surface looks like a pretty abrasive guy," Andy said of Clifton. "But in this movie you get to see his soul. He is a wonderful man. He's the kind of guy who would see a little lost dog on the corner of a city street and would say, 'Ahh, get out of here!' And then, when no one's lookin', at midnight, he'd take the dog home." "He's a lovely guy," Zmuda said, "but very stupid. And Andy becomes his manager to exploit him — like an evil version of Colonel Tom Parker."

To synopsize: *Clifton lives in Philly, works on an assembly line screwing tops on salt shakers (George's idea), is a forty-five-year-old virgin who talks (in his own special parlance) of having laid much pipe and making like a ham sandwich with countless females and his nonsensical bluster is barely humored by those around him. One night, he falls into a massage parlor/bordello and is finally compelled to throw around fistfuls of cash and receives a Jacuzzi bath (while wearing a pink shower cap and singing lounge standards) from four topless scarlet women who happily take his money and claim to admire his voice, telling him that he sounds just like Tony Bennett and/or Frank Sinatra. At which point, a hooker with a heart of gold named Anna (oh!) arrives to see that he is being taken advantage of and she kindly relieves him of his virginity and, thunderstruck by feelings of love for her, he summons courage to quit his job and decides to aggressively pursue a singing career. Andy, meanwhile, comes through Philadelphia on tour and he and Zmuda are accosted by Clifton in an all-night diner, where he is peddling 8-x-10 glossies of himself and repeatedly calls Andy "Mr. Belushi" and Andy is thoroughly besotted by Clifton's idiotic bravura, especially after witnessing him perform to a Frank Sinatra record during an amateur showcase at the nearby Porterhouse Lounge. Andy decides that Clifton will be billed as his special guest/opening act at Carnegie Hall on April 26. Clifton arrives — after much confusion wherein he thinks a ticket is awaiting him at the box office — and performs with usual extravagant badness and the audience eventually storms the stage in riot* and The New York Times *calls Clifton the most obnoxious act in show business history and George is appalled at Andy's lack of judgment and lectures, "Andy, they hate him! They were throwing things at him!" And there is a malevolent glint in Andy's eye as he says, "That's right, and they're going to hate him more and more. They're going to LOVE to hate him. And more important, they're going to PAY to hate him. Gentlemen, I got myself the next Hula Hoop."*

And this comes to pass exactly and, in short order, Clifton is on the cover of Time magazine and there is a run on peach tuxedos throughout the land and his preferred exclamation of paranoia ("Getcha hands off me!") becomes the ubiquitous catchphrase of the moment and he performs at the White House, where he disgraces Chinese diplomats ("What time does da Chinaman go to da dentist?") and he is given his own weekly television show on NBC at which the audience happily comes to boo him as he torments celebrity guests—asking Raquel Welch about her cosmetic surgery and terrifying the San Diego Zoo's Joan Embery, who has brought out a baby seal, which is then chased around the stage by a club-wielding baby-seal-killer from Newfoundland. And it is Andy Kaufman who is the Svengali-producer of this vulgar sideshow and who assures Clifton that it is all meant in fun because Clifton thinks this mania has gone too far and gotten too ugly. (George feels the same way and Andy tells him to relax and to try meditating, but George insists that Andy stop the madness, so Andy fires him.) To distract Clifton from his qualms, Andy has located Anna, the nice hooker, and sends Clifton off to romp with her and she awakens him at last to the notion that he is being used and he decides to do something meaningful in his career, so he tells Andy that he wants to star in a sensitive remake of The Hunchback of Notre Dame (since he feels a tragic kinship). Andy sets up the deal instantly (smelling, in fact, a comedy blockbuster) and now it is the night of the premiere and Clifton stands in the back of the theater and watches the audience scream with laughter at his Quasimodo, who has a cigarette dangling from his mouth, as per Cliftonian trademark, while being whiplashed by tormentors. Aghast that his noble dream has become a laughing-stock, Clifton runs to find Andy in the theater manager's office, where he is barking demands into a telephone ("I want the TV rights sewed up NOW, fucker!"), then, noticing Clifton, changes his telephone manner and says, "Yes, Grandma, I love you, too. . . ."

Clifton wants the movie stopped and Andy—[Well, here was how Andy himself improvised the scene for George back in Lake Geneva, making illustrative use of his writing cigar: "Then Kaufman says, 'Tony, sit down.' 'No, I think I'll stand if you don't mind.' 'Tony, let me explain to you the facts of life. Remember *tenk you veddy much?* You think I *like* doing that, baby? You think I like that—*oh, he's so cuuuute!* I do it for two reasons, baby! For the *moolah* and the *chicka- roos!* That's why I do *tenk you veddy much!* You got a gimmick here, Tony. You gotta play it up! The public is stupid! The public eats it up! Listen to them—they're *laughing* at you! They love you! Take the money!' 'Waitaminute! Lemme get this straight . . .' 'Tony, you have been played for a buffoon jerkoff! You think you could sing? You think you could act? You think people wanna look at you playing the hunchback of Notre Dame serious? Look at you! *You're a buffoon jerkoff!* That's all you are and that's all you'll ever gonna be! I made you! *I made you!* You think you're gonna give me a hard time and blow it for me? I'm making a lot of money on you, pal. I'm not going to have some stupid buffoon jerkoff blow it for me!'" And here Zmuda reminded George: "This, you know, is Andy Kaufman actu- ally talking to *himself* onscreen." And Andy corrected him—"But you *don't* know that. It has to be done very well. No one is going to think that I'm Tony Clifton."]

And Clifton is reduced to tears and he runs back into the theater and leaps in front of the screen and tells the audience that they've all been duped and the audience believes this to be yet another Clifton act of comic obliviousness and they begin cheerfully pelting him with rot- ten tomatoes (supplied by Andy) and he drips with tomato guts and tells them, "I feel sorry for you people . . . I don't think you even know why you did this. . . ." And he pitifully leaves the stage declaring that he will never return and the stage remains empty and then the picture freezes—and the camera pulls back so that the frozen frame is seen on a film-editing console, where Andy sits and now addresses the camera to introduce himself as Andy Kaufman, maker of The Tony Clifton Story, *and he goes on to say that on July 18, 1980, with three scenes left to be completed in the film, Tony Clifton, age forty-seven, died of lung cancer at Cedars-Sinai Medical Center in Los Angeles and two weeks later it was decided by Universal MCA Pictures that, in honor of Tony Clifton's memory, he would play the role of Clifton for the re- mainder of the movie.* [So Andy said to George in Lake Geneva: "And now for the rest of the film, I play Tony Clifton, but the makeup looks like shit—putty on the nose, the wig, no belly, it's very crappy looking. You can see right through it. Like that horrible makeup I wore in the Home Box Office show. And now the film takes a completely different turn; it's going to change from realistic into a complete comedy. Kaufman is taking total liberties with the character. So this is what happens—"]

Andy/Clifton leaves the theater and jumps in a cab and heads for the airport, where he steals a small plane which crashes in a distant jungle where Andy/Clifton emerges unharmed and becomes a tribal god among natives who are impressed with his Sinatraesque chant— do be do be doooo—until he gets word via the jungle paperboy ["Now the film has taken a new turn, like an Abbott and Costello comedy—Clifton asks what the paperboy is doing in the middle of the jungle and the paperboy says, 'Can I help it if they gave me a bad corner?'"] *that Kaufman is staging an elaborate memorial service at Forest Lawn cemetery and selling thousands of admission tickets and various other Clifton paraphernalia, because Clifton was believed to be lost at sea after stealing the plane. So Andy/Clifton charges into the memorial service, riding an elephant, with his tribe of savages in tow, and he clobbers Kaufman* ("I've been waitin' to do this for a long time!") *who falls into an empty grave and then Andy/Clifton sees Anna, the nice hooker, and grabs her lustfully and then the offscreen voice of the real Tony Clifton says, "Getcha hands off her!" And then the real Clifton steps into frame and says to Andy/Clifton, "Where do you get off tellin' people I died a cancer?" And the startled Andy/Clifton gives panicked instructions to his film crew—because this is obviously a movie set—"Keep the camera going! This is gold!" And the real Clifton proceeds to lambast his exploiter for making mockery of the real Clifton life and the "total fabrication" of truths implied therein (including, and especially, loss of virginity at age forty-five!), and then he walks over to "the girl playing Anna" and professes his undying love and the cemetery transforms itself into the set of a magical Busby Berkeley–style leg-kicking musical finale at the close of which the real Clifton announces to the camera that if he has made just one person happy, then it's all been worth it.*

By the time all the rewrites were completed, an evil Andy had been replaced by an evil manager named Norman, who would commit both Andy and Clifton to a sanitarium. But nobody would really care much anymore.

Thom Mount gave them offices next to those of director John Landis—who had originally wanted to do a Clifton documentary but was now filming *The Blues Brothers*. The offices were on a back-lot street near the hospital set. "We thought it appropriate to keep Andy close to the hospital," said Mount. "But Andy took to the lot like a duck to water. He *loved* life on a movie lot—because everything was a façade, was Make-Believe, capital M, capital B, which resulted in a number of odd moments." Clifton was apprehended one night wearing a security guard's uniform and carrying a gun. Mount told the Universal cop who made the arrest, "He works for us. Don't worry." Sean Daniel had assigned a business affairs director to get Clifton membership in the Screen Actors Guild and the Writers Guild—per Andy's instructions. Clifton showed up at many meetings—"He'd be this burned-out, swaggering, brittle, thinly-connected-to-the-planet kind of lounge lizard Lothario with an ego the size of Texas and a bad attitude," said Mount. Such meetings were largely unproductive. Mount also tried to integrate Andy with other comedy stars who worked on the lot—"The other comic artists had enormous respect for him and were also scared to death of him. He was going places they couldn't even imagine going, places that were so potentially dangerous and deadly. People didn't know what to do with him." So he invited Andy and George to a party at his Malibu beach house—"Andy was the guy everyone was most excited to meet and hang out with. But when they would talk to him, he was in what was sort of his internally blissed-out Andy mode: 'Hi, Andy, how are you?' 'Oh, hi, I'm very fine.' He wouldn't give anyone a way in. Halfway through the party, I saw Andy standing in a corner by himself."

Due to the juggernaut of publicity that swarmed the Carnegie Hall event, ABC suddenly felt obliged to schedule the suppressed ninety-minute special, which would air at last on Tuesday, August 28, 1979 (twenty-six months after its completion), and he went to New York to promote it and he took Grandma Pearl onto the locally broadcast *Joe Franklin Show* and told Franklin, "Grandma happens to write all my material and she wrote my special that you're gonna see August twenty-eighth. She's very modest about it." And Franklin asked Pearl for confirmation of this and she shrugged and said, "If he says it." And she said of her grandson's success, "I am very happy. This is my proudest moment." And she told a joke about a dog going to temple and slow-danced with Andy, but no music played and Andy admitted to being forty-three years old, which was something he enjoyed telling all the reporter people lately. Pearl shrugged some more. And then he went on *The Tomorrow Show*, which aired on NBC after *The Tonight Show*, and he talked with host Tom Snyder for close to ten minutes about nothing but weather because Snyder had read the *New York* magazine article in which Andy expressed his dream of hosting a talk show on which nothing would be discussed except weather and so Snyder gamely (even brilliantly) indulged him by traversing the intricacies of rain and snow and sleet and slippery pavement and iced-over bridges until Snyder could take no more, although it was quite clear that Andy could have continued for another hour. And then he wrestled three women—one was a Playboy Bunny who had worked as an extra on *Taxi* the week before (and whom he had flown to New York) and the other two were *Tomorrow* staff members—and he pinned the *Tomorrow* women and came to a draw with the Bunny, but what was most important was that this was the first time he had wrestled a woman, much less three of them, on a television program. Pearl, meanwhile, had sat in the studio that night, out of camera range, and covered her eyes throughout the wrestling segment thank you.

Clifton returned and decimated the Dinah Shore show on September 19 and this was not a good thing for Clifton's career, what with a movie about his life in the works and all. He had gotten separate management by this time—George had handed him off to a Shapiro/West associate named Jimmy Concholla, who became Jimmy C. when dealing on Clifton's behalf and Jimmy C. had a separate telephone line and took on a separate persona to accomplish such dealings. (Clifton liked Jimmy C. to wear black shirts with pastel ties and sunglasses in his presence.) So Jimmy C. and Zmuda, who didn't bother to become Bugsy Meyer, and Linda Mitchell, who didn't bother to become Ginger Sax, and three chickaroonies with whom Andy and Zmuda had recently been dawdling accompanied Clifton (only forty-five minutes late) to the KTLA studios to tape *Dinah!* and Clifton caused a stink during rehearsal of his number, "On the Street Where You Live," which delayed matters further. (He had attributed his lateness to a mix-up at the gate, where his name hadn't been left with security, whereas that-asshole-Kaufman's name was on the drive-on list.) Because Dinah had a cold, her producers told Clifton that she would be unable to sing the duet that he had planned—"Anything You Can Do (I Can Do Better)"—which rankled him more and delayed matters even further, until he had to be shooed from the stage. Finally, the taping began—before a live audience of five hundred elderly people—and Dinah introduced him. "With us today is a special guest. His charm, charisma, his voice, his song stylings—well, let me put it this way: He is beyond description . . ." And he wandered through the audience as he sang what Dinah called "his big hit" and greeted frightened women with the hand that did not hold the microphone and cigarette. (When the show aired about one month later, words would be superimposed below him—THIS IS A PUT-ON and RECOGNIZE HIM YET?) Then he joined Dinah and co-host Charles Nelson Reilly, who stood at Dinah's cooking counter, where he pointed out his three nubile companions in the front row ("Get a shot of the chickies here! Okay, those are my chickies!") and then he took umbrage when Dinah inferred that he had many big-selling records ("I haven't made any records! What kind of crap are you trying to put over on the people here? You're full of crap!") and he implored that Dinah sing their canceled duet and produced a sheet of lyrics for her to follow, which she did, with kindly patience, after which he was to demonstrate his recipe for bacon and eggs—but this segment would never see light of airwaves.

What followed: He dropped a pound of butter into a hot frying pan, then proceeded to crack a dozen eggs, one at a time, then pressed the broken eggshells into Dinah's hands (erroneous tales would later circulate that he cracked the eggs on her head, because she had pushed away a lock of hair wherein a bit of shell stuck) and, at this point, producers wanted to eject him but feared what he would do with the pan of sizzling grease. Dinah, whose eyes belied panic, tried to go to a commercial and he threw a fit and flicked drops of water at her and began inviting the audience down onto the stage to watch his eggs fry, but now the tape had been stopped in the control booth and producer Fred Tatashore and Dinah's business manager rushed down to quell his remonstrations and each man grabbed a Clifton arm—"He was yelling, 'Hey, you guys, what do you think you're doin'! Do you know who I am?! *I'm a big star!*'" Tatashore would recall, "So we said, 'Okay, big star, you're out of here!' And we literally tossed him out of the building, where security guys took him away. He was out there still screaming. I was laughing by then. I said to Dinah, 'I guess we got rid of that!' And I told the audience, 'Well, that's the way it goes with some of these singers!'"

The producers were actually more rattled than was Dinah—one called George immediately to complain and he woefully reported the incident to his tape recorder—**They said that in all the years that Dinah has done her show, nobody treated her as badly as Tony Clifton did. There really was fear of this man. He was insane and unapproachable. He was not funny. He was embarrassing, unprofes-**

sional, and insane. He had no respect for the people over there. Everyone was upset. Jean Stapleton, who was one of the guests, was terribly frightened. (Stapleton, in fact, had locked herself in the greenroom, where, according to fellow guest David Copperfield, "she was weeping and sobbing when all the pandemonium broke loose in the studio. It was amazing.")

George sent flowers the next day and had Andy's name inscribed on the card of apology. He also made Andy call the producers and Dinah herself afterward—which he grudgingly agreed to do. "I called Dinah two days later and I said, 'Listen, Dinah, you have always treated me with such hospitality when I've been on your show. I have a lot of respect for you. And I would never do anything to upset your show. I had nothing to do with it. Tony Clifton is Tony Clifton and I am me.' And she said, 'Oh, that's fine, Andy. I know that you weren't there. I don't know who told you that, but I wasn't upset at you.' Then she said, 'I want you to come on the show,' and I said I'd love to." And, of course, he never returned as any of himselves.

Clifton = buffoon jerkoff = Andy.
Word spread.

He agreed to play a five-night engagement at Harrah's Reno Resort and Casino in Nevada beginning October 6 because Bob told him that the Mustang Ranch was only fifteen minutes away. Harrah's arranged a press luncheon to announce the event a week prior to the Dinah Shore appearance; the luncheon was held in the wine cellar of the tony Blue Fox restaurant in San Francisco, whose proximity to Nevada created puzzlement in itself. Andy showed the fortysome-such reporter people who attended how he could skip rope for ten minutes straight; he did so with his napkin tucked into belt. Milk and cookies were served for dessert. Gerald Nachman of the *San Francisco Chronicle* wrote: "Booking Andy Kaufman into Harrah's is rather like selling Andy Warhol originals at Lucky's [supermarket]."

Andy announced that he was no longer a song-and-dance man. "I'm a wrestler," he said. He also said that he wished to publicly invite the three thousand Russian combat troops currently stationed in Cuba to fly to Disneyland at his expense. "We'll go on some rides and then we'll have milk and cookies. This is my contribution to world peace." He looked stricken, as this was met with chuckling. "I'm serious! Everyone thinks everything I do is part of the act." Zmuda had planted himself as a reporter from the *Norwood Free Press* (based outside of Chicago, he said) and assaulted Andy with many probing questions— "*Is it true, Mr. Kaufman, that you wrestle women only to fulfill your perverted fantasies?*" George eventually went over and slapped him, then threw him out.

Harrah's Headliner Room would be the most commercial venue he had played to date and he did fine but cared more about getting over to the famous Mustang Ranch bordello as soon as the shows were over because this was the most exciting thing that he had ever done in his life. George would get several reports daily. George would sometimes be on the phone with Bob after Andy's performances and he would hear Andy in the background imploding—"Come on, come on, Zmuda! We have to *go*, we have to *leave!*" Andy told George that he had sex with twenty-four Mustang girls that week. Zmuda could not keep up. Sean Daniel and Bruce Berman from Universal came to Reno to discuss the Clifton movie and Andy dragged them to the Mustang, where they could talk while he scoped his slatternly prey. Daniel would recall, "We were there for official business. Andy, on the other hand, was there for love. I think he found much love there." Andy told George, "They loved me! It was truly a religious experience!" Sometimes he would pay them just to talk to him or to wrestle each other for him. He was different, they all thought. So nice, too, they thought, too. He returned to Los Angeles, deliriously happy, and was immediately treated for a red and itchy case of the clap.

On the night that arguably began the spiral toward destiny, he wore Grandpa Paul's elegant calf-length Sulka bathrobe that he had inherited years earlier. Beneath the robe were the white longjohns and the black athletic trunks and beneath the trunks over the white longjohns was the masking tape that Zmuda had wrapped around the groin and pelvic region to conceal the appearance of a televised erection. It was October 20 and it was *Saturday Night Live:* He started out nicely enough, speaking of the olden days when wrestlers had traveled with carnivals from town to town offering money to any man who could last three minutes in the ring with them. His tone was quite pleasant as he explained that he had been doing the same, only with women. ("This is a very legitimate thing and the reason I chose women is because I'm not an athlete. . . . If I chose a man, I might get beaten.") *(. . . rubbing . . .)* He maintained his level tone while sharing his belief that women were best suited for the-scrubbing-the-washing-the-peeling-the-mopping, but lamented that men of late had allowed women to achieve societal status gain—"Men are a bunch of pussycats and pansies for letting this happen. And I think the men in this country are nothing but pitiful specimens of manhood." And, of course, the audience—women and men alike—grumbled and booed, since he had now alienated both sexes and all of North American humankind at once. Zmuda waved the five hundred dollars in the air and five volunteers bounded to the stage and the audience selected a pregnant woman to wrestle him—which he would not do—so he asked for the runner-up, who happened to be prettiest and she was a lithe brunette named Mimi Lambert, heiress to the Lacoste sportswear fortune, who studied dance with Martha Graham and was clad in a leotard because she had danced six hours that day ("My legs were like rubberbands") and she had no idea who Andy Kaufman was because she never watched television but thought he was obnoxious and she lasted well beyond the allotted three minutes, although referee Zmuda neglected to notice, as was his occasional habit, before she was pinned. And during their grappling, he broke away to strut and mug and bait the audience that wanted his blood—"*Shadduppp! Shadduppppp! I'm not chokin'! Come onnnnn! Let's see some competition up here!*"—and after he was declared the winner he gave Mimi Lambert a kick as she began to get to her feet and shoved

her back down on the mat. Then he strutted some more and breath-
lessly issued an open challenge to Olympic swimmer Diana Nyad
("supposedly the world's strongest lady") to wrestle him on a future
show, offering ten thousand dollars if she won. "Not only that—but
I'll have a barber here and if you beat me, I will have my head shaved
in front of everyone right here in the ring! Diana, *any time, baby!* I
don't think you can *dooooooo ittttttttttttt!*" And he clucked like a
chicken. And then he took Mimi out for a very late dinner and they
began dating immediately thereafter and she joined him on tour
within three weeks and returned with him a few more times to
Saturday Night Live, where Bill Murray would send flowers to her in
Andy's dressing room and Andy always walked the flowers directly out
of the dressing room and made sure to give Murray a curious look
every time he did so.

He was throwing fits in hotels. At the Seattle Hilton, the switchboard ignored his requests to have his morning calls stopped. He
threatened to slander the hotel whenever possible, using much of-
fensive language to illustrate his point. George had to make nice. At
the Chicago Holiday Inn, he was asked to relinquish his large room
for a smaller one due to a mix-up. He screamed and kept the big one.
Only four hundred tickets were sold for his Chicago engagement at
the University of Illinois; the auditorium capacity was eleven hundred. A week earlier, only two hundred ninety tickets were sold for a
Boston concert, which was canceled due to lack of interest. (A short
six months had passed since he had sold out Carnegie Hall.) George
believed it was the wrestling. The mail poured in after the *Saturday
Night Live* appearance, all very extremely hostile. George told him to
maybe rethink it. He told George that he had a better idea—a cross-
country tour, underwritten by a sponsor, in which all tickets would
cost only ninety-nine cents apiece. George liked the idea. No spon-
sors would be very interested.

*　*　*

November 17, a brief announcement on *Saturday Night Live*, in response to the negative mail: "So you're trying to get me to stop wrestling on television, huh? Well, there's NO WAY YOU'RE GOING TO DO IT! I will wrestle on *every* show! I will wrestle on every variety show, on every talk show! You will not be able to turn the dial fast enough! YOU'LL NEVER GET RID OF ME UNTIL A WOMAN BEATS ME IN A WRESTLING MATCH!! That's right! But there's not a woman who can beat me BECAUSE WOMEN DO NOT HAVE THE BRAINS!!! *Shadduppppp! Shadduppppppp!!*" And because Diana Nyad had never responded to his gauntlet, he now challenged all of the rest of them out there, offering a thousand dollars and the shaved head and the promise to keep his rubbing off television forever. He asked them to send photographs and statistics and the reasons they wanted to wrestle him and certain people at *Saturday Night Live* (who were amenable to his input) would decide which finalists would be flown in to wrestle him on the program three days before Christmas. (The photographs were imperative.) Guest host Bea Arthur then came on camera and said, "Boy, I hope somebody beats him. And beats him badly!" He screamed at her from the sidelines—"*Shadduppp! Shadduppppp!* I'll take *you* on, baby!"

His sister and his brother collected him on Thanksgiving morning, very early, at Mimi Lambert's Upper East Side apartment, where he had spent the night. Mimi playfully flashed her naked breasts for them as Michael and Carol dragged Andy to the elevator. The three of them rushed to Macy's and boarded a circus float on which they rode in the Thanksgiving Day parade. Andy wore ringmaster togs and Michael attempted to be a juggler and Carol was a trapeze princess in pink and they waved at people for hours. Andy had agreed to be in the parade only if he could bring his siblings. Andy had agreed to perform two nights later at Kutsher's Resort up in the Borscht Belt only if he could bring his family—which meant a complimentary weekend stay for Stanley and Janice and Michael and Carol and Grandma Lillie and Grandma Pearl, who would turn eighty on

Sunday. He brought them all onstage as well that night, which was the twenty-fourth, and each performed acts perfected around the Kaufman dinner table—Michael sang "La Bamba" and Carol imitated Maurice Chevalier and Pearl told the one about the dog at temple and Lillie sang "Row Row Row Your Boat" with her famous grandson and Stanley and Janice wisely opted to remain silent, as did the audience, uncomfortably so, except when Andy polled the crowd as to whether or not they enjoyed his family. They did not enjoy his family. Nor did they enjoy him or any part of his one hour and forty-five minutes (elongated by the wrestling) of meandering stagecraft. He shed conga tears for them. They did not care. They were, for the most part, silver- and blue-haired Jewish retirees who came to Kutsher's for a weekend of bingo and bridge and ballroom dancing. "A bunch of old farts" was what Stanley called them. Gregg Sutton would recall, "I broke a complete sweat. It was the worst gig that I'd ever been a part of. I was dying with Andy and the family up there. The only person who didn't think it was that bad was Andy. He was oblivious and was just going through it. He was getting a kick out of having his grandmothers and his family up onstage, and they were dying." The rest of the band had wanted to quit somewhere in the middle. Sutton said, "You stay right there, fuckers!" That was how bad it was.

Afterward, Andy sat for a filmed interview with Seth Schultz of the Brooklyn showcase club Pips, who was making a documentary about the history of Pips. Andy recalled with delight the free hot fudge sundaes he had consumed there years before. Then he spoke of the audience he had just left and looked tired as he did so and he seemed to be convincing himself that it had not gone well—"Maybe they thought I *wanted* them to boo and hiss at me, but gosh, they were so *rude!*" He repeated the word *rude* five times in two minutes. He said they had been the worst audience he had encountered since he and Little Wendy played for those doctors at the Cedars-Sinai benefit at the Beverly Hilton and Carl Reiner wanted to hide under the table. Anyway, later that night he found a hostile note tacked to his door and various audience members accosted the family in the corridors and Sutton and Zmuda fled in a rental car to go get loaded and Zmuda deliberately drove off the road and through a fence while lecturing to Sutton, "See! The system was made to bend!" And Sutton knew that Andy was in trouble, even if Andy didn't know he was in trouble—"He was already on his way down." As they left the resort the next day, Andy rolled down the back window of the limousine in which he sat and hollered to no one in particular, "It's people like you who give Jews a bad name!"

Simka Dahblitz would be played by Carol Kane and Simka was to be Latka's rib and eventually his wife and they would come together for the first time in the fortieth episode of *Taxi*, which was called "Guess Who's Coming for Brefnish?" to be filmed December 14. Because Simka had recently emigrated from Latka's country, Carol Kane required lessons in dialect known only to Foreign Man and so Andy agreed to help and invited her to his house in Laurel Canyon, where he presented her with various avenues of pursuit—"He said maybe we should go someplace for dinner where no one knew either of us so we could just speak in the language and people would believe that's how we spoke," she said. "He thought we should go to Mexico. It seemed like a big thing, but he stated it as though it made simple logical sense. I figured since he's willing to do this with me, I should just agree to go." Which she did, if a bit warily. Then he said, "I *know!* I've got another idea! A really good way to get to know each other fast is to wrestle together!" She said Mexico was one thing, but wrestling was another, and said she would rather not, but he said oh-come-on-please-it's-really-fun and explained how it broke down inhibitions and he showed her his wrestling room with the rubber mats on the floor, but she still said no and he sulked "like a disappointed kid" and disappeared into the kitchen to make a phone call, which turned into a very long phone call and she finally got aggravated and went in to say, "You know, Andy, I'm thinking it's getting a little late for dinner if we're going to go to Mexico." And he looked at her as though she was crazy and said, "Mexico? We're not going to Mexico. I was just kidding you. You thought we were going to Mexico?" But she took no umbrage and began to better understand his reality such as it was and they went out for Chinese and spoke only in gibberish except for when he translated her dinner order for the waiter and she thought it was an ingenious exercise because the normalcy of a public situation forced a naturalness upon their dithering nonsensical conversation—"You had to make it sound as real as you could." But she never did wrestle with him, never would, about which she was most happy.

He went on Merv Griffin's show and Merv kept asking him about Tony Clifton. He told Merv in no uncertain terms that he wasn't Clifton. He told Merv to invite Clifton on the show sometime so that Merv could see that it wasn't him. He said he would even come on the show with Clifton to prove it. Merv said, "How come you never blink?" He said, "I don't know." Then he wrestled.

"When I win this, I think it would be nice if all you ladies out there get in the kitchen and cook a little meal for your man!" he said before the match on December 22, when he wrestled the finalist on *Saturday Night Live*. She was Dianna Peckham, whose father was an Olympic wrestling coach, and she wrestled him to a draw and it was mostly boring even though his boyhood hero who had started all of this with the strutting and the I-got-the-brains-bad-guy business— "Nature Boy" Buddy Rogers—was standing right there on the stage and had informed the world that he was now Andy's wrestling manager and it was Buddy who held Andy's watch and also Grandpa Paul's robe during the match but it didn't much matter because it was all very boring. And George would report:

After the match, Andy called and when he first got on the phone he said, *"George, I'm going to tell you something that I think will make you happy."* Then he went forth and told me that he felt that maybe the audience was not ready for wrestling and he was going to hold off on wrestling on television for a while. I'm glad he arrived at this decision himself. I felt that it was hurting his career, but the man is creative and has to have his space within which to work.

Grandma Pearl died January 8, 1980.

And he was very disconsolate.

They buried her at the Beth David Cemetery in Elmont, Long Island.

She had given him Hubert's.

Had taken him to the wrestling matches.

Had taken him to see Howdy.

Cut the kiddin', Kid McCoy, she always said.

"I remember he was standing there at the grave site and he looked so pitiful," said sainted former housekeeper Margaret E. English, from whom he had long ago hid in the back of Daddy's car and then surprised Mommy and Daddy while the car crossed the Fifty-ninth Street Bridge and, since they were already late for the formal dance in the city that night, they dropped him off with Grandma Pearl.

Papu Cy was buried there too.

And Grandpa Paul.

The Kaufmans and the Bernsteins were all going to be buried there together, since they always got along so well. Mommy and Daddy also had plots there. Everyone would be together. Eventually.

Anyway, he had not been to the cemetery for a very long time.

So he stood there and looked pitiful.

"He was so sad," said Margaret.

Gregg Sutton always told him that it was Kutsher's that had killed Grandma Pearl.

*   *   *

He immediately went down to see Grandma Lillie in Hollywood, Florida, where he found a JCPenney nearby and bought her a big color television set and also a home movie camera for himself so that he could take home movies of her watching her new color television set (and, incidentally, she did not approve of him spending such a ridiculous amount of money on her and did not understand why he set up his crazy camera to film every minute of every hour that they spent visiting).

He also filmed a nice visit they had with Aunt Esther Denoff—

ANDY: *You watch* Saturday Night Live *when I'm on, don't you?*

LILLIE: *Sometimes.*

ANDY: *You like that show, don't you?*

LILLIE: *No.*

ANDY: *You only watch it for me?*

LILLIE: *Yeah.*

ANDY: *And what about when I wrestle? Do you like it then?*

LILLIE: *No.*

ANDY: *What do you think of it when I wrestle?*

LILLIE: *It's terrible.*

ESTHER: *I never saw you wrestle.*

LILLIE: *You never saw him wrestle? You didn't miss anything.*

But he was her darling grandson and she played along with whatever shenanigans he wished, even when very late that night he kept his camera running while she fell asleep sitting on the sofa holding the remote control to her new television—he liked filming her sleeping very much—so there he was sitting beside his sleeping grandmother for a very long time before he took the remote control out of her hands and watched the television himself and then he woke her when he found the unseemly commercials for the not-very-nice things. "Oh, look! Grandma, look, look! Isn't that terrible, what they advertise on television? X-rated motel? Isn't that something? They put that on television? Look at that! Topless dancing places now! And men! Nude men dancers! Now, look at that! Look at that, Grandma! Only sexy things,

it says. On television! It's terrible!" Grandma Lillie groggily agreed
that it was all very terrible.

On March 1, he made a six-minute-forty-one-second version of
Uncle Andy's Fun House for a proposed experimental ABC-TV program called *Buckshot* on which little films made by interesting people
would be featured. The network people said that if the little version of
Uncle Andy's Fun House was especially good, it could even become a
weekly series. He was very excited. It would be a children's show for
adults, he decided. He had puppets made of Tony Clifton and of
Knuckles, his prime creation, who was a moron, and he would interact with them. He wanted the show to look like it originated from the
basement den on Grassfield Road, so he flew out Stanley and Janice,
who would play themselves sitting upstairs in the kitchen and they
would yell down at him in the basement and tell him to come upstairs
and eat. He would have his own Peanut Gallery in the den with him
and everyone in the Peanut Gallery would wear Uncle Andy T-shirts.
And he would show viewers a twenty-four-second clip of Grandma
Lillie sleeping on her sofa in Florida—which the network hated, but
he insisted that it not be removed because it added to the magic of the
Fun House. George said, **Andy gets locked into what he perceives as
art and every inch and every second of a bit that he does, in his
mind, seems to be perfect. He's not flexible on changes.** In any case,
Buckshot aired and Grandma Lillie was seen sleeping on national
television and *Uncle Andy's Fun House* never returned.

Stanley came to George's office in Beverly Hills to discuss drawing
up Andy's will, since Andy didn't have a will and the accountant
thought it would be a good idea to make out one. Stanley said to his
son, "Why don't you leave something to the Mustang Ranch?" Andy
said, "That's a good idea! Why can't I do that while I'm still alive?"
George said that he could. George said that he could even have a
room there named in his honor. Andy asked George to look into that.

*   *   *

Saturday Night Live celebrated its one hundredth show and he made a tape in George's backyard which was disguised as Andy Kaufman's Wrestling Farm and behind him six women with whom he had recently mud-wrestled at Chippendale's strip club could be seen grappling with each other and he apologized to the camera for not being in New York to help celebrate this momentous occasion and thanked the show for starting him off on his path to success. Unfortunately, the one hundredth show ran long and his tape, which had been a hit at dress rehearsal, was never broadcast.

The robots were ValCom-17485, which was him, and AquaCom-89045, which was Bernadette Peters, and they fell in love and he died at the end (lost battery power, really) before he could pass along life wisdom to the robot child they had made and he cried when he read the script and George told him he would get half a million dollars plus percentage points from Universal—which had now given him an overall deal because once the robot movie *Heartbeeps* was out of the way, they would probably start shooting the Clifton movie in the spring and also use him in other movies. George thought *Heartbeeps* had the makings of a classic, like *The Wizard of Oz*, only more deliberately artful, so he was very optimistic. The movie would take place in the futuristic world of 1995, when everyone had domestic robots tending chores in their homes. Much makeup would be required and it was designed by Stan Winston and applied in daily three-hour sessions by artist Vince Prentice and the process involved gluing pieces of a gelatinous mask (made from ground-up calves' hooves) to the face, then adding eight coats of metallic paint, then dusting it with sparkly Pearl Essence powder (made from crushed seashells). Andy quickly bored of the ritual—he sent Linda to find tapes of Abbott and Costello and Amos 'n' Andy and Brando and Bogart which he could watch to stem tedium—and his latenesses in the mornings became more frequent and more objectionable on top of which he said that he needed to clear his bowels before going into makeup, which meant another twenty minutes wherein an assistant director would always have to bang on the bathroom door and ask, "Is anything happening yet?" and he'd scream "Get away from me!"

He coughed—before he sat in the makeup chair and while he sat in the makeup chair. It was a small, persistent cough. "Gee, what's the matter?" Prentice would ask. "I don't know," Andy said. "It seems the longer I stay in L.A., the more I cough." Prentice figured it was the rubbing alcohol he used as a thinner. "That would irritate anybody's breathing," said Prentice. Besides, Andy said that he had always coughed.

They had started filming in early June up in the redwood groves of Santa Cruz and, on extremely hot days, his gelatin face would melt and his cheeks and jowls would droop and he would age forty years. By the second week on location, he could not stand being without a female. A thirteen-year-old girl knocked on his hotel room door very early one morning and she wanted an autograph and he took her name and phone number and told George that he planned to stay in touch so that he could date her in four years. Out of boredom, he called the *National Enquirer* and told funny lies about how he and Bernadette were having fights and that the director Allan Arkush had thrown him off the set many times. The unit publicist didn't think this was a great idea. The *Enquirer* published the story. Arkush, however, did once wield a gun in order to get him to come out of his trailer. "Look, either you're on the set now or you're a dead man and we're recasting the movie," Arkush told him half jokingly. "Andy thought that was hysterical," Arkush said. Andy had Clifton call Arkush to tell him to lay off. One day, he stepped out of a very dramatic scene because he saw a candy bar on the set and he wanted it. Meanwhile, everyone thought the dialogue was too slow; the dialogue, in truth, was excruciatingly slow. George thought Arkush was utilizing only ten percent of Andy's comic abilities. By the sixth week of filming, back in Los Angeles, a Universal executive cornered George and proposed that if Andy would show up on time for two consecutive days the studio would install a hooker in his dressing room. Andy loved the idea and actually came early the first day of the challenge when the executive informed George that the studio brass couldn't quite justify budgeting procurement of prostitutes. Andy took the news stoically. The Screen Actors Guild went on strike two days later. Andy went directly to Nevada to have sex.

He had looked at his ABC special again, in the makeup chair, on the same day the hooker thing was first mentioned. And he saw the old him on the special. And he had just read something that the critic Marvin Kitman had written about the old him being better than the new him. Marvin Kitman hated the new him. Like all those people who wrote the wrestling letters saying that he was a chauvanistic arrogant idiot asshole now. (George had told Linda to start collecting the letters because George envisioned a book of Andy Kaufman's hate mail, which no publisher would deign to consider.) George told him that there were probably far more people who felt the same way and hadn't sent letters. People thought that he had changed, George said. People didn't think he was lovable anymore. He pondered this for a while and asked George, "Do you think I can still be innocent?" And he sounded a little more worried about it than usual.

Harrah's gave him a free suite and, once he had checked in, he went straight to the Mustang and stayed until six the following morning and called George later and acknowledged, "You're right, I *am* an extremist. Once I get there, I'm crazy and I don't do anything in moderation." He had skinny twins wrestle for him the first night. "I love skinny women," he said, but had other kinds as well. He made Zmuda fly in the next night; they instantly fell in love with the same married hooker. He called his mother from Reno to say that he was having a wonderful time. She reported this to George and George reported this, among other Nevada updates, for posterity—She said, "I asked him if he went to that camp that he goes to," meaning the Mustang Ranch. She said, "When I said that, Andy laughed." He [told] her that he did go to the camp, and he told her about the twins. Andy tells his mother and father everything, or almost everything. He had six girls on the third night, made some wrestle, spent four hundred dollars (they charged thirty dollars per half hour). He says he doesn't treat them like sex objects, he treats the girls like human beings. Sometimes they will just sit and talk for a while and he'll give them rubdowns. . . . He ordered his parents a twenty-five-hundred-dollar Niagara adjustable bed with the cyclo-massaging-vibrating feature—he felt that they are really wonderful parents and it gave him great pleasure to send them this gift. He tried to talk George into a new wrestling scheme—"I have an idea where it will be acceptable! Let's start a new organization, Men for the Promotion of Women's Equal Rights, and then they'll know that I am pro women and won't be angry with me when I wrestle them." I told him it's cockeyed . . . I told him that it's destructive to his career—it's been done, he did it already, there's nothing new. He's got such a fixation on it . . . it's a sexual experience for him. He told George that there was a second, more modern, Mustang Ranch, which was up for sale. He said he wanted to buy it and rename it Uncle Andy's Fun House. Bob, he said, still couldn't keep up with him. "He just conks out very early." The girls had begun referring to Andy as "some kind of superman" by the end of the week. He's real proud of himself.

The SAG strike moved into its second week and he stayed on in Reno and began branching out to other bordellos in Carson City and outlying areas. George worried that all of his whoring was going to knock him out. Andy said, "Let me tell you—I'm a happy man. If I happen to die in one of those rooms, just let everyone know that I died happy. We should tell everybody not to be sad. Everyone should be happy about it." Not that he wants to die. But that's the way he wouldn't mind going. After two weeks of such, he left Reno with a Mustang Ranch hooker named Joanne and, as the strike continued apace, they spent the next two weeks together romping along the California coast and he made a fracas in Sacramento trying to get them into the state fair after hours (succeeding only after he screamed that he was Latka on *Taxi*). All of which delayed an intended trip home to New York to visit his family. Janice told George on August 20, "He was going to come about a week ago, but he got waylaid—and I mean *way* laid!" Anyway, he didn't have to be a robot again for several more weeks, during which time he would promote the release of *In God We Tru$t* and wrestle more women, but not on television. He liked being on strike, although he didn't quite understand what he was striking for—something about residuals from pay television and videocassettes or something.

Merv greeted him and regarded his clothes and said, "You don't have a wife, do you? You do your own laundry?" Mmm-hmmm, he responded. "You're frayed all over!" Merv continued. "I mean, your pockets are ripped!" Andy said, "That's 'cause I wear the same pants for five years." He wasn't trying to be funny but the people laughed anyway and anyway he was only trying to help Marty Feldman sell tickets to a movie that nobody would want to go see.

Mea culpa came that autumn. He had lost everything no really, he said, establishing a landmark in his march of passive-aggressive disregard. David Letterman, a Comedy Store alumnus whom he had known a little in California, was now the host of a new NBC morning program broadcast live from Rockefeller Center, two floors below the *Saturday Night Live* studios, and Letterman's show would be canceled less than a month after Andy visited, which was mostly coincidental but still. The plot unspooled over two appearances in the course of a week or so—he had stopped shaving days before presenting his plan to the producers. "He showed up looking kind of rocky, kind of dirty," said Gerard Mulligan, a writer–talent coordinator for the program. "He said, 'Well, I've been sleeping in doorways the last couple of nights getting ready for the show and what I'd like to do is come out and just look the way I look now, but with a couple more nights under my belt. And David—' (He always called Dave *David*.) '—will ask me what's up. And I would say that wrestling has ruined my life and my career and I only see one way out.' At that point he said he wanted to take out a prop gun and shoot himself in the head. He said he had always wanted to do that on television. We said, 'Well, jeez, Andy, let us get back to you on that.' " And it was decided that he wouldn't shoot himself, but he would panhandle in the audience instead, but that would come with the second appearance—for the first appearance, he would be brought on minutes before the end of the show, as though he had dropped in by surprise, and he looked thoroughly untucked and bedraggled but seemed cheerful enough and announced, "I'm in New York and I've been sleeping in doorways, to see what it's like. It's true! I haven't been in a bed or anything for a few weeks now. . . ." And he excitedly launched into a tale about having been chased off an apartment house staircase, whereupon Letterman said there was no time left in the show and that perhaps Andy could come back another day, which he did, looking far worse—hair standing on end, whiskers thicker, eyes glazed imperviously. Above his lip, the makeup girl had smeared Vaseline to approximate drained mucus, for which Letterman proffered a tissue immediately—"You have a little . . . just a little bit of something here . . . See, people sometimes eat breakfast while they watch the show . . ."

He wiped and remained oblivious and humorless; he smiled never once and said that he had quit *Taxi* and that *Saturday Night Live* hadn't asked him to be on the show for a long time and he coughed in virulent spasms and Letterman said, "But things are okay?" and people laughed. Then he went onto the stage and sat on a stool and said that he wanted to talk about his marriage (and people laughed) and said he had met his wife when he was starting out in clubs and she had been a cocktail waitress and they had two children, Mark and Lisa, and then *Saturday Night Live* discovered him and he then coughed up more phlegm (and people laughed) and he said, "I'd rather . . . if you don't laugh, because I'm not trying to be funny right now." And he said that he went to California and got a manager named George Shapiro, "a wonderful man," and *Taxi* came along— "And I kind of felt inhibited by it, that I was just able to do the one character. I wanted to have more freedom, creatively, to do these other things." So he started wrestling women and received a lot of hate mail and quit the show and had been trying to get a job doing dinner theater in Wisconsin and his wife had finally left him—"She got the kids, the house, she got all my money. Uh, not all my money, but some. Anyway, she got everything. . . . And I, I don't really have anything." And he coughed and coughed. "So, anyway, if anybody could—I know this sounds like a cliché. But if you could . . . uh . . . any extra money . . . I would appreciate it. Don't throw it—I'll just come up . . ." And he staggered up into the bleachers and collected coins and security came to escort him from the studio and the audience made the *awwwww* noise as he left and Letterman said, "Always a pleasure to have the young talent on the show."

"We got instant reaction to that show," Letterman reported not long thereafter. "Phone calls, letters. People were mad at me for having him on, mad at him, sorry for his plight. Other people thought I had not been sympathetic to the needs of this obviously desperate human. [Andy] was real eager to get the hate mail. He made me *promise* to send it. . . . Sometimes when you look Andy in the eyes, you get a feeling somebody else is driving."

Phone call with Kathy Utman, during which he heard no bells but told her about everything that hurt and frightened him, perking up only when he spoke of the Letterman show and how so many people had believed it was really real:

"A lot of people said that was the greatest thing they ever saw me do—people who know me. That and the wrestling thing are both, like, very avant-garde type of off-the-wall humor, you know? And it's not very popular with people in the business, 'cause they don't think it's commercially viable. So I'm having this thing lately . . . like, there was a time when I could have quit *Taxi* and I would have been able to just be an artist—like, you know, do my thing and have confidence in that. But now I'm thinking that there's a lot of people that won't really . . . I mean, if I was to quit *Taxi* which I'm not gonna do— See, I'm not doing what the producers in this business like. They like skits and mindless comedy and I don't do that. The thing is, I've always wanted to have my own show. And for years now no one will give me one. They won't give me my own regular series. And I know that that's what I would do best. George told me the other day that two *cable* companies don't want to give Andy Kaufman a show, because Andy Kaufman performs for himself and not for the public. And that really bummed me out . . . But if everybody in the business thinks that way, then I can't— I mean, if they're all stupid, I'm the one that suffers. You know, also—because when I went up onstage at the Improv in California, I didn't get that big of an applause. And also, Friday night at *Taxi*, I didn't get that big of an applause when I came out onstage, like I usually do. That makes me think, like George says, that because of all the really weird stuff that I do, I'm losing a lot of fans—fans that really like me because of Latka and stuff like that. But if I kept doing Latka all the time, I wouldn't be true to my art, you know? And I choose to be an artist rather than catering to the masses. But, still, I don't want to be losing my career, you know? Ever since he told me that I've been thinking, *Oh, I'm a has-been*. It's in my mind . . .

"The thing is I *don't* perform for the mass public! But as long as there's a group of people out there that understands what I'm doing, I'm performing for *them*. Of course, I perform for myself, too—all good artists do. But it's not like I'm the only one that understands what I'm doing. . . . I just hope that I'm not on the downslide. . . . You know how when someone that you know dies and you *know* they're gonna die a week before they die? So that when they die, it's not really a shock to you—but everyone else is crying and stuff? Well, I think they *should* have realized that the person was gonna die! They shouldn't have been so shocked and be crying at that point. Now, maybe it hasn't happened to my career yet. But, just in case it does, I'm doing it now, I'm realizing there's something wrong. So that if it does happen, I won't feel it as hard. . . . Anyway, it could just be a phase. . . . It might be all in my head, I don't know. . . . Did I tell you about the prostitute that I had . . ."

Suddenly, there in the valley of lengthening apathy, *Rolling Stone* expressed interest in doing a major profile, maybe a cover story— maybe even Andy and Clifton *together* on the cover!—because maybe this destitution thing had some emotional validity and maybe he *was* nuts and what could be more entertaining than chronicling a man bent on destroying himself in public? Writer David Hirshey was dispatched to execute the sleuthing, which began during the first few days of 1981 in New York. It was nearly two A.M. when they arrived at the Improv (in a horse-drawn carriage) and the place was thinning out and Andy took the stage and started hopping and then—"A hunnn-dred bottles of beer on the wall, a hunnn-dred bottles of beer . . ." And Hirshey would report that the reception was understandably anguished at first and so Andy began performing each numeral in a different voice and persona, proceeding slowly at times, quickly at other times, and the people at the tables, who were initially annoyed, now became entranced, then fervid, then frenzied, and then—at fourteen bottles of beer—he walked offstage. At which point, the six remaining people screamed in agony and begged him to finish, which he did and was instantly flushed with euphoria. "That was magical," he said. " 'A Hundred Bottles of Beer' has always been a fantasy of mine. . . . There are such psychological implications to that song, such great things you can do. Once they're hooked, they won't let you stop. Can you imagine?"

On an ensuing night they returned to the Improv, where he wrestled—after they had first dined on Japanese food, which Andy did not consume until he had bowed his head in prayer and then swallowed fifty vitamins, one at a time. "I'm an open book," he said to Hirshey. "I have to be totally honest with you. That's the way I am." Later, however, when he insisted that they look for hookers in Times Square, he asked Hirshey to maybe not mention it in the article so as to not shock his family.

Redemption was offered two weeks later by Dick Ebersol, who had three years earlier left *Saturday Night Live* in the hands of Lorne Michaels. Ebersol had moved to Los Angeles to shape other NBC projects, which now included restructuring *The Midnight Special*, a long-running rock music cavalcade that aired Friday nights following *The Tonight Show*. Beginning in early 1977, Andy had made a handful of appearances on the show—the most memorable of which featured his renditions of "You Light Up My Life" and "Stayin' Alive," for which he accompanied himself on cymbals. Ebersol now proposed that Andy take over an entire ninety-minute installment of the show, which would dedicate itself, partly in documentary style, to answering the ephemeral (and all-too-urgent) question—Who *is* Andy Kaufman? "Andy Kaufman is me," he announced at the outset. "I'm Andy Kaufman." The program would largely serve as an in-studio showcase in which he welcomed many selves onto the stage: Foreign Man would appear and do de Elveece and there would be conga numbers (he beat along to "Tallahassee Lassie" sung by boyhood hero Freddy "Boom Boom" Cannon) and Slim Whitman would teach him to yodel and he would do bad ventriloquism with store-bought Howdy Doody and Little Red Riding Hood puppets and Clifton would perform his usual malevolent set (during which Andy would be seen laughing riotously in the audience). And in the documentary clips he would sit in his sparsely furnished home and explain the evolution of his career and cameras would follow him through the *Taxi* soundstage and through a busboy shift at Jerry's Famous Deli in Studio City, where he now worked Tuesday nights since the Posh Bagel had closed. (Jerry himself would be heard describing him as "an excellent, hardworking, very serious-in-his-work type of man" and expressed interest in hiring him full-time.) Also there would be wrestling footage shot a few nights earlier at The

Comedy Store about which he explained that he played the *role* of the villain to purposely engender audience hostility—"I believe in being a purist and going all the way with the role—and not breaking character or giving away that I'm playing a role. I believe in playing it straight to the hilt." And George would be seen mournfully discussing the hate mail and the loss of fans. And Zmuda would be seen matter-of-factly stating, "The wrestling has definitely cost Andy Kaufman his career. There's no doubt about it. Right now this is the only show that has offered this man to be on in a long time. And we thank you for that."

Clifton, in full persona, checked into the St. Francis Hotel in San Francisco, where he would open, once again, for Rodney Dangerfield during the last three nights of January. The two-show-per-night engagement at the Warfield Theater would be especially historic because now the audiences would actually try to kill him. (Coincidentally, or not, the movie of his life was now two months dead, having been rejected by Universal and then Paramount, Columbia, and Warner Bros. as well.) David Hirshey had flown out from New York to continue his *Rolling Stone* exploration and to search for cracks in the Clifton façade (finding none besides the presence of George and Bob and the occasional backstage disappearance of Clifton's gut). "He looks like Roy Orbison pumped with cortisone," Hirshey would write. On the first night, derision flamed as Clifton sacreligiously mangled "I Left My Heart in San Francisco" and someone screamed TAKE THE DOGSHIT OUT OF YOUR MOUTH! Debris quickly rained from the balcony and, before Clifton had left the stage, twenty people would be refunded their money. Dangerfield found this hilarious—"They *all* hated him, you know? And he kept saying, 'It's too bad that a *few* of you out there have to spoil it for everyone!' I loved it." On the second night, a small German man rushed the stage wielding a penknife and threatened, I CAN'T TAKE IT! NOW GET ZE HELL OFF! Vince Prentice, who had taken over Cliftonian makeup chores, apprehended the perpetrator, whom security mistook as a plant. Clifton then dodged exploding beer cans and a bottle of Southern Comfort—"That was a glass bottle and you're a fuckin' asshole!" he brayed at the assailant, then elected to sing his final three numbers while hiding in the wings. On the third night, triple-folded fishnet would be lowered in front of the stage and Clifton would don a riot-squad helmet with plastic face-guard, which was most advisable, because fruit and vegetables were now on sale in the lobby and much produce was heaved, as were coins and eggs and banana cake. It was a blistering apple, however, that tore through the net and crashed squarely into the face-guard and disintegrated on impact—which sent Clifton teetering off-stage, where he completed his performance and retreated to his dressing room. Hirshey found him there, crowing triumphantly about the whole experience. But Clifton also warned him, "Watch yerself! You print that I'm Andy Kough-man and I'll sue yer ass! I'll sue *Bowling Green's* ass!" Meanwhile, Hirshey had received a phone call in his hotel room earlier that day from Andy, who said he was down in Los Angeles. Hirshey mentioned that someone had thrown a bottle at Clifton the night before. Andy said, "Really? Are you sure it wasn't his manager?"

On Friday, February 20, the disregard found new plateau. *Saturday Night Live* had left him to twist alone toward madness; he had not been asked to return since the wrestling anticlimax fourteen months earlier. (Moreover, the show had fallen into notorious disrepair after the abdication of Lorne Michaels in May 1980.) Thus, Andy trucked with the upstart enemy: He hosted ABC-TV's *Fridays*—a Los Angeles–based live sketch-comedy replication whose limp ratings invited drastic attention-getting measures. He began plotting with producer John Moffitt on the Sunday before the broadcast and said he wanted to open the show by bombing so as to challenge the audience from the outset. George, who was present, tried to convince him otherwise: **I had a disagreement with him again because we both know I hate the bombing routine and he thinks** very highly of it. I find it boring—if you do not entertain an audience, you fail as an entertainer, and I do not want him to fail, even if he is willing to fail. (He would settle, in the end, for opening as Laughing Man, deliriously convulsed and blithering incoherently, whose first intelligible words were *Ohhh, I need help, I need help.*)

He also proposed a piece called the Masked Magician, wherein Zmuda would disguise himself as a disgruntled illusionist (barely obscured in a ski mask) and reveal the secrets of the interlinking rings and basic sword-swallowing; Andy would help plunge a sword—a bit overzealously—down Zmuda's gullet, and Zmuda would then regurgitate blood and intestinal matter and Andy would vomit vegetable soup. (By airtime, network censors would permit Zmuda only bloody spittle and no guts or vomit whatsoever.) *Fridays* writers, meanwhile, prepared two sketch pieces for him—a Point/Counterpoint debate with himself concerning federal arts–funding and a show-closing restaurant sketch called "Marijuana" in which he and three regular cast members, as two couples, would each take turns going into the bathroom, ostensibly to smoke dope, then return to their table quite stupefied.

Andy called a private meeting midweek and suggested a notion to Moffitt, coproducer Jack Burns, and network executive Vic Kaplan. "It *was* his idea," Moffitt would recall. "He presented it in a very straight-ahead and serious fashion. He said, 'This is what I'm gonna do. I want to rehearse the marijuana sketch as planned until we're on the air and then I want to break out of it. I'm gonna say—but only on the air—that it's a silly sketch and I'm just not gonna finish it. I want to break the wall of reality and create a confrontation—and because I just ruined the show, it should end in a fight.' He laid it out point by point, and we agreed to do just that as long as he promised no other surprises in the moment. And he gave his word." No one else on the staff or in the cast would be told with the exception of some writers and the sketch participants, who were Michael Richards, Melanie Chartoff, and Maryedith Burrell—although many would claim that Chartoff and Burrell were also left in the dark. Chartoff, however, said Jack Burns told them just before the sketch, "Stay in character and go with it!"

And so, roughly two minutes into the sketch, it unraveled as planned when he returned from the restaurant bathroom and sat and paused and grinned helplessly and stammered, "I can't . . . I can't play . . . I can't play stoned . . . I feel really stupid . . . I feel so stupid." And Burrell began laughing maniacally as though gripped with actual terror. And Chartoff said to him, "*You* feel stupid?" and quivered. And he remained uncomfortably paralyzed and muttered on about feeling stupid. (Richards would recall, "He just shut down and sat there. And I could just feel that he was just gonna keep on sitting there and let everybody squirm and stink. I realized that he now wanted me to push it to the next level.") So Richards walked off camera and returned with the cue cards and angrily plopped them in front of Andy, who said, "It's all in fun—c'mon!" The actors stayed frozen/panicked, whereupon Andy stood and tossed a glass of water at Richards, and Chartoff rose to push a buttered dinner roll into Andy's hair and Andy threatened to push butter in her face and Burrell kept laughing edgily and Jack Burns, apparently livid, ran onto the set and rushed at Andy, and Andy shoved him and several crew members, who *were* incensed and afraid of further destruction, stormed forth to intercede in the scuffle and Burns screamed for the director to go to a commercial—and it was all very much like the incident on the closed-circuit campus program *Grahm Spotlight* on which Burt Dubrow had tackled Andy and called for a commercial after Andy pulled a gun and tried to commit suicide on camera. But this, of course, was bigger and the network switchboards lit like Las Vegas marquees and *The New York Times* ran a story days later under the headline WAS "FIGHT" ON TV REAL OR STAGED? IT ALL DEPENDS, wherein Tony Schwartz wrote, "It looked like a spontaneous fistfight on live television. Whether it really happened is a matter of interpretation." And Howard Rosenberg in the *Los Angeles Times* wrote, "Was it real? Yes, and the Brooklyn Bridge is in Wyoming. . . . Kaufman, whose schizophrenic comedy consists of reality and fantasy rolled up into one big put-on, convinced a lot of viewers that he had cracked up on the air. . . ."

Stanley and Janice had watched in Great Neck and realized that their son would never work again; Stanley told George that he had decided at that moment not to invest any of Andy's money in the stock market, figuring he would heretofore need it to survive. There was some relief, however, that at least he hadn't wrestled on the show.

The next night, in New York, a new *Saturday Night Live* cast member named Charles Rocket uttered the word *fuck* in the closing moments of the show. It was just a coincidence.

Grizzled, haggard, wretched, unshaven, woebegone—it had worked well before—he tried the following Friday night to read the statement "prepared" by the producers to confirm for viewers that the fight had been a planned improvisational experiment. But then he stopped his monotonous recitation and refused to continue. "This has been a very hard week for me," he said. His job at Taxi *was on the line, he said, and no one would hire him and his friends wouldn't speak to him and his wife had left him and he had only been trying to have fun and the laughter from the audience now was pretty taste-less, he said, because he wasn't trying to be funny. Then came tears. Tears were always easy.*

Two days later, he and Clifton posed together for photographer Herb Ritts in a session that was intended to produce a *Rolling Stone* cover. Vince Prentice had transformed Zmuda into a lippy lounge gargoyle, but it worked and even George thought this Clifton was im-pressive both in look and comportment—Clifton strangled Andy in several shots—and within weeks it was decided that Zmuda would take over the role and be booked on talk shows and perform an en-gagement at Harrah's Lake Tahoe Resort and everyone would con-tinue to think that Clifton was Andy but now it truly wouldn't be Andy. They went to the Japanese restaurant Amagi—George, Bob, Andy—and piled their hands together on the tabletop and vowed that no one but Prentice and a few others would know the truth. **I will not discuss Tony Clifton [even] with my partner Howard, which is his pleasure,** George later dictated. *Rolling Stone* editor Terry McDonell called George the next day and said he had nixed the Andy-and-Clifton cover and instead wanted Andy posed alone strapped into a straitjacket which George nixed—although *Fridays* photographer Wayne Williams had shot him in a straitjacket three weeks earlier and those pictures had appeared as commercial bumpers on the infamous broadcast. They would tentatively settle on using a more straightforward photograph, but it would not matter, because when the April 30 issue of the magazine was published, Ringo Starr was the cover subject and at the very top of the cover were the very small and very provocative words WHY ANDY KAUFMAN IS NOT FUNNY.

As quoted by David Hirshey—

CARL REINER: Unless you let the audience in on the joke, you are making fools of them, and that's what he's doing with this Tony Clifton.

STANLEY KAUFMAN: I never understood why he would want to alienate the audience to such extremes unless he was trying to get them to go from hate to love. Why Tony Clifton? It's possible he created this character to draw hisses for the villain so he can come out the hero.

CAROL KAUFMAN: I don't think anything that makes people uncomfortable is entertainment. Sometimes I just want to stand up on my seat and shout, "He's only kidding, everybody!" I think with Andy, it all goes back to the self, the *I*. What am *I* going to get pleasure out of, not how am *I* going to please the audience. He knows they want to laugh, they want him to tell jokes. But no. That would be selfless.

*   *   *

Two letters to *Rolling Stone* were subsequently published:

One: . . . "As for my not letting people in on the joke, there are times when real life is funnier than deliberate comedy. Therefore, I try to create the illusion of a 'real-life' situation or character. However, it must be believed totally; if I were to let people in on the joke, it wouldn't have that effect. . . . Finally, concerning my 'brief flirtation' with levitation, this is something I have studied and practiced for several years and I take it very seriously. Not only am I able to levitate about eight feet off the ground, but once in the air, I am able to fly about in all directions."

Two: "You promised to put my picture on the cover of your magazine and I flew to Los Angeles at my own expense and I spent a whole evening posing for your photographer standing next to that asshole egotist Kaufman who thinks he's Mr. Hollywood Show Business and I didn't get nothin' out of it and as far as I'm concerned to me that's a waste of time and you're all a bunch of schmucks and you can go fuck yourselves. Incidentally, I am appearing on *The Merv Griffin Show* June 8 all across the country, so could you let your readers know about it."

All things had been well considered at *Taxi*: The sixty-fourth episode—entitled "Latka the Playboy" as written by Glen Charles and Les Charles—introduced Vic Ferrari, a slick, smooth-talking cad who was Latka Gravas's alter ego. It was the first indication of a multiple personality disorder that would possess Latka for much of the next year.

It was nobody's business and he told very few people that he did this, but he did do it and the reason why lived somewhere in a scared and lovely place that was as much a part of him as the other variegated colors. It was early April and his evening flight had been delayed at O'Hare in Chicago, so he decided to take a morning flight instead, because the girl was very sick. He had called her in the

*hospital weeks earlier because a friend of hers got word to him about
how much she loved what he did on television. Her name was Mary
Jean Burden of DeMotte, Indiana, age twenty-one, and she had cys-
tic fibrosis and so he called from the airport and rented a car and
drove forty miles to the hospital in Crown Point, arriving at midnight. A small crowd gathered in the lounge and he visited and
performed for two hours and was Foreign Man and was Elvis—he
serenaded Mary Jean on bended knee with "Love Me Tender"—and
she would tell a local reporter, "He can really talk with his eyes." He
also wrestled two women and let them win. He invited Mary Jean to
come visit the Taxi set when she felt better and he gave her a kiss and
kept waving goodbye as the elevator doors closed. Her mother wrote
to thank him after Mary Jean died six weeks later. "Words could
never say enough," Mrs. Burden wrote. "You'll never realize how
much you helped her."*

He had lately been toying with the idea of reviving the Clifton
movie by giving Foreign Man a co-starring role. Well, it was just an
idea. Anyway, George was encouraged.

Linda made call after call after call until she found Fabian for
him. She finally arranged a lunch at Jerry's Deli because Fabian
Forte lived in nearby Toluca Lake, never mind that he was most wary
about the assignation, fearing put-on, knowing what he knew about
the one who wished to meet him so desperately. He had heard how
his song "This Friendly World" had become Andy's signature closing
number in concert performances—and he never knew quite how to
take that. Andy was late, which angered Fabian, who had been
prompt, and then Andy arrived. "He looked at me like—I hate to use
this word—like he was in *awe*," Fabian would recall. "And I'm still
thinking, maybe he's playing with me and that this was a big hoax.
Like, if he was having this filmed or something, I was going to tear
him limb from limb." But Andy, he noticed, was nervous—"almost

like wringing his hands"—and barely ate his lunch while reciting infinitesimal details about every one of Fabian's records and Fabian laughingly asked him, "Why the fuck do you do 'This Friendly World'? Are you putting me down?" Andy said, "No, you have to understand. That song means everything to me. I wish the world really was that way." And Fabian would always be pleased that he surprised Andy with a bearish Italian hug when they parted that day and would remain touched by the image of the unusual boy in the basement who had sung along with him. "You could see in his eyes that he wasn't kidding," he said.

P-l-o-t-s—there would now be nothing but plots; he pursued old ones and hatched new ones and slipped in and out of view, in and out of towns, in and out of countries; he was mercury and he moved as such. . . .

April: Andy was in New York, which Merv announced (suspiciously), when Clifton taped his first appearance on Merv's program in Los Angeles; Clifton was suddenly fatter and shorter and less nasal and more stupid and slightly nicer; he sang "I Will Survive" and pronounced it *surveeve;* Merv said he looked nothing like Andy Kaufman and Clifton said, *"I am not Andy Kaufman! I want to have nothing to do with Andy Kaufman!"* . . . In New York, meanwhile, Andy spent days wandering into clubs and onto various public access cable programs in the persona of a pompous cigar-smoking monosyllabic Russian who also happened to be himself ("I am Hollywood, I am television star on *Taxi* and I hate when I do not get respect I deserve! I am champion! Champion wrestling, champion many things!"). At the Improv, he burst in on an improvisational class taught by Martin Harvey Friedberg, himself an esteemed madman of performance theory, whom Andy antagonized relentlessly, waving his cigar in Friedberg's face— "Smoke is bother you? Why is bother you?" Friedberg: "You enjoying all that poison that's going down into your system? You're enjoying all that cancer that's getting into your lungs?" Andy:

"Yeah." (He felt that being Russian required a cigar always; but neither he nor Clifton ever actually inhaled the smoke.) On the
Slycraft Hour, a barely seen public access show, he brought on
Stanley and Janice—who did not feign Russian dialects—and he
argued moral decency with a right-wing quack and evinced his
right to destroy *Fridays.* *"Fridays* is rip-off, exactly copy of *Saturday
Night Live.* Is bull. Is lot of bull. So I get mad. I ruin that show. I
will do it again. *Here is my mommy."* . . . Not as a Russian, he
tracked down Alan Abel, a satirist known to be the World's Greatest
Hoaxer, whose *New York Times* obituary on January 2, 1980, had
thrilled Andy, since Abel was not dead but only fooling and had
tricked the paper of record into printing news of his demise.
Among books Abel had published were *The Confessions of a
Hoaxer, The Panhandler's Handbook,* and *How to Thrive on
Rejection*—so Andy felt a very close bond and the two of them became fast friends that spring and they would walk seventy-five
blocks up and down Broadway together. "We talked and talked and
talked and talked," said Abel. "We did have a lot in common in the
sense that he liked the kind of crazy shit—if you'll pardon the expression—that I did. We would compare notes on panhandling—
he was very dedicated to it, you know. He wanted us to collaborate
on something really fantastic and enormous, but we could never
figure out what it would be. He was especially fascinated with my
rejection book and how I had gotten people to believe I was dead.
He'd say, 'How can I do that? I want to do that.' "

Late July: Andy was in London, which Merv announced (suspiciously), when Clifton returned to tape Merv's show in Las Vegas, so
as to promote his forthcoming two-week engagement at Harrah's
Stateline Lounge in Lake Tahoe beginning August 31; Merv asked
him why he had come through the casino that day wearing a bag over
his head and Clifton said, *"Because my makeup man did not get here!
And I don't want the public to see me unless I look right!"* Clifton told
Merv that he was a forty-year resident of Las Vegas and lived in a
Winnebago trailer home and that he had flown the *Spruce Goose*
with Howard Hughes. . . . In London, meanwhile, Andy was enjoy-

ing a stopover on his way to Amsterdam, where he planned to do nothing else but explore the red-light district.

August 30: Before his gig—for which he would receive $7500 per week, performing three shows per night—Clifton checked into Harrah's Tahoe while Andy checked into the Ormsby House hotel in Carson City, which was not close but was close enough; he was more concerned with proximity to his beloved brothels than with proximity to Clifton. He came to Harrah's the first day in order to be seen on the premises and stoke conjecture. According to Gregg Sutton—whom Clifton now called MacNamara (leader of the band, natch)—Andy attended only one show. "He was disguised in a funky beard and weird clothes. He heckled Clifton—'Tell the truth! You're Andy Kaufman, you fraud!' Clifton had him removed from the room." Most other people left on their own; business was light. Clifton told an intrepid local news crew that he was suing Andy—"He's using my name to get places! Makes me feel really *mad*, really *bad*, really *sad*—*clad, had, mad, dad, fad!* That's every word that rhymes with *mad*—from A to Z! Thank you very much!" ("The rhyming thing was the one thing Zmuda invented," said Sutton. The new Clifton also deployed a reptilian tongue which inadvertently slipped out between sentences as means of unpleasant punctuation.) *The Hollywood Reporter* reviewed the show fully duped—"Kaufman establishes nothing with which people can identify. . . ." A showgirl, meanwhile, also fell for Clifton during his engagement, largely because she thought she was falling for Andy; Zmuda received her advances and intimacies without removing his facial prosthetics. "I told her that as an artist, I had to stay in character," he said. "And she actually believed me." Just to be safe, Sutton had advised him to keep the lights out and to make sure that he got her drunk before special moments unfolded.

Halfway through Clifton's run, Andy returned to Los Angeles to prepare to host the season premiere of *Fridays*, for which he had devised a new reality. He told John Moffitt that he wanted to unveil a new him, a Born Again Christian him who would introduce viewers to his fiancée—the woman who had saved him from spiritual ruin.

But first he had to find her, which he did—in the ABC studio directly next door, where *The Lawrence Welk Show* was taped. She was a twenty-nine-year-old featured gospel singer named Kathie Sullivan; he sat her down in the *Fridays* offices, where she nervously accepted his proposal of making televised charade. "He assured me that if I did this he would not do anything like rip my dress off or embarrass me in any way," she said. "He knew that I was Born Again. He was a perfect gentleman." Linda Mitchell asked what size ring she wore and then purchased a cheap but dazzling cubic zirconia for Sullivan to begin flaunting immediately (Andy informed the *National Enquirer* that it was a $10,000 diamond). He had a press release issued—ANDY KAUFMAN TO ANNOUNCE ENGAGEMENT THIS FRIDAY ON THE AIR— wherein Sullivan was quoted professing, "I'm glad God gave me the chance to meet him. I'm so glad I was given the opportunity to change his life."

On Friday night, September 18, he opened the show in a three-piece brown polyester suit; his hair was carefully cropped; he glistened with renewal. Said Moffitt, "He had that look in his eyes that said he had seen God." He began as Foreign Man and also did Mighty Mouse—reestablishing the benign him—then showed a clip of his unshaven self apologizing after the fight imbroglio. "That was a pretty low point in my life," he said. "As you can probably tell, since then I've gone through a lot of changes." Then he welcomed onto camera the woman responsible for those changes, whom he called his fiancée, and Sullivan confirmed her love for him and boasted of his conversion to Christianity and said, "We'll probably end up with a bunch of little kids running around the house saying *tenk you veddy much!*" And they sang a soaring spiritual ballad "that really says just how Andy and I feel—it's called 'Home Again.' " She would recall, "I gave him the easy parts, but he did a real good job, on key and everything." Later in the program, he further promulgated clean living by criticizing a drug sketch that had just been performed, which delayed his introduction of the rock group The Pretenders, which incited booing (just like the good old days), and he closed the show with the rousing gospel standard "By and By." George said it was a very good put-on and thought people believed it. **Well, many people did. Some people just never believe Andy.** *Fridays* writer Steve Adams, author of the notorious restaurant sketch, would remember the universal response to the show somewhat differently—"His finding God didn't work too well. By then the public was on to him. I think he knew it, too."

Weeks later, he issued another press release—ANDY KAUFMAN AND KATHIE SULLIVAN CALL IT QUITS. "Mr. Kaufman," it stated, "wants to keep his once-a-week busboy job at Jerry's Famous Deli in Studio City and continue his intergender wrestling and Miss Sullivan did not approve. Mr. Kaufman found it more and more difficult to give up his own needs and wishes, especially wrestling." Also, he found the three-piece suits too constricting. In truth, it was Sullivan who thought it prudent to cease the deception. "I got a lot of backlash from the Christian community," she said. She did, however, get to keep the ring.

Henceforth, nothing would matter more than the ring. He was back in the ring on October 11—six years exactly since the night he first performed on *Saturday Night Live*—and this ring was in Atlantic City, where he wrestled Playmate Susan Smith (36–24–36, one hundred thirty-eight pounds, blond) at the Playboy Hotel and Casino. Playboy had challenged him, promising a major magazine pictorial feature documenting the event, which would also be taped for broadcast on the cable Playboy Channel—so he could not refuse such exposure (rubbing), and even George agreed. The match lasted eighteen minutes and thirty-five seconds, and she actually pinned him for four seconds, but the referee was distracted and missed the call and so Andy flipped and pinned her and left for Memphis the next day.

Like Columbus before him, he officially charted a new world on October 12. He had been down once already in June and again in July, but those had been brief reconnaissance missions that also involved meeting southern females who had sent him inviting letters.

True cahoots with his future nemesis had begun even earlier. He had wanted to wrestle women at Madison Square Garden, but was told that wrestling despot Vince McMahon, Sr., would never go for such carny in the hallowed arena. But Bill Apter, who edited *Wrestler* and *Inside Wrestling* magazines, had become a friend, and Apter offered another option. Very late one night that spring, after they had seen matches at the Garden, they returned to Apter's apartment in Kew Gardens, Queens—not far from the hospital where Andy was born. Apter told him, "I have a friend in Memphis, Tennessee, who might be interested in your idea. He's a wrestler and a promoter down there and his name is Jerry Lawler." Apter decided that they should call him right then, no matter that it was after one o'clock in the morning. Lawler answered, wide awake, and Apter told him that he had Latka from *Taxi* with him and Lawler said, "Put him on!" Apter would re-call, "They spoke for quite some time. And when he hung up, Andy was very invigorated. He called me a couple of days later and said, 'I'm going down to see Lawler.' And that was the start of the whole thing."

A few weeks later, on June 5, he flew from Los Angeles to Memphis and headed directly over to the Mid-South Coliseum, which was con-sidered Lawler's kingdom since Lawler was considered the King of Memphis now that the other one was dead. (Lawler's local celebrity was such that he had been the first attraction ever to break Elvis's record for consecutive sellouts at the 12,000-seat Coliseum.) Memphis had long been a wrestling mecca and Lawler was regional potentate, a Baby-face (good guy, per parlance) champion muscle-slab who triumphed over serial insidious Tarheels (bad guys, per parlance) throughout the southern territories. But Lawler was also possessed of business savvy and held ranking office inside the Memphis Wrestling Company, which filled the cards and devised all thunderous theatrics that were played out at the Coliseum. And so the prospect of enlisting the lure of the comical maniac who took on the womenfolk was more than exciting. Lawler, in fact, had been made giddy by that first late-night phone call and, upon hanging up, heard himself splutter, "Oh my God!" He would recall, "All Andy wanted to do was experience the thrill of wrestling in front of a wrestling crowd.

That was the whole thing. He had been doing it for people that really came to see stand-up comedy. They didn't come to see him wrestle and they weren't appreciating it. He told me, 'I just want to get the response that wrestlers should get!' " So Lawler told him, "Yes, please! Let's talk about it!" Jimmy Hart, the preeminent southern Tarheel wrestler, had been in Lawler's home when the call came. Per Hart's recollection: "Us being a small territory and Andy being a TV star—well, we knew it would be nothing but big box office business!"

They welcomed him into their fold in June and took him backstage, where he made taunting tapes to broadcast during wrestling programs that would rile the women enough so that they'd want to come whup him when he returned. It was then decided that from that point forward he would (very legitimately) bill himself as the World's Intergender Wrestling Champion—he was, after all, undefeated in over three hundred contests—and everyone thought the title had a perfectly highfalutin ring to it. So the date was picked and it would be Columbus Day and now here he was on that very day in October and they threw a handful of girls at him and he loved the size and the stomp and the roar and the smell of this Coliseum where Elvis had performed and where he now rubbed to his longjohns' content. And none of them could pin him but he pinned most of them. And he brayed at the sea of twisted faces and made his usual affront with the washing-scrubbing-peeling et cetera. And, suddenly, he had become a fully accredited Tarheel! "He had that heeled sense about him and that little prancy, insipid way that he strutted around that ring," said Lance Russell, who called all matches at the Coliseum. "I never saw anybody who loved it any more than he did. He was just great. And, oh God, he wanted to come back!" Afterward, he made some more ornery tapes and said he would return on November 23 and he really couldn't wait.

Budd Friedman asked him to host his syndicated television showcase, An Evening at the Improv, *on October 29, but he would have rather been wrestling back down in that colossal arena, because he hadn't stopped thinking about it, but he couldn't wrestle now anyway because of the cyst on the back of his neck which had gotten so big and so ripe in the last couple of weeks that the doctor wanted to lance it but instead he told the doctor to wait a few more days because he wanted to try something new in the realm of audience participation. Linda made them wash their hands with the hot towels first. They came up one at a time. He told them not to press it too hard, just touch lightly. And he didn't do it to be funny, either.*

Lawler came to the airport to pick up Andy and his brother Michael when they arrived for the November event. Michael had come along to see the thousands clamoring for Andy's blood. They would be joined by Sherry Tuseth of Jonesboro, Arkansas, an art-school student whom Andy had arranged to meet on his June excursion (beguiling fan letter) and who had kept him company during his incipient raids upon Memphis. They went to the Coliseum, where four women wanted a piece of him. He waved the fistful of grand at them and said, as usual, "Any woman that will beat me, as an extra prize, she will get to marry me!" Lawler stood at ringside and watched the first three go down quickly—"So the last one was this heavyset black girl named Foxy Brown—I'll never forget her," he said. "She was the first one that really gave Andy a contest that night. They started the match—and she runs across and grabs Andy and picks him up in the air and drops him for a body slam. I mean, the roof came off the Coliseum! All of a sudden, here's this big mouth getting what he deserves, you know? And he starts scrambling, trying to run out of the ring—and she's pulling his tights down, holding him in the ring. It was just classic." And it was a draw.

Which was when Lawler decided to demand a rematch for Foxy Brown wherein he would become her coach and trainer. Andy loved this idea and immediately made broadcast tapes for Memphis television to say just how much he hated this idea—"I don't know why Jerry Lawler's getting his nose into it! He should keep his nose out of my business! Mr. Lawler, you think you can teach this woman how to wrestle? I will destroy her no matter what you say you can do! Mark my words, Mr. Lawler!" And both men tucked away their secret smiles and waited a week to advance a notion that would grow into a spectacle that was to be theirs alone.

That Foxy Brown went limp and was pinned in eight minutes thirty-five seconds during the November 30 rematch was irrelevant. Andy just sat on her after he won and gratuitously pushed her face into the mat and kept on pushing like the heel that he was supposed to be. And that was when Lawler was compelled to step into the ring and begin his new destiny—"So I just reached down and pulled him up off her. And he flies clear across the ring, falls over, then jumps up. And all of a sudden his eyes get big and he starts screaming at me." And he kept screaming and then Lawler pushed him down again and Andy leapt out of the ring and grabbed Lance Russell's ringside microphone and played his part—"I WILL SUE YOU, LAWLER! I WILL SUE YOU! YOU DON'T TOUCH ME! I AM FROM HOLLYWOOD! I'LL GET HOLLYWOOD AGAINST YOU, BABY! I DON'T WRESTLE MEN! YOU DON'T TOUCH ME, BABY! I'LL SUE YOU FOR EVERY-THING YOU'VE GOT!"

And now that they had established themselves as mortal enemies, they started to think of ways to elevate their feud and sell more tickets and figure out how the fellow in longjohns wasn't going to get hurt. Several meals were shared in the process of discussion. Lawler's wife liked to cook. George, meanwhile, would think it was fortunate that reports of this last occurrence did not filter anywhere north of the Mason-Dixon line.

Heartbeeps opened December 18, one year after its haphazard completion following the SAG strike. *Variety* noted, "Each moment passes like hours waiting for this slumgullion to slide by." Roger Ebert of the *Chicago Sun-Times* wrote, "It's a mystery to me why this film was made." George reported, **Of all the films that opened at Christmastime, it did the worst. Absolutely embarrassingly** bad at the box office, which is a setback for Andy's motion picture career quite considerably.

They were saying he was poison.

They were saying he was impossible.

Simka returned to Latka during the first week of 1982, when the eighty-first episode, "Simka Returns," was filmed and Andy was exceptionally late for an important rehearsal that week and Ed. Weinberger called George and screamed—"Who the hell does Andy think he is? I'm completely fed up with him!"

Taxi had been struggling in the ratings ever since the season before when the network moved it from Tuesdays to Thursday nights. It would rank in the lowly fifty-third position by the end of this season, its fourth, and would be canceled by ABC on May 4 but then rescued (for its brilliance and integrity) on May 21 by NBC, where the series would be permitted its fifth season, which would also be its last.

Simka, meanwhile, had returned to save Latka from his multiple personalities disorder. In addition to the playboy Vic Ferrari, he had also become, in varying measures, Arlo the cowboy, Sir Geoffrey Hypen-Hill, who was British Man, and Alex Reiger, wherein he emulated the Judd Hirsch character. With Simka, he gave them all up for love. They would marry six episodes later.

He returned to *Saturday Night Live,* where it had been more than two years since he wrestled and disappeared from the show. Dick Ebersol had been brought in as executive producer not long after the Charles-Rockett-fuck incident, which had prompted in part a creative house-razing and a fresh start with new personnel. Andy had wanted to host, but Ebersol said no; Andy had wanted Clifton to appear, but Ebersol said no. Elvis appeared, instead, on January 30; he wore a wig now because of his thinning hairline; he also wore a stunning cerulean studded jumpsuit that Bill Belew had recently designed. Elvis lip-synched to the old chicken opera record—which was funny but a desecration—after which Elvis picked two girls from the audience to be brought to his dressing room by Elvis's bodyguard Red West (Zmuda). The cameras followed them inside, whereupon Elvis instructed the girls to rassle—"Whoa! Wait a minute," he said as they began. "Take off your clothes, but leave the panties on." And as they moved to do this, he stopped them and removed his wig and addressed the camera—"Ladies and gentlemen, I'd like to just say something right now. Um, what I just did was based on that book by Albert Goldman about Elvis. And, uh, I would just like to say, all my life I've been a fan of Elvis Presley and, uh, I disapprove of that book and also I disapprove of what I just did."

David Letterman returned to NBC with a new talk-and-comedy show called *Late Night with David Letterman*, which took the place of *The Tomorrow Show* immediately following Johnny Carson's *Tonight Show*. Andy made his first appearance on the program in its third week, February 17, and proudly showed clips of himself wrestling and berating women in Memphis—after which Letterman said, "Andy, you've turned out to be quite a fine young man." He then displayed his brand-new World Intergender Wrestling Championship belt, claiming it was really real. "He's not kidding," said Letterman. "This is molded plastic."

Clifton went on the show the next night. Letterman said, "So there's no truth to the rumor that you're actually Andy Kaufman?" Clifton said, "There's no truth in that whatsoever! That's a total fabrication on your part!" He also boasted, "I've been removed from almost every major motion picture set and TV studio in America!" Andy thought Bob did a wonderful job. Nobody at the Letterman show knew the difference.

Lawler wanted him to send tapes from California. Los Angeles wrestling promoter Larry Burton, who had orchestrated many of Andy's more surreptitious matches around Orange County, invited

Andy and Zmuda to come down to Anaheim, where they borrowed the backyard poolside of one of Burton's neighbors. They shot a great deal of footage there in which Andy—wearing Burton's gold chain around his neck and Burton's rings on his fingers—threatened Lawler with countless law suits and attacked the South in general and *Meeyummmphissss Teeeyennnuuhhhsaaaayyyy* in point and called Lawler a hick and reminded him ad nauseam that he, Andy, was from Hollywood and that he had the brains. Burton found a six-foot three-hundred-twenty-seven-pound woman at a local hardware store and Andy wrestled her on the poolside patio and slammed her head into the concrete repeatedly until she appeared unconscious. "That's what's gonna happen to you, Lawler!" he screamed. "See, I could do anything I want! I'm gonna wipe the floor with you, Mr. Lawler!"

Lawler, for his part, made his own tapes in Memphis with Lance Russell and called Andy a wimp and said to Andy as well as local viewers, "We can settle it two ways, Andy Kaufman. We can settle it in court—which in your case is a joke [since] I barely pushed the guy. Or what I would propose and what I think everybody would love to see is Andy Kaufman come and get in the ring with a real wrestler and let him see what it's like to really wrestle."

The video baiting continued for weeks and they eventually secured the Mid-South Coliseum for April 5, whereupon the grudge match would unfold—smack in the midst of Andy's first club and college tour in more than two years.

George told him that they had lost the engagement in Denver. Only 270 tickets had been sold for an auditorium whose capacity was 2,600. They also lost the Minneapolis engagement—250 tickets sold for a 2,700-seat theater. It was, George knew, the wrestling. Plus, Andy had no new material. Although he did try a couple of new things on March 26 at the Park West Theater in Chicago—he made a telephone call from the stage to someone who had written him a particularly vicious hate letter. Also, the Masked Magician hypnotized plants from the audience. Andy's sister Carol, who lived in Chicago, feigned a trance in which she became Carol Channing and sang "Hello, Dolly!" A stripper from Boston named Princess Cheyenne, of whom Andy was quite fond, feigned a trance and removed all her clothes prompting a calamitous police raid that seemed very extremely real.

On April Fool's Day, he announced the Lawler match on the Letterman show and then returned two nights later to repeat the announcement in case anyone had missed it the first time. He showed clips of them baiting each other. It was very exciting. To him.

He and Zmuda and Sherry Tuseth went to the home of referee Jerry Calhoun two nights before the match. Lawler was there as arranged and proceeded to demonstrate how Andy would survive a suplex and a piledriver because that was what he was going to do to him in the ring and this was a simple matter of remedial choreography and nothing else. The suplex, he explained, would involve Lawler lifting Andy vertically over his shoulders and falling backward together hard—like a pair of toppled trees—which would impact the back of Andy's head. The piledriver, which was illegal in Memphis, was generally performed on opponents who had been rendered limp; the victim would be lifted by the legs and turned upside down and his head would nestle between Lawler's thighs as he fell into a thudding sit. So there on Calhoun's den carpet Andy submitted to Lawler dangling him by the ankles as Lawler talked him through each maneuver—"I told him, 'You know, we'll just keep the match very simple and very basic. You know how to get a headlock around me, don't you?' And he said: 'Oh, yeah, I can do that.' And I said, 'Well, just get a headlock on me, and we'll just go from there. Because I may do a move on you like a suplex from the headlock. If I do, just tuck your chin and try not to let the back of your head hit the mat and you'll be all right, I'll take care of you.' And the move that I'm famous for, if I get a chance, is the piledriver. It's funny—I remember I said, 'Don't worry, I won't break your neck or anything.' But I told him that not much of the head should make contact with the mat, just a little bit. I mean, you could do it and try to protect somebody, or you could do it and make sure their head did hit. It just depends on the placement—on how far you stick their head down between your legs. I showed him how I would keep his head way off that mat."

They went through this a couple of times that night and Sherry Tuseth was struck by Andy's respectfulness toward Lawler and how he relinquished all control to him. "He was pretty much in awe of him all the time," she said. "But what was real surprising to me was just how quickly they could rehearse something like that. It took about five minutes."

George flew in because. Andy had given George assurances, but still. George had not known of the extent of the choreography, so therefore. George was not thrilled. George was very extremely concerned. Zmuda told him not to worry. George sat ringside next to Sherry. George recollected afterward—**He wrestled Jerry Lawler. All the pre-interviews seemed to indicate that Andy was very worried about this guy. . . . There was a guy, Woody Something, from Associated Press, who interviewed Jerry Lawler and he told me that Jerry wasn't kidding around with this wrestling match. Andy went into the ring at the Mid-South Coliseum to a tremendous chorus of boos. For the first five minutes after Andy went into the ring, he was dancing around, jumping around like a monkey, got out of the ring to protect himself, and after five minutes Jerry Lawler offered to let Andy put him in a headlock. So Andy got Lawler in a headlock. Lawler picked him up and threw him right on his back on the canvas. He hit pretty hard. Then Lawler grabbed him and gave him a piledriver, which is an illegal hold. . . . He did this twice. It looked like Andy's neck was broken. He was out for a couple of minutes. Then he woke in a lot of pain and the audience was hooting and cheering and really happy that Andy was hurt.**

*   *   *

Lawler recollected after many passing years:

"We went five to seven minutes before we actually even touched. So I offered him the free headlock and, just as I told him, we went into the suplex. But funny thing was the suplex knocked him out. It really did knock him goofy and he could not get up. I've watched the tape a thousand times. And even though he tried to tuck his head, his head still hit real hard. I mean, if it had been any of the other wrestlers, you wouldn't even have thought anything about it. But Andy wasn't accustomed to taking that type of abuse or whatever. It just knocked him goofy there for a minute. And I had hoped to have a little bit of a match. So I went straight to the piledriver, which meant it was already a disqualification. But now I'm thinking to my-self, Oh my gosh—this has probably been a minute and a half's worth of action for these 12,000 people here. I figured, man, I need to do *something* else. We've cheated 'em out of a wrestling match. And so that's where the second piledriver came into effect. I gave him an-other one. I mean, I've taken probably five hundred piledrivers in my career. You just brace yourself for it, that's just part of wrestling. All of the stuff hurts to an extent, but it's not like a big-injury-type thing. And so I'm telling him while the crowd's screaming, 'Don't worry, you won't feel anything.' Later on he said, 'First of all, the suplex knocked me out. Then both of the piledrivers jammed the heck out of my neck.' And I said: 'Well, you didn't hit, did you?' He said, 'Yes, my head hit both times.' I mean, the wrestlers just don't think any-thing about it. But not being accustomed to that, he thought: Oh, my gosh, this is really hurting big-time."

The ambulance came. Took them about fifteen goddamn min-utes before they came. I almost got into a fight with one of those stupid punk fans there. Andy was taken out on a stretcher. The cameras were all over the place. I was in the ring with him. I was holding his hand. . . . Initially, we were told that he had a com-pressed vertebra and a short disc space between his fourth and fifth vertebrae and severe muscle strain around his neck. Later it turned out that it was primarily muscle strain. He was in traction for three days in St. Francis Hospital and took every kind of conceivable test—cat scans, bone scans, brain scans. The X rays indicated there was nothing serious. It was probably a cervical sprain from an old injury and that was alleviated by the traction. He's supposed to wear a neck brace for a day or two.

He was released from the hospital on the eighth and went home to Great Neck to celebrate Passover with his family, all of whom were mortified and Stanley actually did want to sue and Andy shrugged and happened to tune in *Saturday Night Live* on the tenth, most of which was devoted to a live viewer phone-in poll wherein people were casting votes as to whether or not a lobster named Larry should actually be boiled on television. Larry's life was spared—239,096 votes to save versus 227,452 to boil. He liked this bit very much.

He wore the neck brace in public for the next five months.

He repeatedly announced that he had now officially retired from wrestling, but contended that at least he remained the undefeated intergender champion. He also said, "I just realized after this happened what a delusion I've been going under for the last four years. Just because I've never lost a match, then they gave me this belt—The Intergender Wrestling Champion of the World—I started thinking I was a sports hero. You know, I've just been under this macho delusion that was building up to the point where I could actually seriously think that I could beat a Jerry Lawler in a wrestling match. I mean, that's stupid. I was just stupid."

He was quite gleeful really. As was Lawler.
Lawler told the media that he was glad that he had injured that

wimp and that he was not at all sorry and that he wished that he could do it again.

Then Andy went on the Letterman show five weeks after the match; he went on the program to maunder pitifully—with chin nestled in his woeful brace—and to stammer contrition and welcome empathy. He tried to address the camera to send a heartfelt message and quavered—"Can I say something? Mr. Law— Well, I hate to be hokey about it. But, Mr. Lawler, if you— I wish— Well, I just wish he'd apol—you know . . . I don't want to see anybody suffer. I think he's suffering now enough from people hating him so much for what he did. . . . And *I* forgive him . . . And I think he should vindicate himself . . ." And Letterman nodded along sympathetically and then said, "What about a song, Andy?"

On July 28, they would reunite on *Late Night*—although according to Andy's datebook he had quietly stolen back to Memphis during the last week in June. But they would now appear together publicly for the first time since the night of suplex and piledrivers and sirens and jeers. Andy had called Lawler when the date was confirmed and they both took rooms at the Berkshire Place and went separately to meet with talent coodinator Robert Morton to roughly strategize what would occur on the program. Morton told Lawler, "Andy wouldn't come in if you were in the same room, so we'll just do this individually." The plan was that they would appear in two segments interrupted by one commercial break. In the first segment, Morton said, footage of the Memphis match would be shown and it would be good if he and Andy were antagonistic toward each other. Lawler said that would be no problem. Then, in the second segment, they would finally apologize to each other and Andy said that he would then want to sing "What the World Needs Now (Is Love, Sweet Love)." And Lawler smirked and said fine and went back to the hotel where Andy called him.

Lawler would remember: "So he asked me what I thought about the idea—the apology and the song. I said, 'Well, you know, it's okay

with me.' I figured I'm in his arena now, so I'm not making any suggestions, right? So he said to me—and I'll never forget the way he
put it—he said, 'I wonder what would happen if you hit me instead?
If you just slugged me?' I said, 'You mean *on the show?*' He said,
'Yeah.' I said, 'Well, since we're taping it, they probably wouldn't
even broadcast it. And, second of all, they'd probably have me arrested.' He said, 'No, I would have to be the one to have you arrested.' I said, 'I don't know, Andy, that's pretty strong.' He said, 'I
know—but wouldn't it be great?' But I could tell that's what he
wanted to happen. He didn't want to come right out and tell me to
hit him. Because he never wanted to tell me what to do. He was always kind of shy around me."

They arrived at NBC Studios separately and stayed apart in the
makeup room and also in the greenroom and did not actually see
each other until Letterman introduced them. Andy timidly skulked
out behind Lawler and they sat at the panel and Andy pulled his
chair away from Lawler's chair. And Letterman asked right away
whether he still needed his neck brace and Andy said yes he did and
Lawler smirked. But Andy tried to be friendly about the whole mess
and they looked at the footage—"I was just teasing in fun," he said
about his hectoring Hollywood tapes—and Lawler grumbled and
stated, "I don't want to sit out here and pretend that I'm friends with
this guy, because I think he's a wimp." And it was very uncomfortable and the first commercial break came and Andy left his chair to
gain more distance and Letterman asked Lawler questions about
wrestlers Dick the Bruiser and Bobo Brazil. Then the show resumed
and Andy admitted that he had been wrong to wrestle Lawler and
said that he now felt Lawler owed him an apology. "I don't think I
owe him an apology," Lawler responded, adding that he didn't know
whether Andy was wearing a neck brace or a flea collar.
    Lawler would recall: "If you watch the tape, you can see Dave's
face is like, *Uh-oh, where are we going here?* Because Dave was ex-
pecting the apology from me. So he gets a little worried and I could

tell that he was gonna force the next commercial break early, right? And then Andy starts turning toward me and tries to goad me— 'Whattsamatter, Lawler!' And he starts talking about lawsuit again or something. So Dave said, 'We're gonna pause here for a commercial and get out the hoses. . . .' And right up to that point I didn't know what I should do, but when I heard the music start playing, I knew. I thought, if not now, then never. And Andy gave me this mean look, like he was waiting for something. So I just stood up and slapped the crap out of him, openhanded right across the face, as hard as I could. . . ."

Andy spilled out of his chair to the floor and pandemonium ensued and nobody knew what to believe and Robert Morton rushed forth and Letterman stepped away and the show went to a break—"It was like the President had been assassinated or something," said Lawler. The break would last almost twenty minutes, in which time the studio lights were dimmed and a security guard came for Lawler and escorted him to the greenroom, which had been emptied of its many previous occupants. Lawler said, "I could hear through the door out in the hallway people crying and screaming. And I'm thinking, I just really screwed up here. And then I hear Andy screaming and cussing—'I want him arrested! Call the cops!' Je-sus. And I had already told this goof that if I hit him I'd get arrested! So I'm thinking I'm getting double-crossed here."

And Robert Morton would recall: "During this enormous break, Andy came over to me in the middle of his ranting and kind of whispered, 'Am I taking this too far?' I said, 'No, absolutely not. Just keep going. It's entertaining as hell!' So he just picked up where he left off with his performance. I mean, Andy *knew* that he was performing. He saw that there was entertainment value in this. Whether or not he was surprised by the slap, I never knew. But it was just electric."

Lawler was finally brought back into the studio—"Now the whole audience boos, right? All of a sudden they've turned into a wrestling crowd! So I sit down and everyone is trying to get their composure. Dave is not even looking at me. Andy is over by the studio door, where everybody comes in and Dave says to him, 'Andy, do you want to come back here and sit down or not?' And he said, 'No! If I come out there, I'll say words that I can't say on television!' "

And so the cameras relit and Letterman welcomed viewers back and said, "Andy, are you coming in here again or—" Whereupon, he burst back into the studio and began leaping up and down behind Letterman's desk as he addressed Lawler with a diatribe that would resonate in broadcast history, largely for the number of expletives that were obscured by *coo-coo* noises—"I am sick of this bull*shit!*" he began. "You are full of bullshit, my friend! I will sue you for everything you have! I will sue your ass! You're a motherfuckin' asshole!!!!!!!!! As far as I'm concerned!!!!! You hear me?!!!!! A fuckin' asshole!!!!!!!!! Fuck you!!!!!! I will get you for this!!! [He stormed away, then instantly returned.] I am *sorry*, I am *sorry* to use those words on television. I apologize to all my fans. I'm *sorry*, I'm *sorry*. But *you*—you're a fuckin' asshole!!!!!!!!!!!!!! You're a fuckin' asshole!!!!!!!!! [He slammed his palms on Letterman's desk.] You hear me!!!!!! A fuckin' asshole!!!!!!"

Which was when he took Letterman's coffee cup and sailed its hot black contents in Lawler's direction—"You know," Lawler would say, "if you watch that closely, you can see him make the move to the cup to let me know what he was fixing to do. He threw it so I could get out of the way. It barely went on my left shoulder." So Lawler leapt and Andy scampered out and Letterman said, "Uhh, I think you can use *some* of those words on TV. . . . But what you can't do is throw coffee. I've said it over and over again. . . ." And the segment ended.

Lawler was accompanied to an elevator by the same security guard who saw that he was safely out of the building before asking him to autograph a wrestling magazine. Andy, meanwhile, went upstairs to the *Late Night* production offices to hide from view and to think about what he had done. After the show, Letterman found him up there and Andy eagerly asked, "What did you think?" And Letterman wearily glanced at the neck brace and sighed, "Next time wear a tie."

12

. . . And the people could easily see, now, how noble and
beautiful those episodes were, and remembered with
grief that at the time they occurred they had seemed
rank rascalities, well deserving of the cowhide. The con-
gregation became more and more moved, as the pathetic
tale went on, till at last the whole company broke down
and joined the weeping mourners in a chorus of anguished sobs. . . .

—Mark Twain,
The Adventures of Tom Sawyer

The brace had browned from sweat and folly. He wore it and wore it and kept on wearing it and it became a wreath of perpetual martyr-dom—and martyrs, everyone knew, were supposed to die. Of course, he had been giving it serious thought. Most certainly, it was on his mind. The idea excited him very much. He had discussed it with em-inent hoaxer Alan Abel, who had managed to do it but then called a press conference immediately after his obituary was published. Abel had not properly lingered in death. Elvis, he liked to believe, was doing it well. He had a theory about Elvis, which he shared with a magazine writer named Judd Klinger just one year after Elvis had been gone: He believed that there may have been four Elvises, be-ginning with the original, who had disappeared in 1958. "The man-agers saw that he was getting old so they got rid of him. And then from '58 to '60 they didn't have anybody, so they said that he was in the

Army. In 1960, they got a new guy who played the part of Elvis Presley until '69—this guy, you noticed, didn't look at all like the other guy, didn't have the sideburns or anything. Then, when they saw that his movies were falling off at the box office, they came up with another guy and *he* looked different! He played the part until '73, until they got *another* guy and this guy was overweight, but then they saw that business was *really* falling off—the concerts and the records weren't selling. So they got rid of that guy and they said that Elvis was dead. That was just so they could sell a lot of records, which worked. And in a few years, they'll get another guy and say, 'We were only kidding—Elvis is alive!' "

Well, it was a theory. And, denial notwithstanding, it was a theory of rebirth; it was about returning anew from nadir, about reinvention and rising from ashes. Lately, he could not help but smell smoke, even if he wished to believe otherwise. The slap had resonated across the land and telegraphed excitement and stirred legitimate sympathy. But it had also stirred a deeper concern for his (apparent) wayward psyche; he was *dangerous* now; he was out of control; he had last been glimpsed *raving* on television, which was an uncomfortable image to have pressed into collective memory. Certain people—ones with power—preferred, more than ever, to aggressively avert their eyes from him. George's chagrin was evident when he did not bother recounting the Letterman incident to his tape recorder; in fact, George had been speaking to his tape recorder less and less in the past year, as woe and concern overtook excitement and wonder. By October 1982, he would give up the career chronicling altogether. From that point forward, his foremost responsibility would be that of tending to damage control and soliciting offers that did not often materialize—plus Andy would begin doing things he did not tell George about, such as plotting his own death, which was nothing if not the penultimate bombing.

Earlier in the year, there had been a *Fridays* party at the home of co-producer Jack Burns and, there, Andy took Burns and John Moffitt aside—"He said, 'I want to talk to you,' " Moffitt would recall. "So we went down to Jack's basement rec room and closed the door, figuring he had a new big idea for the show. Then he told us, 'Now, what I want to do the next—within the next year or so—is to pretend I'm dead. I want people to believe I'm dead and so I'm going to disappear. Then a few months later, I'm going to reappear again—hopefully on the show. And I think this is gonna be the best thing I've ever done—this is gonna be the biggest!' " (*Fridays*, however, would be canceled that fall and, anyway, Moffitt and Burns thought he was probably, almost certainly, kidding about the whole thing.) Then, later that summer, after the slap, he met with *Saturday Night Live* producer Bob Tischler and writers Barry Blaustein and David Sheffield to discuss possible ideas he wished to execute in the new season—one of which was to issue a "comedy challenge" (à la wrestling) to Bob Hope, wherein if Hope could get more laughs than Andy in some kind of contest, Andy would have his own head shaved; conversely, if Andy won, he would be called "Mr. Bob Hope" for a week. (Andy quickly reneged on the idea—"I don't think I can win, 'cause I'm not funny," he said.) Tischler recounted, "But then he told the three of us, 'You know, the hoax I'd really like to pull off is my death. But I'm afraid of doing it—because when I do these things, I do them for real, and so I wouldn't even be able to tell my parents. And I wouldn't want to hurt them.' " But throughout the next year he would posit the idea to other people—to Zmuda, certainly, as well as his sister and his brother and also Mimi Lambert. "He said, 'What if I pretended to have cancer or something?' " Lambert would recall. "I was horrified. I said, 'Forget it, Andy. That's revolting, it's not good karma!' " Anyway, by that time she would be more concerned with the fact that he had this cough.

He wanted Latka to wear the brace, too. Ed. Weinberger adamantly refused. He removed the brace before the filming of the first episode of the season and put it back on after they all took bows that night. Cast members just rolled their eyes. He pretended not to notice.

* * *

George did not want him to do My Breakfast with Blassie, *which was an hour-long videotaped movie in which he would eat breakfast at a Sambo's in Hollywood with bombastic former-five-time-heavyweight-wrestling champion, silver-headed bad guy Freddie Blassie, who enjoyed calling people pencil-neck geeks and had made a novelty record called "Pencil-Neck Geek," which Andy admired as much as he admired Freddie Blassie himself. The man who wrote and produced Blassie's record, Johnny Legend (whose real name was Martin Margulies), now wanted to make a very cheap parody of the art film* My Dinner with André, *which Andy hated as much as he respected Blassie. Legend asked Andy if he wanted to do it and Andy said that he did despite George's protests. (George thought that Andy's involvement in anything that smacked again of wrestling—including a boring movie about having breakfast with a crazy wrestler—only invited further destruction. He told Linda Lautrec—who co-created the film with Johnny Legend—"I hope you sell it in a foreign country and everybody makes their money back and no one here ever sees it." But he meant it in a nice way.) So, on August 9, the movie was shot at Sambo's and there was no script because it was going to be an extemporaneous exercise in which the two men—one in a dirty neck brace, the other carrying a cane—discussed life and geeks and fastidious hygiene. "I want my hands to be like a surgeon's when I eat," Andy told Blassie. Both men agreed that it was unwise to shake hands with people in restaurants and then this girl from the next table came over to shake hands and ask for an autograph and at her table were three other girls, and they were all plants, and one of them was Linda Mitchell (who would also play classical guitar on the sound track) and another was Johnny Legend's younger sister, Lynne Margulies, whom Andy had not met until that very moment on camera. And he thought she was very attractive and flirted with her instantly, right there on camera, and she was unamused and truthfully said that she had never seen him on television. "I'm a famous star," he told her, and she said, "Oh." He demonstrated tenk you veddy much for her and said, "When you first walked in, I noticed you right away. And I said to myself, Now, this is somebody who I would give my time to. 'Cause I don't give my time to just anybody. But to you, I would." And he kissed her hand and tried to get her phone number and Linda called him obnoxious and, later, Zmuda came over to the table and pretended to be a hostile fan and pulled several befouled drinking straws from his nose and laid them on the table and also vomited (ice cream) and Blassie said, "I'm ready to puke in that asshole's face!" And Andy also spoke of his late wrestling career and asked Blassie, "Do you think I'm a has-been now?" And Blassie said no, but also said, "It's better to be a has-been than a never-was."*

He reclaimed Clifton for himself one more time. Clifton performed a medley of songs with a troupe of chorus girls on *The Fantastic Miss Piggy Show*, which was an ABC-TV special taped in Toronto a week after the Blassie congress and which would rank fifty-fourth in the ratings when it aired a month later. Horrified Muppets watched him from the control room. Miss Piggy said, "Isn't he something?" Kermit the Frog hemmed and hawed uncomfortably and finally acknowledged, "Interesting." Andy wrote the name of one of the Clifton dancers in his ever-burgeoning phone book—"Darlene, looked sixteen, really twenty-one, Taurus."

There would be no more Clifton. Not for him.

He flew directly to New York to end what he had started precisely where he had started it. *The material—everyone said there was nothing new, that he needed something new. . . .* He was to perform on the HBO taping of Catch a Rising Star's tenth anniversary, which would take place at the Upper East Side club where he had first hauled forth his props and made everyone think he wasn't who he was and vice versa. *So he decided to kill it off, to put the material out of its misery, to expose it as the charade and the lodestone that it had become. . . .* For the sake of nostalgia, he would do what he had done at the outset, what had induced them all into falling down and falling over and falling to the floor and, most of all, falling for him. *He could fool no one anymore, they said, because everyone was*

*"on to" him, they said, and people were even making light of the neck
brace of which he was so proud which seemed very rude. . . .* Besides
him, there would be other Catch alums performing—Richard
Belzer, David Brenner, Gabe Kaplan, Billy Crystal, Robin
Williams, Joe Piscopo, Pat Benatar. *He planted Zmuda up front and
had Rick Newman make sure that a microphone was hidden somewhere on Zmuda's body so that Zmuda could be clearly overheard as
the material was drained of its blood and left for dead. . . .* "Anyway,"
he said, "tonight what I'd like to do is the exact same routine which
I did ten years ago. It's called Foreign Man Turning into Elvis
Presley." At which point there was warm applause. *At which point
Zmuda could be heard throughout the club and, later, on television
saying, "Tenk you veddy much."* And Foreign Man blinked into
character and said, "Tenk you veddy much." *Zmuda turned to a
woman nearby and said, "See, see! Tenk you veddy much!"* "I am
veddy happy to be here but one theeng I don't like about New
York—" *"Ees de traffic . . ."* "Ees too much traffic you know tonight
eet was so much traffic—" *"Eet took me an hour . . ."* "—eet took
me an hour and a half to get here!" *"See! See!"* "Talking about de
terrible theengs—" *"Take my wife . . ."* "—take my wife, please take
her!" *"Her cooking ees so bad eets . . ."*

And this was not mere heckling; it was worse and also better; it was
the act anticipated, performed in parsed phrases, slightly ahead of
itself. It was Foreign Man unmasked and torched and vanquished forever. And the audience laughed with majestic unease as the humili-
ations echoed on—through *"eemetations/*eemetations" and *"de
Archie Bunker/*de Archie Bunker" and *"dingbat get eento de kitchen
and make me de food/*dingbat get eento de kitchen and make me de
food." And Andy was wet; his face was soaked with flop summoned
from trained synapses and abetted by blistering lights and he had to
say something to stop this man down in front of the stage from ruining everything *and he had to say something to push this man down in
front of the stage into now decimating everything that he was and had
ever been* and so he said, "Is there a problem?"

ZMUDA: No, there's no problem. The only problem is that I'm

doing your act for you. . . . If you did some new material, then I wouldn't know what you're gonna do next.

ANDY: Well, uh, I was asked to do this material tonight, okay? This is what the club asked me to do, and I'm doing it.

ZMUDA: Sure, they asked you to do it because your new stuff's a bunch of crap. . . . Can I say something? I was always a big fan of yours, like, I'm talkin' seven, eight years ago. And I just feel that you have been repeating yourself continually. . . . I don't consider wrestling women to be funny, to be creative, to be any of those things.

ANDY: I do a lot of original stuff on *Late Night* . . .

ZMUDA: Okay, so what? What's original?

ANDY: Well, did you see me on *Fridays*? Caused a lot of talk.

ZMUDA: Yeah, I saw you on *Fridays*. A put-on. Pushing people around and actors . . . That's not original, that's not comedy. That's put-on! Anybody could do that. You understand?

ANDY: You're right, it was a put-on.

ZMUDA: I'm telling you, I'm just being honest. . . . I'm not trying to be obnoxious. I'm just saying that you were a very original guy.

ANDY: I was. I was a very original guy. I was considered a very original comic.

ZMUDA: That's right. And *was* is the key word. You said it yourself.

ANDY: Well . . .

ZMUDA: You've lost all credibility. I'm just saying that you used to be an original performer, see?

And, of course, the audience felt embarrassment beyond any embarrassment ever felt for the pitiful Foreign Man when Foreign Man was new and innocent and lost. This was now the disemboweling of an actual life and career—and, whether or not what was happening was real, it was nevertheless all very true and all very profoundly true. What the room felt was hot sticky suffocating devastation and the man down in front of the stage did not stop—he attacked that stupid character Latka and called that movie *Heartbeeps* a piece-of-shit-bomb and said that Andy Kaufman would never make another movie because who would hire him now? And a guy in back, who was Pat Benatar's uncle, who was an off-duty security cop, screamed for Zmuda to shut the fuck

up and Zmuda told him to fuck himself and Zmuda returned to his in-
terrogation and the cop reached for the gun that he kept in his boot
and Rick Newman crawled over and grabbed the cop's ankle and whispered, "Shut up! He's a plant! This is a taping!" And Zmuda demanded to hear new material and Andy responded by doing the twist
while singing *booboobooboobooboo* over and over and the audience
laughed and Zmuda said that they were laughing only because they
knew him from *Taxi* and Andy said, "I guess you're right. I don't have
any new material. I don't have anything new to do." And the tears
started welling and then came the little gulping sobs and Zmuda said,
"See, now this is the old crying routine, the bombing." And Andy
stopped suddenly and said, "You've seen me do that?"

ZMUDA: Yes! Everybody's seen you do that! Kaufman, *look*, call a
spade a spade. You don't have anything new to do. *[Turning to the au-
dience]* As a matter of fact, that is why he hired me tonight to come
here. Look—there's a little mike on me, you see this? He hired me
tonight to come here and criticize him, you know? See, today he was
saying, "Zmuda, *here's what we're gonna do . . . I'll take my old material and I'll call it Variation on a Theme. . . .* " The theme is the old
material and the variation is that I'm told to sit here and criticize it.
[To Andy] Well, it's true. Am I being honest? Am I a plant? Be honest—am I a plant? Come on! Am I a plant? Is this another Kaufman
put-on? Is this more bullshit? Am I a plant? . . . Tell the people . . .
there's a mike here. *[To audience]* Come on, you see it. There's a
mike, they sat me down here to do this . . .

ANDY: Yeah . . . *[sotto voce]* You're not supposed to say anything.

ZMUDA: Fine, then just cut it out [of the tape].

ANDY: *[s.v.]* You just fucked up the act!

ZMUDA: Fine! Fine!

ANDY: *[s.v.]* You weren't supposed to . . .

ZMUDA: Fuck you! Fffff—

At which point, on the tape of the program that was broadcast,
there would be an awkward edit, as though something had happened
and needed to be removed when in fact nothing had happened except the execution of Andy's notion to make an obvious edit to sug-

gest that something had happened—"It was planned that way," said Rick Newman. "The public went crazy when the show was broadcast. HBO and Catch got hundreds of phone calls from people demanding to know what happened. We told them there was nothing to be discussed—'We can't tell you. Just leave it be.' " And when the program resumed, Andy said, "Ladies and gentlemen, right now I'd like to do my oldest routine, which I've done so much that many people are sick of it. Um . . . but I'm gonna do it anyway, and it's my imitation of Elvis Presley. Thank you."

Elvis, bewigged, hoarse, no longer lean or taut—it did not matter, really. Elvis cleansed the palate with familiarity, with "Jailhouse Rock." People still hooted, if not screamed. Meanwhile, many people would consider Variations on a Theme—or whatever he wished to call this act of self-immolation—to be perhaps the most brilliant thing that he had ever done. In any case, he felt very extremely liberated afterward.

The brace finally disappeared. It itched.

New material: the Fakir, mystical Eastern wonder-worker/fraud. Wearing diaper and turban and black socks and brown walking shoes and nothing else, he wordlessly dances forth and ripples his stomach muscles and his pectoral muscles in syncopation with the beat of conga drums (somebody else plays them) and performs a horizontal handstand (yogic coordination) and then stands to swallow a sword (presented by Zmuda in butler's togs) and then fixes a felt mustache above his lip and straps on a guitar and imitates the falsetto of Slim Whitman singing "Rosemarie." ("I'm bringing romance back," he liked to say now.) He had always been a fakir. But he had never worn a diaper and a turban onstage before. He practiced in L.A. at the Improv. He wanted to do it on tour, but George couldn't really line up a decent tour for him anymore, so on September 25, he went on a ten-city bus tour of California to campaign for Governor Jerry Brown, who was running for the U.S. Senate, performing in college and high school auditoriums with musicians Kris Kristofferson and Billy Swan. He did not care much about the senatorial race; he did not care much about pol-itics in general. But it was good to tour again. Mostly, he meditated in the back of the bus in between stops.

The fakir would debut for television on *Saturday Night Live*, where he knew it would remind people of what he had done long ago before making such a racket. The date was set for October 23 and he was advertised as that week's special guest star and he arrived early in the week to begin rehearsal. On Saturday evening, he performed at dress rehearsal as well, after which Stanley and Janice came to Rockefeller Center to watch the live broadcast and they were about to be seated in the studio audience when Andy was told that he had been cut from the show due to time constraints and due to the fact that Dick Ebersol was not thrilled with the fakir. "It was fifteen min-utes before show time," said Stanley. "He was devastated. And I was seething. I'm quick to blow my stack. If I had seen Dick Ebersol that night, I probably would have smacked him." Said writer Bob Tischler, "Andy had never been bumped from the show before. He was legitimately pissed." Tischler had followed him back to the Berkshire Place Hotel to assess the damage and attend to reparations. They went to Ebersol the next week with a plan writhed from the mire. He wanted to be scheduled to appear the following Saturday, October 30—"He told me to bill him at the top of the show as a guest but then he wanted me to cut him again," said Ebersol. "He said, 'While the show's on the air, you'll send somebody to the dressing room to tell me there's not enough time and I'm not going to get on. It'll be a totally normal thing. Then we'll stage a fight out in the hall-way after the show finishes.' "

The premise of the appearance he would not make was to be an explanation of why he had been bumped from the previous week's show and a personal attack on Ebersol—and because it was such a straightforward piece, a monologue, he would not have to be part of the pre-broadcast dress rehearsal that evening, which was a good thing because he would actually be in Gainesville, Florida, at that time, performing an actual concert—a makeup date, really—at the University of Florida. To accommodate the *Saturday Night Live* scheme, the concert had been moved up two hours, after which he would speed to the airport and fly directly to New York so as to be present when he was cut from the show and therefore assault Ebersol outside the studio as the audience filed toward the elevators after one A.M. and thus ignite gossip and scandal. None of this would be known to anyone except Ebersol and Tischler and writers Blaustein and Sheffield and director Davey Wilson. Later, Ebersol would tell Kay Gardella of the New York *Daily News* why he had bumped Andy and his monologue—"He handed me three handwritten pages he planned to do that [were] not only unfunny but also belligerent. Frankly, I felt betrayed. I made my mind up that he was not going on."

And so they fought because he had been cut *twice in a row*; and so they fought in the hallway by the makeup room—"Andy comes out of this makeup room and accosts me," said Ebersol. "Starts screaming at me because I had fucked him and I owed it to him as a friend to put him back on the show. It got worse and worse and I was taking it, but he was good enough to start actually making me angrier and angrier. Finally, I turned my back on him. He never stopped screaming." Said Blaustein, "It was great theater, totally believable. Everyone was sort of spellbound—the audience, the staff and crew that were milling around."

It was happening all over again.

And none of it was televised.

Two Saturdays later, November 13, the plan lumbered forward. Andy watched in Los Angeles and saw, near the very end of the program, Ebersol address the camera and the audience—

"Hi, I'm Dick Ebersol, the executive producer of *Saturday Night Live*. In recent weeks, we have received inquiries from many of you, including even the editors of *TV Guide*, as to why, prior to our last two telecasts, we heavily promoted Andy Kaufman and then failed to present him as advertised. So tonight, let me set the record straight by saying, in my opinion, that in both cases Andy misled us into thinking, right up until airtime, that his material would be up to the show's standards. It was not. It was not even funny, and in my opinion Andy Kaufman is not funny anymore. And I believe *you*, the audience here, agrees with me. So thank you, and I hope this sets the record straight. Good night."

Gardella, afterward, in the *Daily News:* "True or not, it's a cruel blow even if the two were embroiled in a publicity stunt, which Ebersol denies."

The audience at the Letterman show liked the fakir bit just fine. He performed it there five nights later. He was forbidden by the network, however, from mentioning Ebersol or *Saturday Night Live*. But he did tell Letterman, "Lately, it's become a pretty popular thing to say that Andy Kaufman isn't funny anymore. [Audience laughed.] And that Andy Kaufman should not be allowed on television, and that he should be banned from television." He likened it to blacklisting—"It reeks of McCarthyism to me"—and brandished a clipping from the *San Jose Mercury News* whose headline blared, ANDY KAUFMAN SHOULD BE PUT OUT TO PASTURE. [Audience awwwwwwwed.] He told Letterman, "Let's face it—yours is about the only show I'm allowed on right now. And I thank you very much." And Letterman said, "Well, we kinda feel it's a badge of honor, Andy." He also said that he was working with his lawyers on a plan to refund the price of admission to anyone who had paid to see *Heartbeeps*. Letterman said, "Well, make sure you have change for a twenty."

He had buttonholed Ebersol outside the Improv the previous summer and told him that he had very much liked the Larry the Lobster vote in April. "Andy had been intrigued with the vote," said Ebersol. "That had resonated with him. And so he had it in his mind that he wanted to have a vote like Larry." Which had been the crux of the mission from the start. He had wanted to build the rejection of October 23 into a monstrosity of consumptive rejection—from the hallway skirmish to the he-isn't-funny-anymore statement to the cry for appeal on the Letterman show to a culmination in democratic process and telephonic technology. Should he be allowed to return to the show or should he be banished forever? On the November 20 broadcast, the nation would be polled and two telephone numbers would be given out over the air—one to save him, one to punish him for all transgressions in aggregate. The lobster had lived and he insisted to Ebersol that he would as well. "He never thought he would lose," Ebersol said. "I know that as clear as day." Blaustein: "He didn't think he could lose. He was convinced they would vote him on." Tischler: "He didn't think it could backfire."

They tried to talk him out of it.

He camped all week in the Berkshire Place Hotel and received their repeated entreaties to call it off. He told George that he was sure that even if he lost, they would let him return somehow. He wouldn't even have to be him when he came back. Some other him could come back. He had many other hims from which to choose, didn't he? And it was going to be all in fun, only fooling, no really, anyway, wasn't it? He was not worried.

"As the week went along," said Ebersol, "I kept saying to Tischler, 'He's not going to win this.' The wrestling had ticked people off. He was going to lose the vote and then we were really going to be in trouble, because if people vote no, then the vote has to hold." Blaustein said, "I remember late Thursday night we went over to the hotel and said, 'Andy, just as your pieces have to be real, so does ours. And if they vote you off, you can't come back—unless we do something at the end, where you run in and cause a disruption and somehow you say the vote was fixed.' He said, 'No, I want to keep it real. They're gonna vote me on.' We said, 'But if they don't, you realize that you can't ever come back?' "

Clifton could, though—except Ebersol hated Clifton, never wanted Clifton anywhere near the show, nobody liked Clifton, even George had to tell him that Clifton was over, that Clifton did not work, that

Clifton was dead, keep the Clifton puppet from the Fun House show and play with the puppet, but there was no way Clifton would be allowed on the show. . . .

Ebersol went to the hotel very late Friday night. He gave his final plea. He told Andy, "Bringing this into a vote is an enormous mistake." The vote had not been advertised. There would be no loss in killing it. The cast would have time for more sketches. "But the vote is going to lock us in," he said, "and we'll have to live with the results." Andy told him, *"No no no no no no—we've got to do it!"*

He knew he would lose. He told Zmuda. He told George.

George stayed in California. What was the point? They would think of something. Ebersol had discovered Andy, for God's sake. Ebersol had given him *Saturday Night Live!* Time would win out somehow.

Zmuda returned to California after the Letterman show. He was working on a screenplay for a movie called *D.C. Cab* and there was nothing he could do anyway. They spoke on the phone about Clifton, who was dead, which they refused to understand.

November 20, on air, cast member Gary Kroeger:
"... During the next hour, we're going to be counting these votes, and I want you to remember that this show is live . . . we're doing it for real. Andy Kaufman's career at *Saturday Night Live* is in *your* hands. Now, I happen to think that Andy Kaufman is a comedic genius. If you agree with me, call 1–900–720–4101. However, if you think Andy is *not* funny anymore, if you've seen enough of his wrestling women, the Mighty Mouse bits, the phony injuries, the stupid, unfunny hoaxes—if you've had enough of this loudmouth, call 1–900–720–4202. You can call as many times as you'd like, but remember each call is gonna cost you fifty cents. . . ."

* * *

He was never ahead.

Early tally, on air, cast member Eddie Murphy:

". . . This is how you people have voted so far. It's Keep Andy: 38,945 and Dump Andy: 48,838. [Audience cheers] Now, last [season], I asked the people to call in and save Larry the Lobster from being boiled alive. The response to that was overwhelming, and tonight I'm asking you to vote to save a human being. Isn't Andy Kaufman worth as much as a lobster? [Shouts of *NO!*] . . . You people are sick! . . ."

End of program, guest host Drew Barrymore and cast stood at homebase stage, Kroeger reported final vote:

Keep Andy: 169,186.

Dump Andy: 195,544.

The lobster poll had drawn a total of 466,548 votes.

His poll inspired a total of 364,730 votes.

One way or another, people had cared more about a lobster.

Ebersol and Tischler walked to the hotel afterward to check on him. "He was disconsolate," said Ebersol. "He couldn't believe it. He was very sad. Not angry—sad. I think deep inside he figured that there was some way we were going to deal with this whole thing." Over the following Thanksgiving weekend, George called Ebersol and said, "Dick, this is a mess. We're losing bookings. We've got to do something about this. It's really hurting him businesswise." Ebersol suggested that Andy make some commercials that could be aired very inexpensively during *SNL* holiday repeats in relatively smaller markets like Omaha, Des Moines, and Macon, Georgia. Andy returned to California and made twelve of them. Some were pathetic — "Maybe one day *Saturday Night Live* will have a change of heart. Or I'll find another show that I could go on. Until then, I just want to wish you all the best. . . ." Some were indignant — "Sooo, you thought you could get rid of me, you 195,000 people that voted to dump Andy Kaufman! . . . You will never be able to get rid of me! You see my face? You don't like it? Try and turn it off! You can't do it. . . ." Ebersol said he would work one of the commercials into the show's Weekend Update mock-newscast on January 22, 1983, which he did only because it was legitimate news that Andy was mounting this campaign. He told George, "If the fans don't go nuts or get really negative about it, then I'll think there's enough basis to start figuring a way to bring him back."

They ran one of the more pathetic commercials, but the audience did not awwwwwwwwww, which would have helped, and some viewers and press alike claimed the show had welshed on its promise by giving Andy even another thirty seconds of airtime. Ebersol called George and said, "We're going to have to rest this for at least a year or more." Years later, he would concede that *SNL*, which had prided itself on flagrant rule-breaking, had perhaps taken itself a bit too seriously in this matter — "In retrospect, it seems so silly, but we had a loose sort of integrity with this thing. People had spent money voting — about one hundred eighty grand. It seemed strangely unconscionable to do a backflop on the deal. But eventually we would have."

Writers Blaustein and Sheffield met with him in the aftermath. They presented an idea in which he would be disguised as a black cleaning woman in the background of sketches over the course of many weeks until finally he ripped away the artifice and declared himself back. He liked the idea at first, but as time went on he thought it seemed a little too desperate. Plus, the whole thing sort of made him, um, sick.

He had lost his favorite playground.

His father, meanwhile, would nurse a hatred for Ebersol that grew more incendiary with every passing year. "Miserable bastard," Stanley would say. George would also somehow see it all as a double cross. "They could be rightfully pissed at Dick for a million different things," said Tischler, "but in terms of the vote, it was Andy who was really driving it. He refused to understand the reality of it. Reality, however, was something he always had an unusual relationship with."

Before the vote, he kept asking Johnny Legend about that Lynne girl and Legend told him that his sister, that Lynne girl, was helping to edit the Blassie movie and then by late fall they were ready to show him a rough cut of the movie out by Venice Beach so he went and he watched her more than the movie and they all went to a Mexican restaurant that was open until three in the morning. Their first night together they stayed up until dawn watching televangelist Dr. Gene Scott, thereby consecrating their own private unusual relationship with shared realities. Which was to say, they fit. She would let him strangle her in cars to frighten other motorists; she would hang out with him in pinball arcades at ridiculous hours; she would perform screaming fights with him in public; she had posed in Apartment Wrestling *magazine grappling with another girl in bikinis; she had done a nude layout for* Gallery *magazine; and she didn't mind his obsession with prostitutes. The moment she knew they were meant for each other came weeks after they began and they were at the Berkshire Place in New York—"He took his socks off and blew into them and started rolling them up. I recognized that from the W. C. Fields film* The Man on the Flying Trapeze, *and I repeated a line that Fields's wife had said—'Why would the maternity hospital be calling you in the middle of the night?' And his eyes lit up, as if to say, 'Oh my God! She knows what I'm doing!' And that was it—that sealed the deal." He sang her Slim Whitman songs. She liked "Rosemarie" best. He told her he was taking something called the* Making Love *weekend workshop, which was taught by his old TM friend Johnny Gray—who liked to be called John now—and Gray's wife, Barbara De Angelis, both of whom were psychologists. Kathy Utman, who loved to spread love, had urged him to do it, since maybe there had been so many negative things happening to him that maybe he needed to be reminded about love. He told Lynne about one of the exercises where you have to reveal to the person you're partnered with, which was Kathy, the worst thing you've ever done in your life. He said the worst thing that he had ever done in his life was picking his nose when he was alone in the bathroom. "He was completely serious," said Lynne. The workshop also taught him that masturbation was not good for relationships because it drained energy and made one less present with other people. He did not like learning this—he had never liked learning this—since he was a frequent enthusiast of the practice. ("That's one of the reasons he was late sometimes," said Kathy.) But he did stop for a while and people said his eyes became more present and more clear.*

On the seventh day of 1983—which was ten days before his thirty-fourth birthday—he returned to Rockefeller Center, where his banishment from *Saturday Night Live* still hung thick in the air, and visited the Letterman show to demonstrate his new loving nature. He hugged Letterman and bandleader Paul Shaffer and the producers and audience members and said that he loved each one of them and then he called his parents from backstage and announced, "This is Mommy and Daddy." And he addressed them— "Mommy and Daddy, I never told you this before, but I just want to say that I love you both very much. And I'm sorry for if— I know I was a hard kid growing up—I gave you hard times. And I'm sorry for all the hard times I gave you. . . . And I really appreciate you. I'm very grateful to have you both as my parents. . . ." And he hugged them both and Stanley said that they loved him very much, too, and Letterman said, "It's a little like *Queen for a Day* out here." Then they all sat down and Mommy and Daddy told stories about Andy and about how he stood up in the crib and played the records and about how he entertained the little children at birthday parties.

Mommy also said she hated the wrestling with women and Andy pointed out that it had embarrassed her so much that she was afraid to go to the beauty parlor for fear of what ladies would say. And Stanley said he was still incensed at Jerry Lawler and then they called Grandma Lillie on the air and Andy said he loved her, too, and the whole family, including Lillie, sang "Row Row Row Your Boat" for all the nice viewers. And if there was a put-on at all during the visit, it was that this was not the first time that Andy had told Mommy and Daddy that he loved them. He said that all the time always. It was just that maybe 195,544 certain people who watched *Saturday Night Live* might not have known what a lovely fellow he truly was.

He sent the real him onto a television program hosted by a psychologist named Tom Cottle who asked him all about him no really and he told Cottle about the sad little boy who stared out the window when the grandfather died. He told about the boy with the cameras in the wall and the boy in the woods by the playground. He told about the meditating that saved him from becoming a wino in the gutter. He promised that the mean things he said about the women he wrestled were only fooling in fun and that he believed professional wrestling was really real after being thrown on his head three times. Cottle asked him how he felt when Elvis died and he said, "I was sad and, you know, like everybody else, I was a little doubting whether it was true or not, you know? It was a sort of unbelievable thing." He coughed quite a bit while he did all of his telling.

He was a guest referee at the Chicago Amphitheater when Lawler wrestled there on February 12. They yelled at each other in front of everybody. They pushed each other around and he got to do his screaming. He was happy to see Lawler again. The crowd was like thunder, which was exciting again. The media ignored the fact that he was there. He hadn't told many people that he was there, anyway.

☆   ☆   ☆

Latka Gravas donned his coveralls for the last time on earth. The one hundred twelfth episode of *Taxi* was filmed at Paramount Stage 25 on February 18, and it was the final time they would all do this together. Danny DeVito would say, "Everybody was very emotional due to the fact that we were all splittin' up and we knew it and we didn't want to." Tears were easy for Andy, always were, and he shed not one that day. He always felt that he had done his best work as Latka five years before there ever was a Latka.

Five days later he told Letterman that he wanted to film a remake of the Laurel and Hardy classic *Sons of the Desert*, starring himself and Fred Blassie, who sat to his left. Blassie demonstrated—"You've got us into a fine mess again, you pencil-neck geek! Now you're crying again! You hearing that pencil-neck geek crying again?" "Well," said Letterman, "I know people will look forward to that!" Andy also announced that he would be appearing in a legitimate Broadway play called *Teaneck Tanzi*, which would begin previews in April. Letterman teased him—"No wrestling in this?" Andy said, "Um . . . actually, I'd ra— Hmmm. It's hard to— No, I don't know."

The play was set in a wrestling ring and he would portray the belligerent referee who presided over the matches of a woman wrestler named Tanzi (portrayed by Deborah Harry), who would solve her life problems by grappling, in turns, with her husband, her parents, her shrink, her best friend, et cetera. He had lobbied for the role and went to London to meet with the producers in March and began rehearsals in New York shortly thereafter. (The rehearsals, it turned out, had reached a crucial stage by April 9, the night on which *Saturday Night Live* would be hosted by Joan Rivers, who had pluckishly decided to bring Andy back onto the show, and Dick Ebersol had actually acquiesced to her wishes—but Andy could not extricate himself from his theater duties, nor did he leap to try. "By that point," said George, "we were just fed up with the whole thing at *Saturday Night Live*. We didn't go after it anymore because we were still pissed.")

And so *Teaneck Tanzi: The Venus Flytrap* opened at the Nederlander Theater on April 20 and also closed on April 20 and Frank Rich wrote in *The New York Times* that he had found only one high point in the evening and it had nothing to do with the play itself, but with a theater usher—"Slipped in among the bona fide employees of the Nederlander is a ringer—the comic Andy Kaufman. Mr. Kaufman's shtick, as his fans know, is hostility, and here he is, in the highest of dudgeon, a cigarette dangling from his lips, barking at seated customers. He demands to see our ticket stubs, and, should we not immediately locate them, he loudly threatens to eject us clear out to the street. As most of Mr. Kaufman's victims don't recognize him, there's sadistic fun to be had in watching the surly comedian provoke the uninitiated into angry screaming. A critic near me almost slugged him."

Daddy and Michael and Carol had attended opening/closing night but Mommy hadn't been feeling well. She had been experiencing shortness of breath and chest pains for some time and then she and Daddy were playing tennis and suddenly she became so winded that she could barely breathe at all. They went to the doctor, who discovered plaque obstructing one of her heart arteries and said she needed triple bypass surgery and was ordered to take it easy until the operation was scheduled. And she felt it was ridiculous that at age fifty-eight she would need such a thing done. But, just the same, Uncle Jackie Kaufman's wife, Aunt Fran, went to keep her company on the night of the premiere. "She was very jealous, of course, that she couldn't go," Aunt Fran said. To miss her Pussycat's Broadway debut, yet! She went into St. Francis Hospital in Roslyn, known for its excellence in heart procedures, in early May not long before Mother's Day and the operation was a success and on the day she was supposed to come home she suffered a massive stroke, which paralyzed the right side of her body and heavily affected her speech. She couldn't talk for a long while afterward, and when she did she didn't sound much like Mommy anymore. Andy stayed on Grassfield Road all through May and would go to the hospital and pat her hand and tell her that he would find some kind of cure to make her better and she would nod and try to smile. She would be all right, he knew, but she wouldn't be quite the same, which he didn't want to know. All through these famous years, he had always come home as much as possible because Mommy really was his anchor and would always take care of him and make him breakfast in the late afternoon and listen to his ideas. And she was the one who had taught him about vitamins—to take lots and lots and lots and lots and lots of vitamins—and he was the one who had taught her about meditation, just like he had with Michael and Carol, and Daddy would remember driving along with the three of them meditating in the car and always said it was like being stuck in a car full of zombies. The whole family suddenly felt sort of lost, but strong at the same time. Daddy, who was lost and strong, saw that Andy was the same but maybe a little more lost. He said, "I think Andy was very affected by this."

They gave him an installment of the PBS concert series *Soundstage*, for which he was invited to fill an hour as he saw fit and, since this was public television and no serious money was involved, he saw fit to contrive the most elliptical and surreal refraction of existential realities that he had ever attempted. He spent the better part of June working at the WTTW production facilities in Chicago, where the series was produced and where he plotted stratagem as he went along, with George and Lynne Margulies and Elayne Boosler as his sounding board. He would begin the show at the end and start again near the middle and utilize ideas learned as a child from watching *Winky-Dink and You*, wherein viewers were instructed to put cellophane on the television screen and draw on it to help him out of jams. He would have himself arrested and thrown into television court (all with cartoon backdrop) and defend whatever broadcast transgressions he had so far commited on the program. He would have an interviewing desk that was now seven feet high (calling no attention to this) from which he would imperiously interview Elayne, wherein they (candidly, no, really) traversed what had gone wrong with their relationship—"Sometimes I would wake in the morning," he told her, "and I'd think I'd like to tell you that we're gonna break up. I'd say, Well, I gotta tell her tonight— we're gonna break up!" The Clifton puppet would meanwhile stalk the desktop and serve as sidekick.

After the final credits rolled (in which the absent Zmuda was wryly listed as "Invisible Man") and Andy had sung a happy goodbye song and the studio began to empty, he became his dark, snappish incarnation— "Boy, the people out there in public are such a bunch of sheep! They'll listen to anything I say!"—which again was basically his tribute to the duplicitous Andy Griffith character, Lonesome Rhodes, in A Face in the Crowd. At which point, Foreign Man magically confronted him—

FM: Excuse me, eh, Meester Kaufman. Can I talk to you just for one meenute please?

AK: No. Get outta here, you foreign freak!

FM: Please?

AK: No . . . Okay, for a minute, okay?

FM: All right . . . Why do you have to say these kinds of theengs? Such mean theengs about people and you're, you're so mean to people?

AK: So?

FM: You know, I don't care what you do for yourself, but you, you've not only ruined your career, but you ruined my career, too!

AK: So what? Who cares?

FM: Because of you, everybody doesn't like me, either. Why do you do thees? I think I know why. I think it's because you are really, underneath it all—I don't think you're such a bad man.

AK: Oh, thank you.

FM: I think you are a little shy, a shy little man. A little, scared little man.

AK: What do I have to be scared of?

FM: You're afraid of being hurt.

AK: Get outta here—go away!

FM: Because deep down inside you have a gentle soul. And that's why you have to put on thees tough-guy façade. Because you hide your inseeecurity.

AK: [Starting to cry] Really?

FM: You know, when you . . . come to terms weeth your own deficiencies, *then* you'll be able to accept your true self and you won't have to hide behind thees macho act!

AK: [Crying] Right.

FM: Oh, come on—don't cry. Meester Kaufman, don't cry. Oh, eet's all right. . . . Leesten, I'll feenish the show for you, all right?

AK: Okay . . . thank you, thank you . . . [Walking away sobbing]

FM: [To camera] Eh, goodbye, everybody. Eh, be good. And I love you veddy much. Bye bye . . . [Turning to crew person] Okey! Are we off the air? *Okay, who wants to wrestle? Come on! Who wants to wrestle! Come on!!*

He could not help himself.
He joined Lawler on the pro tour.
They wrestled in Memphis and in Nashville.
They wrestled in Indiana and Florida.
He spent most of July wrestling and bellowing.
He and the heel Jimmy Hart formed a tag team.
They plotted and connived to bring down Lawler.
His choreography improved and he now tucked better.
It was a touring carnival.
He climbed on and off the noisy wagons well into November.
Nobody paid much attention.
He kept on screaming and strutting.
He had disappeared.
Nobody cared.

So as to not be from Hollywood anymore, he gave up on Los Angeles, which he had always hated. After Latka went away forever, he got rid of the place in Laurel Canyon and put his stuff in storage and Linda Mitchell left him to pursue her guitar playing and Kathy Utman handled whatever organizational chores arose which were minimal. He resumed the nomadic life that he liked best. Lynne got a place in San Francisco and mostly he was there except when he wasn't. He carted Huey Williams with him wherever he went and was by now well into the fourth book of the opus, having scrawled out a thousand pages of the magical inpenetrable adventure thus far. He found a dessert shop in San Francisco called Carson-York where he loved to write day after day while eating chawwwwklit things. He had always liked San Francisco. He used to visit Gloria Acre there because she had married some guy and moved there and got divorced and so they would get together and he would sometimes stay with her and they would lie in bed and wonder about the baby who wasn't theirs anymore. Because he always did wonder, whenever it occured to him. Anyway, he liked not having to be anywhere and not having to be on time to be anywhere. He liked floating.

On September 22, Letterman said that it had been a long time since he had been on the show. Letterman asked, "What have you been doing since then? What's going on for you?"

"Nothing," he replied.

He then recounted that *Taxi* had been canceled and *Saturday Night Live* had voted him off the air and the Broadway play closed in one night but he said, "I just like to accept things and go on from there. . . . But I'm having a very good time, though, with myself."

He reported that he had been doing some hitchhiking and also that he was in the process of adopting three underprivileged sons whom he invited out onstage and they were three fairly menacing-looking black fellows in their early twenties named George, Herb, and Tony-also-known-as-Tino. Tony explained how Andy came into their lives—"One night I was walking on Broadway, and I was desperate—didn't have no money. And I see this guy walking down the street. And I said, Well, I've been out here all night, and *this* is the guy that I'm gonna mug."

Andy beamed proudly and said, "It's true!"

*   *   *

He had shared the premise with the Letterman producers a week earlier and then cased city parks near Upper West Side housing projects for days until he could find them. He was always meticulous in his planning for the Letterman appearances—since *Late Night* was the only forum he had left. Letterman himself could only marvel at Andy's dedication to comic conceit—"He was the best for us. No one was as careful and thoughtful as was Andy about his appearances and performances. Each one was something that he had orchestrated, rehearsed, and figured out to achieve maximum impact. He would always tell us, almost beat for beat, what was going to happen. And whatever the impact, good or bad, he would just savor it. Nobody could blow the place apart like him."

Before presenting the adopted children idea, he and segment producer Robert Morton had discussed another plan. He wanted to sign his last will and testament on the air with Letterman as witness. He went to Stanley first to see what he thought of this. Stanley suggested that he think of something else to do. Morton witnessed the signing of the will instead in the privacy of his *Late Night* office.

In search of new credibility, he decided that he wanted to go out on the college lecture circuit. That fall, George set him up with a Pasadena lecturing agency called Stofan/Blancarte and postcards were printed and later mailed out to universities everywhere. The postcards featured photographs of him playing Elvis and Latka; of him snarling as a wrestler; of him eating ice cream; of him wearing a straitjacket. The words on the back of the postcard read:

On Creating Reality:

The Physics of Human Response

Andy Kaufman's career of the past 10 years has been a series of experiments which form the groundwork for a thesis. Using film clips and

telling stories, Andy will set you straight once and for all about his con-troversial career and how it relates to the dynamics of human behavior.
For the first time, Andy tells the TRUTH!!

They aimed to send him out on the speaker hustings sometime by the end of the year. "He would have been a smash," George would say. "As for telling the truth, though, I'm sure he would've made something up."

Budd Friedman needed him in Los Angeles on November 7 to per-form for the Improv's twentieth anniversary taping, and so he came back and stayed in Linda Mitchell's small apartment, not far from the club, to prepare his material. He remembered something that he had never used before but had always meant to, which was "Cash for the Merchandise"—the labyrinthine spoken-word multivoiced opening number for *The Music Man,* in which a train car full of nattering trav-eling salesmen bandy about the nuances of hucksterism in impossible syncopation. He practiced and practiced with his conga drum in Linda's tiny guest bedroom/den—*and this felt familiar. . . .*

At the taping, he had a portable clothes dryer waiting for him on-stage. He carried a load of laundry up and threw it in the machine, then pressed the start button. He went to the conga and established his beat and sang the Elvis song "Paralyzed" in his own voice, which was something he had never done before. Then he launched into "Cash for the Merchandise"—which he had transformed into a dizzying spectacle of recitation, a performance piece both thrilling and stupefying. The audience cheered more forcefully than any that he had experienced in a very long while.

He then brought out Little Wendy—with whom he had mended be-cause she was an important part of his world and he was never very good at estranging himself from people who meant something—and he ventured into a new veiled autobiographical fantasy that had been itching to surface. "Ladies and gentlemen," he began, "you know, when I was about fourteen, I was in junior high school, and my first girlfriend—I got her pregnant. And had a little girl—who I have hardly seen, because we gave her away—or *she* gave her away for adoption. And for about twenty years, I have lived with the thought that somewhere in the world there's a little Andy Kaufman running around. So, just recently—a few weeks ago, I was contacted by an agency called Children Anonymous. And that's an agency [to aid] adopted children looking for their natural parents. So, because of that agency, I've spent a very delightful week with my child. Whose name is Wendy Dalton . . . and this is her. She's nearing her twentieth birthday."

And he instructed her to speak with him just as they did when they had been reunited and he asked her questions about her adopted family and about what she thought of his wrestling ("I hated it") and they sang a song called "The Muleskinner Blues" and then she retreated and he performed an anguished dramatic monologue from a play that he made up in his head while he spoke and was heckled by a plant throughout and it all exploded into a mess and he conga-cried and then left the stage with his laundry as the theme from Fellini's 8 1/2 echoed through the club.

On the first night that he came to Linda's, they decided that he would split her monthly rent so that he had a place to stay when he had jobs in Los Angeles. They had gone to dinner at Inaka, his favorite vegetarian restaurant on La Brea Boulevard, and apropos of nothing she asked, "What would you do if you had six months to live?" And he said, "Go somewhere and finish my book. What would you do?" She said she didn't know.

"Within a week," she would recall, "he was coughing. He'd always coughed. But this was a really bad cough."

It would have been a good time and an important time for him to go gather deep silences and he felt it, he felt the real need for it, and there came word of a teacher-training course that had been abruptly scheduled for December and he had just sent a five-hundred-dollar donation and was looking forward to going and he was at Linda's when he heard that they didn't want him to come. This had happened before, even though he was a TM governor, because sometimes bliss people didn't understand that what he did when he performed was only fooling in fun, and someone in the movement would then make a call on his behalf to someone else and he would get to go. But now he learned, vaguely, that a new and powerful woman administrator—who had long hated the wrestling-with-women business—declared that his was not the behavior of a teacher and that his presence was not welcome at this particular course. And he called and called his influential peers in the movement and none of them could do much to reverse the decision. He even called his friend Jerry Jarvis, who had up until recently presided over the entire American TM hierarchy because he knew that Jarvis appreciated his dedication as few others could—"Andy had a more profound understanding of Maharishi's teachings than many people I had ever come in contact with," Jarvis would recall. And Jarvis now spoke with him at length and calmed him and told him that it was a misunderstanding and it would eventually be cleared up by the time of the next training course. But there was nothing to be done about this one. And so he felt hurt and the hurt touched his spirit, which had always been sustained by meditation. He felt betrayed inside his secret soul. "Who are they to tell me how to run my career?" he said over and over. Linda was there while he digested the hurt. "He didn't smash anything or throw anything," she said. "He was angry and then very sad. But he didn't stop meditating."

He and Lynne went back to New York for the one-night-only showing and/or premiere of *My Breakfast with Blassie* at the art theater the Thalia. (*Variety* deemed it an "effective no-budget conversational comedy" with limited home video potential.) A few nights later, on November 17, he reported to David Letterman that the Thalia audience was "rolling in the aisles." He then showed a clip from the film *The Big Chill*, because, he said, "I saw it yesterday and I liked it." Later, his three sons reemerged to display newly acquired trade skills. Andy said, "The adoption papers are now actually legal."

* * *

Thanksgiving on Grassfield Road during which, as per custom, everyone around the table performed for their supper—

Lynne, as a newcomer, observed, "It was a Kaufman family tradition at Thanksgiving. And they were very serious about it. Everyone had practiced their little routines for days." So, with trepidation, she would sing her special version of "I'm a Little Teapot," which Andy loved because she changed the words so that it was about being a little rib from inside Andy. "That came from him always saying, 'I'm the man, you're the woman, you came from the rib!'"

Andy, also as per custom, recorded the festivities on tape.

When his turn came, he said, "Should I read my poetry or do my routine?" Michael said, "Whatever you think better exemplifies your talent." Andy said, "Okay, well, my poetry's from when I was fourteen, so we won't do that." So he elected to perform "Cash for the Merchandise" sans conga and he was spectacular, if a little breathless, and when he finished he was gasping for air. And Stanley teased, "I wanna tell you something—you are so outta condition, it's pathetic! You are really out of condition! Feel his heart. I bet it's pounding!" Andy checked and, still winded, said, "Heart isn't pounding. It's hardly even pounding." Stanley said, "How come you're out of breath? You used to do something like this without even . . . But wow!"

"I gotta jump rope more, right?" he said.

But they were all flabbergasted by his virtuosity.

Lynne said it had also been hypnotic with the conga weeks earlier.

Stanley said it was too damned good for the Letterman show.

Janice could only smile proudly.

He had repeated coughing fits that night.

Maybe, he said, he was coming down with something.

Needed vitamins.

Whenever he left rooms that were meaningful, he would always tell the rooms goodbye. He never left the house on Grassfield Road without

*wandering into every room to say, Goodbye, room, and he would give
the room a little goodbye wave. He went downstairs before leaving
again for California. He waved goodbye to his den just as he always
had. Goodbye, den, he said.*

Lynne returned to San Francisco and he returned to Los Angeles
and to Linda's apartment and he kept coughing. Linda said he had to
go to the doctor, which he had known for weeks but for some reason
hadn't done it. Hypochondria had never been a stranger to him. But
he usually believed that his holistic-macrobiotic-bean-weed-mulch-
vitamin-meditation-sleep regimen (chocolate notwithstanding) sufficiently warded away all dark things. Plus, he had gotten a clean bill
checkup six months earlier.

He had been waiting for the cancer.

He saw something oddly romantic about it.

He was going to use cancer to save his career.

Cancer was how he would fake his death, he told them.

"He had a very strong mind," Lynne would say. "Sometimes I wonder if he just talked himself into it. Because he used to always think
he was gonna get cancer. I remember saying one time that I had
known a lot of people who died of cancer, and he said, 'Yeah, you just
wait and see—I'm going to, too.' I said, 'Well, don't say *that*! That's
terrible!' And every time he went to the doctor he'd say, 'Well, do I
have cancer?' He was just determined that he was going to get it."

Second week in December: Linda drove him to see Dr. Rubins.
Dr. Steven Rubins had an office in Beverly Hills. He had been
Linda's doctor and then, when the hepatitis hit him after the
Huntington Hartford, Dr. Rubins became Andy's doctor as well. He
told Dr. Rubins about the cough and said his left arm hurt, too. "We
did a chest X ray," Rubins would recall. "And we saw a lesion in the

left lung on the left-heart border. And that was suspicious." And Rubins knew what it was and sent him and his X rays to lung specialist Dr. William Young, who also knew what it was—"It was just a question of confirming the diagnosis," said Young. They stuck a camera down this throat—an endoscopy of his trachea and bronchial tubes—and the camera saw the tumor and they sent a needle down his throat to remove a tiny piece of the tumor and they looked at the tiny piece and knew precisely what it was. "Unfortunately, it came back large-cell carcinoma," said Rubins, "which is a fairly highly virulent cancer of the lung that can occur, sporadically, in nonsmokers." In patients under forty, Young would see it approximately once every two years. The tumor was blocking a bronchial tube, which had caused pneumonia, which had caused the cough.

The malignancy had already begun to metastasize.

Which meant that it was now crawling through him.

It swam in his blood.

It was eating his arm in half—a bone lesion, they called it.

An expansile lytic lesion of his left humerus, specifically.

Which was what made it hurt.

Radiation was recommended.

"Upfront, we told him that it was palliative, probably not curative," said Rubins. "And that there were no guarantees. Frankly, it was his option. We thought that maybe it would buy some time."

He heard the word inoperable *but not the word* incurable.
That was all that he heard.
It was difficult to understand anything that he heard.

"He didn't know that there wasn't a difference," said Linda. "He had no idea. They said, 'We aren't going to operate.' And so Andy said, 'Fine. Great.' He didn't ask any questions. He didn't ask anything. He thought, 'They aren't going to operate—that's a good thing.' He didn't know it was terminal lung cancer. Andy didn't know what that was."

* * *

George had come to Cedars-Sinai to hear the diagnosis and sat there with him and they heard. "He said, 'George, you gotta get me on the Letterman show after Christmas so David could ask me, "Andy, what did you get for Christmas?" and I could say, "Cancer."' That was the first thing that he said to me after the doctor told him."

He called Lynne in San Francisco: "He called me and said, 'See? See? I told you. I've got cancer!' You know, it was that type of thing. He knew he was gonna get it and I hadn't believed him. It was like, 'See, I told you so. . . .'"

He wasn't afraid because it wasn't going to kill him because he wasn't going to die because he would do things and eat things and try things and make it go away, so he was, um, fine.

He wanted no one else to know, especially his family. Since he was not going to die, there was no reason to alarm anyone. Lynne came down from San Francisco and moved into the little bedroom with him at Linda's. He did not want the radiation. He drank herbal sludges instead. The arm felt better; then the arm felt excruciating. They went to Dr. Irwin Grossman in Beverly Hills who gave the arm radiation and the pain stopped. "He became my immediate best friend," said Grossman. "He was very sweet, very appreciative." The radiation helped the pneumonia as well, since it shrunk the tumor blockage, thus lessened the cough. Eventually, he would see Grossman every day, receive a one minute dosage of pinpointed radiation and leave. Nausea was ever attendant. He once threw up in Linda's car on the way home. He decided to call and tell Michael on Christmas Eve. Michael heard his brother say the word *malignant*; like his brother, he chose not to fully grasp what that meant. Andy swore him to secrecy and Michael said nothing to anyone.

He slipped in and out of Cedars-Sinai for tests. He wondered sometimes what they were testing for. Some days, he drove himself to his appointments; some days, he was driven. He often made Rubins and Young wait before entering the examination rooms to see him, because he was meditating—"You waited for him," said Young. "Doctors, you know, are not used to waiting." Some days were very extremely angry days. He avoided sadness, however, for the most part, since there were alternatives. "Andy didn't want to hear bad things," said Rubins. He researched alternative treatments, and so did Lynne, and so did Linda. "He was not a person who gave in to failure," said Young. "He believed that, through his spirit, he was gonna win, that he was not gonna die." He listened to visualization tapes constantly and wrote out affirmations—"I'm getting better and better every day." He wrote *better and better* over and over. He also wrote, "I'm not my Papu Cy, therefore I can't have cancer."

"These things are really proven to be chromosomal," said Young. "It's all about just having the wrong genes."

George started talking into his tape recorder again on New Year's Day. On January 7, he reported, I went to bed at 1 A.M. and slept restlessly until 4 A.M. and couldn't sleep after that. I cried my eyes out this morning for the first time since learning of Andy's cancer. It was probably triggered when I became aware that the doctors are giving him only three months of life. I love him so much. He's just like my kid brother—my crazy, creative, unique, lovable kid brother.

Andy walked into the Shapiro/West offices two days later and made calls to nutritionists and to whoever else he could think of who could help him. He called a macrobiotics clinic in Boston. Andy looked pretty good, although he's confused, as he's talking to so many people. . . . He expressed concern that if it got out [that he has cancer] he'd have trouble getting work. I do not feel it would affect the college lecture dates and David Letterman would certainly like to have him. Meanwhile, he looked pretty good.

He told Zmuda on January 10. Zmuda came over to Linda's and Andy told him. Andy smiled nervously when he said the words. Zmuda waited for the *gotcha* but knew there would be none.

He called Gregg Sutton and told him. Sutton laughed and said, "That's hilarious!" Andy said, "No, no, I've really got cancer."

So many of them would laugh when they learned. He liked that part, but it got a little tiring. No really no really no really no really. At least, he had acquired much practice at this.

The family knew nothing, except for Michael, and they went as usual to their winter condo on Singer Island in Florida. Janice's speech had been improving somewhat. Michael sat near her by the pool and she stared ahead into nothingness and into sunshine and two words escaped her lips. "Poor Andy," she said. And that was all she said.

"It was almost like a mother's intuition," Michael would say. "This was a month before she knew anything, but she already knew."

He turned thirty-five on the seventeenth. George brought over a photo album full of pictures from the *Soundstage* taping in Chicago when he had snapped at Foreign Man—"What do I have to be scared of?"

His left eye hurt, he said. It was now inside his head, where all of his other selves lived. *Dhrupick's left eye hurt and it was now inside Dhrupick's head, where all of his otherselves lived.*

*   *   *

George got him an offer the next day—to host the pilot for a syndicated music-video-and-performance showcase called *The Top*; it wouldn't require anything more strenuous than taping introductions to various segments of the program. He could even pretend it was a children's show and call the home viewers boys and girls. "I wanted him to do this," George would recall. "Because performing gave him positive energy which would distract him from focusing only on his sickness." Andy said he would do it and he did, on January 22; a limo collected him with Lynne and Linda and took them to the taping. "All of a sudden, we were out in the world again and it was so bizarre," said Linda. "We were all very nervous. The doctor told me his arm could break if anybody even bumped it or grabbed him to say hi. So I stood there the whole time, next to his arm." George was there to oversee—**The production was quite disorganized technically and Andy was off on his timing and lacked energy at times. On some takes he did well, but he was a far cry from his normal exciting energized self. He was unsure of himself and goofed up several times. I do feel that with sharp editing, the show will turn out quite good. It will be telecast this Friday, January 27. This will be Andy's last show for a while or until he gains his strength.** "He did the show and we went home," said Linda. "He was exhausted."

Life and strength drained as radiation blasted. He stopped the radiation for a while, then felt worse. Often he couldn't move. Lynne and Linda prepared and brewed his placebo gruels for hours at a time—mashes of millet and burdock root and squash; broths of fresh ginger. They shaved piles of ginger scraps to dump into Linda's bathtub, which would be filled with scalding water, where he would steep himself for forty-five-minute purges. "One night he was too weak to get out of the tub," said Linda. "So we had to pull him out, but he was all slippery from the ginger. He kept sliding out of our hands— we couldn't get him out. Suddenly, out of frustration, she and I just burst out laughing. This had all just gotten ridiculous. He was pissed." They tried to explain that the strain was sapping them as well. He yelled, "The only strain that I'm aware of is that I can't have chocolate cake!"

He saw only one reason that this was happening to him. "It's the chocolate," he told them. "Too much chocolate."

George said industry people were starting to hear about it on the streets. On February 10, he insisted that Andy tell Stanley before it turned up in the tabloids. Andy refused, said not yet, because he might get better. George called Michael and urged him to tell Stanley. Michael said he would try, but then he couldn't quite do it, either. "He didn't tell his family for two months," said Lynne. "Finally, I just snuck off to the phone and called his dad and said, 'You better get out here. Andy's sick.' A day or two later, his mom walked into the bedroom— Andy had no idea they'd been told—and he got mad at me."

It was by now the third week of February. Stanley said, "When we saw him for the first time lying on this mattress on the floor, it was devasting. He was already just about gone. He had no use of his arm. Sometimes he couldn't walk or talk. It was a disaster." They hastened him back into radiation. Stanley would lift him up the three steps onto the linear-accelerator table, as Grossman witnessed with over-whelming sadness. "I cried—I mean, there were tears in my eyes. I had to leave the room. It was so sad, seeing a father have to pick up his kid and put him on this table. . . ." Janice would hold his hand every night until he fell asleep. George, Stanley and Linda saw Rubins a week later and Rubins said it could be anywhere from two weeks to a few months.

Andy called psychologist John Gray, whose love seminar he had at-tended just over a year before, and asked for counseling to help him and his family understand what was happening. "He wanted to say goodbye to his family," said Gray, whose work with relationships later manifested itself in such books as *Men Are from Mars, Women Are from Venus.* "He gave them a chance to share feelings and to talk about their life together. Andy was very open to role-playing, which creates a context to express and understand different points of view without aggravation. He responded very well to it." They went to Gray's home office in Brentwood for a few days and in different groupings. Stanley loathed every minute of it—"We called them ten-Kleenex-box sessions. His success was based on the number of Kleenex boxes the clients used. He was trying to bring out our anger toward each other—that we were angry with each other, that we didn't love each other. He wanted hatred and anger to come out, and boy, he wouldn't take no for an answer. This was meant to please Andy because if there was no emotion, then Gray wasn't cleansing our souls. And he had Janice there—who could hardly speak, knowing that her son was in such terrible shape—and he had to make *her* cry! It was cruel." Said Carol, "I remember how awkward it was watching Andy—who had swelling on the brain that day—so he couldn't talk. And my mother couldn't talk. They just looked at each other. It was kind of heartbreaking."

George attended a session with Michael, Lynne and Andy. **In the session, Andy expressed his resentment toward me when I didn't support some of his artistic endeavors like his wrestling, Tony Clifton, his novel, Howdy Doody, et cetera. He opened up his feelings, and during an exercise I played the role of Andy expressing his feelings toward George, telling him I didn't feel enough support from him in my creative efforts as an avant garde entertainer. It was stimulating for both of us. I felt great afterward and so did Andy. . . .**

He heard about the healers who pulled clumps of disease out of bodies by magic. He and Lynne found one in the California desert; some clumps were extracted which looked like animal intestines, but also like red stringy globs of, um, cancer; there was no scarring; he knew it was magic and he believed completely. A woman there told him of the mira-

cle man of Baguio, which was a small town two hours outside Manila, in the Philippines. The woman said she could make the arrangements. They would go March 21 in search of psychic faith-healing miracles.

Stanley rented him a nice house in Pacific Palisades, just steps from the beach, at 300 Lombard. He would be able to watch sunsets on the ocean and have more room to breathe. His family headed home a week before the Philippines quest—about which Stanley banked no optimism—and they would return once he had completed his journey. The night before Andy and Lynne departed, there would be a *Blassie* premiere at the Nuart Theater in West Los Angeles. He would go with some trepidation, for he resembled a wraith, gray and emaciated; he had lost more than twenty pounds and most of his hair and much candlepower in the eyeglow. Lynne shaved what remained of his hair into a renegade mohawk and Gregg Sutton loaned him a studded black leather vest—so he would inhabit one last persona with which to confuse them all. At the Nuart, Lynne and Linda flanked each arm to discourage overt approaches from boisterous friends. Robin Williams came, as did Marilu Henner and director Harold Ramis and Budd Friedman and Elayne Boosler, who fled to the rest room in tears when she first saw him. (Little Wendy followed her in and told her it was cancer.) Afterward, Budd took George aside and said, "Do you think Andy would like to have a little bon voyage party upstairs at the club with some friends and chocolate ice cream?" So a big troop of them repaired to the Improv and the ice cream was plentiful and Andy was happy for the first time in many months and George and Zmuda stoked the room with an effusiveness so relentlessly upbeat as to distract everyone from believing the worst, which they did anyway. "It was like having a wake with the corpse in attendance," said Sutton.

I went to the airport to see Andy and Lynne off on the their trip. The flight was 7:15 P.M. Andy had to use a wheelchair because his leg was hurting and, as always, it was a long walk at the airport. A photographer took Andy's picture in the wheelchair. He *jumped* out of the wheelchair and screamed, "What the fuck are you taking my picture in a wheelchair for?! You fucking leech! You leech!" Andy chased the guy, trying to get to the camera, but he ran away. Bob Zmuda and Elayne Boosler chased the guy to no avail. Andy said it felt great to get so mad. He loved it. Johnny Gray and Linda Mitchell also saw Andy off. I hugged and kissed Andy several times and wished him a good and healthy journey, and asked him to come back well, as we have a lot of good, creative things to do. Andy hugged and kissed everyone and thanked us for coming. It meant a great deal to him and he expressed this touchingly to us. He had shaved his head completely (actually, Lynne did it), and he removed his hat at the departure gate. This cute, loving, bald-headed guy started to board the plane, holding his jacket in one hand and waving goodbye with the other. It was somehow a very touching and beautiful picture.

The April 24 issue of the *National Enquirer* published the wheelchair photograph with a story headlined "TAXI" STAR TELLS PALS: I'M DYING OF CANCER. It was the first time the tabloid had ever run a story about him that he hadn't invented and phoned in himself.

The trip took fifteen hours by air and they stayed nearly six weeks in the largely impoverished town of Baguio, where the renowned faith healer and local politician Jun Labo presided over the unadorned clinic in which patients waited in a queue and stepped forth, one at a time, to receive salvation. Andy received the treatment twice a day. He wore only Jockey shorts and took his turns climbing on and off the operating table on which Labo performed spiritual sleight-of-hand—first dipping his surgical hands into water, then inserting them into a folded towel to dry, then quickly pressing them to Andy's skin and producing the entrails of disease (and/or poultry). Each miracle lasted less than one minute at a charge of twenty-five dollars per. Labo would pluck wet darkness from Andy's brain and arm and chest but mostly from the towel with which he wiped his hands. "He actually seemed to be getting better at first," said Lynne. "He believed it was magic. He was eating, we were taking walks, everything was going great. But then, all of a sudden, he just went down." Zmuda flew over at right about that time to surprise them, which worked, and Andy was buoyant, then faltered again. Zmuda would recall, "Lynne and I told him at one point, 'Why don't you become Tony? Tony couldn't be sick.' And he summoned whatever energy he had left and Tony stepped out of the wheelchair—'*Hey, how're doin'? Where's the chickies. . . .*' And then he collapsed again. For a minute there, we thought Clifton had cured him." Convulsions started a few days later and Lynne said it was time to go home.

George and Linda and Elayne met them at the airport on April 28 and saw that there was now less of him and what there was of him moved more deliberately. Linda would recall, "He was really trying to walk normal. I went over and took his arm to help him and he told me, 'I'm cured.'" They got him back to the Pacific Palisades house (where John Gray had stayed during their absence due to marital separation) and, there, he denied reality—his unparalleled forte—for as long as he could muster strength to do so. "He came back worse than ever," said Rubins. One day, he rallied suddenly and went with Elayne to see three movies in a row which was fun up until sometime during the third one. Also, he briefly flew with Lynne to Denver and back to have crystals laid upon him. But, on May 7, he was admitted to Cedars-Sinai for controlled care and radiation and heavy dosages of Demerol for the pain. He went home five days later (*hated the hospital*) and Michael and Carol and Mommy and Daddy promptly arrived because there wasn't much life left. He was home for only a couple of days.

"Don't worry," Michael told him, saying something/anything.

It was time to go back to the hospital.

"*I'm not worried!*" he snapped.

*   *   *

He went back to the eighth floor VIP wing.

He was registered under the name Nathan McCoy.

Nathan Richards = unctious happy oblivious man.

Kid McCoy = cut the kidding, Pearl would say.

May 16, 6:20something P.M.

Suite was very large. They were scattered in various corners dozing. They had been awake, it seemed, for days. Watching. Waiting. Mommy and Daddy and Michael and Carol and Lynne, they all nodded, eyelids leaden. Linda stood beside the bed, giving him moisture, dipping a cloth into the water, then onto his lips. His brain, hours earlier, fell into ether. Not long before that, however, he and Michael had sung a little piece of a song together. Mostly, for days, he had faded in and faded out and now he had faded out but he breathed through chapped lips, which Linda dampened.

Then his eyes opened and he gasped, but it was a rattle more than a gasp. Linda said/knew it was the death rattle. She woke them up and they came to the bed and each one took a part of him, held a part of him—a hand, a foot, a leg. Lynne pressed her mouth to his forehead. Stanley and Michael and Carol tried coaxing him back—"Come on, Andy, you can stay with us! You can stay!" Janice stroked him serenely. And they all said they loved him. Then Michael said, "Bye, Andy. Have a great trip." And they cried. Because there was nothing left to do. And at twenty-seven minutes past the hour, he had finished.

But his eyes stayed open.

And when a nurse tried to close them, they opened again.

Elayne came in from the lounge down the hall.

She stared into those eyes that would not concede.

"I remembered a reviewer's words," she would later write. " 'This guy doesn't know when to get off.' "

Linda stayed alone in the room with him as the others wandered away to find sense and reason. "I turned the television on to the news because I thought Andy might get a sort of weird kick out of having the news reporting his death while his body was lying there, watching. That was sort of my last little tribute to him."

Stanley called George and George rushed over to Cedars—I felt numb, and the feelings kept creeping in. . . . I touched his face and said "goodbye" and "Andy, I love you." My love is so strong for him. Andy was a unique, wonderful, loving person. He fought until his last breath. I'm so proud to have been his friend. He was a treasure in my life. He stood up bravely for what he believed in as a performer and as a person. He was kind and generous and above all human. . . . I'm so fortunate to have known him.

Zmuda, meanwhile, had gone home from the hospital early that morning and slept all day and woke to hear from Linda two hours after his friend departed. And thus he came late. Which was what Andy had always done, which was, um, fine.

And then the people heard and then the people laughed.
And he could not tell them no really.
And it was almost better that way.
Because no one knew what to believe.
And so he won.

He went back to Great Neck to the Temple Beth-El, where the Rabbi Davidson memorialized milk and cookies and his brother spoke of being fortunate enough to have been the only person in the world who had gotten to be his brother and loved ones wept and also smiled and then he himself sang "This Friendly World" on a tape and people quietly sang along and/or cried along and a local Elvis Presley fan club stood vigil outside. He wore Daddy's old sport coat, which was his now anyway, and he wore no tie because he never wore ties and he went back to the cemetery to be with Papu Cy and Grandma Pearl and Grandpa Paul and to lie next to where Mommy would come later. The stone above him, when it got there, would say that he was a beloved son and brother and grandson and it would also say WE LOVE YOU VERY MUCH and there would be serious discussions beforehand regarding the spelling of *very* about which he would have been thankful.

Dec. 16, 1963

THE EXTREME SUCCESS:

Mr. X was a failure so far,
but hadn't had a chance yet,
for he had just started.
Mr. X is a playwrite;
Mr. X is a poet.
Mr. X is both.
He wrote a poem,
and put it in his play.
It got to be promoted.
And it got to be produced.
It was opening night.
Mr. X was very happy.
With all his friends to come and see,
the stage with actors,
the theater sold out.
It was the largest success
of plays that played.
At end, they called him up.
He then took a bow.
The applause was almost deafening,
and Mr. X went off.
He put his hand in his pocket,
and took out his gun.
He had the broadest smile of anyone,
as he shot into his head.
He was Dead!

ACKNOWLEDGMENTS

Here was a gauntlet thrown and a madness born—to sort and sift through a life of fantasy, but also a life on earth, and locate truths wherever truths had been sent to hide. The sizable task was made navigable due only to the kindnesses and generosities (and sublime patience) of those who truly knew him and deeply loved him. Primarily, there could be no intimacy with subject were it not for his family and those who became his family:

My debt looms most profound for the miraculous nuclear unit members who trusted to share the private wonder of Andrew Geoffrey Kaufman with biographer and world—Stanley L. Kaufman and Michael Kaufman and Carol Kaufman Kerman, each of whom carry the pieces that keep him alive. Then, too, there is the redoubtable George Shapiro, spontaneous diarist/poet, who championed a life and a life story (worth telling and retelling). Those who were peerless compasses throughout the process: Linda Mitchell, Gregg Sutton, Lynne Margulies, Wendy Polland, Kathy Utman, Dennis Raimondi, Mel Sherer, Beverly Cholakian Block, Gloria Acre Schwartz, and, of course, Bob Zmuda.

The author wishes to thank the following for their memories, observations, ideas and time, all of which helped to piece together the lovely puzzle:

The Great Neck Years: Rabbi Jerome Davidson, Cathy Bernard, Moogie Klingman, Richard Corey, Marilyn Blumberg Cane, Jim Krieger, Charley Wininger, Rick Etra, Gina Acre, Gloria Greenberg, Gil Gevins, Ginger Petrochko, Glenn Barrett, Peter Wassyng, Carla Shore

The Relatives: Sam Denoff, Margot Goldberg, Maria Bellu Colonna, Jill Kaufman, Rebecca and Steve Tobias, Susan Lawrence, Jack and Fran Kaufman, Rick Kerman, Prudence Kaufman, Margaret E. English

Grahm Junior College/Boston: Al Parinello, Burt Dubrow, Dick Mallary, Don Erickson, George Schwartz, Marshall Nanis, Marc Summers, Cindy Mace-Arnett, Paul Fusco, Ron Seidle, Ilona Lange Dudasik

Transcendental Meditation: Don Snow, Emily Draper, Jerry Jarvis, Maharishi University of Management, Trisha and Phil Malkinson, Mews Small, Penny Bell, Phil Goldberg, Dean Sluyter, Craig Pearson, Prudence Farrow, Harold Bloomfield, Pamela Paradowski, Kathy Brooks

The Clubs: Budd Friedman, Silver Friedman (The Improv); Rick Newman, Conan Berkeley, Zane Busby (Catch a Rising Star); Seth Schultz (Pips); Eppie Epstein (My Father's Place); Mitzi Shore (The Comedy Store); Jay Leno, Elayne Boosler, Martin Harvey Friedberg, Tom Dreesen, Nancy Redman, Richard Lewis, Richard Belzer, Jimmie Walker, Rodney Dangerfield, Glenn Super, Robin Williams, Johnny Dark, David Brenner

Saturday Night Live: Lorne Michaels, Dick Ebersol, Anne Beatts, Brad Hall, Brian Doyle Murray, Chevy Chase, Gary Kroeger, Jean Doumanian, Joe Piscopo, John Head, Laurie Zaks, Mary Gross, Tim Kazurinsky, Alan Zweibel, Sandra Restrepo, Marc Liepis, Laurie Berden

Taxi: Richard Sakai, Carol Kane, Ed. Weinberger, Howard Gewirtz, Jeff Conaway, Jim Burrows, Jim Brooks, Joel Thurm, Judd Hirsch, Marilu Henner, Mike Binder, Randall Carver, Stan Daniels, Tony Danza, Vicki Rosenberg, Felicia Nalivansky, Larina Adamson

The Productions: Bill Block, Sean Daniel, Thom Mount (*The Tony Clifton Story*); Johnny Legend, Linda Lautrec (*My Breakfast with Blassie*); Larry Cohen (*God Told Me To*); Allan Arkush, Vince Prentice (*Heartbeeps*); Bill Boggs, Paul Noble (*Midday Live*); Harold Ramis (*The Top*); Bob Einstein, Allan Blye, Dick Van Dyke (*Van Dyke and Company*); Greg Garrison, Lee Hale (*Dean Martin's Comedyworld*); Jay Redack, Harry Friedman (*Hollywood Squares*); John Moffitt, Pat Lee, Bruce Mahler, Kathie Sullivan, Melanie Chartoff, Michael Richards, Steve

Adams, Wayne Williams (*Fridays*); Fred Tatashore, Sharon Olson (*Dinah & Friends*); Vince Calandra (*The Mike Douglas Show*); Johnny Carson, Steve Allen, Steve Martin, Peter Lassally, Jeff Sotzing, Susan Rubio, Helen Sanders (*The Tonight Show Starring Johnny Carson*); David Letterman, Robert Morton, Chris Elliott, Gerard Mulligan, Rob Burnett, Rosemarie Keenan (*Late Night with David Letterman*); Chuck Braverman (*Carnegie Hall*); Deborah Harry (*Teaneck Tanzi*)

The Wrestling: Bill Apter, Jerry Lawler, Jim Cornette, Jimmy Hart, Lance Russell, Larry Burton, Sherry Tuseth Jackson, Roddy Piper, Lou Albano, Fred Blassie

Other Voices and Stories: Carl Reiner, Barry Manilow, John Landis, Bill Knoedelseder, Ken Chase, Fabian Forte, Freddy Cannon, Babatunde Olatunji, Merrill Markoe, Alan Abel, Woody Allen, Alan Spencer, Andy Dickerman, Billy Swan, Mimi Lambert, Cindy Lamb, Cindy Williams, Dave Gross, Dustin Hoffman, Murray Schisgal, Eddie Rabin, David Zucker, Elizabeth Wolynski, Emmett Wilson, Gary Lee Fletcher, Greg Gasaway, Janet Coleman, David Copperfield, Jim Walsh, Richard Beymer, Joanna Frank, Joel Siegel, John Burke, John Gray, Mark Perento, Martha Batorski, Sarah Jessica Parker, Shelley Herman, Soupy Sales, Terry Cooney, Terry McDonell, Tom Cottle, Val Shively, Al Garfinkel, Oscar Arslanian, Jennifer Spano, Garn Stevens, Dr. Irwin Grossman, Dr. Steven Rubins, Dr. William Young, Dr. Champion Teutsch, Dennis Hof, George Flint, Peter Guralnick, Joe Esposito, Jerry Weintraub, Bill Belew, Scott Alexander, Larry Karaszewski, Arthur Hull, Sandy Wernick, Albert Brooks, Steve Dahl, Garry Meier.

Additional Research: Comic Relief, Andrea Dennett, Billy Rose Theatre Collection—N.Y. Public Library, Eric Grater, Phil Kruener, HBO, James Taylor, Mike Miller, R. J. Johnson, Rosemarie Garland Thomson, Simeon Peebler, Great Neck North High School, Great Neck Public Library, Brent Zacky, Andy Nulman, Paul Brownstein, David Shayte of the Smithsonian

Shapiro/West & Associates: Howard West, Aimee Hyatt

The Transcribers: Eugene Corey of Brave New Words, Cindy Price of Purposeful Journey, Amy Goldstein, Marcia Smith, and Genelle Izumi, who began it all.

* * *

This book would not exist without the herculean fortitude and journalistic virtuosity of Mike Thomas, ace among copilots, who performed scores upon scores of key interrogations, chased the unchasable, ordered the morass, held the fort, sent for reinforcements, felt the pain and kept his wits about me. (He presently seeks professional counseling.) Chris Calhoun, of Sterling Lord Literistic, came into my life with the birth of this project six years ago; he believed first and has never stopped crashing surf for which I am grateful. At Delacorte, Jacob Hoye—my trusted partner in funhousing—has edited with wisdom and devotion, sustained shrapnel wounds, and made me think very extremely fast; Leslie Schnur took the leap that made the difference. Also Irwyn Applebaum and Nita Taublib were most patient in the face of delay. Richard Sakai of Gracie Films—who was a youth on the set of *Taxi* and who shared his stories first—gave me the idea that Andy belonged in my life; I think I thank him very much. David Hirshey, the Sleuthing Jew (as he wishes to be known), cased Kaufman and Clifton as others might have only dreamed/feared for *Rolling Stone*, then insisted that I take over the job; I think I thank him, too. Webmaster Brian Momchilov—whose Andy Kaufman Home Page, Goofin' On Elvis, (http://andykaufman.jvlnet.com) keeps the torch aflame with uncompromised integrity—is owed a special thank-you for his support and assistance. Ditto Mark Warren at *Esquire*. For their goodwill or enthusiasm or concern or all of the above: David Granger, Mike Sager, Steve Randall, John Rezek, David Rensin, Sandy Holzbach, Melissa Hellstern, Richard Hull, Donna Tadelman, Bill Tonelli, Michael Angeli, Paige Smoron, Richard Raymond, Judd Klinger, Jim Agnew, John Davies, Ilene Rosenzweig, Chris Pallotto and Hugh M. Hefner.

Moreover, I cannot begin to express my love and appreciation for my family, who helped me survive the straits and perils of this journey. And Carrie Lynn Secrist, who bolsters my heart and teaches me life, I thank you for waiting in the tunnel of love.

SPECIAL NOTE: Three volumes of Andy's own writings—*The Huey Williams Story*, *God and Other Plays*, and *Poetry and Stories*—are now available for ordering at http://andykaufmaninprint.com or, for further information, contact Zilch Publishing, 1465 Route 23, Suite 101, Wayne, NJ 07470.

ADDENDUM TO THIS EDITION

A note about source material: In addition to the two hundred-plus interview subjects who recreated their colorful memories of Andy Kaufman for this project, it should be stated that virtually every one of his television appearances described in this book and countless personal audiotapes of concert performances were meticulously transcribed to serve the author. Furthermore, hundreds of print reviews—scores upon scores of which are cited in the text—were also plumbed for content. (Frankly, there are simply too many to list here.) Besides having access to thousands of magical pages that contained Andy's private writings (which opened secret portals into his unique sensibility and fully inspired the intimate prose style of this work), the author found essential pieces of the subject's own musings and recollections captured in the print reporting of the following brave souls:

Allen Steve. *Funny People*: Chapter: "Andy Kaufman." Stein & Day: 1981.

Blumenthal, John. "We Wuz Robbed!: In One Corner a Playmate, In the Other, the Intergender Wrestling Champion of the World." *Playboy*: February 1982.

Bonko, Larry. "Unfunny Funny Guy—That's Kaufman." *Ledger-Star*: March 7, 1979.

Boosler, Elayne. "Andy: A Farewell to Andy Kaufman—By One Who Shared the Ride." *Esquire*: November 1984.

Carter, Betsy. "Hide-'n'-Seek in Andy Kaufman's Fun House." *Washington Post*: July 1, 1979.

Christgau, Robert. "Andy Kaufman's Miracle Show." *Village Voice*: May 14, 1979.

Clifton, Tony (no really). "Laughter from the Toy Chest: Andy Kaufman, Comedy's Stand-up Pirnadello." *Time*: May 28, 1979.

Coleman, Janet. "Don't Laugh at Andy Kaufman." *New York* magazine: September 11, 1978.

Darvi, Andrea. "*Taxi's* Andy Kaufman: He's a Gas!" *Family Weekly*: February 28, 1982.

Firstman, Richard C. "The Lifelong Childhood of Andy Kaufman." *New York Newsday*: June 6, 1984.

Harris, Harry. "The World According to Kaufman." *Philadelphia Inquirer*: October 8, 1978.

Hicks, Jack. "He Loves to Get Hate Mail: Andy Kaufman." *TV Guide*: June 6, 1981.

Hirshey, David. "Andy Kaufman: Beyond Laughter." *Rolling Stone*: April 30, 1981.

Jares, Sue. "For *Taxi's* Andy Kaufman, The Time Isn't Always Prime for His Zany Kitsch-22 Act." *People*: September 7, 1981.

Kart, Larry. "Andy Kaufman: Humor's Con Man Toys with Our Idea of What's Real." *Chicago Tribune*: May 17, 1981.

Kart, Larry. Foreign Man, Tony Clifton, Latka: Kaufman Circles in His Loony Orbit." *Chicago Tribune*: August 12, 1979.

Kilgore, Michael. "Andy Kaufman Takes His Performances to The Edge." *Tampa Tribune*: October 16, 1978.

Knoedelseder, William K. Jr. "The Identity Crisis of Andy Kaufman." *Los Angeles Times*: December 10, 1978.

Kort, Michele. "Andy Kaufman Wrestles with Racquetball." *Racquetball Illustrated*: Decmeber 1980.

Leogrande, Ernest. "Will Carnegie Hall Survive Kaufman's Gig?" *New York Daily News*: April 20, 1979.

Liska, A. James. "Kaufman's Not a Comedian, So Don't You Laugh at Him— Come On Now, Stop Laughing." *Valley News*: August 17, 1979.

Lovece, Frank. *Hailing* Taxi: *The Official Book of the Show*. Prentice Hall Press: 1988.

Mendelsohn, John. "Andy Kaufman Does de Elvis." *Rolling Stone*: January 12, 1978.

Metcalf, C.W. "A conversation with Andy Kaufman." *Oui*: April 1980.

Musto, Michael. "Andy Kaufman: 'I Sing, Dance, Tell Jokes . . .'" *Soho Weekly News*: April 19, 1979.

Nolan, Tom. "All Shook Up! . . . Andy Kaufman Must Be in There Somewhere." *Crawdaddy Feature*: April 1979.

Nolan, Tom. "'I Think They Consider Me Nut': Is It Andy Kaufman's Bizarre Antics That Scare Network Officals? His Latest, Uh, Offbeat Ideas? Or What?" *Panorama*: April 1981.

Nulman, Andy. "Andy Kaufman's a Serious Comic." *Circus Weekly*: May 1, 1979.

O'Melveny, Don and Sheraton, Shelley. "Andy Kaufman." Unpublished article: 1978.

Robins, Wayne. "Andy Kaufman's Complete Variety Show." *New York Newsday*: April 22, 1979.

Sorensen, Jeff. *The* Taxi *Book*. St. Martin's Press: 1987.

Weisbord Cavestani, Laura. "Is This The Weirdest Interview Ever . . . ?" *Los Angeles Free Press*: March 9, 1978.

White Timothy. "Andy Kaufman's Broadway Bout." *New York Daily News*: April 3, 1983.

Young Charles M. "Andy Kaufman's State of Confusion." *Rolling Stone*: June 14, 1979.

Zurawik, Dave. "What's Andy Like? A Good Question." *Detroit Free Press*: July 29, 1979.